American Labor
and
United States
Foreign Policy

AMERICAN LABOR AND UNITED STATES FOREIGN POLICY

RONALD RADOSH

Vintage Books
A Division of Random House
New York

Copyright © 1969 by Ronald Radosh

All rights reserved under International and Pan-American Copyright Conventions. Published in the United States by Random House, Inc., New York, and simultaneously in Canada by Random House of Canada Limited, Toronto. Originally published by Random House, Inc., in 1969.

Library of Congress Catalog Card Number: 75-85605

Manufactured in the United States of America

FIRST VINTAGE BOOKS EDITION, SEPTEMBER 1970

The author would like to offer acknowledgment to the following publishers, individuals and institutions for permission to quote from copyrighted books or articles, and for use of private manuscript collections:

Alfred A. Knopf, New York, for permission to quote from Arno J. Mayer, *Politics and Diplomacy of Peacemaking: Containment and Counterrevolution at Versailles, 1918–1919;* 1967. Copyright © 1967 by Arno J. Mayer.

Duke University Press, Durham, North Carolina, for permission to quote from Robert D. Warth, *The Allies and the Russian Revolution,* 1954.

Funk and Wagnalls, New York, for permission to quote from Serafino Romualdi, *Presidents and Peons: Recollections of a Labor Ambassador in Latin America,* 1967. Copyright © 1967 by Serafino Romualdi.

New York University Press, New York, for permission to quote from Henry M. Pelling, *America and the British Left, from Bright to Bevan*, 1957. Copyright © 1957 by New York University.

Oxford University Press, New York, for permission to quote from N. Gordon Levin, Jr., *Woodrow Wilson and World Politics*, 1968.

University of Pennsylvania Press, Philadelphia, for permission to quote from Austin Van Der Slice, *International Labor, Diplomacy and the Peace, 1914–1919*, 1941.

The Journal of American History, for permission to use sections of Ronald Radosh, "John Spargo and Wilson's Russian Policy, 1920," which appeared in Vol. LII, no. 33, December 1965.

Political Science Quarterly, for permission to quote from John P. Windmuller, "The Foreign Policy Conflict in American Labor," which appeared in Vol. 82, no. 2, June 1967.

V. R.–Leviathan Publishing Company, New York, for permission to quote from Susanne Bodenheimer, "The AFL-CIO in Latin America: The Dominican Republic—A Case Study," which appeared in *Viet-Report*, III, no. 4, September–October 1967.

Henry W. Berger, for permission to quote from "Union Diplomacy: American Labor's Foreign Policy in Latin America, 1932–1955," unpublished Ph.D. dissertation, University of Wisconsin, 1966.

Yale University Library, for the Papers of William H. Buckler and Edward M. House.

Roosevelt University Labor Education Division, for permission to quote from Christos Jecchinis, *Trade Unionism in Greece: A Study in Political Paternalism*, Chicago, Illinois, 1967.

FOR *my Mother and Father,*
Ida and Reuben Radosh

ACKNOWLEDGMENTS

Work on this subject was begun in 1962, while the writer was a graduate student at the University of Wisconsin. Financial aid from that institution was of help in some early research. Financial aid of substance was more recently awarded by the Louis M. Rabinowitz Foundation of New York. Their grants in 1964 and 1965, as well as a Summer Research Grant awarded by the City University of New York in 1967, provided the author with sufficient funds to complete the necessary research for this book.

Many individuals have offered help in the form of suggestions, criticism and by making available relevant material in their possession. These include Michael Ansara of *Ramparts;* N. Gordon Levin, Jr., Leonard Liggio, Joseph Palisi, Richard E. Ward and James Weinstein. The author is most appreciative of the aid given and research notes willingly shared with the author by Professor Henry W. Berger of St. Louis University, Washington. Professor Berger is completing his own excellent study of American labor's foreign policy in Latin America. When this work appears, our knowledge of U.S. labor abroad will be greatly extended and enhanced.

My greatest intellectual debt is to Professor William Appleman Williams, now of Oregon State University, Corvallis. Professor Williams has served as teacher, critic and friend. His work and approach have largely molded my own concept of what is today referred to as "radical history."

Special thanks are due Alice Mayhew, Associate Editor at Random House. It is rare that a new author is given the opportunity to work with someone as gracious, competent and talented.

The encouragement, support and appreciation of this project given me by my family aided immeasurably. For my daughter Laura and my son Daniel, who had to put up with the many hours their father spent writing; and for my wife, Alice, who put up with shortened vacations and numerous research trips, and with whom I share a rare closeness and love, I can only add a succession of thanks.

Indian Lake, New York   RONALD RADOSH
August 1969

CONTENTS

American Labor
and
United States
Foreign Policy

INTRODUCTION

Cooperation between organized labor and the federal government in foreign policy matters has become an aspect of American politics questioned only by radicals and right-wingers.[1] The labor statesman has become such an accepted part of our way of life that all postwar administrations have received unswerving loyalty from the leadership of the American Federation of Labor and the Congress of Industrial Organizations. Indeed, the virtually universal acceptance of cold war diplomacy in American political life has been made possible by the active support at home and abroad of the American labor movement. This was not always the case. Not until the period of the First World War was labor's support in foreign policy matters actively

[1] Criticisms from the Left of labor's foreign policy role include: Henry W. Berger, "American Labor Overseas," *The Nation*, January 16, 1967; Sidney Lens, "American Labor Abroad: Lovestone Diplomacy," *The Nation*, July 5, 1965; George Morris, *CIA and American Labor* (New York, 1967). Criticism from the far Right is presented in Hilaire Du Berrier, *Labor's International Network* (New Orleans, 1962).

sought by the government, and concessions offered in exchange.

From World War I to the present era of Cold War, the
leaders of organized labor have willingly offered their support to incumbent administrations, and have aided the
Department of State in its pursuit of foreign policy objectives. How American labor leaders became involved in
foreign affairs, and the effect their activities had on the
international labor movement, is a complex story that will
be developed in this book. Before beginning, it is necessary
to raise a basic question. What are the factors which motivated American labor leaders to develop a close identification with State Department policy? Workers, after all,
formed the trade union movement in order to better the
economic position of wage earners. No apparent relationship existed between the ability to attain their desired goal
and American foreign policy. Union leaders, however, not
only supported Administration foreign policy; they became
the most vociferous advocates of a firm stand on behalf of
State Department goals. A token gesture was dubbed insufficient. Often labor leaders saved their most militant
posture for diatribes against Administration "enemies"
abroad.

A recent example is the AFL-CIO Executive Council's
offer of total support to President Lyndon B. Johnson's
position on Vietnam. Criticism of the war, George Meany
and his associates proclaimed in August 1966, "can only
pollute and poison the bloodstream of our democracy." In
adopting this position, the labor leaders remained true to
an analysis and outlook held since 1914. Like its early predecessors, the contemporary AFL-CIO Executive Council
spends much of its time and money on behalf of Administration foreign policy. A provocative answer as to why labor
leaders have engaged in such activity was provided by one
observer of the labor scene in the late 1920's. In that era,
the union movement supported what it called "the new
unionism." Labor leaders stressed the need to cooperate
with corporations to attain a high degree of efficiency and
productivity, out of which the employers would gain

enough profits to pay labor adequate and even high wages. Unions, Arthur W. Calhoun wrote, emphasized productivity and labor leaders spoke about the "ways and means of increasing output." Calhoun was not enamored of this conservative approach. But he saw no alternative "but for organized labor to go along with triumphant American capitalism in its conquest of the world." Better to be a "side-partner to American business in its march toward the enslavement of the world," he sarcastically commented, "than to take poor chances in a battle with the employers." Calhoun knew that such a course would prove advantageous to the labor leaders, because American capitalism could "easily afford to hand out a continual stream of material benefits" to organized labor "so that social solidarity might be maintained in the face of an unfriendly foreign world." Calhoun accurately predicted that the corporate system would hand out tangible benefits to organized labor "as the price of loyalty."[2]

Calhoun was wrong in one respect. The adoption by labor leaders of an expansionist course abroad had begun during the period of the Spanish-American War. Samuel Gompers, president of the American Federation of Labor between 1886 and 1924 (with the exception of one year's term), conceived of the trade union movement as an aid to the corporations. "If the devil's advocates had the slightest regard for fact," Gompers wrote, "the development of the past few years would seal their lips and put an end to the baseless assaults upon unionism." It had been proven that American labor was the cheapest in the world, in spite of higher wages prevailing within the United States. American labor was the "most efficient, intelligent, alert, conscientious and productive." American manufacturers "have conquered the markets of the world and have defeated their competitors on the latter's own ground," Gompers boasted. "American supremacy as an exporter of manufactured goods is certain and inevitable. Already all Europe is

[2] Arthur W. Calhoun, "Labor's New Economic Policy," in J. B. S. Hardman, ed., *American Labor Dynamics* (New York, 1928), pp. 320–26.

alarmed and earnestly considering the ways and means of
checking the advance of the United States as an exporter.
In accounting for American success in foreign trade every
competent student pays high tribute to labor." Gompers
agreed with major corporate leaders that industry and
labor could both share the fruits of foreign expansion.
"Never was labor better organized and more alive to its
interests than now," wrote Gompers in 1901, "and never
was America's foreign trade so stupendous as now. If unions are fundamentally injurious, where are the evidences,
the manifestations of the harm done by them?"[3]

Success for unionism was tied up with the view that all
economic groups would benefit from extension of the export trade, and from the growth of an American-style, non-
colonial, informal empire. From 1898 on, Gompers continually reiterated that the American Federation of Labor
did not "oppose the development of our industry, the expansion of our commerce, nor the power and influence
which the United States may exert upon the destinies of
the nations of the world."[4] This commitment to trade expansion paralleled the need of the business community to
find and develop new markets abroad.

It was not until World War I, however, that Gompers
and the AFL saw the policy begin to pay off. The war
created an abnormal demand for labor. After four million
men entered the armed services, the eight-hour day and
forty-hour week became standard in many war industries.
It was the entry into the World War, Joseph Rayback
writes, that "provided organized labor with a fortuitous
opportunity for advancement." The Wilson Administration
"fostered a spirit which encouraged increases in wages,
decreases in hours, and better working conditions."[5]

The *raison d'être* behind the Administration's attitude

[3] Samuel Gompers, "American Labor Cheapest Because Most
Efficient," *American Federationist,* VIII (1901), 261–62.
[4] Samuel Gompers, speech before the National Committee of the
Chicago Peace Jubilee, October 18, 1898, *American Federationist,*
V (1898), 182.
[5] Joseph Rayback, *A History of American Labor* (New York,
1966), pp. 273–75.

toward organized labor was clear. Military victory depended on increased production and the avoidance of domestic labor disputes. The war created a favorable situation in which organized labor could act to obtain basic demands. Since labor was regarded as an uncertain link in the preparedness chain, the Administration was prepared to offer some reforms. Once Samuel Gompers showed his willingness to support Administration foreign policy, Woodrow Wilson acted to give the AFL general recognition. see p. 11

Actually, Wilson had little choice. An example of what the Administration might have faced was revealed when some anti-labor capitalists deported copper workers from Bisbee, Arizona, in 1917. Gompers warned that this harsh policy would only turn workers toward the revolutionary IWW. While leaders of the AFL had nothing in common with the radicals, employers in the northwest encouraged IWW efforts to destroy bona fide AFL chapters. "It may be said as a truism," Gompers wrote to Wilson, "that either the government and the employers will have to deal with the representatives of the bona fide organized constructive labor movement of the country or they will have the alternative of being forced to take the consequences of the so called IWW with all that implies."[6]

From the beginning of the defense effort, Woodrow Wilson took steps to assure the cooperation of the AFL. In October 1916, Wilson appointed Gompers to the Advisory Commission of the Council of National Defense. On that commission, Gompers chaired a Labor Committee that advised the Administration on labor policy. The Council as a whole had the job of preparing national mobilization and coordinating industrial resources.

Gompers' work on the Advisory Commission led him to form close associations with men like Baltimore and Ohio president Daniel Willard, Herbert Hoover, and Bernard Baruch. Gompers soon learned that these men from the corporate community did not hold a hostile attitude toward

[6] Gompers to Wilson, August 10, 1917, Wilson MSS, File 2, Box 124, Library of Congress.

labor. But reciprocity demanded that Gompers stand with them in support of Administration foreign policy. When World War I had broken out in 1914, Gompers had condemned the war and called for its immediate end. By 1916, when he was appointed to the Commission, he had become a staunch advocate of preparedness and an opponent of pacifism within the labor movement. As he informed British labor leader Will Thorne, the lessons of the European war had made him "change many of my former opinions and visions." The job for labor was to see that the "war shall result in benefit and not in retrogression" for the workers. Since the war itself directly affected America, Gompers argued, organized labor had to support an all-out effort against the Kaiser's autocracy.[7]

When the German government resumed its use of submarine warfare in January 1917, Gompers and other members of the AFL Executive Committee urged an American declaration of war to bring "the Kaiser to terms."[8] Gompers moved quickly to show the Administration that the AFL would firmly support any course Wilson decided upon. In mid-February, Gompers convened an emergency session of the AFL Executive Council. At this meeting he explained why organized labor should take a strong pro-Administration position. Addressing his AFL colleagues, Gompers warned that if labor did not take seriously the chance of war breaking out, the government might "as a consequence" have to impose its will upon the workers. Labor could stay aloof and force the Administration to act as it wished. But if the latter course was followed, plans for organized labor would be composed by men "out of touch with the labor movement and out of sympathy with the needs and ideals of the workers." On the other hand, Gompers argued, labor could emphasize the services it could render during wartime. Gompers opted for having labor

[7] Gompers to Will Thorne, October 21, 1916, Samuel Gompers MSS, State Historical Society of Wisconsin, Madison, Wis.; Gompers, *Seventy Years of Life and Labor*, II (New York, 1925), 336–39; Gompers to Ernest Bohm, June 18, 1915, Gompers MSS.

[8] James Duncan to Gompers, February 10, 1917, *ibid.*

"cast our lot with the governmental agencies and help guide them aright." [9]

To gain approval for this decision, Gompers issued a call for a conference with the leaders of all the AFL-affiliated unions. In doing so, Gompers revealed that he intended to take whatever steps were necessary to curb dissenting views of the war effort within the ranks of organized labor. John P. White, president of the powerful United Mine Workers, had from the start opposed both preparedness and military training. Now White found himself "out of harmony with the entire program" proposed by Gompers. He sought to convince Gompers that his own anti-war views were the "result of mature thought." The fact was that White saw "no humanitarian issues in the present war," believing it to be "distinctly a commercial war." White reported that in his travels through the United States, he had found "little sentiment among the working people in favor of this terrible war." The UMW had gone on record against compulsory military training, and White believed "that the great masses of the people should determine whether or not they should engage in this unjust and uncalled for war." [10]

Despite White's strong objections, the AFL Executive Council met privately to draw up a statement about the AFL's projected support of an American war effort. On the 12th of March, Gompers was ready to present the statement to the conference of AFL affiliates. Meeting with the Council were 148 representatives of 79 affiliated unions, 4 unaffiliated, and 5 AFL Departments (Metal Trades, etc.). The statement, entitled "American Labor's Position in Peace or in War," asked that the government recognize the trade union movement as the laborer's representative, and that it grant representation to labor on all defense boards. It asked that the government limit employers' profits, observe union standards and pay scales in defense work, and give women equal pay for equal work. Finally, the AFL statement noted that should the United States be

[9] Gompers to AFL Executive Council, February 27, 1917, *ibid.*
[10] John P. White to Gompers, March 3, 1917, *ibid.*

drawn into the European conflict, the AFL would "offer our services to our country in every field of activity to defend, safeguard and preserve the Republic of the United States of America against its enemies."[11]

To gain passage of this resolution, Gompers had to run roughshod over the existing opposition. Daniel Tobin, president of the AFL Teamsters Union, knew that they would run the meeting as Gompers "wants them to run or they cannot run at all." Tobin was angry because he had been told that the meeting was called so that AFL affiliates could counsel and advise the Executive Council on labor's wartime position. Instead Tobin came to find "a program already prepared, cut-and-dried, to be adopted by the gathering . . . and that we could not, or would not, be allowed to change one word of that declaration." Tobin tried to present an amendment postponing action for a few days. This was voted down "although we were brought there for a definite purpose," and although the Council members had not been given power to act by the membership of their own local unions. Tobin rejected Gompers' request that he serve on the Committee of Labor set up by the Council of National Defense. He let Gompers know that he had "absolutely no confidence . . . in the policy you are pursuing."[12]

Gompers' response to this criticism was to prevent the internal dissent from being made public. James Duncan opposed having the affiliates' meeting open to the press and public, on the ground that certain newsmen wanted "to carry out some hidden line of thought advocated by those socialistically inclined who were opposed to the A.F. of L." These newsmen, the AFL vice-president claimed, would magnify the criticism presented by White and Tobin.[13] Gompers himself refused to discuss the meeting with anyone. The impression he desired to leave was of the "unanimity with which the document was perceived and finally adopted."[14]

11 *American Federationist,* XXIV (1917), 280.
12 Daniel Tobin to Gompers, March 30, 1917, Gompers MSS.
13 Duncan to Gompers, March 17, 1917, *ibid.*
14 Gompers to Duncan, March 23, 1917, *ibid.*

By issuing this document, Gompers was trying to alleviate fears among Administration leaders of labor's taking an anti-war course of action. Irish- and German-Americans were regarded as either anti-English, pro-German, or at best neutral. These nationality groups made up a large part of the AFL rank-and-file. Gompers' statement succeeded in giving the Administration proper reassurance. A flood of congratulatory messages from Secretary of the Navy Josephus Daniels, the financier Bernard Baruch, railroad magnate Daniel Willard, and Secretary of Labor William B. Wilson clearly testified that the ploy had worked.

After the declaration of war was issued by Wilson, Gompers went one step further. Room no longer existed, he now argued, for dissent, debate, or questioning of the fundamental assumptions underlying the decision to go to war. As long as wages, working hours, and union conditions were preserved, labor's loyalty had to be continually affirmed. Since he was convinced "of the justice our Republic had in entering the war," Gompers believed it was improper to discuss whether the war was just. "Time for discussion whether the war should be entered upon was properly before the declaration," Gompers asserted. "After that decision . . . that subject is not further under discussion. We are at war with the Imperial Government of Germany."[15]

In return for the AFL's strict loyalty, the Wilson Administration continued to pursue a policy favorable to organized labor. The concessions offered were real and meaningful. The position of organized labor *was* advanced. In April 1917, the Council of National Defense issued a statement that both employers and workers should continue to observe existing standards rather than try to seek new adjustments. The Council favored maintenance of existing labor standards but opposed union strikes on behalf of advanced benefits such as basic union recognition. Many rank-and-file workers complained that the Administration was asking them to refrain from improving their condition,

[15] Gompers to William B. Rubin, October 15, 1917, William B. Rubin MSS, State Historical Society of Wisconsin, Madison, Wis.

while they were faced with a spiraling cost of living. Secretary of Labor Wilson admitted that there existed "a great many people who have the impression that it will be necessary immediately to break down the standards that have been established." Wilson asked that notice be taken of "a feeling of suspicion, of unrest on the part of the workers, that the first thing we will have to sacrifice will be their standards." Wilson wanted the Committee on Labor to assure workers that the Administration did not desire to reduce the high living standards that unions had already obtained.[16]

Actually, both employers and the Administration desired to curb any labor action that would put what they considered to be undue pressure on industry. Howard Coffin, a member of the Advisory Commission to the Council of National Defense and vice-president of the Hudson Motor Company, asked Gompers' Committee on Labor to be "cautious" and to do "little that is revolutionary." Desiring an "undivided front," Coffin showed his own willingness to achieve this goal by voluntarily shifting his factories from a ten- to a nine-hour day, and eventually to the basic eight hours favored by the AFL.[17]

While some employers voluntarily reduced the hours of labor in their plants, the corporate community and the Wilson Administration *opposed* enforcement of an eight-hour day where it did not exist and where employers did not favor its institution. Gompers had originally asked Woodrow Wilson to support an eight-hour day for industry, arguing that "it would be an inspiring thing" if the government proclaimed an eight-hour day standard for all industry. American labor would be "stirred and stimulated" by such an announcement, Gompers claimed, making any "labor difficulty" an impossibility.

The Administration disagreed. Secretary of War Newton

---

[16] Minutes, Meeting of the Committee of Labor of the Advisory Commission of the Council of National Defense, April 2, 1917, National Archives, Record Group 62, 10a–B2, Box 352. (National Archives material hereafter cited as NA, RG.)

[17] Proceedings, Committee of Labor, Advisory Commission to the Council of National Defense, April 2, 1917, *ibid.*, 10a–B1.

D. Baker told Gompers and Woodrow Wilson that "the *maintenance* of existing standards could hardly be interpreted to mean so revolutionary a change of existing conditions as such a proclamation would entail; that at once, upon such a statement from you being made public, all workers at present employed more than eight hours would feel that they had your authority to demand an eight-hour day and to enforce their demands, no matter what industry might be involved or what disorganization might follow from the unwillingness of their employers to yield the point."[18] The Administration preferred to avoid the friction that might occur between labor and capital if the working hours were lowered. Samuel Gompers and the AFL leadership chose not to contest the Administration's decision—although the eight-hour day had been a traditional labor goal since the 1880's. Gompers was willing to see labor's standards improved, but only when the Administration was a willing partner. Once Administration leaders saw any specific improvement as "revolutionary" (even such a mild reform as the eight-hour day), Gompers chose to abandon his original commitment.

Gompers did manage to show some success in the signing of new agreements with both the War and Navy departments. Adjustment Boards were created to see that in firms carrying out work for defense, union scales of wages, hours, and working conditions in force as of June 1, 1917, would be maintained in the specific locality in which the work was conducted. But while the agreement seemed to be far-reaching, union wage scales already prevailed in the building industry, where craft unions had achieved a great deal of strength. A freeze on the prevailing wage meant that no adjustment could be made to rising living costs. The agreement also sidestepped the issue of obtaining a union or closed shop. The Administration would not sanction forcing a union shop on employers, and the pledge to maintain "conditions in force" as of June *did not* refer to the employer's hiring of non-union labor. In the construc-

[18] Newton D. Baker to Wilson, October 22, 1917, Wilson MSS, File 2, Box 128.

tion industry particularly, the building trades unions had already obtained a closed shop. Since Gompers' agreement did not enforce a victory they had already won, their membership viewed the treaty with Baker as a setback. William Hutcheson, head of the AFL Carpenters, accused Gompers of giving the Administration a green light to sign contracts with firms that hired non-union labor.

After strikes racked the nation during the summer of 1917, Wilson established a Mediation Commission to make further recommendations regarding labor policy. It in turn established a board which presented its suggestions in March 1918. Urging creation of a permanent board that would mediate industrial disputes, the Mediation Commission developed a set of principles to govern labor policy for the war's duration. The principles included prohibition of both strikes and lockouts, recognition of the right to organize unions and bargain collectively through the worker's own representatives, a ban on dismissal of workers for union activity, opposition to workers using coercive measures to induce men to join their organization, maintenance of unionized firms where they already existed, and maintenance of union standards already achieved. The board also recommended equal pay for women, a basic eight-hour day where the law required it, efficient production, and the right of labor to earn a living wage. To implement the proposals, a permanent War Labor Board was established on April 8, 1918.

Under the chairmanship of William Howard Taft and the humanitarian labor lawyer Frank P. Walsh, the Board was given jurisdiction over all fields of production except those handled by existing government commissions. Although the AFL agreed to what in effect was a no-strike pledge, it had gained the most fundamental advance ever granted organized labor by any administration—the right to organize into unions and to bargain collectively, as well as a declaration against lockouts and discharge of workers for union activity. The Board heard 1,250 cases by the year 1919, and made awards affecting over 700,000 workers.

By granting labor its basic demands, the War Labor

Board was able to maintain a wartime continuity of industrial production. In one case, it found that workers objected to a bonus system. They thought that it existed to stimulate them to greater efforts, and that readjustment of their work schedules allowed management to benefit from their increased exertion. The result was that the men slowed down production to what they believed was a fair level. The Board dispelled their suspicion by creating new work schedules with the aid of a committee drawn from the plant's labor force. The result the Board hoped for was that "production should increase astonishingly."[19]

The Board worked to gain maximum production while it increased the morale of the labor force. Part of its job consisted of working out equitable arrangements with unions, and easing unrest which existed because of the previous absence of collective bargaining. "It is surprising," board staff member Charles Sweeney wrote, "how rapidly 'bad unions' become good when they are treated as equals."[20] By establishing the machinery that guaranteed "good" labor unions, Woodrow Wilson and Samuel Gompers each achieved what he desired: the Administration gained relative class peace and industrial harmony along with cooperation from organized labor; the AFL received recognition, participation by its leadership in official Administration bodies, and Administration support of the "responsible," i.e., conservative, union movement. As Secretary of Labor William B. Wilson had put it, it was simply "folly" to repress organized labor. "It would be screwing down the safety valve to the point where an explosion would be almost certain."[21]

The Administration managed to avoid such an explosion. Gompers and the AFL leadership had traded acceptance of State Department policy for acceptance by the Adminis-

[19] Charles P. Sweeney files, n.d., National War Labor Board, NA, RG 2, File 18.
[20] Memo, n.d., *ibid.*
[21] William B. Wilson to Wilson, June 8, 1917, quoted in Dallas L. Jones, "The Wilson Administration and Organized Labor" (unpublished Ph.D. dissertation, Cornell University, 1955), pp. 339–40.

tration of some basic trade union demands as well as an agreement to work closely with the established union leadership. Such an informal agreement was carried out by union leaders outside the AFL as well. In New York City, Chicago, and elsewhere, workers in the men's clothing industry found the opportunity to advance their fortunes. Under the leadership of Sidney Hillman, members of the industrially (rather than craft) organized and immigrant-based Amalgamated Clothing Workers acted to gain strength for their union.

The Amalgamated, unlike the AFL, had a leadership and membership that had developed in the European Socialist tradition. Many of the union's members, as well as most of its top executives, upheld the firm anti-war position enunciated by the American Socialist Party at its Emergency Convention in 1917. The union leaders would soon have to face an important issue: would they be able to stand by their anti-war principles, and still proceed with their campaign to unionize the clothing workers?

Union leaders soon found that wartime conditions provided them with the opportunity to gain union victories. Large clothing contracts were being awarded by the Administration to firms that were hostile to organized labor, that refused to bargain collectively and used their power to force laborers to work under substandard conditions. The government, Hillman wrote to Newton D. Baker, could not "permit conditions to continue which make for the breaking down of the standards of labor established in our industry through many sacrifices and bitter struggles." Workers had to be protected from the greed of employers who tried to enrich themselves through the war. While they could stop such practices by striking, Hillman noted that the Amalgamated preferred "not [to] do anything that might hinder our government." Hillman stressed that he had "entered negotiations . . . in a spirit of cooperation" and had done nothing "that might possibly interfere with the actual manufacture of clothing" or that would "arouse public sentiment against the government." At union meetings he pleaded with the rank-and-file to be patient, but needy workers were arguing that the Administration was "encouraging non-union employers" and was causing unemployment among union labor. Hillman asked that the Government not "directly or indirectly lend its authority to the misconduct of union hating employers."[22]

Hillman's cooperative efforts were successful. In August 1917 Secretary of War Baker established a Board of Control to govern the award of army contracts. Recipient firms had to prove that they respected sound industrial and sanitary conditions, that they had abandoned sweatshops, that they would engage in collective bargaining, and that they would honor an eight-hour day. As a result of the Board's requirements, thousands of new workers joined the Amalgamated Clothing Workers. Within one year the bulk of the men's clothing industry was successfully organized.

While the negotiations were going on with Newton D. Baker, the union leadership was given reason to believe that the Administration did not appreciate the Amalgamated's anti-war position. Editors of the *Advance,* the official union newspaper, complained of facing considerable difficulty from the Post Office in securing second-class mailing privileges.[23] Sidney Hillman himself heard "some rumors that the 'Advance' is being investigated by the Post Office authorities" because of its anti-war stand. If news of this got out, Hillman warned, it might do "a great deal of damage" to the "standing of our organization."[24]

Although editor Joseph Schlossberg called Hillman's story only a rumor,[25] the union leadership took steps to curb the expression of anti-war views. Amalgamated executive Frank Rosenblum wrote to Jacob Potofsky in June 1917 that the paper had "overdone itself in its criticism of the government." While Rosenblum agreed that the war was unjust, he felt that criticism of the war could not be given "the space and prominence it has until now." The

[22] Hillman to Baker, October 6, 1917, Sidney Hillman MSS, Amalgamated Clothing Workers Headquarters, New York City.
[23] Joseph Schlossberg to Fiorello La Guardia, March 6, 1917, *ibid.*
[24] Hillman to Schlossberg, May 14, 1917, *ibid.*
[25] Schlossberg to Hillman, May 16, 1917, *ibid.*

union simply could not, Rosenblum advised, "do anything which will antagonize anyone." To Rosenblum it was "all a question of expediency." To attack the war meant to provide an opening for those who wanted to harm the union, and there were "enough forces in and out of the labor movement seeking to destroy the Amalgamated without getting the U.S. Government on the job to assist them." If it kept asserting its anti-war position, Rosenblum asserted, the union would "lose friends which it might need in the future."[26] The Amalgamated did not undertake further criticism that would antagonize the Administration. As a result, it got an official agreement which afforded the union its great opportunity to complete organization of the men's clothing industry.

The policy pursued by men like Samuel Gompers and Sidney Hillman during the 1920's set the stage for the labor policy followed during the New Deal and thereafter. In the 1940's, war production would once again give a new union movement, the Congress of Industrial Organizations, a massive opportunity. CIO leaders sat on war production boards alongside industrialists and Administration leaders, helping to run the corporate system from the top. Like Gompers before World War I, Sidney Hillman became the goverment's favored labor leader. Franklin D. Roosevelt appointed Hillman to a post on the National Defense Advisory Commission in May of 1940. Hillman worked closely with men like William S. Knudsen, president of General Motors, and the noted corporation lawyer Edward Stettinius, Jr.

By July, Hillman presided over a new Labor Advisory Committee established as part of the NDAC. Members of this board worked according to the procedures set up by the War Labor Board during World War I. Hillman and his associates now formulated a labor policy for the defense industries, and established provisions for the main-

---

[26] Rosenblum to Schlossberg, June 2, 1917, *ibid.* Rosenblum evidently learned from this early experience. In the 1960's, he was one of the few established labor leaders to protest publicly the war in Vietnam, and to urge adoption of a new foreign policy by the labor movement.

tenance of union standards in war material contracts negotiated by the Army and Navy. As was true of Samuel Gompers, wrote Hillman's biographer, Hillman's goal was "to see to it that labor might gain a position as full working partner in government councils, a position commensurate with its decisive role as a producing class."[27]

Desiring that labor be fully integrated into the top levels of corporate capitalism, Hillman set his hopes for labor on the attainment of gains realizable within the existing political economy. Thus, like his predecessors, he was willing to urge a halt to labor militancy when the Administration felt that the boat might be rocked too hard. Nineteen-forty was a year that saw an unusually high number of strikes. A major dispute erupted at a leading defense corporation, the North American Aviation Company at Inglewood, California. Workers at the plant received a wage far below the union minimum. Because the factory was part of the defense system, the national leadership of the United Automobile Workers was pledged to avoid strike action in such plants. Wage and working conditions at the plant, however, led the militant rank-and-file to vote for strike action, against the wishes of both the UAW national board and the Roosevelt Administration. When the workers finally went out on strike, Sidney Hillman blamed "irresponsible and subversive" groups for provoking strike action. Eventually the strike was broken when President Roosevelt ordered the Army to take over the plant and open it by force on the 10th of June. As the major national CIO leader, Sidney Hillman supported F.D.R.'s strike-busting action.[28]

The record shows that the support offered to the foreign policy of various administrations by labor leaders did result in government approval of the established labor movement, as well as the attainment of certain desired concessions. But in order to gain these ends, the labor leaders often hedged on their support of crucial demands desired

[27] Matthew Josephson, *Sidney Hillman, Statesman of American Labor* (Garden City, N.Y., 1952), p. 514.
[28] *PM*, June 10, 1941, and July 21, 1941.

by their own rank-and-file, whether it was the eight-hour day during World War I, or higher wages in a major defense plant before World War II. When these demands conflicted with the orderly development favored by the government spokesmen, the labor leaders proved all too willing to abandon their original commitments.

It certainly is true that many national CIO unions engaged in prolonged acts of labor militancy in the late 1930's and early '40's. But a distinction must be made between the use of militant tactics for essentially conservative ends, and the adoption of a radical line of direction by the union movement. The era of militancy lasted for a relatively short time, and as William Appleman Williams has written, the "labor movement rather rapidly settled down into the syndicalist pattern that was by then clearly emerging from the excitement and flux of the New Deal."[29]

Much of the confusion in the public mind about the politics of industrial unionism has stemmed from the use of many radicals and Communists as organizers for the CIO. While these radicals worked hard to organize workers into industrial unions, and at times even won leadership positions, they became the allies of those who sought to fit labor into the corporate structure. The leadership of the CIO accepted corporate capitalism, and opposed social revolution. As early as December 1935, John L. Lewis warned that the "dangerous state of affairs" in the nation might lead to " 'class consciousness' " and "revolution as well." Lewis hoped that it could be "avoided," and pledged that the United Mine Workers would do "everything in their power to make the system work and thereby avoid it."[30]

The CIO, as labor reporter Thomas R. Brooks has perceptively commented, "was a successful adaptation of revolutionary industrial unionism to the corporate world

[29] William Appleman Williams, *The Contours of American History* (Cleveland and New York, 1951), p. 445.

[30] "John L. Lewis tells of plans in first interview since A.F. of L. Resignation," interview with Selden Rodman, December 20, 1935, William Green MSS, State Historical Society of Wisconsin, Madison, Wis.

of this century. It reinforced corporate welfarism; it did not seek a new world." While socialists and former radicals in the union movement broadened the movement's concern to include political action and social welfare, "they no more succeeded in radicalizing the CIO than did American business in opposing the new wave of unionism."[31]

Having an essentially conservative corporate orientation, the CIO was able to flourish in much the same way as the AFL unions had during World War I. During the 1940's, the major issue facing the unions was job security. While industry wanted to preserve the status quo, union leaders wanted the wartime mediation boards to order a closed union shop where an open shop existed. This issue was dealt with in a context of wage agreements that took place while industry made inordinately high wartime profits. Cost-plus contracts made adjustments fairly easy for industry, and the government provided guidance when the War Labor Board adjusted wage-rates in response to a fifteen per cent rise in living costs from January 1, 1941, to May 1, 1942.

The War Labor Board also took a position on union security. Unionists had already institutionalized the right to organize and bargain collectively in the Wagner Act. They now demanded more than the status quo, which would merely freeze existing union *and* open shops. In a case involving Inland Steel, the WLB declared that it had authority to consider disputes over union status. The Board derived a policy which provided the employee with an escape period of fifteen days, during which he could withdraw from the collective bargaining unit for the duration of the labor agreement. The philosophy behind the policy was explained by Frank P. Graham, in the Caterpillar Tractor case. "By and large," Graham stated, "the maintenance of a stable union membership makes for the maintenance of responsible union leadership and responsible union discipline, makes for keeping faithfully the terms

---

[31] Thomas R. Brooks, *Toil and Trouble: A History of American Labor* (New York, 1965), pp. 178–79.

of the contract, and provides a stable basis for union–management cooperation for more efficient production."[32]

The idea was a compromise between the union movement's desire to extend the union shop and management's opposition. It represented a major advance for unions in the mass production industries, where they had originally enjoyed bargaining rights only for their own membership. As a result, no strong challenges to union recognition took place during the wartime era. "Maintenance of membership," Brooks commented, "helped to dovetail the 'New Unionism' into the new corporatism. What unionists envisaged as 'industrial democracy,' sophisticated management came to view as a practical means for the handling of personnel problems within a company structure that had become too unwieldy for the old-fashioned face-to-face relationship to work with equity or satisfaction. Collective bargaining, in this light, became a system for drawing up the rules for employment; and the unions became agencies for enforcing these rules."[33]

Once the rules were drawn up, the union leaders pledged to abide by them, and to urge the work force to produce efficiently and to work with a cooperative spirit. If individual workers failed to toe the line, the union, not the employer, would then act as the disciplinary agent. This scheme convinced sophisticated corporate employers that unions were indeed responsible, conservative institutions, useful in terms of guaranteeing continuous uninterrupted production. The union leader could show his rank-and-file that they had obtained recognition and collective bargaining rights, and could argue that responsible behavior and increased productivity would keep the employer favorable to the same unionism that had produced direct benefits for the worker. Together with men from the corporation community, the union leader worked with

---

[32] Quoted in *ibid.*, p. 302. For a general discussion of the origins of wartime labor policy and the origins of "maintenance of membership," see Joel Seidman, *American Labor from Defense to Reconversion* (Chicago, 1953), p. 106.

[33] Brooks, *op. cit.*, p. 304.

government spokesmen and made the key decisions that kept corporate capitalism intact.

Basic to the ability to create such an informal working arrangement was the explicit support for United States foreign policy that was offered by the labor leadership. Had men like Gompers during World War I or Hillman during World War II opposed the fundamental assumptions of policy, or even the byproducts of the assumptions, labor–management cooperation would not have existed. Domestic friction would have been the result had Gompers condemned Woodrow Wilson's declaration of war and proceeded to defend the civil liberties of persecuted anti-war Socialists and revolutionary workers in the IWW. Eventually strikes that would have interfered with wartime production would have taken place, and the unions might have issued demands judged to be revolutionary by the corporations and the Administration.

These options, however, were never presented to the rank-and-file for consideration. Whether they would have insisted on waging a fight for the eight-hour day in 1918, even if it meant breaking with the Wilson Administration, is a point only for conjecture. The basic fact is that the union leadership operated in the realm of foreign policy without consulting, and without obtaining the consent of, those rank-and-file workers who paid the steady flow of union dues. The union membership, for its part, looked only at whether the union was bringing them more of the pie; not at how such an achievement was gained. Their leadership did not let them know that the opportunities existed to gain more benefits, if a different course was chosen.

The conservative policy followed by the labor leadership had other ironic overtones. During World War I, the path taken by Samuel Gompers and the AFL leadership was so conservative that Gompers ended up aiding those social groups in Europe who opposed the most moderate social democratic brand of unionism. Gompers' efforts on behalf of a rigid anti-revolutionary policy provided strength for rightist European conservatives, and weakened Woodrow

Wilson's liberal capitalist allies among the European left. This part of the story, and the arduous work done by Gompers in his fight against world social revolution, will be taken up in the following pages.

The reactionary program of post-World War II trade union leaders follows along the path charted originally by Samuel Gompers, with similar effects on the international scene. Rather than identifying with forces of social change in Europe, Latin America, and Asia, the AFL and CIO union leaders have offered their support to any type of anti-Communist regime. Often AFL agents have helped local dictators establish the very machinery they later used to crush independent trade union movements. The AFL-CIO would then propagate the myth that the remaining shadow union—controlled by the local power elites—was a legitimate anti-Communist force that represented the workers' true interests.

In Latin America especially, AFL-CIO unions worked to curb social revolution. Direct agents of American unions helped to overthrow the democratically elected Socialist government of Cheddi Jagan in Guyana (formerly British Guiana), and worked with the most conservative aristocrats in the Dominican Republic against the moderate social democrat Juan Bosch. After Bosch was deposed by the military junta, the AFL-CIO supported intervention by the United States Marines and backed the junta while dubbing the nationalists as Communists. The AFL-CIO leaders opposed cooperation with those workers who sought to end control of their countries by local oligarchies. Instead, George Meany and his associates backed the most reactionary social groups and echoed their propaganda claims. By pursuing such a policy, the AFL-CIO contributed its share to hindering the efforts of non-Communist nationalists who sought a native radical alternative to control by the oligarchs. AFL-CIO activity confirmed the validity of the arguments forcefully presented by Latin American revolutionaries.

By the 1960's, American labor's foreign policy had traveled a complete circle. Samuel Gompers started with the assumption that domestic progress coincided with the growth of an informal American empire. As the export trade grew, American labor would find more jobs and enter into harmonious relationships with the corporations. Domestic progress, Gompers assumed, depended upon continued expansion abroad.

As the union movement grew, its leaders accepted the existing corporate political economy, in return for a minor share in the decision-making process and increasing economic rewards for union members. Its leaders developed organized labor into an institution that functioned to integrate workers into the existing political economy, rather than as a lever for changing it. It was the labor leaders' desire, C. Wright Mills explained, to "join with owners and managers in running the corporate enterprise system and influencing decisively the political economy as a whole." The result was a "kind of 'procapitalist syndicalism from the top.' "[34]

Holding such a conception of unionism, the union leaders understood that a viable movement would aid a statist government to assure the cooperation of a relatively docile labor force. The postwar era, with the Korean War, increased defense spending, a new Cold War, and eventually Vietnam, accelerated the development of a highly bureaucratic and statist corporate capitalist machinery. To keep such a machine functioning smoothly, the corporate national class required the aid of a state-regulated and approved movement. Such a brand of unionism would help the corporations maintain their hegemonic control over American society.

It was essentially for this reason that Franklin D. Roosevelt's administration had aided in the development of the CIO. The new industrial union federation served as a government-created instrument that enabled sophisticated corporate leaders to overcome the resistance to change of both old-style laissez faire capitalists and the old-line

[34] C. Wright Mills, "The Labor Leaders and the Power Elite," in A. Kornhauser, R. Dubin and A. Ross, eds., *Roots of Industrial Conflict* (New York, 1954), pp. 144–52.

craft unions that refused to accept a statist structure. Organized labor could not be integrated into the system via the old craft unions, which were insufficiently structured to aid unskilled labor. Thus the National Recovery Administration turned unionism into a semi-public institution whose organization was part of an official government program. As Benjamin Stolberg wrote in 1933, "in short, the socialist unions, whose militancy has been kept alive these last few years by an inner left wing opposition, fitted very easily into the drift towards state capitalism, which characterizes the New Deal."[35]

In the mid-1950's, both the AFL and CIO mended their fences and merged. The new federation symbolized the attainment of a new consensus. The old AFL had accepted the permanence of an informal corporate state, and it was ready to join with the CIO to centralize control over the American working class. It was not accidental that unity was attained only after the CIO unions had approved the bipartisan Cold War consensus, and had taken the necessary steps to purge their own internal left-wing opposition. The AFL-CIO has since played the role of a "labor front" for the American-style corporate state, and has worked to keep the laborer wedded to the system. As late as the 1968 presidential election, the joint federation did its best to curb any labor sentiment on behalf of a rational foreign policy. The Administration program was endorsed, as was its favored candidate, Hubert Humphrey. The labor leaders failed to express even the moderate criticism of the war advanced by Eugene McCarthy, while many workers were considering support of the populist demagogue George Wallace.

The problem for the unions is whether the time-honored

[35] Benjamin Stolberg, "A Government in Search of a Labor Movement," *Scribner's,* December 1933, pp. 345–50. For elaboration on the above point, see Ronald Radosh, "The Development of the Corporate Ideology of American Labor Leaders, 1914–1933," (unpublished Ph.D. dissertation, University of Wisconsin, 1967), pp. 254–313. The writer is indebted to the analysis presented by the anarchist writer Sam Weiner in *Ethics and American Unionism* (New York, 1958).

formula criticized by Arthur Calhoun in the 1920's is going to be workable in the future. Calhoun, we recall, had predicted labor support for an expansionist foreign policy, since the system would be able to give labor material benefits in exchange for its support of an imperialist program. It is becoming increasingly possible that American unionism may become as impotent as the Fascist unions were in Nazi Germany. The willingness of George Meany to place stringent maxima upon wage increases, at the behest of the Johnson Administration, is a case in point. According to the Administration's proposed "guidelines," wage increases were to be aligned with a small productivity increase. They were not to be geared to the larger general price rise or to the basic rise in the cost of living.

American corporate leaders have been committed to the warfare-welfare state as the best means for stabilizing corporate capitalism. Domestic consensus has depended upon gains being made for all major groups in the economy, within a context of continuous expansion abroad. Today, the basis for such a consensus has begun to collapse. It becomes increasingly difficult to maintain a steady growth rate for the economy. Acute competition develops with European capitalist nations, while at the same time the system's leaders find themselves unable to cope with the upsurge of revolutionary nationalism in the underdeveloped world. The Johnson Administration tried to cope with domestic turmoil by calling for sacrifices to curb inflation—and the brunt of the effort was to be made by the workers who would adhere to government "guidelines" beyond which wages would not be raised. With a productivity increase of 3.2 per cent a year, and prices rising at a rate of 3.3 per cent, wages would have had to increase by 6.5 per cent to equalize the laborer's condition. But the Administration asked that wages increase no more than 3.2 per cent, which in effect asked workers to take no increase in a period when corporate profits were setting all-time highs.[36]

[36] Marvin Gettleman and David Mermelstein, eds., *The Great Society Reader* (New York, 1967), p. 120.

The direction in which the system's leaders were and are moving is toward an administered corporate system in which the power of the state is directly tied to the needs of the large corporations. The new business collectivism, initiated during the presidency of Woodrow Wilson, has come to resemble the type of business-government alliance established by Benito Mussolini in Fascist Italy. In place of old-style collective bargaining, which depended upon the relative strength of the contending functional economic units, more and more corporate spokesmen are moving toward a system of administered wages and prices. As long as the AFL-CIO leadership accepts working within this context, they have actually departed from the traditional standards of Gompers-style business unionism, which was based on labor's use of its economic power to gain demands. And as long as the AFL-CIO leaders favor advances within the context of wage increases that fall behind both price and productivity increases, the only possible result can be the growing alienation of the union rank-and-file from their own national leadership. The future holds out the possibility of massive contract rejections by rank-and-file workers, who are dissatisfied with the advances which their leadership tells them have been made. It should be no surprise that many blue collar workers, out of frustration caused by their inability to control their own destinies, toyed with the idea of giving their support to George Wallace, who made a strong point of promising true advances to union workers.

When such a breakdown occurs, the gains achieved by support of government foreign policy may then prove to not be worth the game. But the labor leaders' approval of a foreign policy designed to bolster the international status quo is *not* a position in itself contrary to the goals of corporate unionism. Rather, labor's foreign policy stems from the conservative union movement as it has been fashioned by the AFL-CIO leaders. In their eyes, labor unions are meant to function as junior partners of the large corporations, and the leaders naturally seek only

"available from"

H w

those gains that are acceptable to the system's top men, men from the corporate community who depend for their profits on the continuation of Cold War politics; the union leaders see the chance for limited gains disappearing if they offer challenges to corporate foreign policy. Just as American foreign policy in general reflects the domestic organization of the political economy—and the idea that domestic progress depends upon foreign expansion—so does the labor leaders' foreign policy reflect the type of corporate unionism that has developed in the United States.

Today the AFL-CIO leaders support waging the Cold War; they favor a vast armaments program, and they approve the use of military force to crush social revolution, be it in the Dominican Republic, Guyana, or Vietnam. Espousal of this reactionary foreign policy reflects the integrative function which American unions fulfill. Unless the entire conception of trade unionism changes, it will be impossible to get the labor leadership to move away from a rigid Cold War position. Since the days of the revolutionary Industrial Workers of the World, there has been no independent union movement controlled by its own rank-and-file and not tied to the machinery of the state. Only with such a union movement, however, will workers be able to mold a democratic movement that will develop leaders who move beyond limited aims that fail to challenge the hegemony of the corporations. When such a new movement is fashioned, American workers will begin a long overdue assessment of the assumptions behind adoption of a backward and reactionary foreign policy.

See p. 19
"exactly"

THE WILSONIAN SOCIALISTS: ORIGINS AND GENESIS OF THE SOCIAL-DEMOCRATIC LEAGUE

The American Socialist Party, unlike many of its European counterparts, took a firm position against both World War I and American participation in that war. Both its left and right wings united and moved in the direction of the European Left, openly identifying with Karl Liebknecht and the anti-war groups in Germany. In the famous anti-war resolution adopted at the Socialist Emergency Convention in April 1917, the Party condemned the war and called for mass movements against conscription and for continuous public opposition to the war through all means in its power. The Party's resolution stressed "allegiance to the principle of internationalism and working class solidarity." It argued that "wars of the contending national groups of capitalists are not the concern of the workers. The only struggle which would justify the workers in taking up arms is the great struggle of the working class of the world to free itself from economic exploitation and political aggression." In support of capitalism, the Party made known, it would "not willingly give a single life or a single dollar; in support of the struggle of the workers for freedom we pledge our all."[1]

Not all Socialists agreed with the St. Louis Manifesto. A small number of prominent party intellectuals, like their overseas comrades, left the Socialist movement and supported the war effort. Socialist writers and intellectuals such as William English Walling, Upton Sinclair, Winfield R. Gaylord, Algie M. Simons, J. G. Phelps Stokes, and John Spargo all offered their support to Woodrow Wilson and his war aims, "justifying their view by the theory that the Allies, being modern capitalist powers, were more progressive than 'feudal' Germany."[2]

One of the most important Socialists to leave the Party after the Emergency Convention's declaration was Spargo.[3] At the Convention, he had authored the minority resolution on behalf of the war effort. "Now that war is an accomplished fact," his resolution stated, "we hold that it is our Socialist duty to make whatever sacrifices may be necessary to enable our nation and its allies to win the war as speedily as possible."[4] Spargo succeeded in gaining for his resolution only five votes out of the one hundred seventy-seven cast. This defeat left the pro-war minority no alternative but to withdraw from membership in the Party.

The war was not the only issue about which the pro-war minority had changed their analysis. They developed a new outlook toward the role of Socialists in the union movement. Socialists traditionally had viewed the American Federation of Labor as an organization to which they had to belong, in order to win the rank-and-file workers away from their class-collaborationist misleader-

[1] James Weinstein, "Anti-War Sentiment and the Socialist Party, 1917–1918," *Political Science Quarterly*, LXXIV (1959), 215–39.
[2] Irving Howe and Lewis Coser, *The American Communist Party: A Critical History* (Boston, 1957), p. 19.
[3] For background on Spargo's role in the Socialist Party, see Ronald Radosh, "John Spargo and Wilson's Russian Policy, 1920," *Journal of American History*, LII (1965), 549–50.
[4] Quoted in David A. Shannon, *The Socialist Party of America* (New York, 1955), p. 97.

ship. The pro-war minority now described AFL policy as
being basically correct.

Spargo expressed his new analysis to Chester M.
Wright, a former Socialist who had become the AFL publicity director. The Socialists, Spargo wrote, should "leave
the unions entirely alone to determine their own business,
contenting themselves with giving support to the unions
. . . when and where such support was welcome and desired." Spargo now felt that the AFL approach was "the
only possible policy for a working class movement in this
country which hopes to achieve anything." He was "deeply
impressed that the actual labor movement" had "instinc-
tively comprehended the real issues involved in the war
and come to a decision consistent with the highest and
best interest of the international working class movement."[5]

In contrast, Spargo believed that the "so-called proletarian philosophy of the Socialists" had not "prevented them
from being practically alienated from the actual working
class movement." Thus his own position was "fundamentally that of the Federation of Labor." Spargo held
that the war would advance the cause of socialism and
that Socialists could contribute to this process by espous-
ing reform within the system. "We should have accepted
the war as a fact," Spargo admonished, "seized upon its
opportunities to extend our collectivist program, and demanded the representation of labor upon all boards and
governing bodies formed during the war." Spargo revealed
that he was trying to line "up the forces for a new party,"
and that he hoped "to enlist a good many of the men of
the organized labor movement in this."[6]

The group to which Spargo referred was eventually
dubbed the Social-Democratic League of America. The
principles of the group were proclaimed by Spargo in
October of 1917. Spargo emphasized the need to attain a
democratic peace at the war's end, one consonant with

[5] Spargo to Chester M. Wright, July 11, 1917, Samuel Gompers
MSS, State Historical Society of Wisconsin, Madison, Wis.
[6] *Ibid.*

the nature of an international fight against autocracy. Praising Woodrow Wilson, Spargo referred to the President as a "splendid statesman" who with marvelous "clarity and inspiration" was voicing the "ideals of Internationalism and of Socialism." Socialists owed it to themselves to support Wilson's call to defend mankind's interest. It was "a duty we owed civilization to support to the utmost the Allied cause." According to Spargo, Wilson had "upheld with rare courage and devotion the ideals of international socialism."[7]

Commitment to the Allies' cause and the Wilson Administration was not to mean that the pro-war Socialists would acquiesce in reactionary assaults. Wholesale criticism of existing policy had to be preserved as essential to the functioning of democracy. It was better to risk giving some consolation to the enemy by allowing free speech, Spargo reasoned, than to fasten a repressive spirit on America. The problem facing the nation, however, was that it seemed to be impossible to maintain rights of free speech and proclaim war at the same time. Spargo noted that official governmental suppression of the Left had made it "exceedingly difficult for men like myself to engage in war work with undivided din and untroubled spirit." They were willing to do such work only because the treacherous policy of the Socialist Party forced them to do so. The Socialist Party was not made up of pro-German agents, Spargo explained, but simply of "misguided

[7] John Spargo, "America's Democratic Opportunities," address before the City Club of Cleveland, October 6, 1917, J. G. Phelps Stokes MSS, Butler Library, Columbia University.

Compare Spargo's evaluation of Wilson with that offered by a regular party member, William Bross Lloyd, on December 27, 1917, at Park Hall, Chicago. Lloyd argued that Wilson entered the war "to export our surplus products, for the profit of their makers and exporters." According to Secretary of the Treasury William McAdoo, whom Lloyd quoted, "the right to export our surplus products is threatened by Germany's submarine edict of last January." The war was fought solely for "economic and commercial objects." Therefore, Lloyd claimed, "examination of the declarations of official proponents for the war will show that it is for the command of world markets and the right to export our goods and nothing else." *Ibid.*

formalists" who were blind to reality. The new Socialist organization he would build would preserve the principles of socialism and serve as a political outlet for those anti-reactionary forces who nevertheless supported the war effort. One of their major goals would be conscription of huge profits and socialization of major industries.[8]

Talk about formation of a new pro-war Socialist group had actually taken place before the Socialist Party held its Emergency Convention. At that time the pro-war minority had distinguished themselves from the bulk of party regulars by giving their support to universal military training and preparedness. They then argued that they would rather sacrifice peace than submit to an incursion upon American liberties. Socialists had to be ready to fight "international crime" and defend their own government from attack.[9]

In early March, the wealthy Socialist intellectual J. G. Phelps Stokes queried William English Walling as to whether or not a new Socialist organization should be postponed until the pro-war group had a chance to see what support they could gather for their minority statement.[10] Charles Edward Russell agreed, but expressed pain at having to dissent from the Socialist Party, a group to which he had given so much of his labor. Yet, Russell held, the Party had destroyed its usefulness and they had to "seek another tool and not blind ourselves to the fact that this tool is worn out."[11] Russell urged that if the Emergency Convention "takes any disloyal action, opposes the war or discourages enlistments," that all who signed Stokes' manifesto should resign from the Party as a group.[12]

At first John Spargo thought that his minority resolu-

[8] Spargo, "America's Democratic Opportunities," *ibid.*

[9] Draft statement, March 1917, signed by J. G. Phelps Stokes, Charles E. Russell, Walter Kreusi, Rose Pastor Stokes, William E. Walling, Robert Bruere, Leroy Scott and William Stoddard. *Ibid.*

[10] Stokes to Walling, March 10, 1917, *ibid.*

[11] Russell to Stokes, March 15, 1917, *ibid.*

[12] Russell to Stokes, April 8, 1917; Stokes to Russell, April 9, 1917; *ibid.*

tion would win a party referendum scheduled for after
the Emergency Convention. But apart from the war, he
felt that "the *general* policy of the party is hopeless."
Spargo desired a "vigorous restatement of Socialism, in
terms which will not repel the American people." Spargo
suggested convening a conference of those Socialists who
agreed with their overall pro-war position.[13] Stokes ex-
citedly replied that Spargo's suggestion for an "entirely
new statement of Socialist faith" would be a fine rallying
point for those opposed to "the fanaticism of the majority." He asked Spargo to compose a preliminary draft of
principles that would serve as a foundation for the new
organization. Stokes made one proposal: that the group
be named the "Social-Democratic League of America."[14]
By mid-April, Stokes had sent an official invitation to a
large group of his supporters, in which he enclosed a
tentative draft of the call to form a new Socialist organization.[15]

One of the main points emphasized by the group was
their allegiance to the principles espoused by Samuel
Gompers and the AFL. Upton Sinclair composed a draft
of the SDL's message to the Federation of Labor, and
stated that Gompers was to be congratulated on his
leadership and that they, too, felt that organized labor
should lead all progressive developments. The SDL opposed what they termed friction caused by self-consti-
tuted political movements whose members refused to
cooperate with labor but who formulated programs in
labor's name. "Either the American labor movement will
lead itself along the road of sound, constructive democracy," Sinclair wrote, "or it will be led by self-declared
'Intellectuals' in the name of the 'dictatorship of the proletariat.' "[16]

[13] Spargo to Stokes, April 18, 1917, *ibid.*
[14] Stokes to Spargo, April 18, 1917, *ibid.*
[15] Stokes to Spargo, Charles E. Russell, William E. Walling,
Walter Kreusi, Archibald Craig, W. P. Montague, Ernest Poole,
Robert Bruere, and Henry Sedgwick, April 24, 1917, *ibid.*
[16] Tentative draft of statement by the Social-Democratic League
to the American Federation of Labor, by Upton Sinclair, April 25,
1917, *ibid.*

SDL members felt that it was necessary to gain AFL support for their endeavors, since it was obvious that little would be forthcoming from traditional Socialist Party circles. Yet Spargo suggested that they hold off from official formation until they had a chance to "look around and see what support we can get from working men and women comrades." If a manifesto was issued by "the little group of Intellectuals primarily concerned" it would hardly make a "ripple in the movement." Spargo still hoped that the Majority Report of the Emergency Convention would be rejected by the Socialist rank-and-file in the scheduled party referendum. At that moment they could submit their proposal for a new organization to the official Socialist Party itself. For the present, Spargo preferred to move slowly and avoid any premature launching of a new venture. It was difficult, he stressed, to break with the movement to which he had given twenty-seven years of his life. "I have no other life," Spargo wrote to Stokes. "It is hard for me to break from the party unless I see something definite beyond me."[17]

Stokes reassured the skeptical John Spargo. He urged immediate formation of the new group. Even if the old Socialist Party repudiated its anti-war stand, Stokes reasoned, an outside group based on new principles could in no way harm their efforts. It might even appeal to a new and larger constituency that the old Party was never able to reach.[18]

Other well-known former Socialists agreed with Stokes. "I thoroughly agree with the tentative draft" and with the criticism advanced of the Socialist Party, Walter Lippmann wrote. "I think it is admirable. I would have nothing to add or subtract. I need hardly tell you that I felt this way myself for a long time and it was this feeling which led to my resignation from the Socialist Party." Lippmann predicted that the country stood "at the threshold of a collectivism which is greater than any as yet planned by a socialist party." Unless the world was "to suffer the

[17] Spargo to Stokes, April 25, 1917, *ibid.*
[18] Stokes to Spargo, April 28, 1917, *ibid.*

most terrible famine it has experienced," Lippmann
thought it would be "necessary to administer collectively
the resources of the whole world—its food supply, its
chief mineral output and above all its shipping." Like
Spargo, Lippmann believed that the war "has really carried
us already beyond the stage of merely national socialism."[19]

Charles Edward Russell, who earlier had urged that a
new tool be found, now had second thoughts. He would
not participate, he wrote, because he could not connect
himself with any group that chose to use the name Socialist. It was the name socialism which guaranteed participation of extreme anarchistic elements.[20] Later Russell
softened, noting that he was definitely through with the
Socialist Party. He therefore again considered responding
to a group that would "harmonize with the organized labor
movement."[21]

By June, Stokes had publicly resigned from the Socialist
Party. Since democracy was the essence of socialism, he
explained, the Party was wrong in failing to support a
democratic war against autocracy. Stokes was particularly
peeved at the Party's expulsion of Russell, which he argued
had taken place without the benefit of democratic procedure.[22] Stokes' resignation moved their plans ahead.
Spargo then sent out a form inviting former associates to
join the new Social-Democratic League. Branding the Socialist Party as "anarchistic and Leninistic," Spargo promised that the new group would do more for socialism than
the Party had ever done. Although it would not bear the

[19] Lippmann to Stokes, May 1, 1917, *ibid.*
[20] Russell to Stokes, April 28, 1917, *ibid.*
[21] Russell to Stokes, May 26, 1917, *ibid.* At the time he wrote
this letter, Russell was on his way to Russia as part of Elihu Root's
government commission that was sent to combat war-weariness and
explore means of cooperation in prosecution of the war. On that
journey, Russell shrewdly began all his speeches by identifying
himself with the Socialist Party, in order to give the false impression that American radicals wholeheartedly supported the war.
Because of this tactic, he was expelled from the American Socialist
Party by its National Executive Commission. See below, chapter III.
[22] Stokes to Socialist Party local, Stamford, Connecticut, July 9,
1917, *ibid.*

name Socialist, for "that word is badly discredited," the "cream of the American movement" would be part of it. A goal of the new organization, Spargo noted, would be to consolidate all radical groups into a new political party, in which the SDL would be merely one participating unit.[23]

The concept of using the SDL to serve as a catalyst for a new political party was Spargo's alone. He considered forging a union of the old Prohibition Party and Theodore Roosevelt's Progressive Party. The three groups could unite around a platform that would be satisfactory to Socialists. The SDL would be independent of the new political party. It was important, Spargo argued, that Socialists who came to the new party's convention appear not as individuals but as part of an organized Socialist group. Spargo felt that he would not be able to act as leader of a delegation of Socialists "without some sort of organization" of which he was actually the chairman. In Spargo's eyes, the SDL would function as the American equivalent of the Fabian Society.[24]

By August, Phelps Stokes conferred with Robert Maisel and Chester M. Wright, former Socialists who were both officially connected with the American Federation of Labor. They told him that they had "no doubt that the League would be made a huge success." Moreover, both "were confident that Gompers, too, would support it, although they felt that for the present Gompers's support might be of the quiet kind rather than open endorsement." Stokes noted that both men had "the disposal of considerable A.F of L. funds in their hands," a good part of which could be used to finance the SDL. Moreover, the name "Social Democratic League would be acceptable to them." Maisel promised Stokes that he would privately interest Gompers in the League.[25]

The conference led Stokes to claim that it was "entirely probable that some extremely strong A.F. of L. officials will

[23] Spargo to W. S. Greeley King, July 17, 1917, *ibid.*
[24] Spargo to C. E. Pitts, July 18, 1917; to A. W. Lever, July 23, 1917, *ibid.*
[25] Stokes to Spargo, August 10, 1917, *ibid.*

be on the list." If Maisel and Wright took part, the SDL would "have the quiet support of an appreciable part, and perhaps a very large part of the AF of L machinery."[26] For tactical reasons, Stokes decided that it would be best to leave the AFL leaders off the official SDL board. He realized that as a Socialist body, the members might decide to carry their program further than the AFL officials desired.[27]

Stokes was correct to claim that Samuel Gompers valued the activity of the pro-war Socialists. At the end of the war, Gompers explained to his AFL associates why he had agreed to abandon his traditional hostility to cooperation with Socialists. "These men who broke away from the Socialist Party," he told the AFL Executive Committee in 1919, "have at the same time become less Socialistic and become . . . more nationalistic." They represented "a large number of influential, thoughtful people, and during the war . . . they have really supported the American Federation of Labor one hundred per cent." They had not entirely broken away "from their Socialist principles or tendencies," Gompers realized; in fact, many of them had "established their reputations before the whole world as Socialists." Though their point of view had "matured greatly," the AFL chieftain stated, they could not surrender or repudiate the idea of socialism because they would then be left without any reputation. Nevertheless, "they have been of real service to our cause, and there are very few actions that they have taken since the time that they left the Socialist Party, but that they have consulted me about it, and there is nothing concerning which I expressed a doubt as to its propriety, its vision, its practicability, but what they have re-considered it."[28]

Smarting under the isolation of the Socialist Party from the leadership of the American labor movement (although

---

[26] Stokes to Walter E. Kreusi, August 13, 1917, *ibid.*

[27] Stokes to Spargo, August 21, 1917, *ibid.*

[28] Minutes of a meeting of a committee appointed by Samuel Gompers, in compliance with directives of the Atlantic City AFL Convention and the Executive Council at its December 11–18, 1919, meeting, for the purpose of carrying on a campaign decided upon on December 13, 1919; February 5, 1920, Gompers MSS.

not from its entire rank-and-file), the pro-war Socialist intellectuals proceeded to subordinate themselves to Samuel
Gompers and the AFL leadership. The pro-war Socialists
saw their moment for contact with the AFL arrive when
Gompers sent his envoys to ask Phelps Stokes to participate
in the Minneapolis conference of the American Alliance
for Labor and Democracy, which had been scheduled to
counter the anti-war conference planned by the People's
Council.[29]

To Spargo, the SDL's participation signified that "American Socialism and American organized labor are joining
hands." He realized that Gompers "needs us and is therefore trying to use us," but he also knew that the SDL
needed Gompers and had to try to use him instead.[30] The
test came when Spargo announced his plan to build a new
radical political party. The terms of the party were so
broad, Stokes had told AFL men, that even Gompers
"might be willing to consider launching such a" party on
the AFL's own initiative.[31] Maisel was not responsive.
Rather than form such an organization, Maisel asked that
the pro-war Socialists "give labor a chance."[32]

Stokes, however, had earlier been told by Maisel that
Gompers would " 'support anything that Spargo and Stokes
stood for.' " Perhaps Gompers did not mean to be taken
literally, Stokes reasoned, but he still believed that Gompers was "very sympathetic in the main with our positions."[33] Spargo was more realistic. He knew that Gompers
did not intend to join them, but only worked with the SDL
members to gain strength for the American Alliance. He
also knew why Gompers opposed building a new political
party. "Nothing could be better than to have us as social

[29] Stokes to Spargo, July 25, 1917, Stokes MSS. The American
Alliance for Labor and Democracy was an organization created by
the U.S. Government, the AFL and the pro-war Socialists to drum
up support for the war effort among labor. The People's Council
was a coalition of anti-war groups. See Chapter II.
[30] Spargo to Roland D. Sawyer, August 23, 1917, ibid.
[31] Stokes to Wright and Maisel, August 1, 1917, ibid.
[32] Maisel to Stokes, August 2, 1917, ibid.
[33] Stokes to Spargo, August 6, 1917, ibid.

democrats, on non-partisan lines, support the administration." Spargo demanded independence for the SDL, neglecting the fact that the SDL had no future unless it touted the Administration line. Spargo attempted to avoid being "ambushed, even by the astute Mr. Gompers."[34]

Spargo tried to work closely with Gompers only because "he represents the mass," and Socialists had to "get into close cooperation with the average Labor Union man." In taking this stance, Spargo withdrew from the traditional approach of Socialists. The Socialist Party had always tried to gain the rank-and-file laborer's confidence by attacking the Gompers machine. Spargo now opted for acceptance by Socialists of the official union federation's leadership. Spargo was motivated by a deep desire to escape the isolation he felt was suffocating the Socialist movement. Yet in doing so, he was acquiescing in Gompers' ideology as well as in his control of organized labor.[35]

Although Gompers opposed their activity, Spargo incorrectly believed that because he needed the cooperation of pro-war Socialists, he would "pass down the line that he favors much of what the new party stands for." The organization of the American Alliance itself proved to Spargo that a new understanding existed "between the official directors of the A.F. of L. and certain Socialists who are actively identified with the new party movement." The close contact with Gompers would lead many from labor's ranks into the new party. Once they entered, it would "be impossible for Mr. Gompers to antagonize us as he has antagonized all Socialist parties heretofore." As long as the war continued Spargo predicted that Gompers would need the support of SDL members and thus he would have to maintain cordial relations with the new party.[36]

While Gompers did indeed use the services of the pro-war Socialists, he was not about to let them build a new political party that would compete publicly with the Democratic Party. As soon as Gompers heard of Spargo's plans,

[34] Spargo to George P. West, August 18, 1917, *ibid.*
[35] Spargo to Benjamin C. Marsh, August 21, 1917, *ibid.*
[36] *Ibid.*

he wrote that they "astonished and perturbed" him. He could not understand "what good purpose can be accomplished by the Socialists who left the Socialist party . . . in the effort to establish another political party." As Gompers viewed it, a party either existed to support or oppose the Wilson Administration. If the new party was organized to support Wilson, it was superfluous. The Democratic Party already existed for that purpose. And if it was organized to oppose the Administration, there already existed the Republican Party. Finally, Gompers informed Spargo that the pro-war Socialists endorsed the AFL program, while the AFL did not endorse the ideology of the Socialists. If a new party was formed, it would only "estrange" Spargo's group from the AFL. Spargo's path was called by Gompers a path toward ruin; the Socialist Party had proclaimed lofty ideals yet had become an adjunct of Germany, and the pro-war Socialists were moving in the same direction. If cooperation was to continue, Gompers ordered them to end their attempt to build a new party.[37]

In numerous letters, Spargo sought to explain that he was only attempting to build a radical party that united various groups, a party that would be non-partisan and that would not contradict American Alliance principles. The issue to Spargo was not whether his National Party was anti-Administration, but whether the Alliance was truly a non-partisan body "as it professes to be." If it was, he could still participate in it and work in a new party. Spargo did not like Gompers' using the Alliance as an AFL instrument against his new party, especially since its war policy followed "lines laid down by [George] Creel" at a conference in the Alliance office. Nevertheless, Spargo was forced to end the short-lived National Party. If the pro-war Socialists were to have any effect, he quickly found that they had to subordinate themselves completely to the AFL, the Gompers leadership, and the Wilson Administration.[38]

[37] Gompers to Maisel, September 29, 1917, Gompers MSS.
[38] Spargo to Gompers, October 9, 1917, AALD Copy Book 1, AFL-CIO Headquarters, Washington, D.C.; Spargo to Wright, October 12, 1917, Stokes MSS; Spargo to Wright, October 16, 1917, *ibid.*

Spargo found that he also faced opposition within the Social-Democratic League. William English Walling refused to back the scheme to build a new party, because Spargo favored free speech for the anti-war minority. Walling had opposed Spargo in 1912 when the latter stood in opposition to Bill Haywood and the "impossibilist" wing of the Socialist Party. He now attacked Spargo so strongly that Stokes felt compelled to ask Spargo to remove his name from the roster of pro-war Socialists asked to be part of the SDL delegation at the Minnesota meeting of the American Alliance.[39]

Spargo and Stokes were forced to give up their plan to use the SDL as a catalyst toward formation of a new political party. But the League itself remained in existence. Members now faced the problem of what position they would take toward the anti-war propaganda issued by the Socialist Party. Henry Demarest Lloyd argued that Socialist Party propaganda had to be met by arguments rather than by suppression. "Loyal radicals," he claimed, are "really the only people who can . . . handle the arguments of people like [Morris] Hillquit." Their theories had to be answered since Hillquit caused a lot of trouble in both politics "and in the production of war supplies."[40]

The dilemma facing SDL members revolved around whether their opposition to the anti-war minority meant that they had to acquiesce in curtailment of free speech. The result of the First World War was a new era of domestic illiberalism. The Wilson Administration gave its blessings to laws which curtailed opposition and dissent. The Espionage Act of June 15, 1917, resulted in many violations of traditional civil liberties. The Act prohibited criticism of the armed forces and interference with recruitment of troops. This section of the Act provided the basis for prosecution of anti-war radicals who spoke out against official government policy. Radical newspapers such as *The Masses* and Victor Berger's *Milwaukee Leader*

[39] Walling to Stokes, August 27, 1917; Stokes to Walling, August 20, 1917; Spargo to Stokes, August 31, 1917; *ibid.*
[40] Demarest Lloyd to Stokes, November 12, 1917, *ibid.*

were deprived of second-class mailing privileges by order of the Postmaster General. Statements opposing the war were termed violations of the Espionage Act, because they could be construed to encourage disaffection in the armed forces. Free expression of ideas hitherto not subject to prosecution was now declared to be a criminal act.

The Espionage Act was superseded on May 16, 1918, by the Sedition Act. This law in effect made any criticism of the government during wartime a criminal offense. Rose Pastor Stokes, who shifted sides as the war progressed and rejoined the anti-war Socialists, was arrested for stating: "I am for the people, and the government is for the profiteers." The most famous victim of the Act was the Socialist Party's top official, Eugene V. Debs. Debs was arrested for a speech given in Canton, Ohio, in which he questioned the talk about patriotic duty presented by some capitalists. "It is not their but your duty that they are concerned about," Debs had stated; "the patriotic duty never takes them to the firing line or chucks them into the trenches." World War I came to a halt before Debs' appeal reached the Supreme Court. Yet his sentence of ten years' imprisonment was upheld on March 10, 1919, in a decision handed down by Justice Oliver Wendell Holmes.

The truth was, as Arthur A. Ekirch, Jr., has written, that American liberalism "had never before been so systematically undermined or suppressed as it was through the official action of the United States government during the second Wilson administration." At the war's end, the "illiberalism that followed the Armistice was worse than that of the war period." Socialists, radicals, conscientious objectors, and political prisoners who had violated the wartime Espionage and Sedition acts were kept in prison. Wilson showed extreme vindictiveness toward Debs. He refused all pleas to issue a presidential pardon. Debs was released only after the more conservative Warren G. Harding became President. Of all the nations that had participated in the war, only the United States in 1920 refused to proclaim a general amnesty for political prisoners. Instead, the country witnessed a new surge of repressive

legislation. This included the refusal of the New York State
Assembly to seat five legally elected Socialist assemblymen, the raiding and closing down of radical newspaper
offices, the denial of his Congressional seat to Victor Berger, and the raids on alien radicals conducted by Attorney
General A. Mitchell Palmer.[41]

The Wilson Administration had clearly revealed that
traditional civil liberties were not to be protected during
wartime. It was logical to expect that in these circumstances, the Social-Democratic League would stand firmly
for the maintenance of civil liberties, even though its members disagreed with the views of those who had been arrested. But the fact that foreign war meant illiberalism at
home had its effect on the policy pursued by the pro-war
Socialists. They could either renounce their approval of
government policy, as did the Socialist Party, or slowly
acquiesce in the violations of civil liberties as "necessary"
measures employed to stamp down the threat of pro-Ger-
man-inspired radicalism. The latter was the path to be
followed by most members of the SDL.

At the start a clear tension existed between the increasingly illiberal policy followed by the Administration, and
the support given to that same Administration by the SDL.
As early as November 1, 1917, Spargo had written the
President and pleaded with him to follow a more lenient
and liberal policy at home. Declaring that he was an enthusiastic and loyal supporter of the war who acknowledged Wilson's leadership, Spargo wrote that "it is quite
obvious that there must be some restriction of the press
in such times as the present, and equally obvious that it
is exceedingly difficult to draw the line." Spargo had no
doubt that Wilson desired to preserve "to the fullest extent
possible our own democratic principles and rights," but it
was "painfully evident . . . that the reactionary methods
of the Postal Department are not only wholly at variance
with the principles of democracy, but are alienating a great

[41] Arthur A. Ekirch, Jr., *The Decline of American Liberalism*
(New York, 1955), pp. 210–20, 233–42.

many earnest men and women of whose loyalty there can be no question."[42]

Spargo informed the President of the dilemma that faced many liberal and radical Americans who supported the war. Because they were loyal to the principles of democracy, they were "forced into criticism and even opposition to the administration." Moreover, the Postmaster General and other censors were out of touch with the liberal and radical movements. Spargo suggested a compromise form of censorship as the way out. Restrictions on freedom, he urged, should be placed "in the hands of a small commission in which well known and trusted liberals and radicals predominate, with the understanding that the commission would trust more to moral suasion and intellectual argument than to repressive force." By free discussion the opposition could be overcome. Wilson could then secure the support of far more radicals who were presently distrustful of the war. Spargo asked Wilson to meet with radicals of various schools so as to understand the difficulties they had in supporting the Administration.[43]

To Spargo's chagrin, he was informed that the President took responsibility for the censorship of the radical press himself. "You are mistaken in supposing that this matter is being handled entirely by the Postmaster General and his subordinates," Joseph P. Tumulty wrote Spargo. The President was "trying to keep in constant touch with it." Tumulty argued that "in the long run . . . the ban is applied to very few papers indeed; only to those indeed whose offenses against the law are manifest and flagrant." The President believed "that experience will vindicate the Government in this matter."[44]

Whether or not Spargo approved of the admission of Administration complicity in repression of radicals, his own position forced him to acquiesce in its occurrence. When Roger Baldwin, the well-known civil libertarian, in-

[42] Spargo to Wilson, November 1, 1917, John Spargo MSS, Wilbur Library, University of Vermont.
[43] Ibid.
[44] Joseph Tumulty to Spargo, November 3, 1917, ibid.

vited Spargo to take part in a conference of "minority groups whose rights have been curtailed during or before the war," Spargo rejected his offer. Spargo expressed fear of the conference because its sponsor, the National Civil Liberties Bureau, had on its committee of directors "men and women prominently identified with the Pacifist propaganda" and none who were involved in active war work. The group's attorneys, moreover, consisted of men whose activities were "calculated to serve the interests of the Kaiser and his minions and to thwart the best interest of democracy." Spargo specifically objected to the participation of Boston Socialist Seymour Stedman, of Job Harriman, and of Morris Hillquit, who he claimed was "in favor of 'peace at any price.' "[45]

Other members of the Social-Democratic League had moved so close to the Administration that they showed no qualms about restrictions put on the anti-war group's freedom of speech. Phelps Stokes argued that he could not defend the right of Scott Nearing to speak at New York City's Cooper Union Hall. The Socialist Party's refusal to aid the cause of humanity was so despicable that patriotic Americans had no right to call for free speech at home while democratic liberties in the world were at stake. It would be a gross betrayal of democracy, Stokes reasoned, to ask trustees of a public hall to give a Socialist the propaganda aid he could not get by himself. It was a gross exaggeration of free speech to hold that any group of citizens should open their doors "interminably to propaganda that they despise."[46]

This, however, was precisely the meaning of freedom of speech, at least before the war changed its meaning to many Americans. Similarly, Algie M. Simons opposed having the President issue a pardon for Eugene V. Debs as well as proclaim any general amnesty for political prisoners. These Socialist opponents of the war, to Simons, were all pro-Germans who had desired a Prussian victory. They

[45] Spargo to Roger Baldwin, November 20, 1917, *ibid.*

[46] Stokes to John and Anna I. Sloan, October 29, 1918, Stokes MSS.

had not repudiated their false wartime stand. If the Social-
Democratic League entered a campaign for amnesty, Simons insisted he would have to leave that organization.
The words he spoke during the war were meant to be taken
seriously. To call for a pardon for anti-war Socialists still
in prison would mean a repudiation of their own pro-war
activity.[47]

Spargo, however, continued to show the trepidations of
one who had fought believing that the war would usher in
a new era of socialism, and who felt betrayed at the reality
of the war's consequences. Spargo sent the President a
memorandum concerning his continued punishment of
wartime offenders. "It is becoming increasingly difficult
for me, and for a great many of my friends," he stated
frankly, "to refrain from joining in some movement of
protest against certain lamentable things which you have
the power to end. We are being driven by the irresistible
compulsion of conscience into a position of opposition to
you at the very time we would gladly be upholding and
helping you." Spargo said he knew of Wilson's devotion to
freedom. Yet he had to report that the President had dis-
appointed his liberal and radical supporters.[48]

Spargo asked Wilson to bring about the triumph of his
avowed ideals over those who assailed them. Noting that
the Germans treated Karl Liebknecht more justly, Spargo
asked Wilson to adhere to the wishes of those pro-war
radicals who supported the Administration during the war,
and who had kept silent during violations of civil liberties
because they expected a general amnesty at the war's end.
It was a mistake, Spargo warned, to wait and appear to
act at the last moment as a result of radical pressure. Because of Wilson's hesitancy, many liberals felt unable to
support the League of Nations as an example of democratic idealism. In the accompanying memo, Spargo argued that many sentences imposed on radicals were sav-
age and were the result of mass hysteria. Radicals were

---

[47] Simons to Henry I. Slobodin, March 19, 1919, Algie M. Simons MSS, State Historical Society of Wisconsin, Madison, Wis.
[48] Spargo to Wilson, August 25, 1919, Spargo MSS.

moving away from Wilson, and he needed their support to gain ratification of the peace treaty. "There is no fact more obvious in our American life today," Spargo concluded, "than the revolt of this very important group against what they have come to regard as a reactionary and oppressive government. The overwhelming majority of liberals and Radicals who supported the war . . . are in revolt."[49]

Spargo still pictured the President as a leader who privately shared Socialist or at best liberal ideals, but who acquiesced in their demise because of the pressure of others. Wilson was content to let Spargo maintain this image. The President wrote that Spargo's words concerned "a matter that I have more nearly at heart, I think, than I have been able to make evident. I assure you that I am going to deal with the matter as early and in as liberal a spirit as possible."[50] Wilson was privately concerned, but instead of acting forcefully, he allowed repressive measures to increase as his term in office neared its end.

Wilson's refusal to curb political repression produced a new split within the Social-Democratic League. Without the war to unify the group, new divisions arose over the Administration's failure to ease wartime restrictions on civil liberties. Spargo openly attacked William English Walling's support of the expulsion of the Socialist assemblymen from the New York State legislature. He claimed that the Socialist Party "had honestly and sincerely conformed to the methods of parliamentary political action." The men whom Walling wanted to keep from taking their seats, Spargo argued, were moderate Socialists. They were not from the irresponsible revolutionary element that Walling himself had defended in the 1912 party debate.[51]

Spargo's efforts produced new attacks from his associates. Stokes wrote that men like Debs had not been prosecuted for their beliefs, but for deliberately obstructing the government during its wartime effort. Thus, they should

---

[49] *Ibid.*
[50] Wilson to Spargo, August 29, 1919, *ibid.*
[51] Spargo to the *New York Tribune*, January 29, 1920, Stokes MSS.

accept punishment for having urged others also to violate the law. A violator of law, Stokes claimed, should not be classified by Spargo as a mere dissenter.[52]

Spargo paid no heed to such advice. He favored an SDL appeal for clemency, but not on the grounds of Debs' stature, age, or service to the nation's workers. That would be an insult to the great Socialist leader. The appeal ought to stand, Spargo urged, "upon the solid ground of the defense of our American democratic rights and ideals." To Spargo, Debs' sentence was an outrage and the imprisoned Socialists were all "victims of war hysteria." If the President did not see fit to pardon them, Spargo warned that he would "lose no opportunity of saying that [Wilson] is no longer a leader of the forces of democracy." Defending the traditional concept of civil liberties, Spargo wrote that the more he disagreed with others, the more "anxious I am to have them enjoy the fullest freedom of utterance for their views."[53] A democracy had to be generously tolerant. While it might restrict speech during wartime as a deterrent, it could not continue to do so after the war. It had to acknowledge that Debs and the other convicted Socialists were not criminals.[54]

In terms of the appeal their own reformist brand of socialism might have, Spargo understood that repression would only widen the appeal of the regular Socialist Party. More restrictions, he argued with Walling, would only lessen their chance of gaining socialism through parliamentary action. It would encourage the belief that only revolutionary direct action would work. While the Socialist Party had failed to identify itself with American "psychology, traditions and ideals," it was never so removed from them as were the reactionaries who moved to outlaw the Party. Whatever his differences with them, Spargo noted he would be forfeiting his own self-respect if he spread the fallacious belief that the Socialist Party did not believe in legitimate political action. Moreover, the Social-

[52] Stokes to Spargo, March 19, 1919, *ibid.*
[53] Spargo to Henry Slobodin, March 15, 1919, *ibid.*
[54] Spargo to Stokes, March 24, 1919, *ibid.*

Democratic League was meant to be an agency for the advancement of democratic socialism. Instead it had become an outfit whose sole purpose was to attack the Socialist Party. It stood dormant at a time when Woodrow Wilson's views had become "reactionary and repugnant to . . . Socialist convictions."[55]

The failure of the war to produce a new liberal atmosphere had succeeded in temporarily disillusioning Spargo. Seeing no recourse, Spargo quit the Social-Democratic League, expressing his view that the "Administration has become reactionary, and deserves no support from any of us."[56] Spargo gained support for his position from the noted pro-war Socialist writer, Upton Sinclair. Walling's position "works against all Socialists," he wrote, "and for the very blackest reaction." Sinclair was shocked that Walling held that "Socialists, duly elected, should be excluded from office" and that he justified "the wholesale jailing of Socialists." Revealing his own bitter disenchantment, Sinclair stated that Walling had "cast in [his] lot with the Allied Governments, and they have become all that Prussia was." Sinclair was hoping, he wrote Walling, "you would get out of the trap sooner."[57]

Spargo did not seem to grasp the ironic overtones of his departure from the League. Despite his protestations, Walling's position was the one truly consistent with the *raison d'être* of the SDL. Had there been no need for creation of a "Socialist" group that supported Administration policy, the Social-Democratic League would not have been organized. At the war's end men like Sinclair and Spargo were acknowledging that the pro-war orientation had not produced the radical future they envisioned. Rather, the war had produced the growth of policies akin to the very Prussianism they had opposed in the Kaiser's Germany.

Spargo was particularly incensed about the renewed restrictions on civil liberties. As Spargo himself knew, all of the SDL members willingly had curtailed criticism of Ad-

[55] Spargo to Walling, January 29, 1920, *ibid.*
[56] Spargo to Stokes, January 29, 1920, *ibid.*
[57] Sinclair to Walling, February 17, 1920, *ibid.*

ministration repression of radicals during the war. But
after the war, the hypocrisy of their attitude became bla-
tantly apparent. This occurred because the pro-war Socialists had high hopes about the triumph of Wilsonian ideals,
which they mistakenly had viewed as akin to their own
Socialist vision. When these ideals seemed to sour into
acquiescence in the Old Diplomacy of European power
politics, and increased domestic turbulence, the pro-war
Socialists felt betrayed. Actually they had only their own
illusions about Wilsonian liberalism to blame.

Rather than repudiate their wartime policy, men like
Spargo began to question their advocacy of socialism. "Unlike a good many of those who were formerly" in the Socialist Party, Spargo wrote to his colleague Phelps Stokes, he
had not "deemed it necessary to recant and repudiate the
principles and ideals for which as Socialists we stood." Yet
Spargo admitted that theories he formerly believed now
seemed "quite untenable." Whether "I can henceforth
fairly and consistently call myself a Socialist," he wrote,
"I must frankly admit that I do not know."[58] Now, he admitted, he found it "exceedingly difficult to keep up my
courage and maintain my faith." Under whatever social
system men lived, Spargo saw "many distressing evils" due
to the "moral and intellectual defects of a large percentage
of the people." All that could be done was to "help advance
the good and check the evil, leaving the rest to time and
Providence."[59]

As for the Social-Democratic League, it collapsed amidst
the dissension of its membership. Aside from a quasi-official mission to Europe during the summer of 1918, in
which Spargo and his comrades sought to drum up pro-
war sentiment among European Socialists, the League had
done very little. By 1920, it died as an almost forgotten organization. Writing to the British Socialist H. M. Hyndman, Spargo accurately noted that in reality there was "no
organized Socialist movement in the United States outside
of the Socialist Party." The Social-Democratic League had

[58] Spargo to Stokes, May 24, 1921, ibid.
[59] Spargo to Stokes, July 12, 1921, ibid.

served "a useful purpose during the war," but was "nothing more than a paper organization." It had less than five hundred dues-paying members in the entire United States. It was "simply a committee of men and women who were formerly in the Socialist Party, some of whom are no longer Socialists, and most of whom have tied themselves to Sam Gompers."[60]

[60] Spargo to H. M. Hyndman, June 30, 1920, Spargo MSS.

CHAPTER

II

LABOR CAMPAIGNS

FOR LOYALTY:

THE WAR AT HOME

The outbreak of World War I, and the subsequent entry into the war by the United States, did not go unchallenged by anti-war pacifists and Socialists. The Socialist Party's Emergency Convention had already strongly condemned American intervention in what it regarded as an imperial conflict. In May of 1917, the Socialists joined with other anti-war groups to hold an American Conference for Democracy and Terms of Peace. Meeting in New York City, the assembled delegates demanded "an early democratic peace, to be secured through negotiation in harmony with the principles outlined by the President of the United States and by revolutionary Russia ... (a) no forcible annexations of territory; (b) no punitive indemnities; (c) free development of all nationalities." At the conclusion delegates voted to create a permanent People's Council.[1]

Out of the May conference, the anti-war movement had created a new national organization, the People's Council of America for Democracy and Peace. The newly formed organization immediately issued a call to hold a national

[1] *Report of the First American Conference for Democracy and Terms of Peace* (New York, 1917), pp. 3, 43–44.

gathering scheduled for Minneapolis during the first week of September. It announced as its aim negotiation of a democratic peace, extension and protection of civil liberties at home, the repeal of conscription, the holding of a national referendum on war and peace, and the safeguarding of labor's living standards and a lowering of the high cost of living.[2]

Generally, as one scholar has written, the Council "sought to turn the American worker against capitalism, to praise the accomplishment of the German and Russian socialists, and to gain a quick negotiated peace by persuading the American worker to hamper Wilson's war program with work stoppages and by any other legal means." The Council also sought to wage "a national anti-war propaganda campaign condemning the capitalist countries of Western Europe for starting a commercial conflict and accusing the Wilson Administration of bowing to Wall Street and leading the United States into an unholy war."[3]

The Council's call reflected the growing strength of the anti-war movement. One key center of this opposition existed among Jewish workers in New York City. Leading Jewish organizations, including the Workmen's Circle and the Jewish Socialist Federation, had approved the Socialist Party's anti-war manifesto. When the People's Council was formed, it had the backing of the International Ladies Garment Workers Union; the United Hebrew Trades; Rabbi Judah Magnes from New York's Lower East Side; Judge Jacob Panken; as well as James H. Maurer, President of the Pennsylvania Federation of Labor; the noted Socialist lawyer Morris Hillquit; and the young Presbyterian minister, Norman Thomas. The Council had 284 branches in New York City alone. These included chapters in 93 unions representing over 900,000 workers. The Council formally argued that Samuel Gompers and the AFL worked

[2] *American Labor Year Book, 1919–1920* (New York, 1920), p. 81.
[3] Frank L. Grubbs, Jr., "Council and Alliance Labor Propaganda: 1917–1919," *Labor History*, VII (1966), 156–72.

with anti-union employers to prevent strikes during wartime. The Council accused the AFL of favoring suppression
of free speech, and of refusing to wage a vigorous fight to
maintain labor's hard-won living standards.[4]

Samuel Gompers was forced to take note of these developments. Robert Maisel, editor of the Socialist *New
York Call*, had informed him of the Council's formation.
The movement was supported by the Socialist Party, Maisel wrote, and meant to infiltrate organized labor with
propaganda that would cause interference with the war
effort.[5] After receiving this information, Gompers left for
New York City. At a meeting with Ernest Bohm, head of
the Central Federated Union, Gompers was told that pacifist elements had actually gained strength in Jewish union
locals. Gompers then conferred with other CFU officials to
discuss formation of a new loyalty group that would be
able to counter pacifist propaganda. He also stressed the
need to "Americanize" the union movement. Noting an
element of treason among Jewish workers, Gompers argued that they were "cowed and dominated by radicals."
The CFU had to oppose the propaganda issued by Morris
Hillquit and the Socialist Party. Gompers met with editors
of Jewish newspapers, established a CFU speaker's bureau
and chose writers to prepare stories that favored the war
effort. Gompers' experience with anti-war sentiment
among Jewish workers in New York was the first step in
the formation of a national pro-war organization.[6]

If anti-war sentiment had been isolated among Jewish
unionists in New York, it might have been possible to ignore it. But information received by Gompers indicated
that the war was highly unpopular throughout the United

[4] *Ibid.*, 157. Cf. Bernard Mandel, *Samuel Gompers* (Yellow
Springs, Ohio), p. 390.
[5] Maisel to Gompers, June 9, 1917, June 26, 1917; cited in
Grubbs, *op. cit.*, 157–58.
[6] Minutes of the conference on Americanization, August 15,
1917, Samuel Gompers MSS, State Historical Society of Wisconsin,
Madison, Wis. Cf. Lewis Lorwin, *The American Federation of Labor*, p. 148; Samuel Gompers, *Seventy Years of Life and Labor*, II,
pp. 379–81.

States. "How to neutralize the campaign now being waged throughout the country in the interest of 'an early peace,' under the guise of the so-called People's Council," wrote Ralph M. Easley, was the question of the day. "Few realize the headway that this movement is making." The National Civic Federation leader reported that "mass meetings are held nightly and are enthusiastically attended in the big industrial centers from Maine to California, and it has an abundance of funds." Easley had received a report from Charles B. Barrett of the Farmers Cooperative Union. The farm group head told him that in travels through Virginia, North and South Carolina, Georgia, Tennessee, Kentucky, Indiana, and Illinois, he had found that " 'the actual disloyalty is appalling,' " and that " '60% of the farmers and 25% of the townspeople are not only opposed to the war but in favor of making peace on any terms.' "[7]

Similar reports reached Gompers from Milwaukee, Wisconsin. Labor lawyer William B. Rubin admitted "that even among the older delegates, Socialism is gaining."[8] Rubin had "one H. of a time holding lines for our friend, Gompers," and chief captain of the molders' union, John P. Frey, confirmed that "the local movement is antagonistic . . . to the Gompers war policy." Frey himself originally felt that Gompers was not "100% right in regard to the situation."[9] Rubin had little success. He was forced to report the "sad fact that Milwaukee labor as an organization has not acted in accordance with your wishes and beliefs along the lines indicated by . . . your various stands on the European crisis."[10]

The widespread unpopularity of the war was of equal concern to Woodrow Wilson and his Administration. The Administration tried to meet anti-war organizations by

[7] Easley statement, August 1, 1917, file on the Committee of 100 on Foreign Relations, National Civic Federation MSS, New York Public Library. (Cited hereafter as NCF MSS.)

[8] Rubin to John P. Frey, September 11, 1917, William B. Rubin MSS, State Historical Society of Wisconsin, Madison, Wis.

[9] Rubin to Frey, June 20, 1917; Frey to Rubin, August 20, 1917, Rubin to Gompers, November 15, 1917, *ibid.*

[10] *Ibid.*

various moves to destroy Socialist and IWW organizations
and journals. But they also moved to form new pro-war
liberal groups that might conceivably gain the confidence
of rank-and-file Socialists, workers, and reformers. After
war was declared, Wilson created the Committee on Public
Information. Assigning money to the group from emergency funds provided by an act of Congress, Wilson appointed George Creel as its administrative head. Under
Creel's direction, the CPI became a propaganda agency. Its
function was to mobilize journalists, writers, artists, and
others to firmly oppose any sentiment that favored a con-
ciliatory policy toward Germany. The CPI published its
own papers, issued press releases, and set up its own
speakers' bureau.

Creel and Wilson realized, however, that a need existed
to create independent pro-war organizations among workers and pro-war Socialists. Such an organization was the
American Alliance for Labor and Democracy. The suggestion for creation of such a group came originally from the
pro-war Socialist leader, John Spargo. Spargo had learned
that Samuel Gompers shared his own analysis of the European conflict. After conferring with Woodrow Wilson,
Spargo was told by Wilson that he was " 'distressed and
troubled by the conditions in certain parts of the country
with respect to the war,' " especially with the " 'very sullen
resentment.' " Spargo promised to approach Gompers and
suggest that members of the pro-war Social-Democratic
League "link up with picked men from the A.F. of L." to
form a pro-war labor organization. Soon the two men informed Wilson of their agreement. The President told
Spargo not to waste time trying to raise money for the
organization, since he had " 'a fund that Congress has
voted that is to be spent at my discretion!' "[11]

Plans for formation of the AALD were also worked on
in National Civic Federation offices by Gompers and Ralph
M. Easley. Easley informed Gompers of the truth that Wil-

---

[11] John Spargo, Columbia Oral History Collections (Special Collections, Butler Library, Columbia University, N.Y.). Hereafter material from this collection shall be abbreviated as COHC.

son "has an appropriation of $100,000,000 to do with as
he pleases." The President had already given one hundred
thousand dollars to George Creel to set up the Committee
on Public Information. Easley suggested that Gompers
phone Creel and have him broach the subject of the Alliance with Wilson. "He has access to the President and this
is the kind of thing his bureau would be glad to promote."
While the CPI would have nothing formally to do with the
AALD, Easley noted it could "furnish the funds for both
the publicity and organization work." Easley volunteered
to attend any meeting with Creel and to handle any follow-
up work that might be necessary. While he was willing to
try and raise money from NCF funds for the Alliance,
Easley noted that "my instinct leads towards the White
House on this matter."[12]

A few months later, Easley revealed to Vincent Astor
that the NCF's work was "bearing fruit." The Civic Federation, he claimed, had "helped to organize . . . the American
Alliance for Labor and Democracy, of which Mr. Gompers
is President and which is made up entirely of wage earners
and socialists who have left the party on account of its
capture by the German 'Hillquits.' " Easley added that the
AALD was "formed in my office and that I advanced the
first $700 necessary to carry it. It is now financed by the
Creel bureau, the money coming out of the President's
$100,000,000 fund."[13]

The American Alliance would actually function as a labor subsidiary of the Administration's propaganda bureau.
Under complete financial control of the Committee on
Public Information, the AALD was an Administration "labor front" meant to drum up support for a pro-war policy
among workers. The Administration might have attempted
this task through the CPI itself. Wilson understood, however, that an institution uniquely suitable to reaching laborers was needed. Gompers followed the advice presented
by Easley and Spargo. After contacting Creel, he learned
that the Administration was willing and ready to assume

[12] Easley to Gompers, July 12, 1917, NCF MSS.
[13] Easley to Vincent Astor, November 14, 1917, *ibid.*

responsibility for the new pro-war organization. Creel wrote that he was "ready to get behind you and the Central Federated Union in your attempt to Americanize the labor movement." Creel added that the "entire movement" had to be "governed and directed by organized labor." He suggested that the AALD offices be set up on the Lower East Side of New York, since he wanted "the meaning of America, and the purpose of America, to be put before the foreign born in all their languages."[14]

Having established the Alliance, Creel revealed exactly how much the Administration valued its work. "This is our most important body," he wrote to Cyrus H. McCormick, "and I am eager to have it stand on its own feet." Creel asked the famous agricultural implements manufacturer to help Frank E. Wolfe, the major AALD fund-raiser, gain financial security for the organization. This would "not only please me," Creel advised, "but others who are above me."[15]

The Alliance itself had its own staff. Gompers functioned as the nominal president, but the outfit was directed by Robert Maisel, a former Socialist. J. G. Phelps Stokes accepted the position of treasurer, after being assured that he would not be held responsible for any debts incurred. The AALD had, Maisel told him, "sufficient money to carry out our work."[16] In reality, both Maisel and Stokes were figureheads. George Creel kept tight control of both financial affairs and Alliance policy. Creel made all basic decisions on matters, including what pamphlets and statements the Alliance should publish. As he later told the League for National Unity, the CPI had "formed an alliance for labor and democracy by Mr. Gompers, and the Government is behind it to the limit of its power."[17]

[14] Creel to Gompers, July 26, 1917 NA, RG 63, CPI 1–A1.
[15] Creel to McCormick, December 4, 1917, *ibid.*, I (A–6).
[16] Maisel to Stokes, August 23, 1917, J. G. Phelps Stokes MSS (Butler Library, Columbia University).
[17] Minutes of the League for National Unity, September 12, 1917, NCF MSS, Box 168. See Maisel to Creel, October 22, 1917, and Creel to Maisel, October 23, 1917, NA, RG 63, CPI 1–A1. When

Formation of the Alliance also marked the first formal cooperation between Gompers and the small group of pro-war Socialists. The acceptance of unity with these Socialists by Gompers and the Wilson Administration revealed a sophisticated understanding of the uses to which the Socialists could be put. The participation of Socialists in the Alliance, Creel and Wilson must have realized, would create the very mantle of legitimacy for an operation that might otherwise appear questionable. Moreover, the Alliance stood little chance of influencing pro-Socialist workers unless it included representation from men who had been traditional opponents of Gompers' form of business unionism. Only men who had themselves been members of the Socialist Party would stand a chance of having their views considered by dissident anti-war workers.

Gompers himself attributed the impetus behind formation of the Alliance to the pro-war Socialists. Pacifists and pro-German groups, he asserted, had assumed "the function of the bona fide labor movement of New York." This development had led him to meet with those Socialists who had broken with the anti-war Socialist Party. Because they were not eligible for membership in the trade union movement, "and in order that they might give good service to the labor movement, and to the country . . . a system of agitation and education in which the service of the people could be availed, the American Alliance, was formed."[18]

The services given to the Administration by these Socialists were even appreciated by conservatives like Easley. The views of Socialists like Algie M. Simons, Easley wrote to Robert Lansing, were quite worthy of consideration. "Of course," Easley argued, "he is still a Socialist and is trying to make Socialism appear important." But Easley understood that if Simons and the other pro-war Socialists "rep-

---

Maisel asked permission to publish an AFL report on the Alliance, Creel replied: "Before giving any such consent I must see what the proceedings are. Please send them to me and I will answer at once."

[18] Report of meeting of the AALD, Assembly room of the AFL Building, February 7, 1918, Gompers MSS.

resented the party in this country," the Administration
could even trust them to travel to Europe for international
Socialist conferences.[19]

For the Socialists concerned, participation in the AALD
meant that the Socialist component of their ideology had
diminished. Not only had they become absorbed in the AFL
machinery, they had adopted Gompers' business union
ideology as well. Phelps Stokes, the new treasurer of the
Alliance, wrote that the AFL policy had his "hearty approval." He had "in mind particularly Mr. Gompers's support of the present Administration at Washington." Stokes
was even less fearful of government regulation during
wartime than most of the labor men. He was convinced
that the Administration was more sympathetic to the AFL
than was generally supposed. Stokes gave his approval to
the new collusion of government, industry, and labor and
to the management of the economy undertaken by the War
Industries Board. "Personally," Stokes explained, "I should
not fear, but on the contrary should approve, the exercise
of a large measure of control over the conditions of labor
in war industries by a joint board representing the Administration, the managers of the industries and the members
of the Federation."[20]

Assured of solid support from both the Administration
and the pro-war Socialists, Gompers was able to launch
the AALD by mid-August. A circular was sent to all local
and international AFL unions, informing them of the
AALD's existence. The Alliance had been built, Gompers
stated, to combat "suspicious bodies in our midst" who were
trying to undermine organized labor, "thus giving aid and
comfort to the forces of reaction and autocracy." All AFL
branches were urged to establish local AALD chapters.
"Minutes count," Gompers emphasized. "The pro-German
cause gains by every moment of American delay."[21]

The first item on the AALD agenda was a massive re-

---

[19] Easley to Lansing, June 13, 1917, NCF MSS, Box 54.
[20] Stokes to Chester M. Wright, July 12, 1917, Stokes MSS.
[21] Circular letter of Gompers to AFL locals, August 15, 1917,
Gompers MSS.

sponse to action proposed by the anti-war People's Council. The Council had announced its sponsorship of a national anti-war conference to be held in Minneapolis the following September. When Gompers heard the news he decided not to "run away." The AFL leader pledged "to be there when they were. The psychology of the time and situation demanded that there should be a clear-cut distinction between what the People's Council represented and what the American trade unionists represented, and because the mind of the people of the United States was focused upon Minneapolis we decided that the conference [of the AALD] should be held there."[22]

The call for an AALD convention, to be held in the same city chosen by the People's Council, was sent out to every central union body and AFL affiliate. But Gompers soon learned that the Minnesota authorities did not approve of free speech for anti-war advocates. They denied the People's Council the right to hold their convention in Minnesota. Gompers did not view this decision as reason to cancel plans for the AALD Convention. Gompers proceeded to contact the pro-war Socialists to formulate plans. Phelps Stokes informed Spargo of the proposed date, and asked his comrade to arrive early in order to hold preliminary meetings with Chester Wright and Robert Maisel. Maisel had told Stokes that he had "come direct from Gompers to ask me to attend the conference, and to ask that I urge you to be there too." Stokes added that "the possibilities in view are immense."[23]

By getting noted radicals to participate, Gompers and the Wilson Administration were making it easier for Socialists and other radicals to support the war. The endorsement of the Alliance by Frank P. Walsh made the Administration's task that much easier. A noted humanitarian labor lawyer, Walsh had previously been appointed by Wilson to be co-chairman (with William Howard Taft) of the

[22] *Proceedings of the 37th Annual Convention of the AFL, 1917*, p. 305. (Hereafter AFL conventions shall be referred to as *1917 AFL Convention*.)
[23] Stokes to Spargo, July 25, 1917, Stokes MSS.

President's wartime labor mediation commission. Now Walsh took part in making arrangements for the AALD Convention and also sought to recruit participants. Walsh especially tried to get Jake Sheppard, a pro-war Socialist from Minneapolis, to speak at the meeting. Walsh thought Sheppard was "the leading Socialist in this part of the country," a man who was "particularly strong with the Socialist crowd and the labor movement in Oklahoma and Kansas" and who "undoubtedly has big influence with them." Walsh wired Chester M. Wright that he would not only appear on the program himself, but would be willing to conduct a speaking tour on behalf of the convention.[24]

The content of the Convention was to be carefully arranged by George Creel. As head of the Administration's massive propaganda agency, and as financier of the AALD, Creel was not about to allow Gompers and Spargo to make preparations on their own. Before the first of the month Creel had "concluded a day with the 'Alliance' putting the last touches to the Minneapolis meeting!" At this conference Creel "explained fully my ideas and wishes with regard to resolution[s]." He advised that the main conference resolution "should concern itself with the war and declare it a *war of self defense*—recite the three years of forbearance that were bloodstained by the brutal aggressions of the Imperial German Government and put the Alliance back of the President squarely." The resolution had to be "an explicit statement of the causes that *drew* us into war—our aims, etc. so that we can see it in leaflet form in all languages."[25]

Creel's additional instructions revealed that he was aware of the danger that the Alliance would be viewed as an Administration front. The Convention, he had instructed, should go on record in favor of free speech and the right of peaceful assembly. It should also urge that the burden of the war should be borne by the wealthy. The delegates should call for a tax on profits that would remove

[24] Walsh to George Creel, August 30, 1917, Frank P. Walsh MSS, New York Public Library.
[25] Creel to Walsh, September 1, 1917, *ibid.*

the greed from war. Resolutions should also support government operation of the railroads and all businesses in which a Federal role was necessary to maintain munitions production.[26]

Creel saw the need for delegates to use the type of radical rhetoric that would establish the Alliance's independence, but which would not threaten its support of the war effort. But while the Convention should go on record in favor of free speech, Creel urged that the resolution not be specific in defense of the principle. The Alliance should not make the mistake of condemning Minnesota's governor for refusing to allow the People's Council to meet in Minneapolis. It was good enough to declare for free speech in the abstract. To help the Convention leaders prepare for the meeting, Creel mailed Gompers a précis of the Administration's labor record. He also sent Spargo a résumé of America's war aims, the bulk of which could be used for material in speeches. Walsh, he advised, could deal with the Irish question. The more radical resolutions that some delegates wished to present could be saved for the last day when publicity waned. "All the luck in the world," wrote Creel. "Stick close to Gompers and see that the program moves with zip."[27]

Gompers did not need Creel's encouragement. He had already cabled his AFL organizers to devote their time to recruiting labor representatives to attend the AALD Convention. The AFL chartered a special train, the "Red, White and Blue Special," that would carry delegates from New York to Minneapolis. Despite these extensive preparations, only 170 delegates attended.

The Convention sponsors had no trouble in steering the proceedings to coincide with Creel's directives. Stressing that the war had to be fought to victory, the AALD Main Resolution argued that any talk of negotiated peace was akin to asking German workers to remain living under slavery. The resolution attacked those "enemies of the Republic who, falsely assuming to speak in the name of

[26] *Ibid.*
[27] *Ibid.*

labor and democracy, are now ceaselessly striving to ob-
struct the operations of the government. In misrepresenting the government's purposes, in traducing the character
of Gompers and his advisors, in stealthily attempting to
incite sedition and in openly or impliedly counselling resistance to the enforcement of laws enacted for the national defense, they abuse the rights of free speech, free
assemblage and a free press. In the name of liberty they encourage anarchy; in the name of democracy they strive to
defeat the will of the majority; and in the name of humanity they render every possible aid and comfort to the brutal
Prussian autocracy." As Creel suggested, resolutions also
were passed urging protection of labor's high living standards, conscription of wealth, the end of profiteering, and
labor representation on all government boards and at the
official peace conference.[28]

The Administration's guiding hand had been felt. Walsh
regarded the Convention as "a great success." He was
"immediately taken with Spargo," he informed George
Creel. "He is the real thing. Gompers was great, too. He
had the thing worked out splendidly in his own head, and
steered a consistent course." As for the points that Creel
had asked the Convention to take up, Walsh wrote Creel
that "you probably noticed that they all went into the resolutions." Material that Creel had sent along had also been
put to good use. Spargo's "epitome of the President's expressed war aims and peace terms was a masterpiece. I
took it to be the joint work of all of you." Walsh expressed
satisfaction that they had "an organization which, if
worked out properly will put an absolute quietus on all
supposed spokesmen for labor and the radical element.
They will continue to look cheaper day by day until they
finally disappear. . . . The whole scheme," Walsh reflected,
"is alive with possibilities."[29]

Equally pleased with the Alliance's possibilities were the
pro-war Socialists. John Spargo believed that participation

---

[28] *1917 AFL Convention*, Report of the Executive Committee, pp.
82–83.
[29] Walsh to Creel, September 10, 1917, Walsh MSS.

of his group was a major victory for the loyal Socialist forces. The AALD was important because it symbolized the new "close union between the more liberal American Socialists and the recognized Labor Union movement."[30] Spargo would soon learn, however, that Samuel Gompers did not intend to allow the pro-war Socialists to engage in independent political activity, especially formation of a new party. Gompers insisted that the pro-war Socialists endorse the AFL's "non-partisan" approach, and he permitted no deviation. It was the pro-war Socialists who endorsed the AFL, he pointed out, not vice versa.[31]

It was left to another pro-war Socialist to inform Gompers about the value that radicals had to the Wilson Administration. W. J. Ghent was irritated at Gompers' calling into question the good faith of radicals who had attended the AALD Convention. Ghent saw no reason why delegates had to offer uncritical support to the Democratic Party. "There is an implication," Ghent complained, "that some special favor was granted the Socialists and radicals in admitting them to participation in the Alliance convention. My belief is that had it not been for their participation the convention would have been a complete failure. The press would have ignored it as an Administration 'plant.' Public opinion generally would have said that the American Federation of Labor had done no more than was expected of it by reason of its understanding with the present Administration, and that it could not have done less." Ghent had put his finger on the importance that the radicals had to Administration plans. "The inclusion of socialists and radicals," he tried to explain to Gompers, "gave it a representative character, which immediately broadened its significance."[32]

Despite the high hopes the Administration had for the AALD, it became a less important organization as the

---

[30] Spargo to Roland D. Sawyer, August 23, 1917, Stokes MSS.
[31] Gompers to Robert Maisel, September 29, 1917, Gompers MSS. For the conflict between Gompers and Spargo around building the National Party, see the previous chapter.
[32] Ghent to Gompers, October 10, 1917, Stokes MSS.

international situation shifted. In March 1918 the German offensive against Russia led to Russian capitulation and the Brest-Litovsk Treaty which Germany forced on the weak Soviet government. The harsh treaty provisions caused many anti-war unionists, particularly those among the Jewish needle trades in New York City, to re-evaluate their attitude toward American participation in the war. Thus the United Hebrew Trades officially reversed its earlier anti-war position. These Jewish workers rallied on behalf of Woodrow Wilson's announced peace terms. The Fourteen Points, they now argued, proved that the President was a staunch defender of peace and an opponent of militarism.[33]

Robert Maisel was able to inform Gompers that they had succeeded in Americanizing the Lower East Side of New York. Indeed, the Hebrew Trades officers had met with him to discuss a new program. Maisel asked for a renewed drive to "get over to our side 200,000 men and women to help the government and its Allies in a successful prosecution of the war." The problem was that finances were low and that George Creel was no longer willing to foot the bill.[34]

Maisel believed, perhaps because he held an executive position with the Alliance, that the AALD's work was as important as ever. Many Lower East Side Jews, he reported, were still not willing to adopt resolutions upholding the government, although they did support participation in the Liberty Loan campaign. Many of them now wanted to build a new Jewish Socialist League. They would argue that the best way to stand by Russia would be through support of the United States government. But for this group to succeed, the AALD had to make new strides "in killing the pacifist movement."[35]

The Alliance did not gain the funds which its officers

[33] Melvyn Dubofsky, "Organized Labor in New York City and the First World War, 1914–1918," *New York History*, Vol. 42 (October 1961), p. 16.

[34] Maisel to Gompers, March 8, 1918, Gompers MSS.

[35] Maisel to Gompers, March 12, 1918, *ibid.*

desired. Between August 25, 1917, and March 8, 1918, general contributions totaled only $11,834. Rent and salaries were still paid by Creel's bureau. This amounted to another $2,500 per month. But Creel was becoming impatient with the Alliance, and was continually threatening to withdraw Administration support. Finally, Creel restricted financial aid to a small amount regarded by AALD executives as insufficient for extensive propaganda campaigns.[36]

Creel himself complained to Gompers about his dissatisfaction with Maisel's vague plans to continue loyalty campaigns at the war's end. Gompers reported that "considerable adverse criticism" had come to his attention.[37] When the war ended, the Alliance experienced the effect that postwar disillusion had on some of its membership. Frank P. Walsh, the labor attorney who had helped Creel arrange the Alliance Convention, became the most prominent member to resign. Walsh left after reading an anti-Bolshevik article composed by Gustavus Myers, which the Alliance published. Walsh considered the article "a vicious onslaught on a great body of people, fighting valiantly to control their own destiny, whether right or wrong." Walsh now felt, as he told Gompers, "very grave doubt" about the Alliance's "utility now that hostilities are over."[38] Walsh seemed to realize, as critics had always asserted, that the Alliance had served to weaken the efforts of all radical and Socialist groups.

With diminishing Administration financial support, and the resignation of key participants, the American Alliance was forced to close shop early in 1919. During the war, it had functioned as the major vehicle the Administration had developed to encourage a pro-war orientation among the rank-and-file of the labor and Socialist movements. Specializing in the distribution of pro-war propa-

36 Lorwin, *The American Federation of Labor*, pp. 151–52.
37 Gompers to Maisel, March 14, 1918, Gompers MSS.
38 Walsh to Frank E. Wolfe, December 30, 1918, Walsh to Gompers, December 30, 1918, Walsh MSS. Maisel to Gompers, January 2, 1919, Gompers MSS.

ganda, the AALD was an adjunct to the larger Committee on Public Information.

The formation of the American Alliance for Labor and Democracy represented more than an organizational means for Samuel Gompers to fight the war on the home front. It represented the domestic use of the organized labor movement by the Wilson Administration for purposes of gathering support for Administration foreign policy. In deciding to support the Alliance, the Wilson Administration began the now common practice of subsidizing the work of seemingly independent organizations that are pledged to defend Administration policy. The secrecy employed by the Administration in its support and control of the AALD was a prototype of the secret subsidies of American labor unions by the Central Intelligence Agency during the 1950's and 1960's.

During the Cold War era, the CIA subsidized unions and labor conferences, sponsored international conferences through front groups, organized magazines that would give a voice to anti-Communist intellectuals, and often used many of the groups they financed to carry out work abroad that could not be conducted by their own agents. In many cases, organizations and individuals who found themselves to have been recipients of CIA funding claimed ignorance of their sponsor. When the old Socialist leader Norman Thomas was informed that the CIA had financed his own activity in Latin America, Thomas responded that if the CIA wanted to finance democratic socialism, it was all right with him. Thomas missed the obvious point: that the CIA had funded his work not to sponsor any form of socialism, but to avail themselves of the talent that would bring new forces (albeit forces favoring reform) into the anti-Communist struggle in Latin America.

The CIA financed those organizations whose work would be useless if the Administration's backing and support were to be made known. While the AALD was not supported on the same vast scale as the CIA was in the later period, the principle employed was the same. Had Administration control of the Alliance been publicly acknowledged, any possible effect the organization might have had would have evaporated. Rank-and-file delegates to the AALD Convention had no knowledge of the extent to which their organization was government-controlled, nor of the fact that the resolutions presented at the convention had been drawn up in advance by George Creel. The method by which the AALD was created, its financial support by the Administration, and Creel's secret control of AALD policy, comprise the first example of how an American administration has used organized labor to serve its own purposes.

The Alliance also forged a new coalition between pro-war Socialists and the organized labor movement. But the consensus was achieved on terms proposed by Gompers and his associates. Each step that the pro-war Socialists took in the direction of unity with the AFL led them to become more absorbed in both Wilsonian liberalism and AFL business unionism, and moved them further away from their original Socialist perspective. Again, the unity of the pro-war Socialists and the AFL served only the Wilson Administration. It enabled them to build a united front with which they could appeal to Allied labor for support of American war aims. Working together, both groups could be of value in seeking to convince European labor groups and Socialist parties to support warfare against the Central Powers. This effort to influence the course taken by Allied labor is the next subject of our investigations.

CHAPTER

III

AMERICAN LABOR AND
THE ROOT COMMISSION
TO RUSSIA *

The unity between the American Federation of Labor and the pro-war Socialists had created a united front with which the Wilson Administration could confront Allied labor. Samuel Gompers had liked to refer to himself as a "pacifist." He had already shown how flexible his "pacifism" was, however, when he gave AFL support to the cause of Cuban independence and favored the Spanish-American war. "Perhaps never in the history of mankind," Gompers had declared to the assembled AFL delegates in 1898, "was a war begun on so high a plane of honor and humanity, or so calculated to be of so great an advantage to the onward march of civilization."[1] But it was the first Russian Revolution, in March 1917, that became the occasion for American labor's entrance on the stage of world diplomacy. Since conventional diplomats felt unsuited to deal with the Russian Socialists, they turned to American labor for help in the execution of Administration policy. For its part, the AFL, under Gompers' leadership, was only

* An earlier version of this chapter appeared in *Studies on the Left*, III (1962), 34–47.
[1] *18th AFL Convention*, 1898, 18.

too eager to put on the garb of labor statesman. As a result, American labor's debut as foreign policy spokesman took shape in the organization of the Root Commission to Russia in the spring of 1917.

The overthrow of the Czar and the accession to power of the Lvov regime was greeted warmly by the liberal supporters of the Allied powers in the United States. The joy of the Wilson Administration at being relieved of the burden of public association with an Allied autocracy was tempered only by a fear that the new popular government might lead Russia out of the war. To prevent such a breach in the wall of resistance to German autocracy, Woodrow Wilson appointed Elihu Root as head of a commission to go to Russia to explore means of cooperation in the prosecution of the war, and to determine the extent to which the Provisional Government might be relied upon to continue military operations against the Germans. Composed of men sympathetic to a liberal revolution, the Root Commission was conceived to urge the Russian people to intensify the fight against the Kaiser.[2]

Historians have treated the appointment to the commission of a labor leader and a Socialist as an afterthought designed to counteract the conservative image projected by Elihu Root, the commission's chairman. George F. Kennan, for example, writes that President Wilson (at Samuel Gompers' request), asked the pro-war Socialist William English Walling to serve as a member for that purpose.[3] In fact, however, the Administration recognized from the outset the prime importance of labor's participation on the commission. Indeed, before the chairmanship was decided upon, Wilson had concluded that trade unionists should be used to gain the confidence of the new Rus-

[2] Secretary of State Robert Lansing to David R. Francis, May 1, 1917, in Ray Stannard Baker, *Woodrow Wilson: Life and Letters,* VII, *War Leader, April 6, 1917–February 28, 1918* (New York, 1939), 45; cf. Robert Lansing, *War Memoirs of Robert Lansing* (Indianapolis, Ind., 1935), p. 334.

[3] George F. Kennan, *Soviet-American Relations, 1917–1920,* I, *Russia Leaves the War* (Princeton, N.J., 1956), 20.

sian government. Administration leaders shared Gompers' belief that because "the revolutionary body in control consists of workingmen, socialists and soldiers, the U.S. Commission, to be most effective, must contain representatives best able to advise with the Council of Workingmen and Soldiers."[4]

On April 10, 1917, three days after the United States entered the war, Wilson's ambassador at Petrograd wired Secretary of State Robert Lansing that Russia's military situation was precarious. Urging that everything possible be done to strengthen the situation, Ambassador David R. Francis warned that Russian Socialist circles were urging peace, and that there was a danger they would succeed in influencing the army.[5] The next day Lansing brought the matter to Wilson's attention, calling for action "to prevent the socialistic element in Russia from carrying out any plan which would destroy the efficiency of the Allied Powers."[6] Fearing that the German Socialists were seeking a separate peace with the Russians, Lansing suggested that a labor-oriented commission of three men be sent to Russia at once. Lansing proposed only one man for the Commission: Samuel Gompers. The AFL president, Lansing be-

[4] Samuel Gompers, "U.S. Labor Envoy to Russia," *American Federationist*, XXIV (1917), 469.

[5] Francis to Lansing, April 10, 1917, printed in *Papers Relating to the Foreign Relations of the United States: The Lansing Papers, 1914–1920*, II (Washington, D.C., 1940), 325–26. (All volumes in this series hereafter cited as *FR*.)

Other evidence indicates that defeat of the Russian Socialists' influence was connected with vigorous prosecution of the war. Cf. Robert Lansing, *op. cit.*, pp. 330–31. Lansing recalled that on the day Ambassador Francis was instructed to recognize the new Revolutionary government, Russian War Minister Gutchkoff told Francis that "the principal menace to a vigorous prosecution of the war was the socialistic element among the workingmen . . . [which] had greater control over the soldiers than the Ministry itself." Cf. Petrograd Consul North Winship to Lansing, May 8, 1917, in *FR, Russia, 1918* (Washington, D.C., 1931), 49–50. Winship reported that the "ignorant Russian masses" believed that capitalist interests of England and France were forcing continuance of the war. Distrust of the Allies and the "feeling of being forced to continue a distasteful and irksome war" was a "tremendous danger."

[6] Lansing to Wilson, April 11, 1917. *FR, The Lansing Papers*, II, 325.

lieved, "would have a very decided influence with the labor element in Russia," and his presence would serve to prevent "the tendency of the socialists toward a separate peace with Germany."[7]

Responding to Lansing's proposal, Wilson decided to send a commission to Russia at once. The President suggested a group of men of broad view and proven discretion, who would be sympathetic to the Revolution. A prominent Jew such as Oscar S. Straus should be included, Wilson wrote Lansing, in addition to a businessman (Willard Straight), an educator (Benjamin I. Wheeler), and Samuel Gompers, whose presence Wilson took for granted.[8] Replying the same day, Lansing noted that it would be inadvisable to overplay the "Jew element." He recommended instead John R. Mott, Cyrus McCormick, and Samuel Bertron as potential members and he assumed Wilson would "agree that Samuel Gompers is as valuable a man as we could get."[9]

Indeed, Gompers had urged the Russians to pursue a moderate course almost from the outbreak of the revolution. On March 23, Ambassador Francis reported that the danger from the Socialist element had not been entirely dissipated and urged Lansing to request Gompers to act. Socialist and labor circles in Britain and France, the Ambassador cabled, had already asked the Russian workers to support their new government in its prosecution of the war. It would be "opportunely helpful," he added, if Gompers addressed such a cable to the Petrograd labor leaders, since "time is precious" and the Socialists among the workingmen and soldiers were holding a "continuous meeting in the Duma," advocating "abolition of classes and the right of soldiers to disobey their officers."[10] Gompers then wired the Russian workers that freedom was the product of evolution, rather than revolution, and that they could

[7] *Ibid.*, 325.
[8] Wilson to Lansing, April 12, 1917, *ibid.*, 326.
[9] Baker, *op. cit.*, 18–19, citing Lansing to Wilson, April 12, 1917.
[10] Francis to Lansing, March 23, 1917, *FR, Russia*, I, *1918*, 15–16.

not hope to achieve their ideal state immediately.[11] Ambassador Francis responded that the cable had been delivered to Duma Chairman Cheidze, and that the message was "excellent" and would "have [a] good effect."[12]

During April, Gompers amplified his comments and suggestions concerning the commission to Russia. Refusing to go himself, he recommended to Secretary of State Lansing that James Duncan, AFL first vice-president, be considered.[13] On May 4, Gompers formally recommended James Duncan and James Lord. Commending Lord as a "constructive radical," Gompers noted that both men were well known abroad, and could do the job of representing American ideals of freedom and justice in Russia.[14] The next day Gompers learned that James Duncan had been appointed as the labor representative on the commission. After hearing the news, Gompers complained to his immediate associates about the appointment of Elihu Root as commission chairman. The selection of Root, he argued, was an unfortunate choice. To carry his work through successfully, the conservative statesman would have to surround himself with a class of people different from those with whom he was accustomed to associate. This would be difficult for Root to accomplish.[15]

While the Wilson Administration and AFL officials were discussing the question of a labor representative, the American Socialist Party began a sustained attack upon the Root Commission. It was this activity which forced Wilson to consider the appointment of a Socialist member to the commission. On May 1, Socialist Party official Morris Hillquit announced to the press that the Russian Socialists would be made aware of his Party's estimate of Elihu Root.

[11] Gompers to N. S. Cheidze, April 2, 1917, *ibid.*, 18.
[12] William Phillips to Gompers, quoting Francis to Department of State (April 7, 1917), April 9, 1917; in NA, RG 59, 861.00/316 (Files of the Department of State).
[13] Gompers to the Executive Council of the AFL, memo of May 9, 1917, Samuel Gompers MSS, State Historical Society of Wisconsin, Madison, Wis.
[14] Gompers to Lansing, May 4, 1917, *ibid.*
[15] Gompers memo of May 5, 1917, *ibid.* Gompers never publicly criticized Root's appointment.

By the time Root reached Petrograd, Hillquit predicted, the Russian people would know of his conservative record.[16] The reasons why the Socialists opposed Root's appointment were explained by the noted Socialist intellectual, Meyer London. Writing to President Wilson on April 28, London asked Wilson, "to revoke the appointment of Mr. Root as Chairman." Root was the "last person in the world to command the confidence of that awakened country." He was not the type of lawyer for whom the Russian people had respect. Root might have a practical mind, London reasoned, but the new Russia had her own standards. "Unless a man's life is associated with some noble ideal, he is not looked upon as a practical man." Finally, London pointed out that the revolution could not have taken place without the Socialists, and any change would not be lasting without their cooperation. Thus they would view "the sending of Root as a calamity."[17] Another Socialist friendly to the Wilson Administration, J. G. Phelps Stokes, felt that "Pro-German" elements in the Socialist Party were unfairly branding Root as an arch-reactionary. But Stokes also felt that it would be disastrous if the commission was made up entirely of men of Root's character, with his strong anti-Socialist bias. Stokes felt that Root could have a place on the commission as a valuable minority member, because of his wide knowledge of international affairs.[18]

The Socialists' opposition was reinforced on May 1 when a noted Russian émigré addressed influential businessmen at a meeting of the Economic Club in New York. Professor Alexander Petrunkevitch warned his audience that because of the Socialist Party's criticism, the Root Commission would be met on its arrival with the distrust of the Russian Social Democrats who held power. Claiming that the Russians might be encouraged to sign a separate peace, Petrunkevitch urged the assembly to offset the danger by

[16] *New York Times,* May 2, 1917, p. 9.
[17] Meyer London to Wilson, April 28, 1917, Wilson MSS, File 6, Library of Congress.
[18] Stokes to the *New York American,* May 4, 1917, J. G. Phelps Stokes MSS, Butler Library, Columbia University.

appealing to President Wilson to place on the commission a man acceptable to the Russian Socialists. Unless such a man was appointed, the Russian press would write that the commission was sent for the purpose of fighting the Social Democrats. With an acceptable man present, it could easily carry the message that freedom depended on victory at the front, not on the building of a Socialist state.[19]

Many members of the audience, one Economic Club member reported to Wilson, "were deeply impressed" by Petrunkevitch's argument.[20] Oscar S. Straus, who was originally considered as a potential commission representative, wrote to George Kennan that if men who could render the best service were not selected, "the mission will be useless, if not harmful." Although he had high regard for Elihu Root, with whom he had been associated in the Cabinet, Straus questioned the wisdom of Root's selection. Straus echoed Petrunkevitch's warning, which he found to be bold and courageous. "The wise thing to do," Straus suggested, "would have been to submit the proposed names to the Russian government, especially as the purpose is to help them, and therefore the personnel must be acceptable in order to be of great service."[21]

Woodrow Wilson took these warnings to heart. On May 5, he invited the pro-war Socialist William English Walling to join the commission.[22] Walling, however, had already announced that he considered it his duty to stay in the United States to combat the anti-war activity of Morris Hillquit and the American Socialist Party.[23] On May 10, Walling wrote to the President that the Secretary of Labor had assured him that Wilson was "willing to accept my standpoint as to my possibilities for personal service as being correct."[24] President Wilson concurred, praising

[19] New York Times, May 2, 1917, pp. 1, 9.

[20] Louis Krower to Wilson, May 4, 1917, Wilson MSS.

[21] Oscar S. Straus to George Kennan, May 2, 1917; George Kennan MSS, Library of Congress.

[22] Wilson to Walling, May 5, 1917, William English Walling MSS, State Historical Society of Wisconsin, Madison, Wis.

[23] New York Times, May 4, 1917, p. 7.

[24] Walling to Wilson, May 10, 1917, Walling MSS.

Walling's "entire action throughout . . . recent consulta-
tions" on the Russian situation as having given him the
"greatest gratification."[25]

Working closely with the Administration and the AFL,
Walling continued his attacks on the anti-war Socialist
Party. On May 5 he and rubber magnate Charles R. Flint
brought Gompers the draft of a cable which Elihu Root
and Melville Stone of the Associated Press had helped them
prepare. Walling claimed that an "exceedingly dangerous"
situation existed in Russia as a result of the anti-war activity of such American Socialists as Victor Berger and Morris
Hillquit who urged their Russian comrades to adopt an
anti-war position. Holding that an anti-war stand actually
meant support of the Kaiser's peace plan, Walling and
Flint urged that a cable be sent to remedy the situation.
Gompers revised the draft and gave the cable to Flint to
send to Russia.[26]

The cable assured the Workmen's and Soldiers' Council
of Deputies in Petrograd that ninety-nine per cent of Americans supported the war against Germany, and that just as
in Russia, the American "agitators for a peace favorable
to Prussian militarism have been allowed to express their
opinions," which was why the "tools of the Kaiser appear
more influential than they really are." Attacking the anti-
war Socialists of the world as German agents, Gompers
claimed that they actually desired a German victory. Finally, Gompers pledged that the Root Commission would
not offer advice on the conduct of Russia's internal affairs,
but would offer only to help Russia combat Kaiserism.
Attacks on the commission from the United States, Gompers explained, were the efforts of "criminal pro-Kaiser"
propagandists, circulated with the intent of "arousing
hostile feelings between the two countries."[27] The message
was sent by cable to Petrograd by Secretary of State Lansing. Lansing suggested "that the delivery of the message

[25] Wilson to Walling, May 14, 1917, *ibid.*
[26] Gompers memo of May 5, 1917, Gompers MSS.
[27] Gompers to Workmen's and Soldiers' Council of Deputies,
Petrograd, May 6, 1917, *ibid.*

be made entirely unofficial so as not to have the appearance of an attempt on the part of this Government to influence their actions."[28]

Despite Gompers' and Walling's efforts to minimize the Socialist Party's attack, American Socialists continued to bombard the Root Commission with criticism. After Walling refused to become a member of the commission, President Wilson substituted another well-known pro-war Socialist, Charles Edward Russell. Lansing had been particularly impressed with Russell's attitude. Lansing believed that, of all the Socialists, "the ideas of Charles Edward Russell are more in accord with what I conceive to be the best suited to influence Russian socialists." Lansing quoted approvingly from some of Russell's writings, in which he advocated a war for victory until Germany's military party and absolutist government were overthrown.[29]

The decision to appoint Russell brought forth a new series of condemnations from the American Socialist Party and its followers. Max Eastman typified the Socialist reaction when he laughed at the "ludicrous touch" of sending an aged emissary like Root to "quiet all this tumult of Marxian lingoes that he can not understand." Eastman also attacked Russell as an "emotional, a sort of journalistic, evangelical Socialist" who could not cope with a revolution conducted according to erudite interpretations of Marxian science.[30]

Similarly, the left-wing socialist *International Socialist Review* attacked Root as a former friend of the Czarist regime who had suddenly been converted to Red revolution. As for Russell, he had lost all contact with workers in the factories. Both men were unable to understand the language of social revolution, the *Review* commented.

[28] Lansing to Embassy at Petrograd, May 7, 1917, NA, RG 59, 861.00/350a—Files Relating to the Internal Affairs of Russia.
[29] Lansing to Wilson, May 3, 1917, Wilson MSS, File 2, Box 118.
[30] Max Eastman, "Syndicalist-Socialist Russia," *International Socialist Review*, XVIII (1917), 78.

Their attempt to caution the revolutionists to act moderately would fail. "Too many Russian exiles," they explained, had "returned to Russia." These IWW's and Socialists would "inform the Russian comrades just what the profit system means in America."[31]

Equally hostile to the Root Commission, the Socialist Party's National Executive Committee attacked Russell as "one of a very slight minority of the members of the Socialist Party who favor the war." Commenting that the Socialist Party did "not consider it as its duty to give advice to the Russian Socialists as to what they shall or shall not do," the committee observed that the Russians were "necessarily much better acquainted" with circumstances in Russia than "any one in this country."[32] The Socialists' scorn was summed up by Upton Sinclair. While the news from Russia showed that the revolutionary forces were vindicating themselves and drawing up "a clear and intelligent revolutionary program," all that the United States could do was to send them Elihu Root and then try to use censorship to keep the Russians from learning out "what Root is!"[33]

The Socialist Party's opposition led the famous revolutionary novelist Maxim Gorky to express astonishment at the absence of genuine representatives of American labor and socialism on the Root Commission.[34] To deal with this problem, Russell made his journey equipped with a score of letters from American Socialists and labor leaders vouching for Russell's authenticity as a genuine American Socialist. Typical was one written by Rose Pastor Stokes, addressed to the famous "grandmother" of the Russian revolution, Katerina Breshkovskaya. Referring to Russell as "one of the best-loved men in the Socialist movement here," Mrs. Stokes said that there was "no one in whom the

---

[31] "The Passing Show-'Root'-ING in Russia," *ibid.*, 5–6.
[32] *New York Times*, May 16, 1917, p. 2.
[33] Sinclair to J. G. Phelps Stokes, May 16, 1917, Stokes MSS.
[34] *New York Times*, May 18, 1917, p. 6.

revolutionary fire burns more purely, yet who is more generally respected, even by the enemies of Socialism."[35]

Evidently the opposition of the Socialist Party succeeded
in making matters difficult for the commission. AFL leader
James Duncan complained that the Russians listened to
anyone who had something to tell them. The IWW's and
radical Socialists with American passports in their pockets
were attacking the commission and playing Germany's
game by destroying all "that is good in the Socialist movement."[36] The International Harvester Company's Russian
agent, August Heid, confirmed that Russians who had
lived in America were stirring up the people. Because they
argued that the commission was not composed of proper
representatives, and that Root represented corporations
unsympathetic to the Russian Revolution, these radicals
seriously endangered the commission's success.[37] On one
occasion, Russian Socialists who had recently returned
from America attempted to persuade the people of Vladivostok to prevent the mission from proceeding to Petrograd. Russell reported that as he was approaching the
mission's train, he was confronted with a Russian-American who claimed to know him from the East Side of New
York. The man then "began a harangue in the familiar
style of the rancorous alien or Pro-German Socialist." This
group of "impossibilists," as Russell termed them, met in
the local Citizens' and Soldiers' Committee, and resolved to

---

[35] Rose Pastor Stokes to Katerina Breshkovskaya, May 3, 1917,
Charles Edward Russell MSS, Library of Congress. For other examples, see Algie M. Simons to V. Bourtseff, May 15, 1917, and to
Alexander Kollontai, May 15, 1917, *ibid.* Simons distorted the truth
when he wrote that Russell spoke "for nearly all the American born
Socialists." More accurately, Abraham Cahan wrote that the Russian Socialists knew to what extent Russell's views differed "from
that of the majority of socialists," but he agreed to put Russell in
touch with those Russian Socialists with whom he was in contact.
See Cahan to Russell, May 17, 1917, *ibid.* See also Allen Benson to
Russell, May 14, 1917, John O'Connell (Secretary, N.Y. Typographical Union No. 6) to Russell, May 14, 1917; Russell MSS.

[36] *The Garment Worker*, XVI, No. 45 (Aug. 24, 1917), 4.

[37] Diary of Cyrus McCormick's experiences on the Root Commission, June 3, 1917, Cyrus H. McCormick MSS, File Box 163, Russia,
State Historical Society of Wisconsin, Madison, Wis.

prevent them from leaving Vladivostok. But the soldiers, then voting with the moderate elements, told them that any attempt to interfere with the mission would be "followed by shooting." Due to the hostile feelings, the mission was quickly moved from Vladivostok to prevent further opposition from developing.[38]

Samuel Gompers also tried to overcome the adverse criticism by cabling the Executive Committee of Workmen's and Soldiers' Deputies that James Duncan was indeed an authorized labor leader. "It appears," Gompers wrote, "that notwithstanding the most altruistic and friendly cooperative action" on the part of the workers of America, the "Kaiser's agents in New York as well as in Russia carry on a campaign of misrepresentation and vilification."[39] Commenting editorially, *The New York Times* urged the United States government to support Gompers' fight against the "treasonable effort" of American Socialists to undermine the Root Commission. If the campaign succeeded, the *Times* added, it would be as serious a blow to the American war effort as defeat of the army in the field. The success of American Socialists in convincing the Russians that Duncan and Russell did not represent American labor was treasonous. It thwarted the Administration's efforts to keep Russia in the war. When a Socialist combined with others to frustrate a war measure, the *Times* concluded, "he is giving aid and comfort to the enemy."[40]

Faced with hostile criticism at home and the opposition of Russian Socialists, the Root Commission had set sail for Russia in May 1917. Aboard ship, Charles Edward Russell warned the other commissioners of the elements within Russia they would have to oppose. "The men whom we most have to fear," he told Elihu Root, "are the radicals who are called the 'reds.'" These were "a class of men who

[38] Charles E. Russell Diary, June 3, 1917, Russell MSS. Cf. Report of the Special Diplomatic Mission to Russia to the Secretary of State, August 1917, *FR, Russia, 1918*, I, 137.
[39] Gompers to the Executive Committee of Workmen's and Soldiers' Deputies, May 18, 1917, Gompers MSS.
[40] *New York Times*, May 20, 1917, Section II, p. 2.

would correspond in Russia to what we know in the United
States as 'I.W.W.'s.'" Trouble makers on any subject,
"they are 'agin the government' whatever that government
is." As influential men in the new Russian government,
their views and their force "must be reckoned with." The
hope Russell held was that these "reds" would be "in such
frame of mind that they can be reasoned with and held in
line."[41] To prepare the ground for this effort, Russell wired
Duma Chairman Cheidze that the American Socialist and
liberal position was being misrepresented in Russia, and
that he was coming "with full authentic information" about
it. Russell expressed his hope that the Russian Socialists
would defer conclusions until he had a chance to present
them with "actual facts."[42]

Russell was privately pessimistic about his chances of
influencing the Russian Socialists. The element in control
of the Russian provisional assembly would probably be
hostile to the United States. Cheidze, the Duma chieftain,
would be a difficult man to deal with because "he belongs
to a class who believes in that pure democracy which
places the workingman at the head of everything." Russell
told the commission members that he planned to assume a
proletarian appearance in order to better persuade Cheidze
to abandon his Socialist beliefs. "I am hoping to have a
talk with him," Russell declared, "and I have brought my
old clothes, so that I can wear them when I see him, and
thus I may stand a chance of getting his free opinions."
Maintaining that part of the Russian Socialist propaganda
was sincere, but that part was derived from German influence, Russell suggested that the commission members
"in our private conversations, as well as in all that we say
. . . meet that erroneous view by emphasizing the fact that
the United States is a real democracy."[43]

The task would be difficult, Russell stressed, because of

[41] Cyrus McCormick Diary, May 21, 1917, McCormick MSS. A
stenographic record was kept of all conferences held by the commission.
[42] Russell to Cheidze, May 16, 1917, NA, RG 59, 763. 72119/
605a—(Files Relating to World War I and its Termination)
[43] Cyrus McCormick Diary, May 22, 1917, McCormick MSS.

the American Socialist Party's anti-war efforts. Character-
izing his enemy Morris Hillquit as "strong, resourceful,
persistent and ingenious," Russell complained that the
Socialist Party leader had warned the Russian Socialists to
beware of "capitalistic propaganda" from the Root Commission, and had asserted that the commission's goal was
destruction of the new republic and the "commercial exploitation of Russia."[44] Russell felt that these reports
"would be industriously spread from one end of Russia to
the other" and would do great harm unless promptly denied. A close connection existed between the East Side of
New York and certain Russian extremists, Russell claimed,
and many "Russian Jews from New York were on their
way to Russia to make us trouble."[45] Unfortunately, Walling's effort at home to fight Hillquit was making little
headway because Walling had "lost a good deal of his influence with the Jews," having "quarreled with them more
or less."[46]

James Duncan stressed his enthusiastic support of
Russian labor's right to strike, pointing out that the right
to strike was not nearly as dangerous as it sounded. When
"men have the right to strike," Duncan opined, "the incentive to strike is taken away from them." What a man
"has the right to do, he is not nearly so anxious to do as
something that he is prevented from doing."[47] Duncan
explained to Root that labor opposed the political strike
so widely used by the Russians, since it did not have any
real grievance as its cause. He promised to instruct the
Russians that the right to strike was "the best move for the
sake of industrial peace." It involved the right of workers
to confer among themselves and with their employers, as
well as the making of agreements and the responsibility
of living up to them. Even when employers broke their
side of the agreement, Duncan emphasized, "we try to get
[the workers] into such a spirit that they will keep their

[44] *Ibid.*, May 26, 1917.
[45] Russell Diary, May 25, 1917, Russell MSS.
[46] McCormick Diary, May 26, 1917, McCormick MSS.
[47] *Ibid.*, May 22, 1917.

part of the agreement anyway." It was hard to get foreign
workers to be tolerant of their employers, Duncan proclaimed. "The 'right to strike' does not mean that we want
to strike." It did mean "the whole question of responsibility
. . . and responsibility always sobers men and makes them
more careful in their action."[48]

Duncan told Root he would inform Russian workers of
the union's benefit fund for injured workers, under which
the AFL had recently given three Finlanders five hundred
dollars to compensate them for the loss of their eyes in a
steel mill. The men returned to their native land, and
Duncan noted with pride that the five hundred dollars
meant "much more to them in Finland than it would in
the United States." Though it seemed beyond Duncan's
understanding that workers—particularly radicals—
might not consider cash adequate compensation for loss
of eyesight, he did realize the difficulty of disentangling
the Socialists and their ideology from the Russian unions.
Orienting Russian labor toward pure and simple trade
unionism, rather than toward political action remained a
great problem.[49]

Both Duncan and Russell addressed themselves to the
question of Russia's participation in the war. Both supported having both the United States government and the
Root Commission come out in favor of the slogan, "no
annexations, no indemnities," which was the position
toward war aims held by most of the Russian Socialists.
Root was hesitant, feeling that the United States could
not withdraw support from Belgium in her demands for
indemnities for the damage done to that country by the
Kaiser. The general sentiment of the commission was that
this subject should be left alone.[50]

Both men were particularly concerned lest anti-war
sentiment prevail in Russia. Russell was upset that the
Germans in "their smooth and clever way [might] deceive

[48] *Ibid.*, May 28, 1917.

[49] *Ibid.*, May 28, 1917.

[50] *Ibid.*, May 28, May 29, 1917; see also Russell Diary, May 18,
May 28, 1917, Russell MSS.

the Russian Socialists."[51] Therefore he suggested that the commission must hold that if Russia did not fully press the war to the end "we must advise against the lending of any money to her by the United States." The commission agreed, and debate then ensued over how they could best ascertain the attitude of the Russian government and people toward the war.[52] Their decision was to inaugurate a publicity campaign to awaken the Russian masses and keep Russia in the war. The commissioners were to reflect a feeling of optimism, and to "think and believe . . . that Russia will stay in the game," that "Russia will stick."[53]

Duncan's and Russell's service was sorely needed. If Russian labor was to continue producing war material, it had to be persuaded to maintain high work standards. E. A. Brittenham, a manager for the International Harvester Company in Russia, reported that the efficiency of men at the Lubertzy Works had been reduced to twenty-five per cent of what it had previously been. The men had no incentive or ambition to work, and were drifting along without any exertion. "This, coupled with their universal desire for a large increase of pay," Brittenham stated, "changes completely the productive value of labor to all manufacturers."[54]

In Russia, Labor Minister Skobelev informed Duncan that Russian workers had received large pay increases, but that they insisted upon discussing shop grievances during working hours and upon receiving pay for the time they spent talking. Entire plants would stop work, and no money was available to pay wages from the output. Duncan suggested that problems be discussed in the evening, and that an adjustment process between worker and employer be introduced. He promised to send on information so that American methods could be put at the Russian government's disposal.[55]

On June 20, Duncan addressed the Council of Work-

[51] McCormick Diary, May 28, 1917, McCormick MSS.
[52] Russell Diary, May 31, 1917, Russell MSS.
[53] McCormick Diary, June 5, 1917, McCormick MSS.
[54] *Ibid.*, June 13, 1917.
[55] *1917 AFL Convention*, p. 330.

men's and Soldiers' Deputies in the Daketsky Korpus.
Here he urged the Russian workers to establish unions
similar in structure to the AFL, and to accept the aid of
American unions so that the Russians might enjoy com-
parable success. Recommending that the eight-hour day
be temporarily suspended so that soldiers at the front
could be adequately supplied, Duncan suggested to the
Council that they use all their influence in favor "of the
full twenty-four hours in each day, six days of the week."[56]
At the All-Russia Trade Union Convention in Petrograd,
Duncan added that Russian workers should support the
Provisional Government, form trade unions, and "work
much overtime."[57] During this speech a Russian sailor
jumped up and "shouted that America was a nation of
capitalists."[58] Duncan, however, believed that he had been
successful. The commission's final report stated that after
Duncan and Russell had explained to the Council of Workmen's and Soldiers' Deputies "the importance of speeding
up work" in railroad repair shops and all munitions industries, "and the necessity for that purpose that workmen
should consent to work in two or three shifts," Duncan and
Russell "secured the adherence of the Council to this
proposition" and influenced Russian workers to favor the
proposed changes.[59]

Russell, because he claimed to represent the spirit of
American socialism, faced a much harder time. In the
town of Irkutsk, as early as June 7, Russell was confronted
by an audience of the two city commissioners who were
both Socialists. The men approached Russell because they
held sincere doubts about the war. "How could a Socialist
consistently support the prosecution of a war," they asked
Russell, since traditional Socialist theory opposed war.
Russell answered that he too disliked war, but that this one
had been forced on the world with the democratic prin-

---

[56] *Ibid.*, p. 337.

[57] Duncan speech of July 5, 1917, *America's Message to the
Russian People* (Boston, 1918), pp. 117–20.

[58] *The Garment Worker*, XVI, No. 38 (July 13, 1917), 2.

[59] "Report of the Special Diplomatic Mission . . . ," *FR, Russia,
1918*, I, 137.

ciple at stake as the result. Its preservation depended upon defeat of Germany, and if Russia withdrew from the war, German triumph would be assured.[60]

Suspicion of Russell's message, however, was evident in the highest government circles. When he met with Labor Minister Skobelev and two other top ministers, Russell noticed that they "showed no enthusiasm about the U.S." because of the "general suspicion of us that has been deliberately created here . . . before our arrival." Since the Russians were Socialists, it was easy to make them believe that the commission was "essentially a capitalistic venture." This was partly accomplished, he claimed, by spreading a false story that when Elihu Root was Secretary of State, he had tried to deliver to the Czar a Russian revolutionist who had sought asylum in the United States. Although untrue, the story was "almost universally believed" and worked to "paralyze most of our efforts."[61]

The interference with commission activity was evident when Russell prepared to address the Congress of the Council of Workmen's and Soldiers' Deputies on June 25. A council representative came to Russell after reading his prepared speech, informing him that Chairman Cheidze had asked Russell "to explain the embarrassing position in which" the Council found itself. Cheidze and others felt that because the atmosphere in Russia was tense, trouble was expected, and that any reference "to the war might start a serious riot and that the consequences might be of the gravest character." Russell was informed that the famous Belgian Socialist, Emil Vandervelde, had addressed the body the previous evening and had "carefully avoided any reference to the war." Cheidze desired that Russell give only a few words of greeting "and cut out all of my speech that dealt with the war." Russell, of course, saw no use in "uttering mere pleasantries," and he argued that when they asked him to speak, his views on the war were fully known.[62]

[60] Russell Diary, June 7, 1917, Russell MSS.
[61] *Ibid.*, June 19, 1917.
[62] *Ibid.*, June 25, 1917.

Cheidze's aide then handed Russell back his manuscript, indicating what passages the Council was asking
him to delete. Russell attacked "the censorship adopted
by the Russian democracy." At that point the aide left
the room. When he returned, Russell was told that the
Executive Committee felt it wise that he not speak at all,
because in fact he did "not represent the Socialist Party of
the United States, but only the United States Government."
If he did represent socialism, the aide suggested that he
wire the United States and receive cabled credentials from
the Socialist Party. Russell then retorted that if they did
not want to hear him, he did not intend to waste his time
by speaking. At that point Skobelev, Fleurot, and other
ministers appeared from another room, and "with every
appearance of concern tended their apologies." They
claimed that their Executive Committee had never objected
to any topic about which Russell wished to speak, that he
was free to talk about the war or anything else, and that
no one feared the consequences of what he might say.[63]

Russell attributed the attempt to prevent him from addressing the Congress of the Council to the "East Side of
New York and men that used to call themselves my friends"
but now were his enemies "because we differ about the
German theory of Government." When he finally spoke
Russell found that the political Right and center "rose and
cheered enthusiastically what I said about the necessity of
carrying on the war," but the extreme Left "headed by the
strange figure of Lenin sat still and did not applaud." Later
Russell was told by Rabitsch, Cheidze's aide who tried to
prevent him from speaking, that he was a friend of Hillquit's. This proved to Russell that the attempt was part of
the opposition's sinister campaign to ruin the commission.
It only showed "the bitter . . . insatiable hatred that many
Jews in America feel for the United States."[64]

When he did give speeches, Russell combined radical
verbiage and emotional identification with the revolution.

---

[63] *Ibid.*, June 25, 1917.
[64] *Ibid.*, June 25, 1917. See also Herbert Bailey, "Russell Foils
Tricks of Socialists Here," *New York Times*, June 28, 1917, p. 2.

At Kamoslav, Russell made "a flowery speech on socialism, congratulating the Russians . . . and welcoming them as brothers into the ranks of socialists. As a climax for his speech he took off the red ribbon which was in the button-hole of his coat, and waved it before the crowd, kissing it and lifting it up in his hands, all of which caused much cheering."[65] As usual, these dramatic gestures brought forth more scorn from American Socialists. Algernon Lee wrote to Hillquit that Russell actually felt uncomfortable when the Root mission was "wined and dined by all sorts of eminently respectable clients." Therefore he had come to Bessie Beattie's room and begged her "to dig up a piece of red ribbon, a red silk neckercloth." An hour later she saw Russell on the street, "with a flaming scarlet necktie and a red rosette in his coat lapel." But Lee reported, this garb did not have the proper effect. "Ignoring these mani-festations of his revolutionary soul, the heathen Bolsheviki snubbed him as cruelly as the rich bourgeois."[66]

Russell usually began his speeches by identifying him-self with the forces of American radicalism, particularly the Socialist Party. By doing so, he falsely gave the im-pression that American radicals wholeheartedly supported the war. Russell's tactic also explains why he was so wor-ried about attacks upon him issued by Morris Hillquit. This bothered him even more after June 12, when he re-ceived notice that the Party's National Executive Com-mittee had voted to expel him from the Party precisely because he was misrepresenting the views of American Socialists in Russia.[67] If this action and Hillquit's criti-

[65] McCormick Diary, June 10, 1917, McCormick MSS.

[66] Algernon Lee to Morris Hillquit, December 17, 1918, Morris Hillquit MSS, State Historical Society of Wisconsin, Madison, Wis.

[67] After receiving notice of his expulsion, Russell drew up the following message to be sent back to the United States: "Your tele-gram says I have been repudiated by the Socialists of America be-cause I accepted a place on this commission without their consent. This is an error. I have not been repudiated by the American So-cialists. It is quite likely that some such action may have been taken by the Germans, pro-Germans, and wild-eyed Kaiserists that consti-tute a wing of the Socialist party of the United States, but these persons are not Americans." Russell tied up their expulsion meas-

cisms were made known, Russell's claim to be a representative of American socialism would be undermined.

Addressing a meeting of the Soviets on June 12, Russell began by holding in his hand the red card of the Socialist Party from which he had been expelled, and a membership card in the International Typographical Union. "I come," he told the Russians, "from the plain people of America, from the workers, the radicals, the American socialists, the champions of democracy." Only through victory against Germany, Russell informed the Russian Socialists, could socialism be built. For years the United States maintained no army. But now "the American radicals, workers and democrats have united fervently to support and uphold this dreadful thing they had always abhorred." After two and a half years of "patient suffering," Russell claimed, American radicals found "that except by warfare there was absolutely no other way to preserve liberty, and we put liberty above life."[68]

Developing the concept that America waged war only to create a world at peace, Russell stressed that such a fight was not a betrayal of revolutionary ideals. Rather, the fight was waged "because of them and for them. We do not despair of the cooperative commonwealth; on the contrary we begin now to see it as a reality and not as a dream." Without democracy there could never be socialism, and there could be no democracy without victory. The war was actually needed to free men from the "cold horrors" of the competitive system. The war against Germany was therefore a Socialist war. "In the name of the social revolution for which we are enlisted," Russell proselytized, "we drive against the monster the sword of freedom." If

---

ure with the action of German agents who had for so long tried to discredit the Root Commission and "frustrate its efforts." These agents had flooded Russia with lies about the commission's purposes, and "boasted they could induce the Russian government to refuse to receive it." Once that failed "they are now trying to make the Socialists of Russia believe I am not a Socialist." This was all part of a "zealous, malignant but futile campaign for the kaiser." June 14, 1917, Russell MSS.

[68] *America's Message to the Russian People*, 143–45.

Germany won, "everything that we care about, as radicals and reformers, would fall into a common abyss of ruin." Americans saw that if Germany won, the thrilling achievement of Russian freedom would be destroyed. Because Americans understood that the Russian Revolution's success depended upon defeat of Germany, they did not hesitate to enter the fight."[69]

Russell's attempt was promptly challenged by the group of Russian Socialists who had recently returned from the United States. Noteworthy was a formal protest printed in the June 18 edition of *Pravda*. Members of the Lettish Federation of the American Socialist Party retorted that while Russell spoke in the name of American socialism, "as a matter of fact he does not represent either the Socialists nor the American laborers or radicals." Calling Russell a "lackey" of America's "imperialistic highwaymen," the group argued that the people had not entered the war on their own initiative. Rather, war was imposed on them without their knowledge or consent "by Morgan and Company, the defense of the interests of which firm has been taken up by the former socialist, the bourgeois renegade and the traitor of the working people, Mr. Russell, for which acts the American socialist party expelled him from its ranks."[70]

Actually, Russell did have some tactical differences with the cautious approach favored by Elihu Root. When the commission had learned that a large labor demonstration had been scheduled for Petrograd on July 1, Root arranged for his group to retreat to Finland, where he felt that they would be safe. Both Duncan and Russell argued that it would be disastrous for their image to retreat at the first sign of a workers' demonstration.[71] When the demonstration did occur, Russell reported that it was not reassuring. Hundreds were marching with signs calling for over-

[69] *Ibid.*, 146–49. Some of the latter sentences are taken from a speech at a soldiers' demonstration at Pavlosk-Voksal, June 30, 1917.

[70] Excerpt from protest against Russell in *Pravda*, June 18, 1917, Russell MSS.

[71] Russell Diary, June 30, 1917, Russell MSS.

throw of the capitalist ministers, for an end to the war, and
for power being handed over to the Soviets. Russell observed that the "frequency of the reference to the Soviet
was the most significant feature," and he hoped it would
not escape the mission's notice. It was these marching
peoples who would "decide the policy and fate of Russia
and not the ministers to whom we pay this much attention." If the masses wanted the Soviet to be "the only power
it will assuredly be the only power and the" attention paid
by them to bureau ministers "will prove fruitless."[72] This
line of thinking removed Russell some notches from Elihu
Root's conservative lineage.

Upon his return to the United States, Russell concentrated his efforts on attacking Senator Robert M. LaFollette
for his opposition to the war. Castigating LaFollette as a
"disloyal American . . . that disgraces the Congress," a
"traitor in disguise" who did the Kaiser's dirty work, Russell told how he wished he could have dragged the Senator
by the throat to Petrograd, to see the "miserable, fawning,
slimy creatures" who went from crowd to crowd quoting
his words. These men used the Senator's words to establish
that the war was waged by a government of munitions
makers. Russia was weary of the war, Russell stressed,
and if she was made to believe that Americans were not
sincere, her strength might waver. Therefore each word
LaFollette uttered served as a "poisoned dagger plunged
toward the heart of [his] country."[73]

After the Root Commission returned to the United
States, the AFL leadership expressed the view that the
members had been more than successful. Displaying an
overly paternalistic attitude, Gompers wrote that the
Russian people were like "a family of children whose
father and mother have suddenly been taken away." Praising James Duncan for acting as a father to these children
who lacked self-direction and responsibility, Gompers
assured his readers that the "children of Russia" would

[72] *Ibid.*, July 1, 1917.
[73] *America's Message to the Russian People*, pp. 151–52. Speech
at Union League Club of N.Y., August 15, 1917.

eventually learn the "lessons of free men and women."[74]

Encouraged by the important role they thought they had played, the AFL leadership concluded that it was necessary to send a new commission to Russia. This one, however, would be composed entirely of American labor leaders and pro-war Socialists. On September 13, 1917, Gompers cabled Premier Alexander Kerensky that the American Alliance for Labor and Democracy had passed a resolution pledging support in every way possible to Kerensky's regime.[75] Soon after, Gompers arranged a conference with President Wilson to discuss how to aid Kerensky.[76] On the 18th, he cabled the Russian workers, urging them to be patient and forbearing in the effort being made to stabilize the regime.[77] Later that day, Gompers conferred with a group of AFL leaders and pro-war Socialists about submitting to Woodrow Wilson the proposal to send a labor commission to Russia. During the meeting, Gompers revealed that his latest message to Russia had been sent at the State Department's request.[78] Later that day, the delegation from the American Alliance and the AFL conferred with the President.

The AFL leadership believed that the new labor mission would correct the impression that American workers did not support the war, that workers who supported the American government were maintaining the ideals of the international working class movement, and that no danger existed of militarism growing within the United States as a result of labor's pro-war policy. In addition, the mission would dispel misrepresentations asserted by "pro-German" propagandists. It would show that the fight for industrial democracy had been carried on by American

[74] Samuel Gompers, "Russia's Travail for Regeneration," *American Federationist*, XXIV (1917), 745.
[75] Gompers to Kerensky, September 13, 1917, Gompers MSS.
[76] Gompers to John Spargo, September 17, 1917, *ibid.*
[77] Gompers to Kerensky, September 18, 1917, *ibid.*
[78] Memo of September 18, 1917, *ibid.* Gompers met with Robert Maisel, J. G. Phelps Stokes, John Spargo, Henry Slobodin, Chester M. Wright, Nathan Syrkin, Morris Kass, and members of the AFL office staff.

labor while it gave its support to the war, and that the U.S. government recognized labor as a definite force in the government. In addition, it accepted organized labor's standards in all government departments. Another purpose of the mission would be to establish communication between the American people and the people of Russia, thus promoting mutual understanding between workers as well as "depriving the anti-war socialist press of the virtual monopoly" it had in describing the Russian movement. If the monopoly established by the anti-war press was broken, readers would be won and they would no longer be influenced to the "detriment of the national cause."[79]

The mission won early support from many in labor's ranks. *The Garment Worker* editorialized that it would correct the false opinion that James Duncan had been an agent of American financial and banking interests on the Root Commission. It would also inspire a stronger determination on the Russians' part to uphold the Kerensky regime and to continue the fight against Germany.[80] Commission members would point out that radical socialism was a failure in governmental administration, and that it divided people into antagonistic groups by accentuating class animosities. The commission would also show that proletarian rule would destroy representative government, and that society would be as autocratic under socialism as it was under imperial power.[81]

John Spargo, the pro-war Socialist who had formed the Alliance with Gompers, reported that President Wilson had raised the question of a government subsidy for the commission. Suggesting that the AFL ignore Wilson's offer, Spargo urged that the Federation raise $250,000 in twenty-five days by getting prominent personalities to endorse the mission's aims. A newspaper fund drive could make it clear that "the result of such a mission would be

[79] "Memorandum in re Proposed Mission to Russia," n.d., Gompers MSS.
[80] "A Mission to Russia," *The Garment Worker*, XVI, No. 49 (September 21, 1917), 4.
[81] "Good Will to Russia," *ibid.*, No. 52 (October 12, 1917), 4.

of more importance than the sending of several army corps."[82]

The AFL leadership did not worry about financing the mission. Frank E. Wolfe, an officer of the American Alliance, explained to Gompers that American industrialists would be quite willing to provide the necessary funds. Rubber magnate Charles R. Flint already had promised to float the commission and to urge New York financiers to make large donations. It was only necessary for Gompers to give Flint his assurance that the Administration approved of their plans, and Flint would "take steps that will enable us to secure large donations in New York."[83]

Wolfe did not consider it extraordinary for business interests to finance a labor mission, especially since the success of the mission would assure access to foreign markets. "There are scores if not hundreds of persons who want Russian markets after the war is over," Wolfe wrote, adding that it "should not be difficult to show them that their interests lie in keeping in good standing with American labor," and "with the Russian people through our efforts." Wolfe had communicated with "some of this class," and he believed that their interests could be "aroused to the necessity for exerting some effort to tranquilize conditions in Russia."[84]

When it became clear that the Bolsheviks were gaining strength, the AFL leadership did its best to curb their influence. A. J. Sack, writing in the *Federationist,* warned that if the Bolsheviks were permitted to exist as a legitimate political party their strength would progressively grow. Attributing Lenin's large following to the disorganization, hunger, and cold in Russia, Sack claimed that the Bolshevik leader would be more successful than Premier Kerensky, who was asking the suffering masses to fight

[82] Spargo to Gompers, September 20, 1917, Gompers MSS. See also John Spargo Reminiscences, COHC, pp. 272–84. Spargo here gives details about the origins of the proposed mission. However, he mistakenly recollected that it was arranged before the Root Commission.

[83] Wolfe to Gompers, September 28, 1917, Gompers MSS.

[84] Wolfe to Gompers, October 29, 1917, *ibid.*

and suffer even more. Nevertheless, Kerensky's position
had to be supported. Lenin wished to establish socialism
immediately, while Kerensky realized that "an apple, sweet
and ready to be eaten in October is sour and indigestible in
June." Warning that it was necessary to eliminate the Bolsheviks from public life by the use of drastic and repressive
measures, Sack claimed that "the Bolshevik danger is like
a cancer. If it is not operated on in time it is bound to grow
till it reaches the vital organs and kills the patient."[85]

The advice offered by the AFL and the pro-war Socialists was ignored by the Russian revolutionists.[86] When the

---

[85] A. J. Sack, "Bolsheviki—The Danger of Russia," *American
Federationist*, XXIV (November 1917), 980–81.

[86] Nevertheless, the AFL leaders and pro-war Socialists did not
stop trying to give their advice. See Russell to George Creel, October
29, 1917 NA, RG 63, CPI, A1(36). Russell believed that had the
Root Commission presented sufficient publicity, Russia would have
remained in the war against Germany; that had they stayed in
Petrograd until the authorities agreed to their plans, Russia would
have continued to fight: if the commission had "refused to be governed by Lansing and stayed in Russia," Russell felt, "there would
have been a chance to get this thing in working order." Russell
urged more propaganda to make the Russian masses understand
that a German victory would mean the overthrow of Russian democracy. See Russell to Woodrow Wilson, November 7, 1917, *ibid.*
Russell still felt that Russians could be made to have heart in the
war. The problem was that the average Russian saw nothing in the
war that appealed "to the soul in him." The war was the Czar's
war and he was prejudiced against it. It was something "opposed
to his dream of universal brotherhood and the instantaneous Republic of the World that came upon him with this Revolution." The
trick was to get the Russian to see that his cherished Revolution's
success depended upon victory against Germany. It was useless to
use the argument that Russia had to fight because of pledges made
to the Allies. The only duty a revolutionist would honor was the
duty to fight for democracy. Russell argued for an education campaign directed along such lines. A campaign addressed to the "Russian's passion for democracy" which showed that his Revolution
was in peril would make him the best fighter in the world. Lectur-
ing the Russians should be minimized; appeals to their democratic
sense increased. Five million dollars for this purpose would obviate
the need for billions thereafter.

Even the success of the Bolshevik Revolution did not make Russell change his mind. See Russell to Gompers, January 2, 1918,
Gompers MSS. Russell wrote that the "general mass of the Russian
Bolsheviks honestly and conscientiously believe that they are serving the cause of the workers in other lands," and that the American

Bolsheviks took power in November 1917, the proposed AFL labor-Socialist mission died stillborn. The Bolsheviks did not desire the advice of reform unionists. Realizing that the Bolshevik program conflicted directly with his principles, Gompers pledged American labor to unrelenting hostility towards the Soviets. The Bolshevik "pirates," Gompers wrote, had run "up the black flag over helpless Russia and declared war upon the established order about which the fabric of civilized life had been woven and Russia was transformed from an ally into a menace."[87]

The participation of James Duncan and Charles Edward Russell on the Root Commission marked the beginning of the era of the labor statesman in international affairs. For the first time, an American Administration requested that the labor movement and its leadership aid in the conduct of American foreign policy. If a labor member was not included on the Root Commission, the Wilson Administration feared that it would be unable to implement policy and deal effectively with the new revolutionary Russian government. Sharing this view, Samuel Gompers wrote to Secretary of State Lansing that the participation of a labor leader on the commission would do more than any other step to cement the bonds between Russia and America.[88]

In fact, however, the effort to create rapport with Russian Socialist groups by the inclusion of Duncan and Russell on the commission was a failure. George F. Kennan has written that the choice reflected President Wilson's lack of appreciation for the defiant bitterness of Russian radical opinion, its contempt for the moderate reformist philosophy of American labor, and its strong sentiments

---

workers were in reality opposed to the war and would say so if they dared. What was required was a new delegation from American and Western workers demanding that Russian labor not abandon their brothers to the German autocrats. Russell felt such a statement would "have a most powerful effect upon the rank and file of the Russian proletariat," and that if Gompers was in charge it would have a chance of success.

[87] Samuel Gompers, *Seventy Years of Life and Labor*, II, p. 400.
[88] Gompers to Lansing, April 19, 1917, Gompers MSS.

against the war. "The thought that men like Duncan and Russell would have any natural intimacy with Russian socialists," observed Kennan, "was indeed farfetched."[89] Actually, President Wilson had few illusions about the effectiveness that AFL leaders would have in Russia. To Lansing, Wilson observed that "Gompers himself and the leaders immediately associated with him are known to be pronounced opponents of Socialism and would hardly be influential in the present ruling circles of labour at Petrograd."[90]

The anti-war agitation of the American Socialist Party forced Wilson to appoint a pro-war Socialist in addition to a labor commissioner. The President realized that the Administration's best hope lay in having its policy presented in the name of socialism. For their part, on the other hand, the pro-war Socialists believed that their acceptance of the war would enable them to further socialism by achieving representation of labor on all boards and governing bodies formed during the war.[91]

Representation was obtained on various government boards during the war, but cooperation with the administration did not increase the real power of either labor or the Socialists. Rather, their activity enabled the Wilson Administration to undertake programs which would have been difficult to execute had they refused to partake in pro-war activity. The experience of Duncan and Russell illustrates how such men were used by the administration to execute policy, rather than being involved in its formation.

Despite the failure of their approach, evident in the occurrence of the Bolshevik Revolution, the AFL and pro-war Socialists based their future policy on the belief that the program of the Bolshevik regime would inevitably cause it to wither and fail. Anticipating the analysis advanced by George F. Kennan in his 1947 containment

[89] Kennan, *Soviet-American Relations, 1917–1920*, I, 22.
[90] Wilson to Lansing, April 19, 1917, in Baker, *Woodrow Wilson*, VII, 28–29.
[91] Spargo to Chester M. Wright, July 11, 1917, Gompers MSS.

memorandum, Charles Edward Russell explained to Cyrus
McCormick why it was inevitable that the Soviet power
would collapse.[92] "The Bolsheviks are doomed," he wrote
to McCormick, "and we should be prepared to become
effective as soon as their reign of madness passes. There
are two reasons why we can be confident they will have
only a temporary sway. They are a minority of the population and the scheme of society they advocate and the way
of making peace they have started out to follow are alike
utterly impossible and preposterous. Hence, they are certain to fail."[93]

Having accepted Woodrow Wilson's rhetoric regarding
America's war aims, the pro-war Socialists and AFL leaders placed themselves at his disposal in carrying out Administration policy. Convinced that an Allied victory would
assure the triumph of democracy in Europe and the world,
Russell and Duncan attempted to persuade the Russians
to follow Allied leadership. For their part, the Russians
believed that they had little at stake in the war. After three
years of bleeding and dying they had overthrown the Czar
precisely because they had no interest in suffering to preserve an alliance system which had served only to oppress
them in the past. The arrogance of the Americans in attempting to impose their will upon the Russians only endangered whatever feelings of friendship existed between
the two peoples, the more so because of Russell's misrepresentation of the position of American Socialists. In
effect both Russell and Duncan had simply allowed themselves to be used as agents of Wilson liberalism, without

[92] X, "The Sources of Soviet Conduct," *Foreign Affairs*, XXV
(July 1947), pp. 566–582. In his famous anonymous article, Kennan argued that "the future of Soviet power may not be by any
means as secure as Russian capacity for self-delusion would make
it appear to the men in the Kremlin." Kennan saw a possibility that
Soviet power "bears within it the seeds of its own decay." He urged
that the United States "continue to regard the Soviet Union as a
rival, not a partner," and therefore urged a policy of "firm containment, designed to confront the Russians with unalterable counter-
force at every point where they show signs of encroaching upon the
interests of a peaceful and stable world."

[93] Russell to Cyrus McCormick, December 2, 1917, McCormick
MSS.

in any way advancing the interests either of socialism or
the labor movement in whose names they spoke. The
Administration, on the other hand, had reason to be satisfied. Although the Root Commission failed to achieve its
primary objective, the precedent of having labor leaders
pursue Administration policy in the name of American
labor and socialism had been established. It is the development of this precedent to which we must now turn our
attention.

IV

AMERICAN LABOR
AND THE STOCKHOLM
CONFERENCE

The policies pursued by American labor leaders and pro-war Socialists can only be understood within the context of Wilsonian diplomacy during the war. In response to the twin challenges of war and revolution, Woodrow Wilson sought to construct a new world order in the form of an international liberal capitalism, an order that would be safe from the old imperialism of the Right and the revolutionary forces of the Left.

Wilson desired to use American power to force the practitioners of imperialism into a stable international system that would be based on an Open Door commercial policy, international free trade, and recognition of a community of interest among the developed nations of the world. Wilson's hope of creating such a new liberal world order was decisively challenged by Lenin and the Russian Bolsheviks. The Russian Marxists argued that international capitalism was unable to resolve its own internal contradictions through peaceful and gradual reform. Hence, Wilson's program for world peace was by nature anti-Leninist. In terms of the First World War, the approaches taken by Lenin and Wilson led to different conclusions. Lenin hoped to turn the war into a civil war between the European workers and their capitalist over-lords, while Wilson wished to turn it into a crusade for a new liberal order. Wilson's "crusade" thereby offered a way for Allied Socialists to endorse the Entente's war effort. The moderate Socialists could claim that they were not fighting for the old imperial concerns, but for a new order based on peaceful reform. If the Allied Socialists were to take such a course, they would be moving further away from the Bolsheviks than they were originally. For the Wilson-oriented Socialists, the war became the prerequisite for future progress.

Wilson's dilemma and program have been succinctly summarized by N. Gordon Levin, Jr.:

Wilson's non-revolutionary anti-imperialism sought to use America's moral and material power to create a new international order, safe from the related threats of war and revolution, in which America could serve mankind from a position of political and economic pre-eminence. Yet the attainment of such a stable American-inspired world order was dependent, ultimately, on the Administration's ability to contain the world's anti-imperialist forces within the confines either of orderly liberal reform or of legitimized liberal war. Indeed, Wilsonians feared that unless America could remain in control of all progressive international movements, Leninist revolutionary socialism might capture Europe's masses and destroy not only atavistic imperialism, but all liberal values and institutions as well. Somehow, then, Wilson had to use either liberal war or liberal reform to destroy traditional imperialism, while at the same time maintaining the inviolability both of the nation-state system and of world capitalist order in the face of the challenge posed by the more radical anti-imperialism of Leninist revolutionary-socialism.[1]

It was the Wilson Administration's desire to control all

[1] N. Gordon Levin, Jr., *Woodrow Wilson and World Politics* (New York, 1968), pp. 7–8. My discussion of this question is highly indebted to Professor Levin's insights. See particularly Chapter II of his work, "War and Revolution II: Wilsonianism and the Rise of Bolshevism," pp. 50–73.

progressive international movements, as Levin has put it, that defined its attitude toward both American and Allied labor and socialism. First, Wilson provided an ideological component to the war that could be accepted by the Allied Socialists—the theme that the war was a conflict between an aggressive German autocracy and a defensive Allied democracy. This theme was reinforced and given further validity, the Wilsonians claimed, by the German resumption of submarine warfare, and by the occurrence of the liberal March Revolution in Russia.

Once the United States had entered the war, however, a new problem arose for Wilson. The use of military power against Germany and her allies encouraged those extreme Old World powers in the Entente who sought a pure military victory, and who were unconcerned with or opposed to Wilson's program for a new liberal capitalist order. If Wilson shifted to the left to oppose these traditional groups, however, he faced other dangers. Any seemingly revolutionary gestures would tend to encourage Wilson's Socialist enemies on the Left, and their program was the opposite of Wilson's. This meant a rather ambivalent relationship between Wilson and Europe's moderate Allied Socialists.

Wilson tried his best to meet the dilemma by steering a middle course, that is, by creating a moderate anti-German liberalism that would avoid old-style imperialism and anti-war revolutionary socialism at the same time. In setting out upon such a path, disagreement arose among some of the President's leading advisers. His intimate associate Colonel Edward M. House preferred to influence the Allied Left and to bring Russia back to liberal nationalism through liberalizing Allied war aims. Those following Secretary of State Robert Lansing, on the other hand, had grave suspicions of the Allied Left and favored an overt anti-Bolshevik course.

The House-Lansing conflict was of a tactical nature. Both House and Wilson wanted Wilsonian liberalism, and not socialism, to lead the anti-imperialist movement in the world. Wilson wanted to create a peaceful world order in which American commerce and liberal ideals would be dominant. Wilson, as Levin has shown, sought to reform old structures rather than initiate radical changes in existing societies. Wilson's liberalism was thus of a limited nature, and was easily able to accommodate itself to an alliance with the Old World powers in a war against Germany.

The problem was that Wilson and House faced a grave challenge from the European Socialists, who argued that imperialism was an inevitable stage of capitalism, not a policy emanating only from the Kaiser's Germany. Somehow, Levin writes, "the American and European Left had to be convinced, through the orderly and sympathetic guidance of Wilsonian ideology, that the defeat of German arms and the democratization of German politics were the essential prerequisites to the attainment of a peaceful liberal international system." House and Wilson believed that liberalized Allied war aims would undermine German imperialism, and at the same time would channel "the anti-imperialist passion of the Allied-American Left away from radical goals and into the more moderate pro-war path" of Wilsonian liberalism.[2]

To deal with the Allied Left, House believed that it was necessary to undertake war aims revision. Only such a move would be able to purify the Wilson-Entente cause so that moderate democratic Socialists in the Allied nations would see that support of an anti-German war effort did not contradict their desire for a new world free of traditional imperialism. House, for one, was sure that if the war aims were successfully modified, there would be little trouble in co-opting the Allied Left.[3]

To some extent, House's tactic worked. The revision of war aims enabled Allied moderate Socialists to support

[2] *Ibid.*, p. 52.
[3] Edward M. House Diary, August 19, 1917, Edward M. House MSS, Yale University Library; and House to Wilson, November 11, 1917; in *The Intimate Papers of Colonel House* (Boston, 1926–28), III, 133, 282–84. Cited in Levin, *op. cit.*, p. 55.

their own governments in a fight against German imperialism, while hoping that Woodrow Wilson would be able to exert sufficient pressure to curb the imperial appetites of their own Allied governments. The success of this tactic was indicated by the American Ambassador to France, William G. Sharp, in the summer of 1918. "Paradoxical and strange as it may seem," Sharp wrote to Lansing, "the counsel of President Wilson . . . exert[s] a vastly greater influence upon shaping the thought of the socialistic mind in France—sometimes of an iconoclastic tendency—than do any other leaders of the Allied Powers. The reason, perhaps, is not far to seek; it has confidence in his motives. In my judgment, that influence has been a valuable asset, and far more powerful in restraining the radical actions of this particular group than is generally understood. They have time and again reiterated their own principles as being in full accord with those enunciated by President Wilson."[4]

Wilson's problem in courting the European Socialists was to avoid offending the traditional European Right in the process. Wilson was actually willing to adopt House's approach of co-opting the Left only up to a point. Wilson would easily move to the position taken by Secretary Lansing, who had always been skeptical about the ability to unite the Allied Left behind the war on Wilsonian terms. This Wilsonian dilemma was first revealed in the response to the Allied Socialist demand for a peace based on no annexations and no indemnities, and on their plans to hold an international Socialist conference at Stockholm to discuss peace terms.

The Provisional Government of Russia operated according to a three-point program: it worked to stabilize its power, to continue the war against Germany, and to pacify and subdue its revolutionary Left. To gain these ends, it accepted a Wilsonian program which sought to create hostility to German imperialism while at the same time it favored modification of Allied war aims. Colonel House

4 FR *The Lansing Papers, 1914–1920,* II (Washington, D.C., 1940), 135.

and the Provisional Government's Ambassador at Washington, Boris Bakhemeteff, both favored anti-imperialist war aims as the best way for the Allies to prevent a radical-based, separate Russo-German peace.

The Russian government had announced that it would uphold commitments made to the Allied powers by the Czar, and that Russia would remain in the war against Germany. At the same time, War Minister Alexander Kerensky officially dissociated his government from secret agreements formulated by the Czar, and announced his government's support of an exclusively non-annexationist peace. This decision led the other Old World Allied leaders to fear that Russia's Provisional Government was being pushed by extremists who favored a separate peace with Germany, based upon acceptance of the slogan: "No annexations, no indemnities." These concepts, however, had been used by Woodrow Wilson himself to express Allied war aims. Now, some Allied leaders feared, they were being used by European Socialists for their own radical purposes. Members of Wilson's Administration, like Secretary of State Lansing, agreed that Wilson was being exploited by pro-German elements.[5]

Woodrow Wilson was alerted to the dangers inherent in the Provisional Goverment's policies by the pro-war Socialist William English Walling. Writing in the *New York Times*, Walling set forth the arguments that would be consistently voiced by both Social-Democratic League and American Federation of Labor officers. According to Walling, both the official Socialists in Germany (permitted to function as a legal entity by the Kaiser) and the opposition Socialists headed by Karl Liebknecht, favored a peace based on "no annexations, no indemnities." Walling feared that Lenin and the Bolsheviks would be able to gather strength on the basis of that slogan. Many of the Russian masses, he claimed, favored signing a peace with the Kaiser in order to gain strength to fight their own rulers.

[5] George F. Kennan, *Soviet-American Relations, 1917–1920*, I, *Russia Leaves the War* (Princeton, N.J., 1956), 134–39, 142–46; Levin, *op. cit.*, p. 57.

It was the duty of the West to arm itself against "the minds of the ignorant and inexperienced Russian masses" by rejecting this new peace formula, unless it was clearly specified to mean only "no forcible annexations, and no punitive indemnities."[6]

After making his views public, Walling moved to gain acceptance for them from the Wilson Administration. Walling first cabled Gompers that immediate renunciation of the "no annexations–no indemnities" slogan was necessary to "save Russia." Gompers responded by urging Walling to proceed to Washington where they could both confer with the President.[7]

After presenting their views to the Department of State, Walling and Gompers found that they had met with official approval. Secretary Lansing informed Wilson that certain phrases the President had used were being misconstrued "by the radical socialists (probably under German influence) to force the Provisional Government to declare a policy which will remove the chief incentive to Russian offensive operations, namely, control of the Dardanelles and possession of Constantinople." Lansing was clearly concerned that concessions to anti-imperialist ideology would aid Germany by robbing the Russian masses of their desire to fight, which was based on the hope of territorial annexation. Radicals, Lansing continued, were asking why Russia should continue fighting if she could not be compensated in territory or by indemnities for the "enormous expenditure of life and money" that a hard fight would entail. The slogan "no annexations–no indemnities" was an attempt by radicals to win the masses to a separate peace policy. It was a "real danger . . . that ought to be avoided."[8]

Wilson may have been torn between the different approaches favored by House and Lansing. In this case, he

[6] William E. Walling, "The German Socialist Peace Intrigue—A Warning to Be on Guard Against the Second Phase of the Kaiser's Propaganda," *New York Times*, April 26, 1917, p. 12.

[7] Walling to Gompers, May 16, 1917; Gompers to Walling, May 16, 1917; Samuel Gompers MSS.

[8] Lansing to Wilson, May 17, 1917, NA, RG 59, 861.00/361, 338.

accepted Lansing's judgment. Wilson informed George
Creel that he would "attempt some statement to correct
the misapprehension aparently existing in Russia." He
intended to take Lansing's suggestion that the message be
sent via Ambassador David Francis who would make it
public in Russia.[9] Before acting, Wilson received a long
memorandum from Walling. In this report, Walling offered a detailed presentation of the political and ideological disputes ranging among European Socialist parties.
Many of them, Walling attempted to show, were moving
toward a separate peace position based upon approval of
the "no annexations–no indemnities" slogan.[10]

On the 22nd of May, Wilson sent his message to the
Provisional Government. It was clearly based on acceptance of the analysis shared by Walling and Lansing. The
objective of the United States, Wilson told the Russians,
had been "beclouded during the past few weeks by mistaken and misleading statements." The United States
sought no aggrandizement or profit from the war. It fought
only to gain the liberation of all peoples from subjection to
autocracy. The basic motivating principle of the United
States was that "no people must be forced under a sover-
eignty under which it does not wish to live." No indemnities were to be "insisted on except those that constitute
payment for manifest wrongs done."[11]

Wilson revealed that adherence to self-determination
did not mean that the Allied governments would be unable
to claim indemnities for damages inflicted by the Central
Powers. Wilson trod a thin line between appeals to the
internationalists and Socialists, and the demands of those
who practiced international power politics. While he
affirmed the right of just indemnities, he also tried to keep

[9] Wilson to Creel, May 18, 1917, George Creel MSS, Library of
Congress, Washington, D.C.
[10] Walling to Wilson, May 21, 1917, NA, RG 59, 763.72110/612;
cf. Walling to Wilson, May 21, 1917, Gompers MSS.
[11] Message of Woodrow Wilson to the Provisional Government of
Russia, enclosed in Lansing to Francis, May 22, 1917, *FR, The
World War, 1917*, I, Supplement 2 (Washington, D.C., 1917), 70–
73.

alive his interest in a just peace. A few days later, in a second message to the Provisional Government, Wilson again tried to counteract the peace program of the Russian Left, by putting his stress on Germany's interest in an early peace:

The war has begun to go against Germany, and in their desperate desire to escape the inevitable defeat, those who are in authority in Germany are using every possible instrumentality, are making use even of the influence of groups and parties among their own subjects to whom they have never been just or fair or even tolerant, to promote a propaganda on both sides of the sea which will preserve for them their influence at home and their power abroad, to the undoing of the very men they are using.[12]

These two speeches revealed an extreme reluctance on Wilson's part to compromise with the Left, even to the slight extent desired by Colonel House. While Wilson did reveal a certain ambivalence, on key issues he sided with Lansing, out of fear that any movement toward the Allied Left might encourage extreme revolutionary forces.

In addition to the demand for a peace based on no annexations and no indemnities, the Allied and Russian Socialists posed another additional problem for the Wilson Administration. In May of 1917 the Soviets, then under control of moderate elements, had issued a call for an international Socialist congress in which the European workers could assess where they stood in relation to the war. Unlike smaller meetings held by Socialists at Zimmerwald in 1915 and Kienthal in 1916, the proposed conference would not be confined to minority Socialists from the left and center factions. A broad meeting of European Socialists was made possible for the first time because of the impetus given world socialism by the success of the first Russian Revolution.

The call for a meeting at Stockholm produced an early

[12] Ray Stannard Baker and William E. Dodd, eds., *The Public Papers of Woodrow Wilson* (Garden City, N.Y., 1927–1939), V, 49–50; cited in Levin, *op. cit.*, 66.

opposition from both the Allied governments and the moderate European Socialists. One of the first to oppose the call was Arthur Henderson, leader of the Labour Party and a member of Lloyd George's War Cabinet. While Henderson was visiting Russia in June of 1917, he joined the French Socialist Albert Thomas and the Belgian Socialist Emil Vandervelde in drawing up a statement terming the Stockholm Conference "useless and dangerous" because it could not end in positive action and "would give rise to misunderstanding and would lead the working and peasant classes to think that a just and durable peace was possible before aggressive imperialism is destroyed."[13]

Henderson was prominent among the centrist defenders of Wilson in the Socialist movement. At home, he waged a two-front struggle against Britain's Conservative government and against those further to the left. Men like Henderson, Arno J. Mayer explains, "trusted in the President to block a punitive peace, thereby thwarting the offensive of the Allied Right, consolidating the reformist regimes in the defeated nations, and giving the lie to Lenin's charge that Wilsonianism was but an insidious bourgeois-capitalist smoke screen."[14]

Henderson's Wilsonian outlook caused him to rapidly change his approach toward the proposed Socialist conference. He spent many days touring Russia, addressing the Soviets, and talking with diplomats and Cabinet members. He soon found an almost unanimous feeling among the Soviets on behalf of a Stockholm meeting. Understanding that the absence of Allied Socialists would create a bad impression in Russia, Henderson and Thomas shifted and began to offer vigorous support to the proposed meeting.

The majority of European Socialist parties followed the

[13] Quoted in Robert D. Warth, *The Allies and the Russian Revolution* (Durham, N.C., 1954), p. 72. The genesis and development of the Stockholm proposal is treated by Warth in Chapter IV of his book: "The Allied Socialists and the Stockholm Conference," pp. 66–88.

[14] Arno J. Mayer, *Politics and Diplomacy of Peacemaking* (New York, 1967), p. 16.

lead taken by Henderson and Thomas. After receiving their enthusiastic support for the meeting, leading moderate Socialist parties voted to endorse the conference. The French Socialist Party voted to send Jean Longuet and Pierre Renaudel, their two most prominent members, to confer in Russia about arrangements. While the majority Socialists of the British Labour Party still disapproved, the Independent Labour Party and Socialist Party announced their concurrence, and voted to send Ramsay MacDonald, Fred W. Jowett, and E. C. Fairchild to Petrograd.

The new endorsement of Stockholm by moderate Allied Socialists caused pronounced anxiety among the American pro-war Socialist group. It was their analysis of the Stockholm meeting that conditioned the response of both Secretary of State Robert Lansing and President Wilson. Speaking on behalf of the AFL, Samuel Gompers cabled the Petrograd Workmen's and Soldiers' Council of Deputies to disregard movements for peace that emanated from the Kaiser's agents.[15] He then addressed telegrams to Léon Jouhaux, secretary of the French General Confederation of Labor, and to G. J. Wardle, chairman of the British Labour Party. Gompers informed them that "insidious influences" were working to create pro-Kaiser propaganda, meant to divide those who were fighting for democracy. The proposed Stockholm meeting did not represent the working classes of Europe or America. Rather, it was called "by German socialists and pro-German agitators to bring about [a] Kaiser-dictated peace under [the] catch phrase no annexations, no indemnities." It was meant, Gompers argued, to deceive the Russian Socialists "into betraying the great western democracies into consenting to a separate peace."[16]

Gompers was joined in his attack on Stockholm by his allies from the Social-Democratic League. Walling, Charles E. Russell, and Ernest Poole issued a public state-

[15] Gompers to Workmen's and Soldiers' Council of Deputies, Petrograd, May 6, 1917, Gompers MSS.
[16] Gompers to Jouhaux, L. Dubreuilh, and Wardle, May 7, 1917, *ibid.*

ment decrying the conference as the most dangerous plan
issued by the Kaiser on behalf of a German military victory. While it would not fool those in the experienced
democracies, the SDL members claimed, it might very well
"deceive the inexperienced democracy of Russia, putting
it completely in the hands of the Kaiser." The result would
be a separate peace that would assure a German triumph.[17]
Unlike Colonel House, this loyal Left had no desire to even
try and unite the Allied Left behind the war under subordination to Wilsonian principles. Rather, they believed
that the Allied Left was serving the aims of the Kaiser,
albeit unconsciously. Both Gompers and Walling thereby
took positions that worked to undercut Wilson's key areas
of support abroad, and to strengthen the hands of the Allied Right. Their position had deep ironic overtones, since
the European Socialists were trying to rally the entire Allied Left behind an advanced Wilsonian program. By taking this stand, Gompers and Walling made impossible any
united action with moderates like Henderson, Jean Longuet, or Camille Huysmans, even though an alliance with
these forces might have meant success for Wilson's program of a revived, international liberal capitalist community.

The arguments presented by Gompers and Walling were
vigorously challenged by Morris Hillquit, the lawyer who
led the New York Socialist Party. As a member of the
International Socialist Bureau that was arranging the
Stockholm Conference, Hillquit assured Secretary of State
Lansing that "there is not the slightest foundation in fact
for any of the charges" made by Walling and his associates. The conference did not emanate from German or
pro-German sources, Hillquit noted, and plans for a separate peace between Russia and Germany were not part of
the scheduled deliberations. "In view of the unfortunate
impression prevailing here and possibly abroad that the
intemperate and unwarranted statements of Messrs. Walling, Russell and Poole have received the official sanction
of the administration," Hillquit asked for the opportunity

[17] *New York Times,* May 9, 1917, p. 3.

to speak with Lansing in order to acquaint him with the real facts.[18]

Hillquit was to learn that both Lansing and Wilson shared Walling's view of the Stockholm Conference. "I do not like the movement among the Socialists to confer about international affairs," Wilson confided to Lansing. "They are likely to make a deal of mischief, especially in connection with affairs in Russia. I think our own people would warmly resent any encouragement by our government of the American Socialists who may seek to take part, especially after their recent almost treasonable utterances in their convention." For the time being, Wilson felt that the government should "neither give them leave nor seek to restrain them," since the Socialists would on their own "make themselves either hated or ridiculous."[19]

Wilson's view was reinforced when he received confirmation from Charles E. Russell. The millionaire pro-war Socialist took note of the denials that the conference was pro-German in origin or significance, but his long acquaintance with "controlling influences in the Socialist movement" made him certain "that the entire conception of the Stockholm conference is of the most sinister nature." Loyal American Socialists held no illusions. The denials were issued by men who previous to the declaration of war were "outspoken German champions." Russell hoped that Wilson's "own clear vision concerning" the conference would not be affected "by denials of its true character." The conference was "essentially pro-German" and this sympathy was its "mainspring." Stockholm was meant to "endorse a policy that would mean the defeat of the Allies' cause and the triumph of the basic principles of German imperialism."[20]

The last assessment of Stockholm to reach Lansing and Wilson before they were to take action came from Walling.

[18] Hillquit to Lansing, May 10, 1917, NA, RG 59, 763.72119/595.
[19] Wilson to Lansing, May 11, 1917, in Ray Stannard Baker, *Woodrow Wilson: Life and Letters*, VII, *War Leader, April 6, 1917–February 28, 1918* (New York, 1939), 65.
[20] Russell to Lansing, May 15, 1917, enclosed in Lansing to Wilson, May 19, 1917, Wilson MSS, Library of Congress.

In his memorandum of May 21, Walling expanded on problems he had taken up with the President during a personal meeting earlier in the week. Walling warned that the French Socialist Party was holding its National Council meeting on May 27, and that it would probably decide in favor of participation at Stockholm. Walling hoped that while the President would deal with Russian misinterpretations of the Administration position, he would also deal a blow to the French Socialists "at this critical moment."

The problem stemmed from what interpretation the Stockholm meeting would give to the "no annexations—no indemnities" formula. In Germany the minority Socialists, led by the imprisoned leaders Karl Liebknecht and Rosa Luxemburg, had endorsed the Zimmerwald program and were in close contact with Lenin. They favored revolution "in Germany regardless of the justified or unjustified claims for territory or indemnity on the part of the other peoples of Europe." The larger factions favored some indemnity to Belgium, but demanded some concessions from the Entente powers in return for an indemnity.

While the British and French majority Socialists did not accept the slogan of no annexations–no indemnities, Walling predicted that they probably would adopt the liberal interpretation given this slogan by Alexander Kerensky. Kerensky opposed all annexations against the wishes of inhabitants and all punitive indemnities. Above all, the Entente Socialists stressed the right of all peoples to decide their own allegiance. The pro-German groups at Stockholm were trying "to make this phrase comparatively meaningless by substituting the word nations for peoples," thereby rationalizing the continued subjection of ethnic nationality groups to remain under the domain of the existing states of Austria and Hungary.

Most dangerous was the position taken by the French minority Socialists. They favored Stockholm if the conference adopted the views of the revolutionary German minority. But, argued Walling, they hid the fact that the German minority had exactly the same peace program as the majority, although the latter supported the Kaiser. The position of the French minority, headed by Jean Longuet, was termed "most dangerous" by Walling, "since it brazenly denies the opposition between the German Socialists, as represented by the Minority, and the Socialists of the Entente countries as represented by the British Labor Party." Moreover, continued Walling, the French minority claimed that "President Wilson, as well as the Russian Government, has adopted the interpretation of the German Socialists." They were using Wilson's popularity for their own revolutionary ends. Walling noted one possible opening for Wilson. The French minority did favor free development for peoples and nationalities, not only nations. This divergence from the German majority gave Wilson the chance to agree with them on this one point, while at the same time developing a "reasonable interpretation" of the no annexations–no indemnities formula. Unless this was done, Walling warned, the French Party was likely to endorse the Stockholm Conference.[21]

The Allied Socialists found many problems facing them. The opposition of many Allied governments and the hesitancy of Allied leaders to allow their own Socialists to attend caused the conference date to be repeatedly postponed. Delegates, however, had been arriving in Stockholm as early as the end of May. Socialist delegates from the Central Powers were readily given permission to attend by their respective governments.

As the conference arrangements developed, Woodrow Wilson was forced to take an affirmative position. His decision revealed little faith in the ability of his own ideas to curb prospective extremism in the ranks of Allied and domestic Socialists. On the 22nd of May, Lansing reported to American representatives in Europe that "under the direction of the President no passports will be issued to Socialists intending to attend the Stockholm conference."[22]

[21] Walling to Wilson, May 21, 1917, enclosed in Walling to Gompers, May 21, 1917, Gompers MSS. Cf. Walling to Lansing, May 21, 1917, NA, RG 59, 763.72110/612.

[22] Lansing to Nelson Page, May 22, 1917, *FR, The World War, 1917*, I, Supplement 2 (Washington, D.C., 1917), 730.

The United States became the first nation to issue such a prohibition formally.

Wilson's decision was warmly applauded by many of the Administration Left. Ralph Easley of the National Civic Federation praised the order as "vigorous and clear-cut." The whole "socialist contingent here is a joke," he wrote Lansing.[23] J. G. Phelps Stokes was also pleased. The SDL leader regarded American Socialist Party members as enemies of the United States. Stokes could not see how after revealing "utmost hostility to the present course and purpose of the government of the United States," the Socialists could "ask the government for letters of recommendation to a foreign power to be used under conditions that can reasonably be believed to harbor purposes hostile to the purposes of the United States." It would have been more surprising had the government aided them in their efforts by allowing them to travel to Stockholm, Stokes reasoned. Democratic principles simply forbid a government to "aid a minute fraction of the people to thwart the aims and flout the law of the nation."[24]

The Administration gave its action the color of law by citation of the Logan Act—a law which made it a crime for an American citizen to negotiate with a foreign government in a dispute concerning the United States government. The law had been lying unenforced on the statute books for over one hundred years. The Administration managed to dig it up and to offer it as a reason for its action. Morris Hillquit retorted that the European Socialist parties were not governments, and were not involved in any disputes with the United States. Hillquit's plea for permission to attend the conference was firmly rejected.[25]

Had Hillquit been allowed to attend, his delegation would have taken the exact position at Stockholm outlined by Wilson in a recent address on American war aims. Like

[23] Easley to Lansing, May 24, 1917, NA, RG 59, 763.72119/611.
[24] Stokes to the *New York Evening Post*, May 24, 1917, J. G. Phelps Stokes MSS, Butler Library, Columbia University.
[25] Morris Hillquit, *Loose Leaves from a Busy Life* (New York, 1934), pp. 156–57.

Wilson, the Socialist Party claimed, its delegates only wanted to prevent enactment of punitive peace terms and to provide future safeguards, for international democracy. In fact, Hillquit stated, Woodrow Wilson's "attitude has been officially endorsed by Socialists on both sides of the conflict."[26]

In taking this position, Hillquit aligned himself with the moderate majority of European Socialists, with men like Henderson, who viewed Wilson as the last defender of democratic war aims against the traditional imperial goals of their own Allied governments. In acting to cancel the passports, Wilson inadvertently provided strength for the Allied Right, and weakened the base of his most staunch defenders. Wilson understood that if he did permit the American Socialists to participate in the conference, that decision might have produced serious division among the Allied governments. It might have had the effect of encouraging those who favored a separate peace, and those who held overtly revolutionary beliefs. While Wilson did at times support Colonel House's efforts to absorb the Allied Left in a Wilsonian war consensus, he was too fearful of revolution to risk going over the heads of the established Allied governments to work with the moderate Wilsonian Socialists of Europe.

At home, Wilson continued to receive the backing and encouragement of the Administration Left. Walling saw to it that no misunderstanding of Wilson's position was allowed. Hillquit was evading the real question, Walling charged, "by saying that the Russian Socialists, the Stockholm Conference and the American Party are not for a separate peace." What these Socialists were trying to do was "annex" Woodrow Wilson by making it appear that even the French and Austrian Socialists agreed with Wilson's program. "It would be just as accurate," Walling retorted, "to claim the President's assent for the near-treason resolution of St. Louis." Walling noted that while the German majority Socialists favored free development for great nations only, the President had "referred to prospec-

26 *New York Times,* May 23, 1917, pp. 1, 5.

tive territorial changes and demanded the same rights for weak peoples as for large nations."[27]

If Wilson had any qualms about his decision, they were set aside when further congratulatory messages appeared. "Nothing recently has given me more comfort and satisfaction," the noted Russian expert George F. Kennan informed Lansing, "than your refusal to issue passports to the Socialist delegates to the Stockholm Conference." Kennan did not believe that the action would have an unfavorable effect in Russia. Rather, he claimed it would "have a *good* effect" since it would discourage "the pacifists and pro-German schemers" and would strengthen the hands of Miliukov, the army officers, and millions of thinking men in the educated Russian classes. It was these men, Kennan stressed, who stood for democracy, "loyalty to the western Allies and a vigorous prosecution of the war without futile or treasonable parley."[28]

Soon after Wilson announced his decision, other Allied governments followed. Marshal Henri Pétain frightened the French Cabinet into believing that the army would collapse if French representatives attended the Stockholm meeting. The Italian government also banned participation at Stockholm by Italian Socialists. Only in Britain did the passport issue remain unresolved, and in August, Lloyd George announced that he would not tolerate any communication with German Socialists at Stockholm or anywhere else.[29]

In the long run, Wilson's decision began a rapid loss of influence for the United States among labor and Socialist groups in Europe. The Stockholm Committee, Warth has written, "declared that the American government was largely to blame for the passport difficulty and was all the more bitter about it because of the liberal pronouncements on war aims which President Wilson had made in the

[27] William E. Walling, "The Stockholm Conference," *New York Times*, May 26, 1917, p. 12.

[28] Kennan to Lansing, May 24, 1917, George Kennan MSS, Library of Congress.

[29] Warth, *The Allies and the Russian Revolution*, pp. 72, 76.

past." Had the Allied governments issued passports, they would have "more easily avoided the imaginary terrors of the 'Stockholm plot' than by refusing them and thereby alienating relatively small but influential segments of public opinion." Rather than strengthen the Russian pro-war groups, as Kennan had predicted, Wilson's decision allowed the Bolsheviks to chide the Allies for refusing to "allow even their patriotic socialists an opportunity to explore the ground for a general peace settlement." The Mensheviks and Social Revolutionaries "suffered an irreparable loss of prestige through the Stockholm failure and were forced to give way to socialists promising action instead of words."[30]

Because of the Allied governments' action, the Stockholm meeting did not take place. Its failure only strengthened the traditional groups in the Allied Right, and weakened the Wilson-oriented Left that sought to put teeth into Wilson's pronouncement of democratic war aims. The demand for some form of international Socialist conference, moreover, remained a constant problem for the Allied powers. European labor developed a new militancy, as more Socialists began to call for immediate peace negotiations and formulation of just and democratic peace terms. Wilson's action had only produced dismay among the very groups on the Left who were looking to the American President for leadership. Action that had been partially inspired by the analysis of the American pro-war Socialists and the AFL further divided European labor, and produced a new skepticism about the validity of Wilsonian liberalism. The ban on Socialist participation at the Stockholm Conference had backfired. A growing demand for peace had to be faced anew by both the Allied governments and by Samuel Gompers and his pro-war Socialist allies.

[30] *Ibid.*, pp. 87–88.

V

THE AFL AND WARTIME DIPLOMACY: THE FIRST LABOR MISSION TO WARTIME EUROPE

The advent of the Bolshevik Revolution was met by Wilson and Lansing with firm opposition. From the start, the Wilson Administration viewed the Bolsheviks as dangerous social revolutionaries. The Administration attitude toward Bolshevism had been clearly defined by Secretary Lansing in a memorandum written during January 1918. The Bolsheviks, Lansing warned, appealed "to a class and not to all classes of society, a class which does not have property but hopes to obtain a share by process of government rather than by individual enterprise. This is of course a direct threat at existing social order in all countries." Lansing feared that Bolshevik doctrine might "appeal to the average man, who will not perceive the fundamental error." Moreover, the Bolsheviks interfered with nationalism by advancing "doctrines which make class superior to the general conception of nationality." To Lansing, these theoretical views were "utterly destructive of the political fabric of society" and had to be defeated if order and governmental "stability are to be maintained."[1]

[1] Lansing to Wilson, January 2, 1918, Wilson MSS, Library of Congress, Washington, D.C. The basic exposition of Wilsonian pol-

As in the past, differences arose about the best approach to be taken in dealing with the radicalism of the Russian Bolsheviks. Colonel House believed that liberalization of Allied war aims could bring even the Bolsheviks back to liberalism; that even Lenin could be persuaded to support a war by a new liberal nationalist Russia against German autocracy. Lansing, on the other hand, did not believe that Lenin could be domesticated. Lansing frankly preferred to wage a joint campaign against German imperialism and Bolshevism. He had no faith that Lenin could become a reincarnation of Kerensky. If forced to choose between the Kaiser's autocracy and Bolshevism, Lansing had no hesitations. The despotism of the Kaiser was preferable to a "despotism of ignorance . . . productive of disorder and anarchy."[2]

Wilson's Fourteen Points speech of January 4, 1918, reflected the early reliance on Colonel House's tactic. The purpose of the speech was to present Allied war aims in an anti-imperialist framework, so that Bolshevik extremism would lose its force and become absorbed into the pro-war liberalism of the March Revolution. Acting upon the suggestions of many of his advisers, Wilson believed that war aims liberalization would succeed in channeling the anti-capitalist radicalism of the Russians into the anti-autocratic crusade against the Kaiser's Germany. Instead of attacking the Bolshevik regime head on, Wilson seemed to offer hope that the leaders of Russia would see the mistake in negotiating with German imperialism and come over to the values of Wilsonianism. In his famous Sixth Point, Wilson had said that policy toward Russia was the "acid test" of American and Allied ideals. America, Wilson stated, wanted to give Russia "an unhampered and unembarrassed opportunity for the independent determination

---

icy toward Bolshevik Russia, and the roots of American intervention are to be found in William A. Williams, "American Intervention in Russia: 1917–20," in David Horowitz, ed., *Containment and Revolution* (Boston, Mass., 1967), pp. 26–75.

[2] *FR, The Lansing Papers, 1914–1920,* II (Washington, D.C., 1940), 352–53. See also N. Gordon Levin, Jr., *Woodrow Wilson and World Politics* (New York, 1968), pp. 64–69.

of her own political development and national policy," and desired to provide "assistance also of every kind that she may need and may herself desire." In this manner America and the Allies would reveal "their comprehension of her needs as distinguished from their own interests, and of their intelligent and unselfish sympathy."

Wilson had adopted House's tactic of purposefully failing to offer a clear-cut distinction between the liberal Russia of the March Revolution and Bolshevik Russia. The assumption was that the Russian moderates would be able, on the strength of Wilsonian ideals, to lead the Bolsheviks back to a liberal capitalist anti-German crusade. In no way, however, did Wilson's speech reveal any subservience to Leninism. Rather than Wilson being converted to the doctrines of revolutionary socialism, Wilson and House hoped that Lenin would be absorbed into a pro-war democratic nationalist consensus. House's tactic was meant to be anti-Bolshevik. Lenin was to adapt to Wilsonian liberalism, not the other way around. Revolutionary ideals were to be moderated by an Allied version of anti-imperialism.

With the Bolshevik dissolution of the Constituent Assembly later in January 1918, Wilson and his Administration would drift away from reliance on House's approach to that favored by Lansing: trying to find a liberal nationalist alternative to Bolshevism and developing its own independent base. But while the House approach was being developed, it led to serious misunderstandings about the Administration's intentions toward the Bolsheviks. The Fourteen Points speech led many to believe that Wilson was seeking a *modus vivendi* with the existing Bolshevik government, and was thinking in terms of according it recognition.

These beliefs were stressed in an interview which William Boyce Thompson, an industrialist who was friendly with Raymond Robins, held with the noted journalist Herbert Bayard Swope. Thompson's claims were vigorously denied in an article written for the *New York Times* by William English Walling. Again, the true anti-Bolshevik stance of the Administration was set forth in accurate terms by one of the key members of the Administration Left. Taking issue with the view that the Fourteen Points speech was meant to endorse "the Bolsheviki and the Bolshevist peace terms," Walling asserted Wilson meant to work with the Bolsheviks only "in so far as the Bolsheviki showed themselves in the future willing to work with us." It was "utterly impossible," Walling wrote, that the Bolshevik government "should be recognized by America or any democratic government."[3] Walling recognized "fully the wisdom of the President's diplomacy," he wrote to George Creel. "But he is not a pro-Bolshevik."[4] The evidence indicates, as George F. Kennan has written, that Walling "was in fairly close touch with the Administration on Russian matters during the winter of 1918." It is not known whether Walling conferred with Wilson after the Fourteen Points speech was delivered. But, as Kennan notes, it was evident that Walling's "boldness in undertaking to say publicly what was in the President's mind when he spoke on January 8 did not meet with Mr. Wilson's disfavor. Had his interpretation of the President's thoughts been incorrect, the results would surely have been different."[5]

Walling, a pro-war Socialist, had thus provided the necessary backing for Wilson's policy, and had encouraged the President to stand firm against those who sought some accommodation with the Bolsheviks. As if to prove that Wilson was turning away from House's method of fighting Bolshevism, and adopting Lansing's view that Bolshevism could not be transformed via the rhetoric of liberal anti-imperialism, Wilson and Lansing offered a positive response to an overtly anti-Bolshevik memorandum submitted to the White House by Walling and Samuel Gompers.

[3] William E. Walling, "Move to Recognize the Bolsheviki?," *New York Times*, January 14, 1918, p. 4. For the basic discussion of Walling's fight with Creel over pro-Bolshevik influence in the Committee on Public Information, see George F. Kennan, *Soviet-American Relations, 1917–1920*, I, *Russia Leaves the War* (Princeton, N.J., 1956), 264–73. Cf. William A. Wiliams, "American Intervention in Russia," *op. cit.*, p. 44.

[4] Walling to Creel, January 17, 1918, NA, RG 63, CPI I, A1 (43).

[5] Kennan, *op cit.*, 273.

The Gompers-Walling memo, dated February 9, 1918, arrived at a moment when Wilson was under strain from his constant grappling with both the war effort and the problem of Russia. "Hence it may have been particularly encouraging," William Appleman Williams writes, "to have Gompers come forward in vigorous and determined opposition to recognition of the Bolsheviks and to any kind of dealings with them."[6] In the memo, which was obviously composed entirely by Walling, the argument was developed that the Western democracies had more to fear from revolution than the German autocracy. War-weariness in the West was causing the demand to grow among Allied labor for a Stockholm-type conference to demand an immediate peace. In France and Italy, Walling and Gompers claimed, Socialists and unionists had resumed "their previous revolutionary pacifist activities." In England one-third of the unions adopted a pacifist program, while Arthur Henderson was repeating "almost daily that an international conference can bring an early end to the war." Walling and Gompers saw the danger of revolutionary upheaval spreading to England, Italy, France, and on to the United States. The danger was that even if the war was to end, labor strikes would develop before American power had been fully developed, and before Germany lost any of her conquests. The result would be the failure to curb German militarism, since even Karl Liebknecht's program did not provide for relinquishment of German domination over her Allies. Germany would be less weakened than Italy or France. The Allies might see a revolutionary upheaval, while German militarism remained strong. To aid the Bolsheviks in any manner, Walling warned, was "playing with fire," since it would lead to an end of the war before a German defeat or an American victory.[7]

The memorandum, as Woodrow Wilson put it, issued a

---

[6] Williams, *op. cit.*, 45.

[7] "The Chief Danger of Revolutions and Revolutionary Movements in Eastern Europe: Revolutions in Western Europe," Samuel Gompers MSS, Box 52, State Historical Society of Wisconsin, Madison, Wis.

warning "against encouraging the Bolsheviks, since any
such policy would be interpreted as an acknowledgment
by the 'Imperialist' governments of partial defeat." Informing his Secretary of State that the memo "deserves a very
careful reading," Wilson noted that it "seems to me to
speak an unusual amount of truth and to furnish a very
proper basis of the utmost caution" in formulating policy.[8]

The memo served as reinforcement for the strong anti-
Bolshevik program that Secretary Lansing had been urging
upon Wilson for quite some time. Walling "had a keen
appreciation of the forces which are menacing the present
social order in nearly every European country," Lansing
answered Wilson. "It is really a remarkable analysis of the
dangerous elements which are coming to the surface and
which are in many ways more to be dreaded than autocracy." Autocracy was at least "intelligent despotism,"
while the other was based on "ignorance." One, to Lansing,
had "the virtue of order, while the other is productive of
disorder and anarchy." As for Walling's views on the Bolsheviks, Lansing found them "helpful and sound," and felt
"more than ever convinced that our policy has been the
right one and should be continued." Any meeting of Socialists imbued "with the idea of an international social revolution," Lansing believed, "might become a very real menace to all existing forms of government, democratic as well
as monarchical."[9] Walling's memorandum had led to a
vigorous reaffirmation of the basically anti-Bolshevik
attitude taken by the Wilson Administration.

Having served the Administration in a time of indecision,
by acting to strengthen the chosen anti-Bolshevik course,
American labor leaders and pro-war Socialists had come to
be highly valued by Wilson for the potential services they
could offer. As for the AFL leadership, they needed no
coaxing to make their views known. Their activities had
won a new acceptance for labor, and the need to maintain
wartime production had resulted in new concessions and

[8] Wilson to Lansing, February 13, 1918, Wilson MSS.
[9] Lansing to Wilson, February 15, 1918, NA, RG 59, 861.00/
133a. Cf. *FR, The Lansing Papers*, II, 352–53.

contracts for AFL unions. The labor leadership therefore
welcomed the opportunity to be of service to the Department of State. The method chosen was to influence European labor to support the Allied governments and the war
effort. The job was to be done, as was the case with the
Root Commission, by sponsoring different American labor
missions to Europe.

The Wilson Administration saw a great need to have
organized labor undertake diplomatic missions on its
behalf. Such a need developed because of the shift in opinion within the ranks of Allied labor. In Britain particularly,
trouble was brewing. While the bulk of the Labour Party
threw its support behind the war, a minority did not. Representatives of the Independent Labour Party opposed Britain's entry into the war and devoted themselves to trying
to obtain an early peace settlement. This group, headed by
ILP leader Ramsay MacDonald, linked efforts with pacifists
in the Liberal Party. Together they formed the Union of
Democratic Control, which agitated for peace negotiations
and an end to secret diplomacy.[10]

Before the United States had declared war against Germany, members of the UDC favored using Woodrow Wilson as a mediator between the belligerent powers. W. H.
Buckler, an American graduate of Trinity College in Cambridge and a special assistant at the U.S. Embassy in
London, kept Colonel Edward M. House in touch with the
views of this anti-war group. Recent events, Buckler wrote
toward the end of 1916, had encouraged the negotiation
group. Although they had only forty votes in Parliament,
"they carry weight." But Buckler added that the group was
"so friendly to the President's policy" that they desired all
peace terms to be stated "frankly but confidentially to
Uncle Sam as the 'honest broker.'"[11]

After the United States entered the war, the attitude of

[10] The account of British labor policy during World War I is
drawn from Henry M. Pelling, *America and the British Left* (New
York, 1957), pp. 108–29.
[11] W. H. Buckler to House, December 27, 1916, W. H. Buckler
Collection; "Political Reports from London" folder, House MSS;
Yale University Library.

the "negotiation" group within Britain changed from one of support to Wilson and confidence in the American program, to anxiety about the war fever which swept the United States. As ILP leader Philip Snowden expressed it, there was "little reason to believe that America will long remain actuated by the noble impulses which breathed in President Wilson's speech. There are signs already that war fever is raging in the United States."[12]

The shift in opinion was indicated when Arthur Henderson offered his support to the Stockholm Conference. Henderson had changed his original opinion because he thought it the only means left for placating the Soviet and for keeping Russia in the war. Nevertheless, Lloyd George and other British ministers feared the outcome of the Stockholm Conference, believing that it was "now tainted beyond hope of redemption by the presence of the 'Kaiser's hirelings.' "[13]

By August, Lloyd George made it clear that his government was opposed to Stockholm and would not allow any "sectional conference" to decide or dictate peace terms. Because Henderson supported the conference, conflict arose between his role as a Labour Party officer who worked for Stockholm, and as a War Cabinet minister in a government whose leaders were opposed to the conference. Henderson refused to abandon his support of Stockholm. As a result, he was forced to resign his post in the Cabinet in August of 1917.[14]

With Henderson out of the War Cabinet, a vacancy existed which British labor sought to fill. Heeding their demands, Lloyd George appointed G. N. Barnes to Henderson's old office. Barnes was a former officer of the Amalgamated Society of Engineers. Ostensibly, Labour Party participation in the government was carried on. Actually, Henderson's dismissal meant that the most powerful and experienced officer of the Labour Party was formally es-

[12] *Labour Leader*, April 12, 1917; cited in Pelling, *op. cit.*, p. 110.
[13] Robert D. Warth, *The Allies and the Russian Revolution* (Durham, N.C., 1954), p. 78.
[14] *Ibid.*, 81–83.

tranged from the government. It also meant that Henderson was in the position of working for a foreign policy contrary to the position taken by Lloyd George's government.

These developments led to efforts by the two governments to promote exchanges of British and American labor leaders for the purpose of stiffening the ardor of British Labourites. At the end of November, Secretary Lansing forwarded to Wilson a report from the Office of Naval Intelligence. The report indicated that "the fight of labor" against Lloyd George "may be very far reaching in its effects." Most troublesome was the fear that if Arthur Henderson succeeded in becoming prime minister in a new government, "he would be in favor of Peace." The report suggested a possible way of dealing with Henderson. The British labor leader was "quite interested in Samuel Gompers and has considerable admiration for him." Therefore it "would be of unquestionable advantage to the Allied cause to have Mr. Gompers go to England." Wilson asked that the report be shown to Gompers, and that he be consulted "as to whether he knows of any means by which he could help to steer Mr. Henderson."[15]

Gompers responded immediately. His first suggestion was that Barnes, the new Labour member of the War Cabinet, be invited along with a delegation of British labor leaders to visit the United States.[16] Gompers asked that W. A. Appleton, general secretary of the General Federation of Trade Unions, be included on this delegation. This suggestion was meant to be a slap at Henderson and British organized labor, the bulk of which was represented by the massive Trades Union Congress. Appleton, however, opposed both socialism and a negotiated peace. He was the only British labor leader who shared Samuel Gompers'

[15] Lansing to Wilson, November 30, 1917, enclosing the confidential report from the Office of Naval Intelligence; Wilson to Tumulty, November 30, 1917, Wilson MSS, File 2.
[16] Gompers to G. N. Barnes, January 5, 1918, Samuel Gompers, "International Labor Relations," *American Federationist*, XXV (April 1918), 295.

total outlook. Barnes, taking his cue from Gompers, appointed Appleton to lead the delegation to the United States. The problem was that Appleton in no way represented British labor. "The G.F.T.U. of which he was the secretary," Pelling points out, "was no more than a strike insurance fund to which few unions were affiliated." The appointment was due only to Gompers' intention "to regard him as his own counterpart in Britain." But Gompers was well aware "that the T.U.C. was the truly representative body of British trade unionism."[17]

The announcement of Appleton's visit brought a hostile response from many pro-labor Americans. The liberal journalist Lincoln Colcord showered attacks on the delegation, arguing that "these men were chosen by the British government without consultation with British labor groups, and they have come to America primarily on a political mission for that Government."[18] To deal with this response, the National Civic Federation scheduled a debate between Gompers and Paul Kellogg, a journalist who supported the policies of Arthur Henderson. Easley explained to Gompers that a "serious break" had occurred between the pacifist-Bolshevik factions and the legitimate ranks of organized labor, and the former "had already inaugurated from England an attack on the American Federation of Labor and especially on Mr. Gompers, as well as on the British labor delegates now in this country."[19]

At the meeting, Paul Kellogg argued that Henderson only desired a just peace and a commitment from Lloyd George that his government would stand behind such an anti-imperialist policy. His efforts were "in no sense to down arms or down tools in an effort to bring about a premature peace." Instead British labor was trying to force the Allied governments to stand united behind the anti-imperialist settlement. For this end, they favored holding an inter-

---

[17] Pelling, *op. cit.*, p. 114.
[18] Colcord to Ralph Easley, March 10, 1918, National Civic Federation MSS, New York Public Library. (Cited hereafter as NCF MSS.)
[19] Easley to Gompers, March 10, 1918, *ibid.*

belligerent conference at which Allied labor could openly confront its German counterparts.

Gompers and the pro-war Socialists could only see this division in terms of black and white. The only course for labor, Gompers asserted, was to fight the war "until either autocracy is crushed or democracy enthroned." He would not "encourage my fellow countrymen in a discussion of peace when there is no peace possible." William E. Walling argued that Henderson actually favored the same Stockholm Conference which President Wilson had already disapproved. Any meeting, he claimed, would appear as a semi-official gathering. While Henderson obviously believed that British labor could drive a wedge between the German government and the German working classes, actually the German Socialists were driving a wedge between British labor and the British government. Pacifist sentiment would lead to a general strike in Britain and France, an event toward which the German military looked forward.[20]

Privately, Walling had informed Gompers that he wished to "lay special emphasis on the extremely dangerous character of Henderson's revived agitation for a Stockholm International Socialist Conference." Because Henderson adopted a friendly attitude toward Woodrow Wilson the danger had increased, for he now advocated such a meeting "as a disciple of President Wilson." Walling asked Gompers to take "some suitable action" since "a more important labor crisis" had not occurred during the war. "These fanatics never know when they are beaten," Walling reflected, "and I believe Henderson is more aggressive at the present moment than he has ever been."[21]

The attacks on Henderson by Gompers and Walling were misplaced. Throughout the war, Henderson was most interested in wooing Gompers and satisfying the Allied

[20] Addresses by Paul Kellogg, Samuel Gompers, and William English Walling on the British Labour Party's Program of Reconstruction after the War and the Stockholm Conference, March 16, 1918, *ibid.*

[21] Walling to Gompers, January 10, 1918, *ibid.*

cabinets. What Henderson hoped was that Gompers would give his endorsement to war aims as defined by British labor, in order to unite the entire Allied Left behind a more advanced Wilsonian program. Henderson's politics were not subversive of the existing international status quo. To prove how much he desired Gompers' cooperation, and acting on behalf of the TUC Parliamentary Committee and the National Executive of the Labour Party, Henderson invited Gompers to attend an Inter-Allied Labour and Socialist Conference to be held in London in February of 1918. The meeting was to consider Britain's war aims, the convening of an international Socialist conference, and arrangements for representation of the working classes at the official peace conference. Henderson urged that even if Gompers did not agree with the meeting's sponsors, he should come to put "the American point of view." More-over, Henderson let Gompers know that he favored exclud-ing the American Socialist Party from official participation. Although they had received "a request from the American Socialists," Henderson wrote Gompers, they had decided "that your Federation was the only body to be invited to this conference to represent America."[22]

Despite Henderson's overtures, Gompers was not about to work with the European centrists. Henderson's invita-tion, although mailed in early January, did not arrive at AFL Headquarters until the 9th of February. Its late arrival allowed Gompers to argue that no time existed to gather together an AFL delegation. Gompers also showed his dis-approval of the European labor leaders who opposed his own program. "American labor believes," he answered Henderson, that "German influences have inspired the London conference and until this is disproved will avoid the conference."[23]

The absence of an AFL delegation did not deter Hender-

[22] Henderson to Gompers, January 16, 1918, Gompers MSS.
[23] Paul U. Kellogg and Arthur Gleason, *British Labor and the War* (New York, 1919), pp. 57, 61–62; Samuel Gompers, *Seventy Years of Life and Labor*, II (New York, 1925), 403–04; *1918 AFL Convention*, 40–50.

son. The Labour Party decided to send its own mission to
visit the United States and to try and settle its differences
with the AFL. Since Henderson viewed himself as an avid
Wilsonian, he believed that he would be able to gain the
support of American labor for a policy of negotiations
with German workers. In March he informed A. H. Frazier,
the American liaison officer with the Supreme War Council, that he would follow any course suggested by Wilson.
The President need only "signify his wishes," Henderson
wrote, and he would "endeavor to comply with them."[24]

Woodrow Wilson was not as willing to utilize Henderson's offer of cooperation. He found Henderson's attitude
"interesting," Wilson explained to Colonel House, but he
did not know what reply to make. While Wilson understood
that it opened a "channel of influence which may upon
some occasion be very useful indeed," Wilson realized that
if he met Henderson halfway and got "into confidential
relations" with him, it would likely "embarrass my dealing
with Lloyd George and the rest of the Ministry, to whom
Henderson is in opposition."[25]

Two days later, Wilson met Gompers and learned that
the American labor leader vigorously opposed Henderson's
policies and his planned labor mission to the United States.
Gompers had argued that the mission might destroy the
positive effects of Appleton's visit, and would make it appear that socialism and pacifism were strong in Europe.
Wilson agreed that any negotiations with enemy Socialists
were "outrageous and fraught with the greatest mischief."
The President asked Colonel House to express his "sincere
appreciation" to Henderson for the confidence he had in
Wilson, but that the President felt it would "make a bad
impression in this country if any group of men were to visit
it who would be understood to represent a party, whether
that party be national or international, the people of this
country being just now intolerant of parties and impatient
of special missions, and this quite irrespective of the wel-

[24] Ray Stannard Baker, *Woodrow Wilson: Life and Letters*, VII,
War Leader, April 6, 1917–Feb. 28, 1918 (N.Y., 1939), 38.
[25] Wilson to House, March 20, 1918, in *ibid.*, 38.

come they might in other circumstances wish to extend to the individuals composing the group."[26]

In his reply to Henderson, Wilson had revealed that he did not desire to attain international solidarity among Wilsonians if it meant going over the head of the established Allied governments. Rather than come to terms of agreement with the moderate democratic Socialists in Europe, Gompers preferred to work through the conservative AFL and the Administration Left. Wilson, like Gompers, did not want to risk supporting informal conferences with enemy Socialists. Instead, they tended to view those who supported such a course as potential, if not actual, traitors.

Wilson stood with Gompers despite reports which indicated that "all groups of British labor, rank and file, as well as leaders regard the President as their leader." Yet, House had been informed, the "feeling of weariness among labor is widespread, and of enthusiasm [for the war] there is practically none." British labor did demand, however, "that democratic war purposes be expressed, be adhered to and pursued by every effort. The Government is thoroughly discredited," Walter Hines Page and Felix Frankfurter reported, "but for the present it is safe because there is no alternative and Lloyd George is deemed strong in France and Italy. However the elements of opposition are many and labor discontent, the food problems, doubts as to the war aims . . . may all bring a change of ministry." Their report indicated that the purpose of Henderson's proposed mission was to gain Gompers' approval "so as to present a united front of labor for the Wilson principles both to the Allied Governments and to the Socialists of the Central Powers."[27]

Wilson's domestic supporters in the Administration Left did not share this analysis of Henderson's motives. As

---

[26] Wilson to House, March 22, 1918, in *ibid.*, 44; House to Frazier, March 27, 1918, *FR*, I, Supplement I, 1918 (Washington, D.C., 1918), 177.

[27] Felix Frankfurter and Walter H. Page to House, March 1, 1918, NA, RG 59, 763.72119 So/76.

Easley wrote to House, "the visit of these delegates from the socialist-labor groups in Europe at the present time will be fraught with serious consequences. It challenges at once all the forces of law and order in this country" and would mean a confrontation of the trade union movement "by the socialists of Europe." Easley hoped that the government could indicate that it did not want Henderson in the United States. "I realize," he told House, "that the British Government could not afford . . . to refuse to give these men passports, but, if it were feasible for our Government to indicate to Great Britain that the coming here of these men . . . would make for disunity in this country, the British Government might be glad to put a stop to their coming." Easley added that he was not misrepresenting "our loyal labor leaders when I say that they would like to have these men kept at home." Easley feared that Gompers' re-election as AFL president might be threatened if the Socialists were able to seize "upon this Arthur Henderson commission as a rallying point in the fight against Gompers."[28]

Easley put great stress on the above point when conferring with Gompers. Writing before Wilson's decision to oppose the mission, Easley argued that a visit by the "Henderson-Pacifist Menagerie" would serve as a radical rallying point at the AFL's expense. Easley played upon Gompers' own fear by arguing that the Henderson commission would "get into a number of Central bodies, where their views . . . would be endorsed." Since Henderson had already criticized Appleton, the only choice left for Gompers was to protest his planned visit and let the British government know his feelings. Easley predicted that if an "intimation came from over here," Lloyd George would stop Henderson from making his visit.[29]

Easley was correct. Wilson's opposition forced British labor to change its plans. Henderson agreed to wait and confer with AFL leaders when they arrived in Europe in

[28] Easley to House, March 14, 1918, NCF MSS.
[29] Easley to Gompers, March 4, 1918, *ibid.*

the spring.[30] Having stimulated the patriotism and productivity of their own workers, the AFL leaders turned their attention to Europe. Gompers decided to send labor missions abroad that would "inspire the workers in Allied countries to the same single-minded devotion to prosecuting the War that characterized the American workingman."[31] The mission was to be sent at a time, as Arno Mayer points out, when Germany's offensive was at its peak, and when the Allied governments wanted aid in the taming of their own dissidents. For this purpose, the aid of American labor leaders was highly desired, since their own "war enthusiasm knew no bounds." The cabinets were also prodded on by the Social Patriots who needed reinforcement in their own fight against left wing *minoritaires*.[32]

Unlike the American Socialists who had been unable to obtain passports to attend the Stockholm Conference, the AFL group experienced no difficulty. Lansing sent Wilson a file of papers applying for passport applications for the seven labor men and two women who had been chosen for the delegation. Lansing noted that he was "not sure what your views are upon this matter," but that "Gompers by his letters favors the granting of the passports."[33] The next day Gompers was received at the White House. After he discussed international relations with the President, Wilson gave the mission his approval.[34]

To indicate the Administration's approval, Lansing wired Ambassador Walter Hines Page announcing the mission's plans. "As Mr. Gompers assures me of their intense loyalty to this country," Lansing explained, "and their unswerving devotion to the cause of democracy, it would

[30] Gompers to Henderson, March 13, 1918, *1918 AFL Convention*, 50.
[31] James T. Shotwell, ed., *The Origins of the International Labor Organization* (New York, 1934), I, 99.
[32] Arno J. Mayer, *Politics of Diplomacy and Peacemaking* (New York, 1967), pp. 40–41. For Mayer's discussion of this first mission, see pp. 40–43.
[33] Lansing to Wilson, March 21, 1918, NA, RG 59, 763.72119/-1529.
[34] Gompers to James Duncan, March 24, 1918, Gompers MSS.

be well to show them such courtesy and consideration as you properly may in your official capacity." Lansing noted that previous instructions forbidding discussion of policy with members of another government did not apply to this commission, since its members went "abroad to discuss labor conditions and to seek the most effective way in which the laboring classes can cooperate with and advance the policies of their respective governments in prosecuting the war. There is no purpose on the part of the American delegation to consider or discuss the policies or in any way to interfere with the avowed purpose of this Government or of any Government of the Allies."[35]

The mission, which visited Britain and France during April–May 1918, consisted of James Wilson, president of the Patternmakers; James A. Wilcox; William H. Johnston; Martin F. Ryan; William Short; Chester M. Wright; Belinda Scott; and Agnes Nestor. Its chairman was John P. Frey, head of the AFL Metal Trades Department and an officer of the AFL Molders. Frey had already corresponded with Arthur Henderson the previous October. In that month, Henderson sought to explain his position to Frey. "We have now had over three years of this terrible war," Henderson had written, "and I am no longer a believer in the 'knock-out' blow." Sacrifices made by workers led Henderson "to the conclusion that every effort should be made to shorten the war if only by a single day, and that such efforts should include not only the military, but political, diplomatic, economic, and any and every means." Although he supported the Stockholm Conference, Henderson clarified that he did not wish the meeting to settle peace terms. That job rested with the governments concerned. But what the Socialists could do was to gain a uniform consensus on war aims and then attempt to line up the governments behind them.[36]

[35] Lansing to Page, April 2, 1918, *FR*, 1918, I, Supplement I, (Washington, D.C., 1918), 189.

[36] Henderson to Frey, October 1, 1917, John P. Frey MSS. (Library of Congress).

Frey did not accept Henderson's logic. The first labor mission, he recollected, "had the task of influencing English and French leaders to adopt the American position": to "continue the war until German arms were no longer effective."[37] Frey had serious reservations about the mission's potential. He believed that the European and American Left would try to undermine their work in advance. "I am inclined to the thought," Frey stressed, "that upon my arrival in Great Britain, efforts will be made by men who are dominating figures in the political movement to either endeavor to discredit the representatives whom you appoint . . . or else to make such use of us as would enable them to leave the impression in the workers' minds that we were in sympathy with their program."[38] Frey left for Europe in a pessimistic mood. As he informed the group before its departure, he had "seen a change come over" Arthur Henderson in the past year. It was necessary to guard against being put in a position "where it would appear that we are giving at least moral support" to Henderson's ambition to become prime minister of a new British government.[39]

After finding that the European labor leaders did not agree with the AFL position on the war, Frey explained their divergent approach by claiming that they were agents of the German government. There was a "distinct element of opposition to the [American] government on the part of many of the leaders of the movement," Frey later reported. The European labor chiefs did not understand why American unionists did not press demands upon their government in return for a pledge of loyalty. Frey was convinced "that there are men in the socialist movement of France who have German gold jingling in their pockets." In Britain they were simply "doing the work" of Germany "without

[37] John P. Frey Reminiscences, COHC (Butler Library, Columbia University).
[38] Frey to Gompers, March 12, 1918, Gompers MSS.
[39] Conference with members of the Labor Mission, AFL Headquarters, March 28, 1918, *ibid.*

being paid for it." Peace through negotiation could not be supported. The war "had to be fought to the finish on the battle field."[40]

Frey maintained this view despite Henderson's attempts to point out that he adhered to a Wilsonian program. At a dinner meeting on April 17, Henderson informed Frey that British labor "desired to lay before representatives of Labor from enemy countries the Allied view, of a settlement calculated to produce an enduring democratic peace." To do this they favored an international labor and Socialist conference. Any "speeches referring to the necessity of crushing Germany, or of having no dealings with any Germany [sic] working men till Germany is crushed," Henderson argued, "would not be well received by British working class audiences."[41]

Henderson's warning was in vain. He had to note that the AFL group "indulged in flamboyant language about crushing Germany" which caused Henderson embarrassment. Henderson attempted to argue that if the Allied governments could be in touch with Germany about peace terms, labor could do the same. Even the AFL, he claimed, favored holding a labor conference simultaneously with the official peace conference. But to achieve this it would be necessary, Henderson believed, to hold preliminary meetings with German labor. They too had to be united in favor of a democratic settlement.[42]

It was clear, as W. H. Buckler reported, that a "deep cleavage" existed between British labor and the AFL on the question of an inter-belligerent labor conference. Moreover, "the American delegates . . . are known to have been carefully picked by Mr. Gompers, who is very widely regarded here as the Rip Van Winkle of the Labor movement." While Henderson did not actually expect to win their approval, he did hope to widen the AFL's point of

[40] Meeting of the National Civic Federation, August 13, 1918, NCF MSS.

[41] W. H. Buckler, "Labor Notes for Week Ending April 20, 1918," House MSS.

[42] Buckler, "Labor Notes for Week Ending April 27, 1918," ibid.

view and to give them a better understanding of European labor.[43]

If Henderson was trying to make the AFL delegation show more tolerance, his purpose had failed. The AFL mission also met with the TUC Parliamentary Committee, which besides Henderson, included Ramsay MacDonald, J. H. Thomas, Stewart Bunning, and Sidney Webb. When the AFL leaders heard more talk of an inter-belligerent conference, James Wilson insisted that any meeting was impractical as long as the German military machine remained intact. Only military defeat of Prussia would give the workers the opportunity to establish a democratic government in Germany. The American AFL delegates, George Berry added, were "with their government, because they believed it was in harmony with the ideals of the Trade Union movement in America."[44]

At the end of April, the British labor leaders tried again. The Americans listened and said nothing, showing their evident desire "not to commit themselves." William Gillies of the Labour Party staff noted that "they sat like 'Sphinxes,'" an attitude which antagonized the British Labourites who knew the readiness of the AFL men to declare their own position at public meetings. The British labor men were not impressed. Writing about this meeting, Buckler reported to Colonel House:

The relations between the British Labor leaders and their American guests were entirely friendly, but from the intimate comment of Webb, Gillies, and Henderson, it is evident that the Americans impressed them much as shrewd, intelligent backwoodsmen might impress a New Yorker. Their point of view struck the English as provincial, and the extreme caution with which they declined to give any expression of personal opinion, but insisted on reading long and tedious extracts from the proceedings of the American Federation of Labor savored

[43] Buckler to House, May 4, 1918, *ibid.*
[44] The Trades Union Congress Parliamentary Committee, 30th Quarterly Report, June 1918, "American Mission and British Labour Movement," pp. 35–39, Frey MSS.

of antiquated formality. The English were bored with the views of the American Federation of Labor which they knew beforehand. What they wanted was a free exchange of opinion with the American delegates. As they put it, 'We outsiders know what resolutions amount to, and we wanted to get at what the Americans really thought.'[45]

The British labor leaders expected a better reception from the AFL because they mistakenly felt they could establish bonds of solidarity with their fellow Wilsonian allies. The problem was, as Henry M. Pelling has observed, that they held "an exaggerated idea of the extent to which President Wilson's policy" agreed with their own. Sidney and Beatrice Webb even believed that Wilson so desired to use the strength of Allied labor for his own cause, that he might "join hands with the British Labour Party . . . and instruct Gompers to link up with the [Socialist] International."[46]

The truth was that the AFL, with Wilson's blessings, firmly argued that discussion of war aims should not take place between the Allied and enemy labor movements. Rather, Wilson hoped that Allied labor would speak only of the need to gain a military victory over the Kaiser's forces. This position by necessity widened the gap between the AFL delegation and the Allied labor leaders. While Webb and Henderson held illusions about Wilsonian policy, Ramsay MacDonald did not. MacDonald summed up the mission by writing that while his associates "tried to give them a few facts to digest to set into their sonorous professions of faith and their adjectives and adverbs," the British government was "looking after them pretty closely."[47] The feeling of hostility was mutual. Men who used to be good unionists, Frey wrote, had become politi-

---

[45] Buckler, "Labor Notes for the Week Ending May 4, 1918," House MSS.

[46] Beatrice Webb, *Diaries, 1912–1924* (London, 1952), p. 114; cited in Pelling, *America and the British Left*, p. 118.

[47] *Forward* (Glasgow), May 11, 1918; cited in *ibid.*, p. 119.

cians. The more he saw of British labor, "the more I feel proud of the A.F. of L. and in particular of Gompers."[48]

After their stay in Britain, the AFL delegation moved on to France. They were welcomed by those dissident members of the French Socialist Party who endorsed the AFL stand. These forty members of the French Parliament were led by the noted French Socialist, Albert Thomas.[49] As in Britain, George Berry reported, "we endeavored to . . . convert them to our point of view." Berry found, however, that the French workers were "not over enthusiastic" although he believed they did favor prosecuting the war. Berry and the AFL delegation persisted in calling the forty French pro-war Socialists the "real representatives of the French movement."[50]

The French government was satisfied with the backing they obtained. Ambassador William G. Sharp reported that the mission took the only course compatible with America's position, "that of complete loyalty to the policy of the President in [the war's] prosecution." Only such a position, he emphasized, would "have been tolerated for a moment by the French Government in extending a welcome to them." Sharp felt that the men were "sound, patriotic and very helpful to the morale of the French people." Only when the German army approached Paris did French radicals loudly oppose the mission.[51] Sharp also reported that "many members of the French Government, among them Mr. Clemenceau and Mr. Pichon, expressed to me their greatest satisfaction over the helpful influence which these delegates had exerted among the labor elements in France."[52]

On their way back to the States, the mission returned for yet another visit to Britain. TUC and Labour Party leaders

[48] Frey to William B. Rubin, May 2, 1918, William B. Rubin MSS, State Historical Society of Wisconsin, Madison, Wis.

[49] *New York Times*, June 24, 1918.

[50] Meeting at AFL Headquarters, June 1, 1918, Gompers MSS.

[51] Sharp to Lansing, June 9, 1918, NA, RG 59, 763.73/10304.

[52] Sharp to Lansing, May 12, 1918, *FR, 1918*, I, Supplement 1 (Washington, D.C., 1918), 230.

had prepared documents showing that the TUC had 3,677,-000 members and the Labour Party had 2,415,000. These figures compared favorably to the scant 796,000 who were enrolled in W. A. Appleton's GFTU. And only 81,000 of the latter group were also *not* enrolled in either the TUC or Labour Party. Despite the new proof of the representative character of the two large British labor federations, the AFL delegates remained adamant. Frey reiterated their position. He also supported appointing labor ambassadors to all American embassies, in order to prevent division among Allied labor. As he saw it, the "enemies of Labour had taken advantage" of a lack of knowledge "to prejudice the American movement in the Allied countries."[53]

The AFL members proved that they could not learn from their contacts with British labor. The conservative ambassador Walter Hines Page, who had been attacked by the AFL as an enemy of organized labor before the war, now praised the AFL delegation as "admirable representatives of the bone and sinew of American manhood."[54] The AFL members did not show any hesitancy because of this praise from unexpected sources. They believed that their mission had been a complete success. Samuel Gompers greeted them upon their return with the admonition that a "pacifist and a socialist are nothing more than pro-Germans." James Wilson told his chief that "only a small minority" of British and French labor wanted negotiations. Moreover, these men were "leaders of political parties, who are talking peace at any price." Wilson conveyed to Gompers the appreciation of Lloyd George, who had obtained AFL support against his domestic labor critics. The Prime Minister had indicated that he appreciated Gompers' "patriotic stand in this war" and "hoped that he would have the opportunity to take" Gompers personally "by the hand" in the near future. George L. Berry reported that the TUC was "diametrically opposed to our position." But the AFL leaders had not en-

[53] TUC Parliamentary Committee, 30th Quarterly Report, pp. 35–39, Frey MSS; Labour Party's 18th Annual Conference Report (1918), p. 10. Cited in Pelling, *op. cit.*, p. 120.
[54] Page to House, May 27, 1918, in Burton J. Hendrick, *Life and Letters of W. H. Page* (London, 1924), II, 387.

gaged in a dialogue to find out what the TUC position was, nor had they ever had any intention of doing so. They were in Europe only "to convert [the TUC] to our point of view."[55]

It was more than naïve of Webb and Henderson to think that they could have broadened the AFL leaders' understanding. Frey explained that true union groups were cooperating with their governments. Only labor leaders "permanently engaged in the political field" supported negotiations with the enemy. The problem which Frey bypassed was that the majority of European labor held precisely a "political" rather than a bread-and-butter unionism perspective. Despite this truth, the AFL delegation nourished the myth that the "true" representatives of European labor were those who subscribed to AFL policy. The workers were loyal, Martin J. Ryan told Gompers; only their leaders spoke "about peace conventions and several things that I did not seem to understand just what they had in mind." Contrasting their own approach to that of the Labour Party leadership, William Short informed Gompers of what he considered to be a major triumph. He had personally visited the front, fired a machine gun, and thrown a hand grenade at German soldiers. Gompers' satisfaction was complete. "No effort," he told the returning mission, "since the outbreak of the war has been of greater importance than the American labor Mission's visit to Britain and France."[56]

The point of view taken by the AFL delegation and by the pro-war Socialists revealed a frank rejection of any desire to meet their European counterparts even halfway. William English Walling, the pro-war Socialist who had drawn close to Gompers, explained that "not only the Socialists but the labor unions of the Continent" were tied to the old Socialist International, and held an ideology "even more terrible and menacing than that of the Bolsheviki." The only path for European labor to follow, Walling pro-

[55] Meeting upon the return of the labor mission to Europe, AFL Headquarters, June 1, 1918, Gompers MSS.
[56] *Ibid.*

claimed, was to extend to Europe "old fashioned Jefferson-
ian democracy" with "organized labor of the A.F. of L.
type" being "taken into partnership with the government."
Walling admitted that such a prospect was "scarcely inspiring" for a "genuine Socialist and internationalist," but
it was preferable to chauvinist socialism, Bolshevism, or
sterile loyalty to the old Socialist International. Like Gompers, Walling argued that the war itself was "bringing
about a large part of the vast changes we have desired"
and it was the duty of Socialists to further that development.[57]

This attitude only deepened the blindness to reality of
those who adhered to AFL ideology. The belief that the
political unionism of Henderson had to be fought and that
AFL unionism had to be spread in Europe only further
antagonized European moderate labor. Sidney Webb thus
told W. H. Buckler that "in the interests of Allied unity it
would not be desirable that any more American labor delegates, preaching the doctrine of the 'Knock-out blow' and
of complete non-intercourse with German socialists,
should come to this country or to France at the present
time." Webb stated that the AFL mission "did not tend towards harmony, but had on the contrary a somewhat dis-
turbing effect on French socialists and labor circles."[58]

The left-wing minority in Britain was even more vehe-
ment in their protest. MacDonald wrote Adolph Germer,
secretary of the American Socialist Party, that Frey's group
had "convinced most of the Labour leaders here, irrespective of their views upon national policy at the present
moment, that the American Federation is hopelessly out
of date and has no grasp of the realities of European politics." MacDonald called the delegation "a profound disappointment" and termed their press interviews back in the
United States as "grotesque in the extreme." The Labour

---

[57] Walling to Algie M. Simons, April 29, 1918, Algie M. Simons
MSS, State Historical Society of Wisconsin, Madison, Wis.

[58] Buckler to House, June 18, 1918, Buckler Collection, House
MSS; Laughlin to Lansing, June 19, 1918, *FR, 1918*, I, Supplement
1 (Washington, D.C., 1918), 259.

Party could either negotiate with the AFL and ignore European labor, MacDonald suggested, or deal with European labor and ignore the AFL. He opted for the latter choice, although, he explained, "I regret it very much as I wished to see American labour and Socialism march along with us and help us to secure after this war democratic freedom and permanent peace."[59]

In France the Belgian Camille Huysmans also commented "with scorn on the farcical inaccuracy of the reports which have appeared in our press of the attitude of socialist and labor opinion on this side of the ocean as interpreted by the labor delegates who recently visited London and Paris." Huysmans, as well as Webb and Henderson, now realized "the limitations, intellectual and otherwise, which made it practically impossible for these American delegates to carry back to America an accurate report of the attitude towards war problems held by their European colleagues."[60]

Henderson was particularly dissatisfied with the reports of British labor opinion presented by the mission once they had returned to America. The group claimed that since their mission, the movement favoring negotiations with German labor had disappeared, and that "Henderson himself . . . now declares his unwillingness to negotiate with the Germans, saying 'we are willing to converse, but we are not willing to negotiate.'" Henderson attacked the AFL mission for inaccurate reporting that was meant to misinform the public. He never had supported a conference that would negotiate peace terms, Henderson informed House, and only desired a consultative meeting whose decisions would not be mandatory. Such a conference would issue a full statement of each side's desire for a democratic peace. "These decisions," Henderson noted, "completely dispose of the suggestion that we seek to enter a plenary congress to negotiate peace over the heads of responsible govern-

[59] MacDonald to Germer, June 5, 1918, Socialist Party MSS, Duke University Library. From the notes of James Weinstein.
[60] Buckler to House, June 28, 1918, Buckler Collection, House MSS.

ments." Henderson added that if British labor thought that
Woodrow Wilson's "high ideals" could be fulfilled by fighting, they would favor such a course. But since they were
not convinced of that, they sought to "reinforce military
effort by conversations, informal conferences," and diplomacy.[61]

The AFL mission had refused to endorse the Memorandum on War Aims that was adopted by the Inter-Allied
Labor and Socialist Conference which met in London during February 20–24. They preferred to adhere to the AFL's
own policy on war aims, which they argued was inspired
by similar Wilsonian principles. Agreement existed between Allied and American labor solely on one issue—that
labor should be represented at the official peace conference
and that a labor meeting should be held concurrently in
the same country as the regular peace conference. This
agreement on a minor point was overshadowed by the
irreconcilable divergency on the issue of holding an inter-
belligerent labor-Socialist conference before the war's end.
"These two issues," Arno Mayer has put it, "were but the
occasion for the manifestation of fundamental ideological,
political and social divergencies between American trade
unionists and Allied Socialists. The former were syndical,
nonpartisan, and pragmatic in outlook; the latter were
Socialist, political and ideological."[62]

Rather than convince Allied labor leaders to adopt the
AFL's view of Wilsonianism, British and French labor and
Socialist leaders maintained their own chosen course. Both
sides, however, were prone to illusions of their own making. The Henderson-Webb-Longuet group believed that
Woodrow Wilson pursued revolutionary or at least humanitarian goals opposed by their own Allied governments, and that the AFL would help them gather support
for commonly shared Wilsonian goals. The AFL leaders,
on the other hand, viewed Allied labor leaders as a group
of politicians who had succumbed to revolutionary Social-

---

[61] "Allied working class policy," interview with Arthur Henderson, n.d. [1918], file drawer 34, House MSS.
[62] Mayer, Politics and Diplomacy of Peacemaking, p. 42.

ist ideology. To Frey and his associates, this explained why they were dabbling in such "dangerous" ideas as peace conferences with enemy labor leaders before a military victory. Gompers and Frey, moreover, allowed themselves to believe that it was only a minority of misguided and unrepresentative leaders who shared these "incorrect" and objectively pro-German ideas.

Despite the AFL mission's failure to convert Allied labor, the Wilson Administration had benefited from its work. The group of labor leaders had traveled to Britain and France for the purpose of defending Administration foreign policy. It had been given official permission to engage in the type of conversation and meetings forbidden to the opponents of official policy. Frey and his colleagues had carried out their task admirably. The praise bestowed upon them led them to a new conclusion: that similar missions were needed if their purpose was to be fulfilled. In the near future, Samuel Gompers himself would decide to head yet another, and more important, labor mission.

The Frey mission revealed that American labor leaders had formally arrived. Endowed with government and private approval, it had earned the labor leaders a new status and position. Not only did they work at home to defend the rank-and-file laborer by demanding collective bargaining and union contracts; they worked with the United States government itself to guarantee labor's loyalty at home and abroad. Labor leaders had begun to function as links in the American foreign policy machine. They had entered the era of the labor statesman.

British labor leaders believed that as a result of the first AFL mission to Europe, the gap between Allied and American organized labor had widened. The AFL leaders held a different view. In spite of the Labour Party's destructive efforts, W. A. Appleton wrote John P. Frey, the AFL mission "had a very beneficent effect." Much had been done to belittle its work, but there could be no question of "its real value." Yet, there was more to be done. Allied labor continued to use its influence "mainly in the interests of Germany." French Socialists had adopted the "no annexations—no indemnities" formula, and were demanding immediate peace negotiations. Appleton suggested that Samuel Gompers himself "come this way as soon as possible." He was aware of the difficulties Gompers would face, but felt that "we can rally the Trade Unionists to his support." They would "find a common denominator that would hold them together as against the wiles of the malcontent politicians." Once Gompers arrived he could offset the call for a labor-Socialist conference with enemy labor, by calling for an inter-Allied conference composed only of trade unionists.[1]

Appleton's desire to see Gompers in Europe was held as well by many other prominent Allied government and labor officials. The first labor mission had been urged by Lloyd George, as well as others, to have Gompers accept their pleas for having him travel to Europe. Since Gompers believed that in America the labor situation was "in a fairly satisfactory condition," and that the declarations of American labor "stood out in sharp contrast to the hesitant attitude of labor in other countries," he decided that "the service he could render by going to Europe would be more than he could at home."[2]

Gompers went to Europe with the express purpose of heading a "Paul Revere" mission to warn workers against the influences of those labor leaders who held a political, pacifist, pro-German or Socialist approach. As a frank advocate of his own brand of conservative syndical unionism Gompers hated above all the intellectual Socialist leadership of the Allied labor movement. Gompers' forthcoming visit stirred up grave worries among Allied labor leaders, especially when they saw conservative Allied opinion praising the mission as an anti-pacifist effort. Moreover, Gompers' anti-radicalism made it appear that he was trying to destroy the Labour Party and break up the Socialist International that was led by men like Arthur Henderson and Jean Longuet. [3]

Gompers' decision to lead a mission to Europe, therefore, immediately created a fight between Appleton and C. W. Bowerman of the Trades Union Congress. The question arose as to which group would welcome the Gompers mission as the representative of British labor. Ambassador Walter H. Page reported that Bowerman and the Labour

---

[1] Appleton to Frey, July 23, 1918, John P. Frey MSS. (Library of Congress).

[2] Samuel Gompers, *Seventy Years of Life and Labor,* II (New York, 1925), 407–09.

[3] Arno J. Mayer, *Politics and Diplomacy of Peacemaking* (New York, 1967), p. 43. Mayer's account of Gompers' efforts in Europe may be found on pp. 42–52.

Party "would be particularly glad to confer with Mr. Gompers" in the hope that a frank discussion of labor policy could take place. But Page also reported that Gompers' impending visit was hailed "with special joy by the Northcliffe and conservative press as an antidote to pacifism in the British labor party."

Page raised the issue of whether the use made of Gompers' visit by elements hostile to Labor would "annoy their rank and file, and thus accelerate their political movement to the left which has been a marked feature in the development of British labor policy during the past year." Henderson and Bowerman held the "majority of labor votes," Page admitted, and Gompers would "require all his diplomatic skill to avoid antagonizing the majority represented by those leaders, while at the same time co-operating with the minority led by Appleton and Thorne." Although, according to Sidney Webb, there was no chance that British labor would change its position on an inter-belligerent Socialist conference, Gompers would nevertheless "be welcomed and listened to with the greatest respect by all British socialists and labor men."[4]

The problem was, as W. H. Buckler reported, that Gompers' "visit may be used by the influences and press hostile to the Labour Party for the purpose of belittling Labour by attempting to discredit the Executive Committee of the Labour Party and the Parliamentary Committee of the Trades Union Congress whose policy Mr. Gompers is believed to disapprove." Buckler was privately informed by Colonel A. C. Murray and Lord Eustace Percy of the British Foreign Office that they "thought there was a considerable danger of friction through the labor world being stirred up by Mr. Gompers's visit, and the danger namely lest a considerable part of Labor which is now working smoothly in support of the war may be moved . . . into changing its attitude."

They both think, therefore, that it is of great importance to keep the British Government in the background and not to let

---

[4] Page to Lansing, August 20, 1918, NA, RG 59, 763.72/11050.

British Labor suppose either that the Government or that the Northcliffe and Beaverbrook press is backing or pressing Mr. Gompers' views on the British Labour Party. They understand that if Mr. Barnes entertains Mr. Gompers he will do it as a representative of Labor and not as a member of the Government, though it is not clear that this distinction can be plainly marked. They say that the Northcliffe and Beaverbrook press has been privately warned not to indulge during Mr. Gompers' visit in the expression of ecclesiastical approval which they have used on several occasions recently.

Henderson was convinced, Buckler reported, that the government would make capital of Gompers' visit to discredit Henderson. Gompers had already made his personal attitude clear by choosing to correspond with Appleton while purposefully ignoring Henderson. There was little doubt, Buckler remarked, that Henderson "fears the result of Gompers's visit and [that] if Gompers assumes a position of hostility to him and his associates in the Labour Party, Henderson is likely to retaliate so far as is possible."[5]

Despite such advance warnings, Gompers was indeed traveling partially to attack the ideology of men like Henderson. Gompers had even been forewarned that Henderson would attempt "to exploit the visit . . . in the interests of" Labour Party propaganda.[6] The mission led by Gompers was on guard against such possibilities. Its purpose, Ralph Easley wrote, was to attempt to counter the efforts of "the pacifist-socialist movements in England and France [which] threatened to undermine the working classes there, practically along the lines pursued by Lenin and Trotsky in Russia."[7]

Conservative British sources had actually favored a Gompers visit since early January. As a confidential memo indicated, plans for Gompers' visit had been formally approved by the British government. Speaking through Sir

---

[5] Buckler to House, August 24, 1918, W. H. Buckler Collection, Edward M. House MSS, Yale University Library.

[6] Appleton to Frey, August 20, 1918, Frey MSS.

[7] Easley to G. Agar, August 10, 1918, NCF MSS, New York Public Library.

William Wiseman, Lord Northcliffe stressed his desire to have Gompers visit England so that "the persistent and consistent efforts of a commission" could hold "the industrial situation in check until the American forces in France are sufficiently strong to morally offset any rupture that might percipitate [sic] a revolution."[8] On behalf of the Wilson Administration's propaganda agency, George Creel had also urged Gompers that "it is of the utmost importance for you to go abroad very soon."[9]

While conservative British statemen desired Gompers' presence in Europe, a different reaction was forthcoming from Ray Stannard Baker. Wilson had sent the famous muckraker journalist to act in England, France, and Italy as a special commissioner of the State Department. Baker's task was to survey and contact elements of the Left in the Allied nations, in order to provide balanced information to State about their role in European politics. As for himself, Baker personally wanted the Allied war cabinets to take their Wilsonianism seriously, before a military victory had been achieved. He viewed the Allied leaders as simple realists who wanted a pure military victory, and who were unconcerned with the achievement of Wilson's ideals. Baker worried that their demands for trade preferences and more territory made labor restless and increased its hostility to the Allied governments. To deal with this problem, Baker wanted Washington to support Socialists and radicals in their fight against conservative governments and left revolutionaries. He wanted Wilson to help Henderson hold the allegiance of doubtful labor elements. Since he believed that the Allied governments in power never meant to give Wilson their full-fledged support, Baker did not want Wilson to allow the democratic Socialists to drift away from him.[10]

[8] "Confidential Proposal for Labor Propaganda," n.d. [1918], Gompers MSS, State Historical Society of Wisconsin, Madison, Wis.
[9] Creel to Gompers, February 14, 1918, NA, RG 63, CPI I, A1 (17).
[10] Mayer, Politics and Diplomacy of Peacemaking, pp. 34–40. The above account of Baker's purpose in Europe is based on Mayer's information and analysis.

As for Gompers' forthcoming journey, Baker observed that quite a number of men "feel that the American delegation will do more harm than good." They thought of Gompers as being "of the old aristocratic school of labor leaders" that did not "understand or sympathize with the new democratic forces that are stirring underneath." This sentiment, Baker noted, was not "confined merely to the socialist which recognizes . . . an opponent in Gompers," but was equally the view of "the middle group of leaders." They felt that British labor had " 'gone beyond the Gompers stage' " and that the presence of the mission, "picked out by Mr. Gompers with its expenses paid by the Propagandist Department of the British Government, which they greatly distrust, has small chance of influencing British labor and still less of learning what British labor thinks."[11]

The problem was compounded because British labor was becoming skeptical of American war aims. While they sympathized with Wilson's ideals and had incorporated them into labor's own war aims memorandum, there was "a strong element that now begins to fear that the war-spirit will run entirely away with America, and that America . . . will become so intent on a 'knock-out-blow' that it will fail to seize upon opportunities that may arise to secure a democratic peace by diplomatic means." Distrusting capitalist governments, Allied labor did not feel that a military victory presented assurances of a democratic peace. Therefore, Baker reported, they favored holding an inter-belligerent labor-Socialist conference. At present the middle group of labor leaders such as Hjalmar Branting of Sweden and Jean Longuet of France supported the war effort, but at the same time sought to use their influence to maintain a democratic purpose on the part of the Allied governments.[12]

As he stayed on, Baker reported that British labor was growing more impatient. "Wilson is apparently losing

[11] Ray Stannard Baker, "My Mission to Europe, 1918–1919," unpublished manuscript, Ray Stannard Baker MSS, Box 171, Series 2, p. 83, Library of Congress. (All material from this source cited hereafter as Baker, "My Mission.")
[12] *Ibid.*, p. 184.

something of his hold on the democratic groups here," Baker observed on August 6. "They think he is being used by the government groups in behalf of their own selfish interests."[13] Labor was also growing disenchanted with the policies of their own government. During the first week of August, Arthur Henderson and C. W. Bowerman asked to obtain passports for travel to Switzerland, where they were to confer with the Dutch Socialist Troelstra. But he had just returned from meetings with German Socialists. Lloyd George refused to issue the passports, on the legal grounds that Troelstra had entered Switzerland by way of Germany. Such action led to determined opposition from labor ranks.[14]

The problem was that Henderson and Bowerman were "better trusted among a very large group of people than Mr. Lloyd George and those around him." In addition, labor unrest was growing. Coventry workers in munitions industries were on strike. They argued that the government asked unlimited sacrifices from labor but allowed the capitalists to profiteer. As Baker saw it, responsible leaders like Robert Smillie of the mine workers wanted to carry on the war. Yet Lloyd George's leadership made many workers " 'hopeless and reckless.' "[15]

The truth was, according to Baker, that labor in both Britain and France felt that a pure military victory meant a peace dictated by reactionary governments. They looked to Wilson because they thought he advocated a democratic peace and would use America's power to obtain it. But the reactionary governments played fast and loose with labor by denouncing them at one moment as defeatist, and by flattering them the next. When they appointed weak and non-representative labor leaders to government posts, they only widened the breach with the real forces of organized labor. Baker saw it as urgent that Woodrow Wilson "fire labor with the conviction that it is really fighting for

13 *Ibid.*, p. 201.
14 *Ibid.*, p. 219.
15 *Ibid.*, pp. 219–20.

a democratic peace." Only such a program, he believed, would allow "disruptive and defeatist dangers . . . to disappear."[16]

Baker put stress on placating the Allied Left because he saw their support as crucial to the success of Wilson's program. Baker hoped that radical forces would continue to rally around Wilson, and he consistently exaggerated their importance and power. He worried less about the strength and influence of the Right. Instead, his concern was with a restlessness in the movement which tended to the advantage of Lenin and the revolutionaries. To prevent the defection of the Socialists, Baker wanted Wilson constantly to reassure the Left that he stood by the Fourteen Points. To Baker, the Left was a major pressure group behind a non-punitive peace. Without their backing, he feared that the Big Three would move in a conservative direction at the peace table.[17]

Baker was so concerned with labor's lessening enthusiasm for Wilson that he wrote personally to Colonel House. When he first arrived in March, he informed House, "the whole labor and liberal group were strongly with us, but of late there have been many doubtful voices and a decided tendency to question our purposes." Baker saw that "a tremendous amount of unrest is seething just beneath the surface here and there is a great deal of anti-war and anti-government feeling which at any moment may develop serious results." Baker warned that "this unrest cannot be cured by attempts at mere stupid coercion."

Baker tried to warn Wilson that perhaps it would not serve his ultimate aim to send Gompers to Europe. "If the more conservative leaders cannot control these masses of workers," Baker observed, "one wonders what effect Mr. Gompers will have on the movement!" A great deal of warweariness existed, and Americans found it difficult to understand. But "to bring these men only a message of interminable war, for no clearly democratic or socially

---

[16] Notes of August 17, 1918, *ibid.,* pp. 220–22.
[17] Mayer, *op. cit.,* pp. 40–41.

constructive purpose, as Gompers with the best intentions in the world will probably do, is not very promising."[18]

Baker's concern was brought directly to the President by House. Wilson should step up his efforts to commit the Allies to democratic goals. "While the liberals are largely with you at present," he informed Wilson, "I have a feeling that you are not so strong among labor circles of either France and England as you were a few months ago." Labor support was "uncertain and erratic." House did not believe that Wilson would be powerful enough to "compel the reactionaries in authority to yield at the Peace Conference to American aims." It was necessary to try and commit the Entente to goals essential "to the reconstruction of the world."[19]

Despite the expressions of doubt and the strong words of advice, Gompers sailed for Liverpool on August 16, with the support and good wishes of the Wilson Administration. Wilson may have been personally displeased with Gompers' vanity and arrogance. But the President needed the political support of American organized labor. He also knew, as Arno Mayer writes, that "Gompers had his mind set on the trip, that the Allies wanted him in their service, and that Colonel House had promoted the enterprise. Thus America's most prestigious labor leader embarked on a mission that would fire the war enthusiasm of Allied workingmen at the cost of simultaneously sapping the political and social forces favorable to a Wilsonian settlement."[20]

Gompers' official visit began on August 30 when the British government honored the mission with a luncheon. At the affair, George H. Roberts, secretary of the Norwich Typographical Association and Minister of Labor in the Cabinet, told why the mission was regarded so highly by the Lloyd George government. "The contacts of our guests with patriotic labor in this country," Roberts stated, "will

[18] Baker, "My Mission," pp. 222–23; Baker to House, August 19, 1918, in House to Wilson, September 3, 1918, Wilson MSS, Library of Congress. Cf. Henry M. Pelling, *America and the British Left* (New York, 1967), p. 123.
[19] House to Wilson, September 3, 1918, Wilson MSS.
[20] Mayer, *op. cit.*, p. 45.

help us to defeat the efforts of those who would trick us
into meeting with enemy subjects."[21] The luncheon, and
dinner the following evening, were presided over by George
Barnes. Although he was Minister of Pensions, Barnes
appeared in his Labour Party rather than his ministerial
role. The Cabinet's concern for the mission was reflected
by the list of dinner guests, which included Lloyd George,
Arthur J. Balfour, Sir Alfred Milner, Winston Churchill,
Robert Cecil, Austen Chamberlain, Lord Reading, General
Jan C. Smuts, and William H. Hughes.[22]

During the first week of his visit, Gompers traveled about
Britain, where he visited his old home in Spitalsfield and
the Bell Lane elementary school he had attended as a child.
This itinerary pleased Ralph M. Easley, who thought that
"the political psychology of Gompers going to the neighbor-
hood where he was born and having his old chums surround him was certainly effective in neutralizing the rapidly weakening hold of Henderson on the British labor
movement. For was not Gompers born in London," Easley
asked, "as well as Henderson, and has he not still the
interests of 'Old England' at heart, the same as Henderson?"[23]

Easley's comments revealed that those who supported
the Old World governments were most pleased with Gompers' efforts. Easley was particularly overjoyed because of
the support given by Gompers to Lloyd George. "Whatever
differences there may be between the President and Lloyd
George," Easley commented to Theodore Roosevelt, there
were fewer differences between the British Premier and
Gompers. While the "Henderson 'bunch' " was "patting
President Wilson on the back at the expense of Lloyd
George," the British chief of state was "patting Mr. Gompers on the back at the expense of Woodrow Wilson."[24]
William Howard Taft agreed with this observation. Dis-

[21] Paul M. Kellogg and Arthur Gleason, *British Labor and the
War* (New York, 1919), p. 27.
[22] Gompers, *Seventy Years of Life and Labor*, II, 416–17, 437,
447, 460; cf. Mayer, *loc. cit.*
[23] Easley to Roosevelt, August 31, 1918, NCF MSS.
[24] *Ibid.*

senting from Roosevelt's "off-hand observation" that Gompers was a " 'cog in the Wilson machine,' " Taft noted that Gompers exerted "an important influence over the President concerning the Bolsheviki situation in Russia and the Arthur Henderson situation in England." He had also taken "a strong stand for Lloyd George," which was "more than the President has done."[25]

Gompers' efforts in England gained the approval of conservative Americans as well as the Lloyd George government. At the annual Derby conference of the Trades Union Congress, Gompers told delegates that American labor would be unwilling to shorten the war "one hour if it meant that the German military machine remains unbroken."[26] To increase his chances of influencing British labor, Gompers abandoned a head-on fight against Henderson. By merely consenting to appear at a TUC meeting, Gompers was acknowledging that this body did indeed represent British labor. Ambassador Page reported that "as a means of tactfully presenting the war aims and methods of American labor their visit to that congress has been a great success." While Gompers vigorously portrayed "the energies, the warlike ardor and the loyalty to the Allies of working men in the United States, he did not say a word which could offend either the Appleton, Havelock Wilson or Henderson-Bowerman faction." Noting that the London *Times* had commented on a lack of incisiveness in his speeches, Page attributed this "to the neutrality which Gompers strictly observed as between the minority and majority sections." Yet, Gompers did not succeed in changing the position taken by British labor. The TUC conference passed resolutions supporting an inter-belligerent Socialist conference "almost unanimously."[27]

After the close of the TUC meeting, Gompers attended a joint meeting of the TUC Parliamentary Committee and the Executive Committee of the Labour Party. There he entered into debate with Henderson about the forthcoming

[25] Taft to George W. Perkins, September 10, 1918, *ibid.*
[26] Gompers, *op. cit.*, 418.
[27] Page to Lansing September 12, 1918, NA, RG, 59, 032/G58–.

Inter-Allied Labor and Socialist Conference. Gompers informed those present that he objected to representation at the meeting for the Labour Party, because of its political approach. He also objected to the presence of French Socialists. Henderson retorted that the French labor and Socialist groups were as critical of the scheduled conference because the American Socialist Party had not been invited to attend. To this Gompers charged: "There was no such thing as an American Socialist Party but a German adjunct in America of the German Socialist Party."[28]

Gompers' obstinate stance only further inflamed British Laborites. The moderate Gillies told Baker that Gompers and his associates were generally "'kept so busy seeing the military activities that the government agents want them to see, and so occupied with dinners and teas . . . that they cannot get any real understanding of what British labor really wants.' " Baker recorded that "these American labor men did seem curiously naive, evangelistic, full of optimistic generalities." Baker himself felt that British labor had "gone a long way ahead of the labor movement in America." It was "grappling with far broader social and political problems, and it has made a real attempt to draw together all the working class forces in the kingdom on a social and political program." Men like G. N. Barnes had "lost their hold on the labor movement to a large degree."[29]

Gompers' main activity in London was to take part in the Inter-Allied Labor and Socialist Conference scheduled to meet on September 17–29, 1918. Before attending, he tried his best to divide the unionists and Socialists. Thus, Gompers wired Bowerman, Appleton, and Jouhaux—not Arthur Henderson—that the AFL would appear only if the conference was restricted to "*bona fide* Labor Representatives." The move failed. Bowerman and Henderson responded that the TUC and Labour Party had called an "inter-Allied Conference of *bona fide* Labour Representatives including all Parties at the inter-Allied Conference in Feb-

28 Gompers, *loc cit.*, p. 418.
29 Baker, "My Mission," pp. 83–86.

ruary, which you were unable to attend."[30] On the opening day, Gompers arrived at Central Hall at Westminster to find that the credential cards bore the inscription "Inter-Allied Socialist Conference." Gompers stubbornly refused to accept them, and insisted upon showing only his AFL membership card. Bowerman directed that Gompers and his associates be admitted. Later, Henderson apologized to Gompers, explaining that cards from former Socialist meetings had been mistakenly sent to the printer and no one had checked them. To this explanation Gompers responded that the "politicians" felt labor to be of such little importance that the absence of its name did not strike their conscience.[31]

At the conference, moderate elements were in a superior position. The AFL delegates had put American organized labor in the same ranks as the European Social Patriots. At the same time, the official Italian Socialist Party did not attend the conference, particularly because they objected to Henderson's failure to invite both the American Socialist Party and the Bolsheviks. The AFL, the Italians argued, was far removed from Socialist principles, and the conference would only give credence to Gompers' belief in class collaboration. The Italian Party also opposed the formation of war aims by the workers. The war, they believed, could not result in any democratic arrangements, because of its imperialist nature. Moreover, Italy was represented at the meeting by the Reform Socialists, a group improvised during the war to oppose the actual Italian Socialist Party. The only conference favored by the Italian Socialist Party was an inter-belligerent meeting which met to force immediate peace and which had an agenda of anti-capitalist action.[32] This stand of the Italian Socialist Party thereby weakened the far Left, just at the time when Gompers' presence strengthened the far Right.

[30] Labour Party: Minutes of the Executive Committee, p. 14 (Minutes of August 8, 1918); cited in Mayer, *op. cit.*, p. 47.

[31] Gompers, *Seventy Years*, II, 428–29; cf. Bernard Mandel, *Samuel Gompers* (Yellow Springs, Ohio, 1963), p. 408.

[32] Edward Strull and J. Hearley to Creel, September 25, NA, RG 63, 1918, CPI 20-B3.

Gompers' attitude was one of caution. He entered the conference with the view that most delegates "were prejudiced againt our men." He insisted, therefore, that all sessions should be open to the public.[33] Gompers instructed John P. Frey, who also was part of this second mission, that he should fight as hard as possible for the AFL position. Frey recalled that a "battle was waged relentlessly and without quarter in the committee room." Sidney Webb had expected to write and read the major report to the conference. Gompers, however, advised Frey to insist on his prerogative to perform that function. Frey was put on the crucial committee on war aims. He claimed to have been shown dossiers of his fellow members, who subsequently feared what Frey had learned of their records from Scotland Yard. Therefore Frey was allowed to write the committee report.[34]

On the second day, Ambassador Page reported, "Gompers put forward a full statement of the views of American labor on the war and of the fundamental principles which might underlie the future treaty of peace. The conference urged that the 14 points be adhered to, and that enemy socialists be interrogated in regard to their adherence to Allied war aims, so as to impose upon the working classes the responsibility of choosing between solutions."[35] Again, the question of an inter-belligerent conference became the central point at issue. The previous February, the Inter-Allied Labor and Socialist Conference had instructed the British delegation to send the memorandum on War Aims to enemy Socialist parties and to ask for a response. The Bulgarian, Hungarian, and Austrian parties accepted the memorandum as a basis for discussion, but the German Social Democrats did not. Henderson had since concluded that their negative response made it "futile and harmful to make any attempt to organize an immediate interna-

[33] Minutes, Executive Council Meeting of the American Alliance for Labor and Democracy, December 1, 1918, Gompers MSS.
[34] Frey, speech to the Literary Club of Cincinnati, January 1, 1927, Frey MSS; Frey, COHC, 366.
[35] Page to Lansing, September 20, 1918, NA, RG 59, 032.G58-.

tional conference." He now feared further divisions and a
split among the parties that had united at the February
conference.[36]

At the September meeting, Henderson therefore favored
trying to change the German Socialists' view, by insisting
on a change in the German attitude prior to holding any
inter-belligerent conference. Henderson's moderate view
was attacked from both the Left and the Right. Jean
Longuet and the French Socialists advocated immediate
convocation of an inter-belligerent Socialist conference.
Gompers and Frey, on the other hand, called for meetings
between Allied workers and those of the Central Powers
only if the latter "were in open revolt against their autocratic governors." Gompers received support only from the
four right-wing Italian Reform Socialists and one Cana-
dian delegate.[37]

On the two other major areas of concern before the
Conference, Gompers and the AFL proved to be a moderating influence. Gompers had been asked by the Labour
Party and TUC executive bodies to prepare some comments on the inter-Allied war memorandum that had been
prepared in February. Henderson hoped to gain Gompers'
total endorsement of the statement, in order to rally the
Allied Left around a Wilsonian-oriented program. In presenting his own war aims, Gompers ignored the February
memorandum entirely, since it both criticized the Allied
governments and supported an inter-belligerent meeting.
Gompers, of course, was not going to approve a statement
emanating from his major enemies in the international
labor movement.[38]

Instead of supporting the February memo, Gompers

[36] "For the Executive: Private and Confidential Memorandum by
Arthur Henderson on Inter-Allied Conference Decisions, February
20–24, 1918," submitted and discussed on September 4, 1918, at
joint meeting of the Parliamentary Committee of the TUC and the
Executive Committee of the Labour Party, in Labour Party: Minutes of the Executive Committee, p. 14. Cited in Mayer, op. cit., p.
48.

[37] Labour Party: Report of the Nineteenth Annual Conference
(Southport, 1919), pp. 4–11; cited in Mayer, op. cit., p. 48.

[38] Mayer, op. cit., p. 49.

called for endorsement of Wilson's Fourteen Points. He also presented proposals that sought to discredit political unionism. Gompers urged that the peace treaty include an economic and political bill of rights for labor, one that in the words of the American Clayton Anti-Trust Act of 1914, declared that "the labor of a human being was not a commodity or article of commerce." It would also call for the rights of free association, assembly, speech, and press. Finally, the resolution would call for a basic workday that would not exceed eight hours per day.[39]

These resolutions were presented to the sub-committee on war aims over which John P. Frey presided. This same committee also was considering the replies of the Central Powers' Socialist parties to the February inter-Allied war aims memorandum. The sub-committee brought to the floor a resolution meant to blend the two different approaches. The September conference was now asked to welcome Wilson's Fourteen Points as a program which affirmed the proposals of their own February memorandum. The Fourteen Points were to be accepted as "a concise summary of the main principles which" the February memorandum "expounded in detail [in regard] to the various questions to be dealt with." The workers were to pressure their own governments to adopt these principles in a joint statement of Allied policy. The sub-committee's resolution also expressed sympathy for Gompers' proposed new bill of rights, although it stated that "most of these aspirations found expression in general terms" in labor's February memorandum.[40]

This text, as recommended by the war aims sub-committee, was adopted by the conference by a vote of 57 to 10. The extreme Left voted against it, but the French and British independents abstained, out of fear that a negative vote would encourage their own conservative governments. Gompers and the AFL delegates also abstained, since the AFL did not want to reveal their failure to cause a split

[39] Kellogg and Gleason, *British Labor and the War*, pp. 288–89.
[40] Labour Party, *Report of the Nineteenth Annual Conference*, pp. 7–9; cited in Mayer, *op. cit.*, p. 50.

between the Social Patriots and the majority that stood
behind Henderson. Moreover, Gompers wished to exert a
moderating influence within the old International. The
delegates had voted to put Gompers on a committee with
Henderson, Albert Thomas, and Emil Vandervelde, to
lobby with the Allied governments for inclusion of labor
representatives in the official peace conference delegations,
and to help organize a labor conference to meet concurrently with the official peace conference. Gompers had
always favored these two moderate goals, and as Mayer
writes, he now welcomed "this opportunity to join two
steadfast Social Patriots [Thomas and Vandervelde] in
keeping a close check on Henderson."[41]

The third day of the September conference was high-
lighted by debate over the position to be taken toward the
Bolshevik Revolution. The majority resolution was favored by all the major factions except the AFL delegation.
Supported by Henderson, Longuet, Renaudel, Huysmans,
and Popovitch, the resolution offered Allied labor's sympathy to labor and Socialist groups in Russia that were
continuing the struggle against German imperialism. It
denounced the Brest-Litovsk Treaty that Germany had
forced upon Russia, and warned against the dangers of
intervention in Russia as a step that would strengthen
reactionary tendencies under the pretext of fighting Bolshevism. "To such a policy," the resolution stated, "the
working classes of the Western democracies would have
the elementary duty of offering opposition without stint."[42]
In presenting the resolution, Henderson explained that it
was not meant either to approve or condemn intervention,
only to accept it as an accomplished fact and to warn the
Allied workers against possible counter-revolutionary
implications.[43]

The majority resolution, therefore, took an equivocal

[41] *Ibid.*
[42] "Proceedings of the Inter-Allied Conference, London, Sept.
17–19, 1918," AFL Publication, n.d., Frey MSS.
[43] Resolution passed on September 18, 1918, at the meeting of
the Labour Party Executive Committee, Minutes of the Executive
Committee, p. 14; cited in Mayer, *op. cit.*, p. 51.

position on a crucial issue. At the same time, Gompers and
the AFL delegates offered their own resolution. Their statement supported Allied intervention in Russia if it was
carried out "with the hope of counteracting the sinister
influence of the Central Powers upon the so-called Bolshevik Government, which has suppressed the utterances and
the aspirations of the great majority of the Russian working classes."[44] Both resolutions were judged to be unsatisfactory by Jean Longuet, who represented the French
minoritaires. Any Allied intervention in Russia, Longuet
countered, was contrary to Socialist principles and played
into the hands of imperialism. Despite his own feelings,
Longuet withdrew his own motion explicitly condemning
intervention, and gave his support to the majority resolution. Longuet argued that the official resolution included
the Bolsheviks among those who would receive Allied labor's sympathy, and that it also made it clear that intervention violated the principle of self-determination. Longuet's interpretation was immediately challenged by the
French Social Patriot Albert Thomas, and by the Belgian
Emil Vandervelde. If Longuet's interpretation was accepted, the two powerful delegates threatened to shift
their support to the AFL resolution.[45]

The conflict was to be settled by returning the resolutions to committee. Again Longuet maintained his position. The result was that Henderson moved to satisfy
Thomas and Vandervelde, who had threatened to ally
themselves with Gompers. The amended resolution
brought forth from committee omitted any expression of
sympathy and all warnings about the possible reactionary
consequences of Allied intervention. Avoiding mention of
the word intervention altogether, the new resolution urged
that any Allied effort to aid "the Russian people must be
influenced only by a genuine desire to preserve liberty and
democracy in an ordered and durable world peace in which
the beneficent fruits of the Revolution shall be made per-

[44] "Proceedings of the Inter-Allied Conference, London, Sept.
17–19, 1918," Frey MSS.
[45] *Ibid.*

manently secure."[46] The result was a new round of argument. Finally the Henderson-Vandervelde majority secured cloture and had the amended resolution adopted by a large majority of delegates. Rather than risk a break with the Henderson center, Jean Longuet abstained as a form of protest.[47]

In gaining a major victory at the conference, Arthur Henderson had emerged as the most powerful figure in the effort to build up the Second International. Henderson had hoped to gain Gompers' cooperation in the effort. At least he desired to head off any attempt by Gompers to build a rival Allied trade union international based on conservative business-unionist principles. Had Gompers actually moved in this direction, the new organization would have weakened Henderson's efforts to put the International firmly behind Woodrow Wilson. Henderson counted on Wilson to force a just peace. Since the Allied governments now believed that victory was near, Henderson was counting on the Second International and Wilson to curb the appetites of Lloyd George.

Gompers' presence in Europe, however, had the effect of weakening Wilson's supporters and strengthening the Allied Right. In the politics of European Socialism and labor, as Mayer puts it, "Gompers strengthened those leaders and forces which were least inclined really to oppose their own governments and to appease defeated Germany as well as revolutionary Russia. He thereby aggravated internal antagonisms which undermined the unity and effectiveness of the recuperating [Second] International on the eve of the Armistice. And just as Henderson was reluctant to break with Gompers, so Longuet and Mac-Donald were reluctant to separate themselves from Henderson. The net result was that the center faction which triumphed stood right rather than left of center in the Allied Socialist and labor movements."[48]

In this respect, Gompers' presence in Europe had been

[46] *Ibid.*
[47] *Ibid.*
[48] Mayer, *op. cit.*, 50.

successful. Gompers' presence had pressured Henderson to water down his own pro-negotiation stance. William S. Sanders reported to G. N. Barnes that "the influences of the American delegation found expression in the resolutions passed by the Conference, which were of a much less pacifist tendency than those of the last Conference." Gompers' position "helped to rally the anti-pacifist sections at the Conference, who were much more vigorous than usual in the debates which took place."[49]

Henderson had backtracked, W. H. Buckler claimed, because he had always purported to be a loyal supporter of Woodrow Wilson. If his forces had criticized Gompers too strenuously, Buckler reported, they would "have stultified their own claim to being loyal supporters of the President." The AFL had forced both Henderson and Albert Thomas to dissociate themselves from Longuet and those of a more radical bent. "Had Henderson and Thomas not assumed a distinctly anti-pacifist attitude," Buckler explained, "they would have placed themselves in the foolish position of openly antagonizing Mr. Gompers, the ardent supporter of President Wilson whom Henderson and Thomas are constantly extolling."[50]

This tactic worked only because Henderson and the center had indeed consistently invoked Wilsonian goals as their own. Indeed, Woodrow Wilson and Gompers held a position that was more rigid than Henderson's. Henderson argued that the German Socialists could be won for Wilsonian war aims. Actually, William English Walling argued, their peace terms were equally remote from those of both Wilson and the Allied Socialists. Henderson believed a victory was not desirable. Wilson, on the other hand, saw military victory as indispensable and "as worthy of a perfectly stupendous price yet to be paid." Henderson wanted peace through conciliation; Wilson through military defeat of Germany. "It is a blessing that Henderson has expressed himself so clearly," Walling wrote, "for Mr.

[49] Sanders to Barnes, September 24, 1918, Gompers MSS.
[50] Buckler to Irwin Laughlin (American chargé d'affaires), London, October 29, 1918, *ibid.*

Wilson's prestige has become so great that all the pacifists seek to cloak themselves under his name."[51]

Having taken Walling's advice on how to deal with Henderson, Gompers viewed his participation as a success. The AFL, he wrote, "accomplished so much toward shaping the action of the conference that the opponents of our policies have since made the assertion that it was 'a Gompers Conference.' To us, however, it was apparent that the soundness and righteousness of our position . . . was a dominating power." Gompers was especially pleased that he had blocked acceptance of a "peace without victory" resolution, and that the original resolution on Russia had been modified.[52]

Fresh from his victory at the Inter-Allied Conference, Gompers and the AFL delegates moved on to France. Special reasons existed, according to AFL leader George L. Berry, that made a trip to France necessary. The French Confederation of Labor, Berry informed Gompers, was led by men "opposed to the government and who seek peace, even a Russian peace." Moreover, the French industrial situation was chaotic and bordered on revolution. A systematic effort was needed to put forth propaganda by "responsible laboring men to assure the effectiveness of the French government as an ally in the prosecution of the war."[53]

Gompers had received similar advice from his trusted associate, William English Walling. The French Confederation had already endorsed convening an international Socialist conference, Walling reported. Calling this "the most dangerous and treacherous" proposal that could be made, Walling argued that the conference would revive Bolshevism because most Socialists were "damn fools enough to honestly believe" in such "insane" ideas. Like

51 Walling, "Arthur Henderson versus Woodrow Wilson," August 10, 1918, *ibid.*
52 Report of the AFL Mission to Great Britain, France and Italy, 1918, *ibid.*
53 "Confidential Proposal for Labor Propaganda," memo submitted by the British government, based on an investigation conducted by George L. Berry, n.d., *ibid.*

Henderson, the French Socialists argued that they favored
a Wilsonian program. Yet their opposition to war credits
for their own government amounted to an "out-and-out
threat of revolution." This attempt could be checked, Walling believed, if it was made perfectly clear that President
Wilson had no sympathy for Bolshevism, and that he
opposed an international Socialist congress.[54]

Using the material supplied by Berry and Walling,
Gompers was ready to confront the French workers. As in
Britain, Gompers was entertained by French government,
military, and labor leaders. He was greeted by Premier
Georges Clemenceau. During his stay, he continued to attack supporters of peace through negotiation. After listen-
ing to a speech by French Syndicalists, Gompers related
that he heard "their fantastic and irrational proposals as
long as I could endure them and then I tersely told them
they were traitors to the cause of the people of France.
This remark brought the meeting to an abrupt end, for
such a verbal tumult followed that speeches were no longer
possible."[55]

Gompers faced strong opposition, since French trade
union and Socialist leaders like Jean Longuet, Marcel
Cachin, and Pierre Renaudel were all left of center. Compared to Gompers, unionists like Léon Jouhaux and Al-
phonse Merrheim were also radical. "There are amusing
aspects to the attempt of Mr. Gompers to find kindred trade
union spirits in France," Ray Stannard Baker observed.
"When he treats with M. Jouhaux, who is indeed the only
representative with whom he can treat, he is about as far
from any real meeting of minds as he could get." French
unions also rejected business unionism, and workers
espoused attainment of social goals. That is "where Mr.
Gompers makes his mistake," Baker concluded. "He is

[54] Walling to Gompers, August 6, 1918, William English Walling
MSS, State Historical Society of Wisconsin, Madison, Wis. Walling,
"The French Confederation of Labor and the War," *ibid.*; Walling,
"The French Bolsheviki," Gompers MSS.
[55] Gompers, *Seventy Years*, II, 440–46; Sharp to Lansing, September 29, 1918, *FR, 1918*, I Supplement 1 (Washington, D.C.,
1918), 330–31.

looking for the same kind of movement here that we have
in America where the social pressure has never been anything like as severe as it is here, and where escape from the
working class has, until recently, been easy. In America
the labor movement is still something more or less added
on, another and powerful weapon for economic improvement . . . and Mr. Gompers apparently thinks he can
change these deep things with speeches."[56]

Since Gompers detested the political approach taken by
French labor leaders, he tried to confine his meetings to
members of the minority pro-war faction. His guide in
France was Adolphe Smith, who placed himself at Gompers' command in order to "prevent the *camouflage* of
yourself and what you say." Smith arranged a meeting
between Gompers and the pro-war Socialist group in the
Chamber of Deputies.[57]

Most of Gompers' time in France was spent in dramatic
but useless excursions to the front. On September 24 they
inspected the Citroën munitions works, and drove on to
American army headquarters at Chaumont. The next day
they proceeded to Neufchâteau, where the mission heard
the first bombardment before the St. Mihiel advance. The
AFL delegates toured areas that had been covered by
victorious American troops, visited the home of Joan of
Arc, and U.S. air service headquarters. The group toured
the British, Belgian, and American fronts, met King Albert
of Belgium, and had lunch with General Douglas Haig on
the battlefield at Bourlon Wood. They inspected the Hin-
denburg Line and talked with soldiers who were eating
lunch during the thick of the fighting. Finally, they
watched the assault on Cambrai as planes flew ahead and
bombs fell around them.

The tour gave Gompers the feeling that his pro-war
commitment had been proved. However, it did little to
reach the anti-war French workers. Much of Gompers'
stay in France amounted to little more than a glorified

[56] Baker, "My Mission," pp. 233–36.
[57] Smith to Gompers, September 24, 1918, Gompers MSS.

official sightseeing tour. The climax of Gompers' journey took place on October 4. On that day, W. H. Buckler related, they had "so wonderful a day at the British front near Cambrai." The mission motored from "our Chateau to Amiens, saw that well, including the Cathedral . . . and came up by rail to Paris where I ended the day by guiding the party through the murky streets to the 'Casino de Paris' for a very pro-American show, full of rag-time." Buckler concluded that Gompers was "a very nice kindly, human old boy"; perhaps an honest estimate, but hardly one about which French labor cared.[58]

After leaving France, Gompers and his mission proceeded to Italy. In that country, both the Socialist Party and the trade union movement were anti-war and anti-government. Because of concentrated peace efforts, work efficiency was at a great low and support for the war effort had never been weaker. To deal with these problems, the Italian Ambassador to the United States had requested that Gompers tour Italy. Gompers rejected an official government invitation, however, because he realized that the "reaction might not be helpful." However, the Italian government placed at Gompers' disposal a sum for compensation, subsistence, and travel expenses, as well as an additional bonus of ten dollars per day for extra expenses.[59]

On Sunday, October 6, Gompers arrived in Italy. He was met in Rome by government leaders, including the ministers of commerce and labor, the Undersecretary of State for Foreign Affairs, and the chief of the government propaganda bureau. As Ambassador Thomas Nelson Page reported, "the workingmen's representatives at the station were conspicuous mainly by their absence." They had not attended because of concerted attacks on Gompers' visit which appeared in *Avanti,* the Socialist Party newspaper. Moreover, the day of Gompers' arrival brought news that Germany had requested an armistice and offered its ap-

[58] Buckler to Georgina Buckler, October 4, 1918, Buckler Collection, House MSS.
[59] Gompers memo, August 6, 1918, Gompers MSS.

proval to terms based on Wilson's Fourteen Points. This
news had produced a new wave of strikes and disorders in
Milan, Turin, and Florence.[60]

The disorders led Buckler to comment that the "warnings
of the American mission were much needed." Later that
same day, Gompers attended a luncheon given for the
mission by the Italian branch of the Committee on Public
Information, at which Gompers and John Spargo made
speeches. In the evening, Gompers, Frey, and Spargo dined
together at the American Embassy. The next day Gompers
stressed that his object in Italy was to inform workers of
"the solidarity of the labor organizations of America with
the President and the Government and its war program."
Buckler thought Gompers was proving that "the attitude
of vigorous and militant labor leaders need not necessarily
be hostile to the Government of their own country." For
Italian labor, which "was apt to believe only in revolutionaries, iconoclasts and enemies of its own government,"
Buckler wrote, "this demonstration could not fail to be
extremely instructive."[61]

How instructive Gompers' efforts in Italy were is open
to question. His first public address was scheduled for a
mass meeting in the Augusteum, Rome's largest auditorium. But the *Messagero,* Rome's leading morning paper,
ran a story announcing that the mass meeting had been
indefinitely postponed. The meeting had already been
shifted from the second to the third day of Gompers' visit,
because the mission felt that "some influence was at work
to prevent their reaching the laboring people." Page had
the CPI staff give adequate notice of the meeting by putting up posters and by distributing handbills. Nevertheless the story about cancellation appeared, although it was
without any foundation.[62]

On the morning of the scheduled rally, it was found that
the posters put up by the CPI had been covered up with

---

[60] Page to Lansing, October 11, 1918, NA, RG 59, 032.G 58-.
[61] Buckler to Irwin Laughlin, October 29, 1918, Gompers MSS;
Page to Lansing, October 11, 1918, NA, RG 59, 032. G 58-.
[62] *Ibid.*

others which stated that Gompers had not arrived in Italy and that the meeting was postponed. Page then conferred with the head of the Italian propaganda agency, "and arranged with him to see that the mass meeting set for that evening should not be a failure."[63] It was decided, among other things, to advertise the meeting in the afternoon papers. It was too late, however, since printed notices about the rally's cancellation were now being distributed. "Mr. Gompers was like a caged lion," John P. Frey recalled. "His enemies had tricked him and brought about a situation which, in addition to being a personal humiliation, would work against the patriotic purpose which had brought him to Italy." Gompers was determined to speak, "though under the circumstances he dreaded the occasion."[64]

Gompers had feared that the seats in the huge auditorium would remain unoccupied. When he arrived, he found to his satisfaction that the arena was filled with throngs of people. But the seats were not taken up by the workers and Socialists whom Gompers had meant to reach. Page and the propaganda bureau had arranged to have companies of Italian soldiers and sailors marched in to fill the auditorium. Gompers remained unaware of the nature of his audience, and presented a strong oration. Page reported that the "address was received with great applause and enthusiasm. His speech, which was translated, paragraph by paragraph . . . was a ringing defiance to the anti-war official Socialists, and an endorsement of our Government's war policy and the President, and was directed pointedly against the defeatist organ, the *Avanti*." Page was satisfied that the speech received prominent place in the press, and that the only criticism came from the Socialists.[65]

Gompers' speech had only received such great applause, however, because an Italian officer stood in a flag-draped

[63] *Ibid.*
[64] Frey, "When Gompers Spoke Before the One Packed Meeting of His Career," Gompers MSS.
[65] Page to Lansing, October 11, 1918, NA, RG 59, 032.G 58-.

alcove behind the platform and gave signals to the audience of military men. After Gompers left the stadium, a
bugle was sounded and the audience left, marching in
two through the exits which were guarded by military
police.[66]

Gompers' conquest of a captive audience symbolized
how far removed he was from the thoughts of Italian workers. His speech received its sharpest criticism from *Avanti*.
The Socialist organ spoke proudly of the Confederation of
Labor's refusal to take part in the official reception given
Gompers. The AFL president, the paper declared, was the
representative of millions of dollars and of three and one-
half million organized workers. While they had little
money and only half a million organized workers, they
never permitted anybody, "not even the leader of the North
American Mission, to insult our ideals and faith, our Party,
and the newspaper which is loved and respected by the
greater part of of our organized laborers . . . .the truth is
we need no one to instruct us in our dignity."[67]

Gompers' failure was recorded for posterity by Ray
Stannard Baker. "So far as having any effect upon the labor
situation in Italy," Baker observed on October 13, the AFL
mission "was a complete fizzle." Instead of "trying to do
the thing he came over to do, namely to understand and
influence European labor, it has been, in Italy . . . one
grand junket, with official receptions and dinners. Gompers was entertained yesterday by the King. In Rome he
set the socialist elements—and here labor is socialist—
by the ears. I went to one of his meetings, half the audience
was made up of soldiers sent in by the Government to prevent possible disorder. One of the infuriating qualities of
some of my beloved compatriots," Baker complained, "is
to talk down to people upon subjects which their auditors
understand far better than they do. Everything in America
is better than anything in Europe, so they preach!"[68]

[66] Frey, *op. cit.*, Gompers MSS.
[67] "The 'American' and the Confederation," *Avanti*, October 16,
1918, in North Winship to Lansing, NA, RG 59, 032. G58-.
[68] Baker, notes of October 13, 1918, "My Mission," p. 258.

After the Rome rally, Gompers went to Padua where the AFL mission dined with King Victor Emmanuel at his royal chateau. They visited the Italian and American front lines, witnessed shelling of Austrian troops, and were the guests of two generals for dinner. Next they proceeded to Milan, for a round of more speechmaking. Here Gompers argued that Woodrow Wilson was "the loyal interpreter and symbol of democracy for all, and he will give a clear and solemn reply in the name of allied democracy, to the ambiguous proposals of our enemies." Addressing himself to the boycott of his speech by the Socialists, Gompers argued that those absent from his rally were "German in sympathy." This comment backfired, and later that evening Gompers offered to meet some Milan Socialists. They refused, however, because the AFL opposed free immigration to the United States from Italy. Gompers again claimed that "no discussion of a political character was possible between" the AFL and the Italian Socialists. Calling the Socialists "an organization of slaves," Gompers stated that it would "be useless to waste our time in speaking with them" because their master was Germany.[69]

Some American diplomats believed that Gompers' visit was producing worthwhile results. Consul North Winship expressed his view that the speeches in Milan "left a very good impression among all circles except that of the Official Socialist Party. He and his commission were received not only by the Civil and Military authorities, but by all the patriotic and labor organizations except the Confederazione del Lavoro." But since the Confederation and the Socialists were the major influences among the Italian working class, Winship inadvertently had revealed the limitations of Gompers' mission. Winship, however, believed that Gompers had delivered "one of the best pieces of American propaganda that has been delivered in this city." He was not the only person to appreciate Gompers' performance. Benito Mussolini's newspaper printed the text of his speech in full. "It is interesting to know also," Winship reported, "that Mussolini, who is a patriotic Social-

[69] Gompers' Milan speeches, NA, RG 59, 032. G58-.

ist, attended the official reception on Monday afternoon
making an excellent address of greeting to the Gompers'
Commission, and of parase [sic] to the American people."[70]

In Genoa, the mission was met by the mayor, the president of the Chamber of Commerce, and other high digni-
taries. Gompers informed the group that his trip had been
a success, "giving encouragement to perplexed and perhaps discouraged minds." It was necessary to force a German retreat or to "destroy her completely," Gompers told
his audience, and he was proud that for this task Woodrow
Wilson knew he "could count on the hearty cooperation of
the working classes." Since the United States would be the
last power to be fighting, they had a right to put Italy,
France, and Britain on guard. Gompers accused the Italian
Socialists of being cowards and chided them for refusing
to attend the Inter-Allied Labor and Socialist Conference.
Finally, he argued that international peace could not result from negotiation. "Germany must be destroyed; she
must not only have the consciousness of her defeat but
also the suffering." Only a dictated peace, Gompers argued,
would make human brotherhood a living reality. In taking
this position, Gompers had even more firmly lined himself
up with the existing Allied governments and with the
European Right.[71]

Gompers had completed his visit to Italy, and had taken
a strong pro-war stand. Ambassador Thomas Nelson Page
saw his journey as beneficial, "particularly in impressing
upon the minds here America's determination to win the
war and bring about a peace that will be lasting and just to
all."[72] W. H. Buckler believed that the mission had strengthened the hands of pro-war Socialists "at the critical moment when the possibility of peace came suddenly into
view and when firmness among the Allies was of special
importance." Gompers, Buckler felt, had upheld "the

[70] North Winship, "Gompers' Visit to Milan," October 17, 1918,
NA, RG 59, 032. G58-.
[71] David F. Wilbur (consul general), "Mr. Samuel Gompers and
his Mission in Genoa," October 19, 1918, Gompers MSS.
[72] Page to Lansing, October 11, 1918, NA, RG 59, 032. G58-.

hands of pro-war Italians and" had aided doubters to "assume a pro-war attitude."[73]

While some of the more shortsighted diplomats felt that his mission had been an unmitigated success, Gompers himself was aware of the great opposition shown him by Italians, as well as the critical reaction to his mission offered by other Americans in Italy. Gompers let word reach Woodrow Wilson that some critics made it appear that the President was dissatisfied with Gompers' performance in Europe. Because Wilson needed Gompers' domestic support, he tried to ease whatever distress Gompers might have suffered from "any false impressions as to what had been told me over here about your visit to Italy." The President claimed that he "had received the fullest assurances of the high value and the entire success of your mission, notwithstanding the few unpleasant instances like that at Milan."[74]

Woodrow Wilson had good reason to encourage Gompers' continued allegiance to his Administration. As the time for the official peace conference drew near, Wilson preferred to mitigate any possible opposition that might emanate from AFL quarters. But it was not true that the President had received only laudatory accounts of Gompers' visit to Italy. Writing to Undersecretary of State Frank L. Polk on October 26, Ray Stannard Baker revealed that in Italy "the whole labor and socialist group is not only intensely anti-government but is far more war-weary than either the French or the British," and was permeated "with a peace-at-any-price spirit." Baker thought it impossible for Americans to realize "how inflammable and dangerous the situation is." Italian Socialists believed that Wilson accepted the revolutionary Zimmerwald anti-war platform, and questioned only whether the President really would adhere to it. Soldiers were bitter, and severe repression of Italian radicals made martyrs of their leaders and fanned the faith.[75]

[73] Buckler to Laughlin, October 20, 1918, Gompers MSS.
[74] Wilson to Gompers, January 11, 1919, *ibid.*
[75] Baker to Polk, October 26, 1918, in Baker, "My Mission," pp. 284–92.

But unlike Gompers, Baker realized that the anti-war sentiment was not a result of German propaganda. To use such an argument only obscured the root causes of discontent. Baker concluded that the working class movement was not "the mere wild agitation of a few leaders, who can be clipped off and sent to jail"; nor was it a "flimsy and weak-minded thing to be easily dominated by German propaganda." It was, rather, "a deeply rooted movement among the people. The idea that it can be squelched by force of government, or turned over in a day by a visit from Mr. Gompers is of course absurd. I don't think Gompers so much as touched the outer fringe of the movement," Baker told Polk, "and I was in Italy when he was here and saw his work."[76]

Baker's account, as biting as it was, was underscored by the report of John H. Hearley, acting commissioner of Creel's Committee of Public Information in Italy. Gompers' success "as a moral and democratic agent," Hearley reported to George Creel, "was limited; for Gompers was—as he always is—Gompers." The fact that he traveled from London with W. H. Buckler, an attaché of the American Embassy, "gave the mission a governmental and official atmosphere" which Hearley understood "was unfortunate." After leaving Rome, Gompers had visited the front, dined with the King and some generals. Only afterward did he return to industrial centers like Milan, Genoa, and Turin. Once there, Gompers "only stopped a day in each place." It would have been "better from a propaganda point of view," Hearley noted, "if he had reversed the order, seeing the workers first and the king afterwards."[77]

Hearley had attempted to persuade Gompers to follow a course more suited to reaching the anti-war Italian workers. "I personally advised—in fact, pleaded with him," Hearley reported, "to refuse to be directly or indirectly steered by officialdom and forget municipal receptions, and in centers of labor like Milan, Genoa and Turin to go right into the factories and see the workers at the benches or

76 *Ibid.*
77 Hearley to Creel, October 25, 1918, Wilson MSS.

machines and afterwards assemble them together and talk with them." Hearley emphasized that "this was the only way to have reached large numbers of them and to have come into direct contact with them." Hearley realized that Gompers "did not have the time to do this adequately." But Hearley felt that Gompers "apparently would not have been liberal or democratic enough to have done this successfully if he had had time." The only popular contacts made by Gompers, Hearley claimed, were those arranged by the CPI. These did not affect Gompers. "His vanity . . . seemed to come out, and while here he was apparently much more concerned with ambassadorial luncheons, ministerial meetings and an official and aristocratic reception in the capital than with anything else." The Italian workers, Hearley emphasized, were "for the most part . . . socialistic and anti-government, and this behavior was not calculated to win them, especially since Gompers has long been regarded here as being 'anti-socialistic and anti-Italian.' "[78]

In terms of affecting the anti-war position of French and Italian labor, Gompers' mission had clearly been less than successful. Nevertheless, the members of the AFL mission indulged in a constant stream of self-glorification. Basic to their approach was a belief in the omnipotence of the AFL and Gompers' ideology. European labor, AFL vice-president James Duncan noted, "required the steadying hand of the leader of our movement on this side to encourage and keep the workers upon the other side in the true and correct position." To the American labor leaders all evil was abroad; all innocence at home. As Gompers told an audience who met to celebrate the mission's return to the United States: "America is more than a country. America is more than a continent. America is . . . an ideal, America is the apotheosis of all that is right."[79]

[78] *Ibid.* For a different estimate, see Mandel, *Samuel Gompers,* p. 415. Mandel's assertion that "there was universal agreement that Gompers' mission had been a great success" is obviously in need of correction.

[79] National reception for Gompers and the American Labor Mission to Europe, Chicago, Ill., November 8, 1918, Gompers MSS.

Such remarks revealed the true nature of the extensive gap that separated European and American organized labor. The gap was based upon more than a different policy toward the World War. It resulted not from Gompers' ineptness, as Norman Angell had put it, but from a "wider difference of outlook and social policy."[80] Gompers did object to those who desired conferences between Allied labor and "enemy" Socialists. But his basic objection was to the advocacy of Socialist ideology by European labor leaders. That the variety of socialism espoused by men like Arthur Henderson was centrist, moderate, and pro-Wilsonian did not minimize Gompers' dissatisfaction. Gompers was carrying on his early fight against socialism in the international arena. Socialist influence within the British Labour Party, on the French workers, and particularly on Italian labor, became a new challenge to Gompers' desire to create a labor international based on AFL principles. European labor's political approach, Gompers complained, was formulated by professors and intellectuals who had got their "fangs into the labor movement and usually poisoned and destroyed it!" An ideal labor movement had to be composed of workers from the shops and mines. This, Gompers stated, did not "sit well in the crop of the so-called intellectuals."[81] Socialism, he had told the Inter-Allied Labor and Socialist Conference, "is the fad of the fanatics, the sophistry of the so-called intelligentsia, and it has no place in the hearts of those who would secure and fight for freedom and preserve democracy."[82]

Gompers' rigid objection to all forms of socialism led him to look askance at any policy proposals emanating from Henderson and his moderate Socialist colleagues. Gompers set out to attack firmly all proposals for any kind of inter-belligerent Socialist conference. Had Gompers been willing to cooperate with Henderson, it is quite likely

[80] Norman Angell, *War and Peace* (London, 1918), p. 274.
[81] National Reception for Gompers and the American Labor Mission to Europe, Gompers MSS.
[82] Gompers, *Seventy Years*, II, 431.

that chances for a sane Wilsonian peace would have been quite improved. But Gompers' stance enforced the position of the Allied Right, and weakened the moderates who stood behind Woodrow Wilson. In terms of the effect he had on Allied labor and socialism, Gompers had acted to considerably weaken Wilson's most sincere allies. As the period of armistice drew close, the Allied governments faced only a moderate opposition to a Carthaginian peace. Gompers' opposition was ideological. Ramsay MacDonald was correct in his observation that the differences with Allied labor did "not originate in war policy," but came "from fundamental diversities of attitude that have been intensified by different war experiences up to date."[83]

Gompers' approach made it virtually impossible for him to understand what motivated the policy of Allied labor leaders. It was predictable that Samuel Gompers would not be able to get Allied labor to adopt the AFL position on world affairs. War-weary European laborers desired a quick end to the war, a just and democratic peace, and repudiation of their own conservative governments so that they could proceed with social reconstruction on the basis of labor governments. They were not about to adopt business unionism domestically, and to favor a policy of all-out military victory and a dictated peace. Gompers' insistence that they follow such a conservative path only reinforced their view that the AFL was a half-century out of date.

Despite Gompers' failure to point the direction for Allied labor, Woodrow Wilson had gained the satisfaction of seeing the official organized labor movement act as his agent abroad. While Gompers had weakened the impact of Allied Wilsonians, Wilson himself preferred to deal with the existing Allied governments, and did not want to risk the dangers of revolution that were hidden beneath the surface of moderate socialism. Once again, Gompers and the AFL had shown that they were reliable agents of Wilsonian liberalism, and that they could preach Administra-

[83] *Forward*, May 25, 1918; cited in Pelling, *America and the British Left*, p. 128.

tion policy in the name of labor. Unlike European organized labor, the AFL had tied its destiny to that of its own government. It even preferred to arouse the animosity of the Allied labor majority in order to serve Woodrow Wilson.

VII

THE ORIGINS OF STATE DEPARTMENT SOCIALISM: THE SOCIAL-DEMOCRATIC LEAGUE AND WARTIME DIPLOMACY

Woodrow Wilson had learned a valuable lesson from his experience with the Root Commission. It had been clearly established that representatives of the American Federation of Labor were out of touch with committed European Socialists. With the failure of the two labor missions to Europe, Wilson again sought to influence Allied labor by securing the aid of American Socialists. Since any AFL leaders were automatically discredited in the eyes of Europe's political unionists, the Administration saw its best hope in having its policies presented abroad in the name of socialism.

The existence of the Social-Democratic League offered a ready vehicle for this purpose. Its leaders had formed the association precisely because of their disagreement with the anti-war platform of the Socialist Party. The SDL program offered support to the Administration's war effort and to Wilson's peace aims as interpreted by the September 1918 Inter-Allied Labor and Socialist Conference, and also supported the social reconstruction program of the moderate British Labor Party. But like the Wilson Administration, the League viewed the war as a simple struggle between democracy and autocracy. It supported a conference with enemy Socialists only if the Central Powers delegates supported immediate overthrow of their existing governments.[1]

The League, as Austin Van Der Slice has written, presented "a number of interesting angles." It was "organized just in time to send its government endorsed mission to Europe. The government made use of its 'quasi-socialist' character to select it as the approved representative of American socialism. It was the one kind of socialist organization that Samuel Gompers could work with. And finally several of its most prominent members were at one time or another directly connected with the government's propaganda efforts." Van Der Slice suggests that, although seemingly independent, some of its missions "were frankly government enterprises" or at least "received the encouragement and support of the governments." Any mission "that actually received passports was likely to be following a policy endorsed by the Allied governments."[2]

Like Gompers and the AFL leaders, the Social-Democratic League would serve Administration policy by forming a Socialist mission to wartime Europe. Fortunately, direct evidence exists which reveals the actual extent to which the SDL mission was a government affair. "The idea of a socialist delegation," William English Walling recorded, "was approved by [George] Creel in conversation with J. I. Sheppard of the *Appeal to Reason*." The group would be permitted to gain rapport with Allied Socialists by advocating an international Socialist conference. But even Gompers approved of this tactic, Walling noted. The group would insist upon acceptance of Woodrow Wilson's entire

[1] *New Appeal*, November 16, 1918 (Girard, Kans.). This paper was the pro-war successor of the old Socialist *Appeal to Reason.*
[2] Austin Van Der Slice, *International Labor, Diplomacy and the Peace, 1914–1919* (Philadelphia, London, 1941), 276–77.

program by all conference delegates. This would set up "such conditions that it would never take place." Secretary of State Lansing personally requested that Sheppard recommend personnel. After they were chosen, passports were issued on one hour's notice, instead of the usual forty-eight. The mission was "in accord with the general ideas expressed by Creel to Sheppard and by Gompers to me." Moreover, the League had received ten thousand dollars from industrialist William Cochran and Chester M. Wright to reinforce its ties to the American Alliance for Labor and Democracy.[3]

The original idea for an SDL mission had come from John Spargo. Spargo feared that the SDL was entering a period of decline. While it functioned as a group that was critical of the old Socialist Party, it did not have its own "definite and useful policy." Spargo felt that the League might still have "a very great and useful future." Developments abroad imposed upon it the responsibility of acting "with other Socialist bodies in the new international organization of the movement." By arranging an SDL mission abroad, the organization might be able to get itself off the ground."[4]

Spargo proceeded to send Secretary of State Robert Lansing a memo on behalf of the League. Spargo informed Lansing of "the growing disaffection and Bolshevism among the Socialists of France and Italy." Lansing could gain corroboration from the first AFL mission that Allied morale was weak and that a Socialist "delegation . . . will be very helpful and cordially welcomed." Spargo asked Lansing to grant Walling an interview to discuss the proposed SDL mission. Since many Allied Socialists advocated peace through negotiation, the morale of armies on the Western front was low. The SDL had reached the conclusion that "a delegation should be sent to France, England

[3] Memo of Walling, text of phone conversation with Ralph M. Easley, June 28, 1918, National Civic Federation MSS, New York Public Library.

[4] Spargo to Stokes, May 1, 1918, J. G. Phelps Stokes MSS, Butler Library, Columbia University.

and Italy to confer with the Socialists of those countries, interpret to them what we believe to be America's sincere and democratic policy in the war, present to them our reasons for taking the stand we have taken in support to the Allied cause and beg our comrades to stand with us solidly for victory."[5]

To be successful, Spargo suggested, the mission had to be composed of well-known Socialists with a definite standing in the international movement. They also had to represent an actual Socialist organization. They could not stand open to the charge of being paid by a capitalist government. Thus they could not have an official designation or status. It would have to be a free commission of pro-Allied Socialists whose only purpose was to convince their comrades to support the war. Since the members had to be reliable and loyal, however, it could not "be composed of Socialist Party members." Spargo noted that the Social-Democratic League was a natural medium for such a mission. It was a national group recognized by some Allied Socialists, and had familiar figures in its organization. If the government approved, the SDL would be willing to assume the expense for such a journey.[6]

It evidently did not dawn on Spargo that the quasi-official character of the mission would be easily detected. By appealing to Lansing, the organization from the start was violating its own criteria of independence. Spargo agreed that any members chosen would have to be approved by the Department of State, and would have to be men "of unquestionable loyalty." Spargo also asked that the mission members receive passports, letters of introduction, and identification from the government, as well as a private letter from the President approving the mission. "Such a letter," Spargo told Lansing, "might well be written by the President in reply to one calling his attention to the fact that so many of the European Socialist conferences have officially commended his stand." It could also be

[5] Spargo to Lansing, June 9, 1918, NA, RG 59, 763.72/10310.
[6] *Ibid.*

used "with great effect in the meetings of Socialists addressed by the American delegates."[7]

Lansing responded favorably. On the 12th of June he met with Walling to discuss the mission, and gave it his approval.[8] Later that day, the League issued a public letter announcing the mission. Because of the Socialist Party's anti-war efforts, the SDL stated, French and Italian workers had the mistaken idea that American labor was opposed to Woodrow Wilson's war aims and they believed that the United States would sign a punitive peace treaty. The SDL mission would back Wilson's war aims, and would advocate that these aims "be accepted by the European Socialists as a minimum peace program." According to the SDL, their announcement was sent to President Wilson, and he sent back "the statement that he was heartily for the Mission and that he approved of the names submitted."[9]

Actually, Spargo himself had conferred with the President about the forthcoming mission. Wilson confided to Spargo that he worried about reports from the front, which indicated low morale among many of the troops. To deal with this, Spargo suggested that they create friction among the Allied Socialists in order to divide them. Wilson approved the idea and offered to give the SDL members diplomatic passports. Spargo vetoed this since it would undermine their influence with European Socialists. "These men belong to unions," Spargo told the President, "and they would pass it on that we were stool pigeons traveling with diplomatic passports." Spargo preferred to get the money from William F. Cochran, the Baltimore industrialist. But mission members did carry a letter from Wilson, in which the President referred to Spargo as "in some ways" Wil-

[7] *Ibid.*

[8] Lansing to Spargo, June 13, 1918, Spargo MSS, Wilbur Library, University of Vermont.

[9] Emanuel Haldeman-Julius, "Loyal American Socialists Send Mission to Europe with Message of Encouragement to War-Torn Toilers," including Walling, J. I. Sheppard and Henry Slobodin to Lansing, June 12, 1918; *New Appeal,* June 22, 1918.

son's "personal representative" who would function as the Chief Executive's "eyes and ears."[10]

The mission's goals were elaborated upon by Walling. A key aim was to bring about better understanding between American workers and those of France, England, and Italy, "a majority of whom speak and understand no language but that of Socialism." The Entente Socialists argued that their peace aims were identical with those of Wilson. "Pacifist fanatics" had persuaded the Allied Socialists that the American people did not support the President, and favored the Socialist Party's anti-war position. The danger was that the "Hillquits and Bergers may largely counteract the immense and beneficent influence of Woodrow Wilson in Europe." A disloyal one per cent might negate the effect of the loyal majority. Since Allied labor was Socialist, if they got it "fixed in their heads that the American people are for a Bolshevik peace they may jeopardize the whole Entente cause."[11]

Since most Allied Socialists favored an inter-belligerent Socialist conference, advocacy of the Stockholm idea was a prerequisite for gaining the confidence of the centrist Allied Socialist majority. Hence the SDL mission decided to also favor such a meeting. This stand seemingly differentiated the SDL group from Samuel Gompers and the AFL. The latter had obstinately opposed any such move and had branded advocates of a Stockholm-type conference as defeatists.

But as noted above, the SDL would be careful to set such conditions for an inter-belligerent conference that it could never take place. They would insist that all delegates attending from the Central Powers support rebellion against autocratic governments. This provision would automatically exclude the German Socialists, pacifists, and Bolsheviks, all of whom put attainment of peace above democracy. Delegates would have to pledge to accept Wilson's war aims, would have to agree that the war was a fight between democracy and autocracy, and would have

10 Spargo, COHC, 287–88.
11 Walling memo, n.d. [1918], Samuel Gompers MSS.

to favor immediate overthrow of the autocratic Central Power governments. The mission, stressed William E. Walling, in effect rejected any conference "with subjects of an autocracy who are still under the iron heel of the despot." No conference could really be held, under that condition, with the official Socialists of Germany. If such strict provisions were not made, Walling claimed, any conference would end up being controlled by the Kaiser's Socialists, pacifists, and neutrals, "treacherous forces" which could not be underestimated.[12]

The SDL mission also followed a different tactic than Gompers' on one other major issue. Gompers consistently attacked the control of Allied labor by intellectuals, theorists, and politicians. Gompers never lost the opportunity to lecture Allied labor about the evils of socialism. But since the SDL mission was composed of Socialists, they were not in agreement with Gompers on this issue. This meant that the SDL mission had to find a different way to attack Arthur Henderson and his followers, who vociferously advocated an inter-belligerent Socialist conference. They did this by espousal of the traditional Marxian critique of the moderate nature of German social democracy. The SDL group took the position that they "share the view of [Karl] Liebknecht that the war was launched by the militarists and imperialists of Germany." The American Socialist Party, on the other hand, "shares the view of Scheidemann and his followers that all of the belligerents were and are equally guilty." The SDL tried to give the appearance that they supported the revolutionary left socialists in Germany—men who had been imprisoned by the Kaiser and who would not have been granted permission to attend any inter-belligerent Socialist meeting.[13]

That Walling, Spargo, and their comrades spoke favorably of Karl Liebknecht might have given Samuel Gompers and the Wilson Administration reason to pause before ex-

[12] *Ibid.*
[13] Statement of Allen Benson, *Social Democratic League of America—One Year's Activity of the Reorganized Society—July 1918–May 1919* n.d. [1919], pp. 6–7.

tending their hand to the SDL. But Walling privately made
it clear that any international conference would also exclude "Karl Liebknecht and his faction." Walling understood that Liebknecht's group did "not regard this as a war
of democracy against autocracy," but in fact called for
"revolution against Woodrow Wilson and Lloyd George"
as well as the Kaiser.[14]

If Walling and Spargo thought that Allied Socialists
would not investigate the preconditions they were setting
up for an international Socialist congress, they were mistaken. "Suppose Germans invite Americans to a conference on the condition that they repudiate the American
government, pledge themselves to establish an autocratic
Monarchy in America and openly refuse to support their
Republican Government," Adolphe Smith wrote. "We may
declare that Germans cannot be admitted till after their
revolution, but we cannot invite them to commit high
treason; nor would it be any use for them to do so merely
to attend a congress." If they were willing to risk their lives,
Smith suggested, "let it be for a complete revolution."[15]

Despite this kind of response, the SDL leaders believed
that they could succeed where others had failed. "It is a
bigger thing than I thought," commission chairman Algie
M. Simons of Wisconsin revealed. "Lansing and President
Wilson have both said they consider it the most important
mission that has yet gone across. There will be ample
funds for any work to be done, and an elaborate system of
propaganda has been planned." Simons informed his wife
that she could come along for the journey; whatever funds
were needed would be supplied since the mission had "the
full backing of the government."[16]

Following Spargo's suggestion, the SDL tried to obtain independent financial support. To prospective backers, they
urged the importance of telling Allied labor that the Ameri-

[14] Walling to Gompers, August 9, 1918, Gompers MSS.
[15] Smith to Woodroffe, August 2, 1918, Algie M. Simons MSS,
State Historical Society of Wisconsin, Madison, Wis.
[16] Simons to May Wood Simons, June 18, 1918 (two letters),
ibid.

can worker supported Woodrow Wilson and Samuel Gompers, not the disloyal Socialist Party. "For obvious reasons," a fund-raising letter signed by William Cochran stated, "the Government could not undertake the financing of this mission. The effect of a mission of Government paid Socialists on foreign Socialists, whose point of view is often radically opposed to their own Governments, would have been discredited by the criticisms of the enemies of the mission."[17] But when money failed to pour in, the SDL did not hesitate to ask the government for aid. J. G. Phelps Stokes wrote Cochran that he and Henry Slobodin would run down to Washington "to see whether George Creel could in any way help out in the matter of financing [William] Bohn's [preparatory] trip, in case our S.D.L. funds ran out."[18]

The bulk of the funds were supplied by Cochran, who contributed a check for ten thousand. But the mission itself was nevertheless controlled by the Administration. This was revealed by the Administration's decison to exclude William Bohn from participation in the SDL mission. Bohn favored establishment of a working group of Socialists who would keep in touch with the Department of State regarding the activities of Allied Socialists. The group would be put in charge of propaganda work among Austrian and German Socialists. They would eventually organize exiles in neutral nations to permeate Germany and Austria where they would preach the doctrines of revolution.[19]

Bohn took seriously the SDL's emphasis on the Kaiser's support of the official German Socialists, and on the supposed agreement with Karl Liebknecht's group. Even though Bohn called only for revolution against the governments of the autocratic Central Powers, Woodrow Wilson distrusted this position. He asked Joseph Tumulty to write

[17] Fund-raising letter by William Cochran, August 1, 1918, Stokes MSS.

[18] Stokes to Cochran, August 6, 1918, *ibid.*

[19] Bohn to the Social-Democratic League, July 5, 1918, NA, RG 59, 811.202/19.

Stokes that the President's judgment was "against sending
anyone upon such a mission as you suggest that Mr. Bohn
should undertake." Wilson argued that although Germany
was fomenting revolution in countries with which she was
at war, "it has been the pride of the United States not to
engage in such endeavors." Wilson did not wish to encourage Bohn to do anything that would "directly or indirectly bring about revolution, even in an enemy country."
Wilson favored "direct" remedies he considered to be "more
efficient."[20]

Wilson had again revealed that he stood committed to
inter-Allied unity and military defeat of Germany. He in
no way favored an alliance with the centrist moderate
Socialists in Europe. Despite this, the SDL proved willing
to put itself into Administration hands, and to do the
bidding of the Department of State. Henry Slobodin, one
of the SDL officers, provided the major rationale for his
group's support of the war effort. Marx, he reminded
Socialists, was not a pacifist. In fact, he had supported the
North in America's Civil War. Once again, pure pacifism
had become an instrument of German militarism. The
German Socialists shared their ruler's desire to run the
world. They were being used to spread propaganda that
would weaken the Allied worker's morale. The Socialist
International had previously been a first-class power as
strong as any nation, with many zealots ready to stake their
lives at its command. But now Germany had secured its
hold on the International, and the Allies had failed to deal
with the power it still had.[21]

While the Department of State was favorably situated
to make appeals to the democratic elements in Europe,
Slobodin pointed out, it neglected to make proper arrangements to deal with these groups. "The Socialist masses of
Europe," he informed Lansing, "view with hostility anything that comes from other than Socialist sources." The
Department could not influence the European masses until

---

[20] Wilson to Tumulty, September 6, 1918, Wilson MSS., Library
of Congress.
[21] Slobodin to Lansing, July 18, 1918, NA, RG 59, 811.202/19.

it recognized this truth. The only group that would receive a hearing from Socialists in the central empires and Slavic nations were American Socialists.[22]

The problem was, Slobodin continued, that the American Socialist Party "could not be used by the State Department for these purposes." Slobodin informed Lansing, however, that "there is a large number of American Socialists who would be eager to co-operate with our government in that work." The job of carrying Administration policy to Europe should be the task of Socialists only. It was futile, Slobodin argued, to give that duty to those "who have never before come into contact with the Socialist movement." Slobodin offered the SDL's services to the Department for the duration of the war. The destiny of the nations, he believed, would be affected by the ability to reach Europe's revolutionary masses. Slobodin suggested a formal liaison of pro-war Socialists with the Department. State should select several Socialists whom it trusted to take charge of revolutionary propaganda among the central empires. These would be, in Slobodin's words, Socialists *"under the control of the State Department, but otherwise free to use the traditional methods of Socialist propaganda."* Their work would ostensibly be carried out by the SDL, in order to present a picture of independence from the Administration.[23]

Having won Administration support, the SDL leaders got ready to undertake their mission. They expected "to combat what I venture to call war neurasthenia," Spargo reported, since the war had got "on the nerves of the people." The mission would combat defeatism by speaking frankly to the Allies. It would ask them to keep fighting, and would point out that "revolutionary action in democratic countries . . . is vastly different from revolutionary action in a country like Germany or Austria" where Socialists did indeed have the duty to wage revolutionary warfare. But in the United States, it was "treason to the International" to urge revolution against a democratic

[22] *Ibid.*
[23] *Ibid.* (Emphasis added).

government. In Germany, it was treason for a Socialist to refrain from the revolutionary course.[24]

Precisely because they thought themselves to be Socialists, the SDL members believed they would be able to convert those Allied Socialists who had disapproved of John P. Frey's labor mission. The SDL group arrived in Britain shortly before Gompers was scheduled to arrive with his group. Algie M. Simons complained that although the Inter-Allied Labor and Socialist Conference was set for September, "the situation was made very much harder by the A.F. of L. mission." Frey's group had made "every break and mistake possible," Simons claimed, and had "balled up everything it touched." Simons had not heard "a good word for it from any of the 57 varieties of opinion we have sounded." His group, however, would be in close sympathetic contact with all the factions in the labor and Socialist movement.[25]

Much to their surprise, some of the SDL members found that they did not have extensive disagreements with their European counterparts. Gompers had not been willing to forge an alliance with the moderate European Socialists, who were his major competitors for international labor's allegiance. Despite Henderson's appeals, he would not join the British labor leader in his efforts to rebuild the International along Wilsonian lines. But the Social-Democratic League members found that they actually shared Henderson's vision and goals. In some respects, a man like John Spargo was an American equivalent of Henderson.

The SDL mission soon learned that Allied labor feared that Wilson would compromise his war aims, and that he would not be able to control the official peace conference. When the group met with Henderson, the British labor leader told them that he favored prosecution of the war, just as they did. He also favored what he called "interbelligerent 'conversations.' " These were meant to supplement Wilson's war aims. Henderson also doubted that American labor would gain representation at the peace

24 *New Appeal*, July 6, 1918.
25 Simons to Stokes, July 9, 1918, Stokes MSS.

conference, and therefore he favored holding a simultaneous labor and Socialist conference. As for the present, Henderson simply said: " 'Let's meet the Germans face to face and tell them what we think of them.' " The conference did not have to include any voting on resolutions. It would merely consider exchanges of opinion. The argument that such a conference would be a sounding board for a German-inspired peace was thought by Henderson to be an insult to the intelligence of the Allied delegates who would attend.[26]

The group also met with the official labor representatives of Lloyd George's government. Thirty members of Parliament attended a dinner for the mission that was presided over by War Minister G. N. Barnes. The mission told the M.P.'s that they were indebted to Allied labor for helping to make the war a struggle for democracy. They noted their agreement with the goal of "complete democratization of government and industry so that the workers may get full economic and political justice." Louis Kopelin, editor of the *New Appeal,* told the group that they had "letters from [Newton D.] Baker and Mr. Lansing asking General Pershing to arrange mass meetings for us so that American fighting men know what the Socialists of America really feel about the war they are waging."[27]

After Britain, the group made a short stop in France. Even the Social Patriot Albert Thomas told the group that increasing American activity meant a new danger of imperialism. Thomas, however, strongly admired Woodrow Wilson for attempting to stand firm against such a development. Thomas told the mission that the French Socialists supported the war effort and that there was no French equivalent of a Victor Berger or Morris Hillquit. Simons recorded that the French Socialists universally accepted Woodrow Wilson's war aims.[28]

Simons' conversations made him immensely pleased

[26] Journal of Algie M. Simons, notes of July 2–24, 1918, Simons MSS.

[27] *New Appeal,* July 27, 1918.

[28] Journal of Algie M. Simons, July 1918, Simons MSS.

with the mission's progress. Conferences with the Belgian
Socialist Emil Vandervelde particularly led the group to
believe that they could build a new pro-Allied Socialist
International, an organization dedicated to the fight
against "German influence." They had the support of the
forty pro-war French Socialist deputies, as well as G. N.
Barnes in England. Simons saw the new group as an "effective fighting organization of several million Socialists,"
which would "prove worth several thousands of soldiers in
the ranks."[29] Their mission, Simons believed, was "really
changing the current of public opinion and producing a
far greater affect [sic] than any other body that has gone
over." Simons predicted success in the effort to build a
pro-Allied Socialist International.[30]

The mission's major effort to influence Allied labor
would take place in Italy. Success there was of greater
urgency, Charles E. Russell stressed, than "trying to cut a
wide swath" in Great Britain, where the SDL was unable
to get much propaganda into the British newspapers.
Russell advised that attention should be paid to Italy,
where the situation was quite bad. "It is much more important that Italy should be brought into line," he informed
George Creel, "than that we should be trying to influence
British public opinion in our favor."[31]

Charles Merriam, the chief of the Committee on Public
Information in Italy, agreed with Russell's estimate. Since
Italian labor was committed to a revolutionary anti-war
position, Merriam urged Russell to get the SDL mission
into Italy. The CPI, he wrote, would arrange a conference
with Bissolati, head of Italy's pro-war Socialists. A new
spirit in the official Socialist party, he noted, had created
an excellent opening "which should not be neglected."
Merriam asked that "every effort" be made to bring the SDL
mission to Italy.[32]

    29 Simons to May Wood Simons, July 28, 1918, *ibid.*
    30 Simons to May Simons, August 5, 1918, *ibid.*
    31 Russell to Creel, June 19, 1918, NA, RG 63, CPI 17-A2 (21).
    32 Merriam to Russell, July 4, 1918, transmitted by Thomas
Nelson Page, Charles Edward Russell MSS, Library of Congress.

Writing from Italy, Algie M. Simons revealed why visiting Italy was so important. In Italy alone, Simons reported, "the great mass of Italian workers" followed doctrinaire Marxism and Bolshevik leaders. In Milan, Naples, and Bologna the unions were both anti-war and Bolshevik. "Everywhere there are whispers of a general revolution. Economic conditions aggravate this—almost no coal— little food—*no participation of labor in handling of relations of labor and capital.*" There were three types of Socialists in Italy: the pro-war independents around Labriola; the Reform Socialists headed by Bissolati, the Minister of War Pensions; and the official Socialist Party that was opposed to the war. The reform group had twenty deputies in the parliament and were a component of the Italian Union of Labor. This union, however, was a small body meant to counter the anti-war Confederazione del Lavoro, to which most of Italian labor belonged. "Unfortunately," Simons wrote, "the power of 'reform' Socialists is far greater in governmental circles than throughout the country."[33]

The Italian Socialist Party, dubbed the "official" Socialists by observers, was the most powerful organization of the Italian Left. The Party opposed participation in the war, and its deputies refused to vote on behalf of war credits. Simons praised the pro-war Socialist Benito Mussolini, a man who was "outraged by the neutralist attitude of the party, its absolute refusal to take sides, to condemn the invasion of Belgium or blame the German comrades who voted the first war credits." Mussolini had left the official Party and had founded "a democratic pro-war paper . . . which has become famous for its enthusiasm and for the insistence upon the vigorous conduct of the war."[34]

Despite vigorous activity by the pro-war minority, the official Socialists advocated neutrality and induced the Confederazione del Lavoro, "the only important labor organization in the country, to follow its decision and refuse to co-operate with the government." Members who fol-

[33] Memo of Algie M. Simons, September 12, 1918, Gompers MSS.
[34] *Ibid.*

lowed the pro-war leader Turati were "disavowed by their
followers and had to resign." Members of the official Socialist Party found that their officers were arrested, that local
organizations were dissolved by government edict, and
that large meetings were forbidden. Members of the Party
were "firmly convinced they are the victims of deliberate
persecution and that under pretext of war the Government
is making an attempt to extirpate them entirely." Their
members were proud that among all the belligerent Socialist parties, theirs alone was true to the "promise of the
International." They reveled in their persecution, Simons
wrote, "fully realizing that each condemnation throws an
aureole of martyrdom about the head of the condemned
and strengthens his prestige with the masses." The government, on the other hand, blamed the Socialist Party for
fomenting riots in Turin, and for staging a strike among
the army that led to the defeat of Italian troops at
Caporetto.[35]

The Socialists held this position, Simons asserted, because of blind loyalty to Marxism. They believed that it
did not matter whether Germany or the Allies won, since
both represented imperialist powers. They wanted their
own party to become the nucleus of a new left-wing International. They desired an indecisive end to the war, and
felt kindly toward Germany because it was Marx's birth-
place. Because the official Socialists were so important,
Simons advised that the SDL mission avoid being used by
the "reform Socialists" for local political purposes. If they
let themselves be used, the official Socialists would become
bitter, and would be "firmly convinced that the pro-war
socialists in America have sold out to capital." Simons
suggested provoking discussions with the official Socialists
to prove that an Allied victory "will be followed by a dim-
inution of imperialism" since Woodrow Wilson was
pledged to such a course.[36]

While many official Socialists viewed Woodrow Wilson
as a true democrat, Simons pointed out, they believed he

[35] *Ibid.*
[36] *Ibid.*

was limited in his actions because he led a bourgeois republic. The problem was that many held this view, since the official Socialists were an influential political group. Their strength, Simons held, "is very great and probably growing." The Party had conquered labor, had gained the peasants' esteem, and was growing "principally because *it is against the war and draws around itself all those varied elements . . . who would indeed like to see peace at any price.*" It would be a great accomplishment, Simons believed, if the Social-Democratic League mission could convince Italians to "hold on a few months longer."[37]

To achieve this effect, Simons told his audience that the SDL had not come to Italy to interfere with policies that Italian labor had determined for itself. Nor did they arrive to urge the workers to make more sacrifices. They came only to bring cheer; to assure Italy that American labor stood firm in its desire to fight till victory. Emphasizing that the SDL members all believed in socialism, Simons assured his listeners that the majority of American Socialists "are now supporting the position of President Wilson and his peace demands, which are practically identical with those set forth by the inter-allied Socialist Congress of London." The United States, he asserted, had no imperial aims. Its only goal was to free the world from autocratic domination. To leave the military power of the central empires unbroken meant only a truce before a new world war. It was the duty of internationally minded socialists to avoid such a development. The only way to "prevent the coming of this militarist state," Simons concluded, was the "way that leads through military victory."[38]

John Spargo used a similar tactic in his speeches. As Socialists, Spargo told a Milan audience, the SDL mission did "not comprehend the attitude of those who also claim to be socialists and yet oppose the war. No neutrality is possible," Spargo insisted, "between the enemies of liberty and its defenders." Those who opposed the war were the natural allies of Central Power autocrats, and they had

[37] *Ibid.*
[38] Simons speech in Italy, n.d., Simons MSS.

abandoned "the sacred ideals of socialism and humanity."
The only way to make socialism a reality was to first destroy the Teutonic autocracy. Following the tactic devised
by Walling, Spargo praised Karl Liebknecht because he
was imprisoned for his revolutionary opposition to the
Kaiser. Such praise was meant to appeal to the Italians
who considered Liebknecht to be a major hero of the
Marxist movement. "Today," Spargo concluded, "we constitute the Inter-nationality of Civilized Peoples fighting
against that infernal machine and we shall not desist until
we have broken it down."[39]

When he wrote to defend the mission from critical
attacks, Spargo always pointed out that their journey was
not inspired by the American government. The SDL, he
stressed, had paid its own expenses. Moreover, they did
not seek "to meddle with the party affairs in this country."
Their only goal was to make known the true position of
American Socialists; to point out that "American labor is
solidly for the war." This did not mean, Spargo claimed,
that they had forsaken their Socialist principles. They were
actually supporting Socialist internationalism, since
Woodrow Wilson had "better expressed the ideals of international solidarity than any other statesman in the world."
Only German propagandists made it appear that a reign of
reaction existed in America. The prosecution of Tom
Mooney was an exception to the rule. Those Socialists who
supported the war effort also worked on behalf of Mooney's
freedom.[40]

In some Italian cities, the mission was prevented from
holding public meetings. At Turin they were able to confer
privately with Italian Socialists, but rioting earlier in the
year made a meeting impractical. Although they found less
pacifism than they had expected, Spargo noted that they
had discovered "a good deal of war-weariness and dissatisfaction with the government." The mission members did

[39] Spargo speech, Milan, Italy, August 20, 1918; translated from
"Il Popolo d'Italia," enclosed in North Winship to Lansing, August
26, 1918, NA, RG 59, 763.72119 So/23.
[40] Spargo article, September 7, 1918, NA, RG 63, CPI 20 B-4.

their best, and believed that they had made a "profound impression."[41]

At Genoa, the group addressed a rally of two thousand people. In Rome, they actually met with leaders of the official Socialist Party. The Party's officer again informed the mission that while they believed Wilson to be sincere, they thought he could not help being used by America's capitalist ruling class. But the SDL group, unlike the AFL mission, did not attempt to convert these Socialists to a pro-war viewpoint. They met with them only to prevent *Avanti* from making "capital out of our association with the pro-war Socialists. We had demonstrated our desire to meet all sides."[42]

The SDL mission believed they had accomplished some good. "It has been repeatedly said," their year-end report stated, "that the Mission helped materially to keep the Italian people in the war up to the end." The largest meeting they had addressed was in Milan, where over three thousand heard them talk. The SDL claimed that the crowd's enthusiasm was at such a high pitch that when they arrived on stage, the audience rose and cheered for several minutes. After Simons presented his speech, the group received an even larger ovation. Even in pacifist Bologna, the SDL claimed, fifteen hundred "wildly enthusiastic" people turned out to greet them.[43]

This type of reception led Simons to reflect that they had "fought a good fight here and those who claim to know currents of opinion are wildly enthusiastic over the results." Simons believed that their mission had thrown "a sort of panic into the anti-war Socialists." They were attempting to block the Inter-Allied Labor and Socialist Conference in London, and "some ridiculously overenthusiastic Socialists in Italy" feared they might succeed, thereby causing the failure of "the allied cause in Italy."[44]

[41] Spargo to Charles E. Merriman, n.d., NA RG 63, CPI 20-B4.
[42] *Ibid.*
[43] Benson, in "Social Democratic League of America—*One Year's Activity of the Reorganized Society*," July 1918–May 1919, pp. 6–7.
[44] Simons to May Wood Simons, August 21, 1918, Simons MSS.

The mission's claims of great success and "wildly enthusiastic" audiences were tempered by the reports of Administration observers. North Winship cabled that the
most striking aspect of their Milan visit was that the SDL
was greeted by the mayor, an avowed anti-war Socialist.
But Winship contradicted Simons' account of their day in
Milan. The auditorium at which they spoke was only
half-full, Winship reported, and there was "little enthusiasm shown." Contact with the official Socialists, moreover, had an effect opposite to that intended. The pro-war
minority was angry and did not come to hear the mission's
speakers. The group actually got a poor turnout because
of "their visit to the Mayor and the fact that they did not
get in touch with the best Socialists here who usually
arrange patriotic demonstrations."[45]

While the speeches were "good in their way," Winship
reported, repetition made them lose all effect. The local
Socialist who served as interpreter was "not aware of the
object of the Commission, or the sentiments of the
speakers." Publicity was so poor that the newspapers did
not even comment "on the Commission or its activities,
not even the Socialist journals." Winship concluded that
the SDL mission "only helped to encourage and stimulate
the Socialists here probably due to the misinterpretation of
their views."[46]

Towards the end of the mission's European journey,
internal divisions arose. A split emerging within the group
actually reflected the international divisions between the
Administration Left (e.g., Samuel Gompers, William E.
Walling) and the moderate centrist Socialists in the Allied
camp (e.g., Arthur Henderson, Jean Longuet). The differences came to light when John Spargo approved a press
interview in which the SDL leader summed up his impressions of Allied Socialist politics.

In the interview, Spargo stated that whereas he had expected to find Allied Socialists filled with hope for the fu-

---

[45] Winship to Lansing, August 26, 1918, NA, RG 59, 763.72119
So/23.
[46] *Ibid.*

ture, he had found all of them "doubting the power of democracy to control and direct the forces of the storm." They pointed especially to the existence of "secret treaties and intrigues." To question that these Socialists wanted to win the war, Spargo came to realize, was to "believe that it is 'defeatist'" simply to favor a compromise peace. The great fear of the Allied Socialists was that the imperialist powers would have their way at the peace conference. This suspicion aided the advocates of immediate negotiations with enemy Socialists. To counter their arguments, Spargo had pointed out that American Socialists insisted upon a just Wilsonian peace. But Spargo's American critics maintained he had neglected to add that they insisted upon fighting Germany to victory in order to achieve their goal. The impression given, they believed, was that the SDL favored peace so badly that they were only lukewarm in their support of the war.[47]

Spargo's interview aroused the immediate anger of both Samuel Gompers and William E. Walling. Since Spargo had been associated with Gompers in the American Alliance, Gompers believed that he had a veto over the policies espoused by the pro-war Socialists. The press interview with Spargo had carried a headline indicating that Spargo now held an anti-war position. While the body of the dispatch did not justify the headline, Gompers told Walling, "it is just as incongruous a statement as can be made and gives the newspapers the opportunity of writing the headings. I can scarcely believe," Gompers wrote, "that Mr. Spargo gave expression to the utterances attributed to him—at least I hope he did not."[48]

Walling had already erupted in anger at Spargo's interview. As the SDL officer in charge of the organization back in the United States, Walling insisted that from that point on, press correspondents speak only to Simons for the mission's views. All other releases were to be wired back home for Walling personally to look over before publication. Walling was especially upset that Spargo had

[47] Stokes to May Wood Simons, August 20, 1918, Stokes MSS.
[48] Gompers to Walling, August 10, 1918, Gompers MSS.

claimed that Jean Longuet and his allies were not pacifists.
If Spargo had said that, Walling wrote, the SDL "delegation
might as well return to America."[49]

The divergent approach taken by Walling and Spargo
reflected the broader division between Gompers and
Arthur Henderson. Gompers' activity in Europe destroyed
any chance for an alliance of American and European
Wilson-oriented Socialists, who were seeking to unify the
Allied Left around an advanced Wilsonian program. Like
Henderson, Spargo and a few of his associates realized
that the moderate Centrists were not Bolsheviks. Rather,
they were Wilsonians who supported the war effort, and
who desired to pressure independently their own governments to adhere to the promise of a just peace. While Gompers worked to strengthen the hands of the Allied Right,
and rejected any form of unity with Henderson, Spargo
favored an alliance with Henderson and Longuet as a
means of building up centers of support for Wilson. Had
Spargo's position been approved by Wilson, it would have
meant that the Administration accepted a moderate form
of class politics for its own ends.

Spargo was equally upset about Walling's and Gompers'
attack. It was "monstrous," he replied, that any member
of the SDL "should be capable of the sort of thing Walling
has done." Spargo noted that he had engaged in long fights
with the extreme Left; with men like Ramsay MacDonald
and with the official Socialists in Italy. The trouble with
Walling was that "practically all the men in the Socialist
movement of the different countries are, to his mind, pro-
Germans and pacifists, peace-at-any-price men." The
simple truth was that "they are not so." The centrists were
only trying to assure a just Wilsonian peace, a goal which
Spargo thought the SDL also favored. "We found men
whom we had regarded as pacifists," Spargo reported, "to
be as strongly in favor of the war as we were." They differed only on the tactical question of holding an inter-
belligerent Socialist congress. But Spargo knew that this
difference did not make the Allied Socialists anti-war. Even

[49] Walling to Simons, August 2, 1918, Gompers MSS.

Gompers, Spargo incorrectly believed, had "found that the realities are quite different from the long-distance appearances." There were many men in the Labour Party with whom even Gompers saw he could work.[50]

The division now threatened to interfere with the unity obtained between the SDL and the American Federation of Labor. Phelps Stokes urged Algie Simons to meet Gompers personally in London, and to use every opportunity to "show publicly appreciation of Gompers' services to [the] democratic cause."[51] Walling, in addition, now urged that Spargo be removed from the mission. Simons alone should function as mission spokesman, Walling advised, and the delegates had to act as a single body.[52] As a result of this pressure, Spargo decided voluntarily to leave the group. Instead of going on with them to Britain, he remained in Italy as a member of the Committee of Public Information office. He felt that as a CPI staff member, he could draw up a manifesto declaring ringing support of the war that would do "immense good in [a] critical situation."[53]

Spargo's decision to stay in Italy did not put an end to his confrontation with the rigid Administration Left. The conflict that would break out between Gompers and Spargo was a prototype of the contemporary division between George Meany and Walter Reuther over how best to fight the Cold War in the 1960's. Since Spargo was a CPI staff member when the Gompers mission arrived in Italy, it meant that Spargo had a role to play in making arrangements for the Gompers delegation.

Insult was added to injury when Gompers saw the newspapers after his mission had arrived. Press reports of the CPI luncheon given for Gompers were concerned with Spargo's speech, "while Mr. Gompers, Mr. [James] Wilson and the labor Mission were almost ignored." Later, when the papers printed the phony story about cancellation of Gompers' major speech in Rome, they also featured a long,

---

50 Spargo to Stokes, September 22, 1918, Stokes MSS.
51 Stokes to Simons, August 20, 1918, *ibid.*
52 Walling to Simons, September 2, 1918, *ibid.*
53 Spargo to Stokes, September 6, 1918, *ibid.*

two-column interview with Spargo. The interview "had
taken place some days previously," Nelson Page reported,
and included a portrait of Spargo "while . . . Mr. Gompers
and his mission were relegated to an inconspicuous position with a most inadequate report."[54]

Gompers believed that his trouble was purposefully
caused by Spargo. He was furious to learn that arrangements for Gompers to visit Milan, Genoa, and Turin had
been completed by Spargo. When Spargo then offered to
accompany Gompers to the front, the AFL president made
clear his disapproval. Ambassador Page did not "concur in
the belief held by some members of the mission that Mr.
Spargo was personally concerned in the manifest effort
to minimize the effect of the Labor Mission's effort." He did
feel, however, that some Socialists had played a part, and
that some CPI members "were not displeased at anything
that led the public to think that the Gompers Mission was
less important than the Spargo Mission of Socialists which
visited Rome during August."[55]

Gompers himself believed that he had been received in
Italy with the greatest acclaim by the people, the American
colony, and all prominent officials. Thus he felt highly
humiliated to find a letter in the press by Spargo, aiming to
"give me a clean bill of health," vouching for Gompers'
"worthiness and honor of purpose." Having any Socialist
—even a pro-war Socialist—vouch for Gompers' honor
was too much for the AFL president. Gompers was enraged
that Spargo's letter received a prominent spot in the news,
despite "the enthusiastic reception which was tendered
the Mission and myself." With Nelson Page present, Gompers demanded to know why "the American Labor Mission
seemed to be under the wing and guardianship of Mr.
Spargo." Page was indignant and according to Gompers, he
supported the AFL mission's desire for independence.[56]

Gompers' fury was understandable. The newspaper
story introduced Spargo as "perhaps the best known and

54 Page to Lansing, October 11, 1918, NA, RG 59, 032.G 58.
55 Ibid.
56 Gompers memo, December 20, 1918, Gompers MSS.

most authoritative exponent of Socialism in the United States." Spargo had tried to use this prestige to create a sentiment favorable to Gompers. The AFL chief, he wrote, was "one of the foremost men in America's public life today, and one of the stoutest and most trusted of President Wilson's supporters." Decrying Socialist attacks on Gompers, Spargo praised him for building "the most powerful organization of workers in the world." Although as a Socialist he did not always agree with the AFL leader, Spargo stressed, he had "never doubted his sincerity, his loyalty to the working class or his courage."[57]

Gompers would inform his audience, Spargo wrote, of how his leadership of American labor had "been a great boon to the working class of America." Spargo assured the Italians that most American Socialists shared his estimate of Gompers, "notwithstanding the long years of bitter strife" in which both sides had fought each other. Referring to the American Alliance, Spargo praised the AFL and pro-war Socialists who were "united in a concerted movement to inspire the workers of the nation with a strong determination to win the war." In that work, Spargo stated, "I was able to co-operate with Mr. Gompers and came to understand him better." Spargo ended by calling Gompers "incorruptible" because he was "rich in the confidence and the affection the workers freely bestow upon him."[58]

Spargo had a hard time writing his eulogy of Gompers, since in reality he had almost destroyed their wartime unity in conflict over the political policy to be followed by the SDL. He wrote the piece only out of a sense of duty that he could make things go more smoothly for a mission that would be greeted with unanimous hatred by Italian labor and socialism. Spargo knew that as a result he would be "placed in a rather difficult position." But the official Socialists attacked Gompers and the AFL every day, and he felt compelled to defend them against such revolutionary attacks. As a result of his defense, Spargo himself be-

[57] Report of interview with Spargo, n.d. [1918], *ibid.*
[58] *Ibid.*

came a "scapegoat" and soon was "denounced every day nearly in 'Avanti' and other papers."[59]

Spargo was willing to take the risk of incurring these attacks, because he felt that the Gompers mission was "composed of men who represent the most conservative side of the American Federation of Labor." Since all labor was "permeated with Socialism" in Italy, they would find it impossible to communicate with the AFL mission. Protest against the Gompers visit had been so strong, Spargo noted, that even Italian pro-war Socialists had complained. The official Socialists so resented the AFL that they had refused to send delegates to the London Inter-Allied Labor and Socialist Conference, as a protest against Gompers' participation.[60]

Spargo recommended that "in view of the fact that all the unions in Italy . . . are dominated by Socialists, it seems advisable to exercise greater care in sending labor delegations here. It can hardly be doubted," he wrote, that Frey's first AFL mission "has done harm and not good." Spargo urged that the Administration encourage only "the more radical union men, Socialists or Socialist sympathizers" to visit Italy. They at least would not be subject to attack on ideological grounds. The missions, he suggested, should not be supervised by the Italian government, but should be subordinate to the CPI. The local office would decide where to send them. Spargo reiterated that the Italian Socialist Party was "the crux" of a serious situation. He suggested establishment of a regular department, in the charge of a well-known Socialist, that could "do a great deal of effective work among Socialists."[61]

On the basis of Spargo's reports, the Administration had put him in charge of a CPI desk in Italy and assigned him to supervise the Gompers mission. Spargo felt that his efforts would make things easier for Gompers, although

[59] Spargo to Stokes, September 22, 1918, Stokes MSS.

[60] Spargo, "Observations on the Italian Socialist Situation," week ending September 21, 1918; NA, RG 63, CPI 20 B-4; report to Charles E. Merriam.

[61] Ibid.

he doubted the mission's efficacy in advance. By the end of September, Spargo reported that due to his work, the anti-Gompers campaign had "entirely ceased." He cited the article he wrote as having provided an "antidote to the poison already spread by 'Avanti.'" But Gompers—who self-righteously saw no need for help—rejected Spargo's services as meddling by an ill-meaning Socialist intellectual.[62]

While Spargo was in Italy, the original SDL mission had returned to Great Britain. After attending the Derby meeting of the Trades Union Congress, they reported that resolutions passed were less pacifist in spirit than those of previous TUC conferences. Arthur Henderson had previously scoffed when the SDL argued that Germany had to be driven out of France before any peace negotiations could take place. But now an almost unanimous vote revealed that the TUC itself favored a German withdrawal from France and Belgium. Even Ramsay MacDonald, they claimed, had told Algie Simons that an Allied victory was certain.[63]

Henderson's position, however, came under criticism from some who were favorable to the Administration. Russell described Henderson's views as an "amazing thing." He skillfully made statements that seemed loyal, Russell reported, but that cast doubt on the course taken by the Lloyd George government. "He seems to have meant," Russell explained, "that British labor support[s] the government in the war but without any enthusiasm and" that it is ready "to take advantage of every opportunity to advance its own interest."[64]

The entire SDL mission now felt that pacifism was diminishing "largely because of a growing knowledge of American military and financial strength and even more because of faith in the sincerity of America's democratic war aims."[65] Whatever changes had taken place in British

---

[62] Spargo to Charles Merriam, September 30, 1918, NA, RG 63, CPI 20 B-4.
[63] Simons to May Wood Simons, September 4, 1918, Simons MSS.
[64] Charles E. Russell Diary, September 4, 1918; Russell MSS.
[65] *New Appeal,* September 28, 1918, report of Louis Kopelin.

labor, however, were due primarily to Henderson's desire
to placate American Wilsonians and to gain their cooperation in rebuilding the old Socialist International. British
labor, moreover, still supported the idea of holding an
inter-belligerent Socialist congress. But after the Allied
offensive, it became fairly obvious that the war was drawing to a close. Many Allied labor groups shifted their emphasis to the need for a democratic and just peace, and
they downgraded their calls for immediate inter-belligerent conversations. But it was the Allied offensive, and not
the work of any American Socialist or labor missions, that
produced this tactical change.

The Social-Democratic League members were completely satisfied with the accomplishments of their mission. President Wilson spent one hour with them to hear
their personal report, and told them that "he had kept in
touch with" the SDL's work "abroad and thanked the Mission." Secretary of State Lansing added that he had
received reports of their work with the greatest interest,
and hoped that they would continue their work so that all
Americans would understand the just aims of the Administration. Lansing told the group that they had committed
"a great service not only to the allied cause but to humanity."[66]

Writing personally to Russell, who remained in Britain
with the CPI, Lansing noted how "effective the work of
you and your colleagues was in Europe." Thanking the SDL
mission for its efforts on behalf of the Department of
State, Lansing wrote that he appreciated "the wise and
patriotic influence which you have exerted."[67]

Before going in to talk with Lansing and Wilson, the
SDL mission had prepared a formal written report on their
efforts. The report indicated that some of the mission
members had been able to report objectively the position
taken by Allied Labor. British labor, they pointed out, de-

[66] Louis Kopelin, "Socialist Mission Makes Personal Report to
President Wilson," New Appeal, October 5, 1918, reporting on meeting with Lansing on September 25 and Wilson on September 26.
[67] Lansing to Russell, September 23, 1918, Russell MSS.

sired an inter-belligerent Socialist congress because they felt it would weaken German morale and expose the German Socialists to condemnation from their comrades. Only a military deadlock, domestic depression, suppression of labor's rights, and its exclusion from directive roles in war industries—along with a gain in the strength of Allied imperialist interests—would strengthen the standing of Allied anti-war groups.[68]

Turning to France, the SDL reported that Jean Longuet's Socialists were called defeatist since they did not believe that the Allied forces could win a military victory, and because they made a fetish out of holding an inter-belligerent Socialist conference. But in Italy, they argued, the situation was at its worst. Italian labor and Socialist movements were "frankly hostile to the prosecution" of the war, and they threatened "revolution to bring about its conclusion." The government there was "extremely sympathetic with the Bolshevist movement and demands an immediate convening of an International Socialist Congress."[69]

The Allied Socialists, they continued, were not pro-German. Like Ray Stannard Baker, the SDL group argued that all anti-war sentiment would dissolve if the Allied Socialists were given assurances that Woodrow Wilson's democratic war aims would prevail at the peace conference. The SDL had tried to make these aims clear and had also explained that American labor "shares in the management of industrial relations and aided in the prosecution of the war." Even now, their report argued, the mass of Italian workers who "undoubtedly still give their allegiance to the closely disciplined revolutionary anti-war position" could be "turned either way." The mission urged concentration upon Italy since it was "the most explosive and dangerous element in the whole interallied Socialist situation." If their forces were released, "a world-wide,

[68] Algie M. Simons, Charles E. Russell, Alexander Howat, and Louis Kopelin, "Report of the American Socialist Mission," September 25, 1918, NA, RG 59, 763.72110 So/79.
[69] *Ibid.*

desperate and almost blind destructive upheaval might result."[70]

The SDL urged creation of a new propaganda bureau that would deal with the job of answering pacifism and Bolshevism in Allied countries. Controlled by Creel's CPI, this bureau would be made up of men with experience in the Socialist movement. Their goal would be to show the sincerity of the United States' exposition of democracy. Since all Socialists swore allegiance to Wilson's war aims, the SDL noted, they had only to allay doubts that the United States would not be powerful enough to achieve these aims. If the belief grew that the war was fought for classic imperial ends, "revolution is almost inevitable."[71]

Like Baker, the SDL mission ignored the growth and power of the Allied Right, and worried instead about the restlessness and fervor among Allied labor. They did not consider that the Left might be ineffective due to fragmentation and sectarian squabbles. And like Henderson, they seemed to think that Woodrow Wilson was seriously contemplating an alliance with the moderate centrists in the Allied Socialist movements.

This possibility also struck fear into the hearts of some American conservatives. The mere fact that Wilson worked with the SDL and toyed with Arthur Henderson was upsetting. Writing to Theodore Roosevelt, Ralph M. Easley indicated that he did not understand Wilson's use of the League as a means of reaching Henderson. At the meeting with the SDL mission, Easley believed, Wilson had "expressed some very strange views, particularly that he was in sympathy with the peoples of Europe who were against their imperialistic governments. He said that the alleged 'statesmen' of Europe started this war but it was going to be ended by the people." Easley felt that such comments were "exactly on a level with . . . the Arthur Hendersons and the socialists of France and Italy." It appeared, he thought, that Wilson was "accepting the lead-

[70] Ibid.
[71] Ibid.

ership of the anti-government factions of the various European movements."[72]

Wilson actually never contemplated that kind of alliance. But he appreciated that the moderate Socialists eschewed revolution and looked to American liberal capitalism for leadership. If they could be kept believing in the validity of his war aims, Wilson realized, Allied labor could be kept in line. Thus Wilson approved of the SDL mission's attempt to keep Allied moderates behind him.

Wilson's desire to keep the moderate Socialists on his side, however, was not appreciated by the more dogmatic members of the Administration Left. William E. Walling, who by then had drawn quite close to Gompers, felt the need to send a corrective memorandum to Lansing. "The trend towards an international general strike to bring about an early compromise peace," he warned Lansing, "continues unabated." Unlike the SDL mission, Walling argued that Allied victories in July had not affected the pacifism and Bolshevism of European labor. The strength of the movement for a compromise peace, Walling insisted, was shown by the resolutions passed at the September Inter-Allied Labor and Socialist Conference. Gompers had proposed that "there should be no meeting with representatives of the Central Powers in a labor conference except with such as were 'in open revolt against their autocratic governments.'" Aside from the AFL votes in support, Gompers received only six other votes "in the entire European Socialist and Labor movements, with sixty-three votes against it!"[73]

Walling neglected to note that even Arthur Henderson now favored holding off on any immediate convocation of an inter-belligerent conference. Moreover, on the issue of war aims and intervention in Russia, the AFL had indeed acted as a moderating influence. But Walling insisted that the French Socialists had been completely captured by pacifism. Longuet, who had been in the minority at the

[72] Easley to Roosevelt, October 1, 1918, NCF MSS.
[73] Walling to Lansing, September 24, 1918, NA, RG 59, 763.72119 So/81.

Inter-Allied meeting, demanded an immediate inter-belligerent conference. This was a Bolshevik declaration of insurrection, according to Walling, and he accused Longuet
of waging war against the Clemenceau government. Insur-
rectionary strikes and sabotage were prolonging the war,
and were putting German labor into a dominant position
in the European movement.[74]

According to Walling, a Socialist could not both support
the war and favor an inter-belligerent conference. Men
like Longuet wanted peace at any price. Their acceptance
of Wilsonian war aims was a ruse meant to gain support
for discussion with enemy Socialists. Most odious was their
call for an international general strike and an early end to
the war. Their Bolshevism, moreover, was proven by their
opposition to Allied intervention in Russia. They opposed
it although the Bolsheviks had been exposed as German
agents. They did not make an exception "even for an intervention called for by the Constituent Assembly or the
combined non-Bolshevik parties." Walling was particularly
disturbed to hear Longuet's claim that Woodrow Wilson
sought to recognize the Bolsheviks. Longuet's misunderstanding was due to a literal reading of the Fourteen
Points. Walling correctly pointed out that Wilson did not
intend to seek a *modus vivendi* with the Bolshevik
regime.[75]

The Administration's basic agreement with Walling's
conservative orientation was made known by Lansing.
After reading the memorandum, the Secretary of State
thanked Walling and told him he had studied it "with the
greatest interest and with much profit. It is," Lansing
wrote, "a very clear exposition of the situation."[76]

Walling's exposition was challenged by those who still
sought to unite the Allied Left behind the war, under the
guidance of Wilsonian ideals. Writing to Joseph Grew,
William C. Bullitt took up the assumptions shared by Walling and Lansing. "Neither the calm assurances of the

[74] *Ibid.*
[75] *Ibid.*
[76] Lansing to Walling, October 3, 1918, *ibid.*

Embassies . . . that the pacifist-socialists are unimportant, nor the alarmist opinion of Mr. Walling that they are exceedingly dangerous seems to me to be true," Bullitt wrote. He agreed that the Labour Party, the Longuet group in France, and the Italian Socialist Party were "all so powerful" that their reactions had to be considered when planning diplomatic moves. But Bullitt still believed that so "long as the President follows his clear liberal policy . . . they will stay in line."[77] Bullitt's emphasis was not to be pursued by the Administration. Nevertheless, he had given an insight into why the Administration attached so much importance to the services of the pro-war Socialists.

Bullitt also challenged Walling's reportage of the Inter-Allied Conference. Walling neglected to point out, as Bullitt accurately reported, that the meeting adopted a motion opposing immediate convocation of an inter-belligerent Socialist conference. As for calling Longuet a Bolshevik and an advocate of peace at any price, Bullitt pointed to the evaluation presented by the entire SDL mission. They had noted that Longuet hoped only for revolution in Germany, and wanted favorable Allied military movement to be used to negotiate a peace. Quoting Algie Simons, Bullitt wrote that Longuet had stated only that he believed that " 'the workers should not rely on governments and should work through an International Socialist Conference.' " Moreover, the SDL had reported that Longuet was " 'doubtful of his position.' "[78]

Bullitt himself had been told by a member of the SDL mission that he had "gained a favorable impression of Longuet," and that the French Socialist had denounced the position taken by the American Socialist Party. Walling had refused to publish his remarks because he wanted no endorsements of Longuet presented in America. Bullitt agreed with the SDL's contention that imminent Allied victory was causing the so-called pacifists to modify their position. Walling, he argued, took his evidence of "defeatism" from positions espoused before August. As long as

[77] Bullitt to Grew, October 7, 1918, NA, RG 59, 763.72119 So/81.
[78] *Ibid.*

Wilson followed a liberal policy, Bullitt concluded, there
would be no upheaval in France, England or Italy. "For
the moving spirit of the radical movements in all those
countries is distrust of the intentions of Lloyd George,
Clemenceau and Sonnino." Only if the United States did
not remain true to its ideals would trouble arise. If one
hint occurred that the war was being fought for imperialist
purposes, there would take place "just the upheaval which
Mr. Walling fears."[79]

Bullitt and Spargo were more accurate observers of
Allied Socialist politics than Walling and Gompers. The
forces that the AFL attacked were only moderate Centrists
who looked to Woodrow Wilson for leadership, and who
were fighting domestic revolutionaries as fiercely as they
did their own Allied governments. But the observations of
men like Bullitt were undercut by the Administration's
reluctance to forge any alliance with moderate Socialists.
Wilson preferred to maintain his ties with the existing
leadership of the Allied governments, and to use American
pressure to obtain a moderated peace.

Spargo and his associates had avoided the difficulty
encountered by Gompers. They had been able to communicate with their counterparts among Allied labor. The gap
had widened, however, between the Social-Democratic
League and the more radical Allied Socialists. Ramsay Mac-
Donald, head of the Independent Labour Party, doubted
the SDL mission's claim of independence. How, he asked,
had they received passports? "When Spargo and his friends
came here," MacDonald wrote Adolph Germer, "we were
very anxious to hear what they had to say, and I did what
I could to let them put their case before my friends, as we
are always anxious to hear and discuss every point of
view." The IPL stated their views to the SDL Mission. They
were surprised to find that the League then sent "an un-
truthful letter to the newspapers in which our views were
misrepresented and our confidence dishonorably betrayed." The SDL, MacDonald assured Germer, "had no
influence." It "impressed nobody," and every "half penny

[79] *Ibid.*

spent by it was wasted." Its statements were "absolutely unreliable."[80]

MacDonald's attack indicated that the League had not succeeded in its attempt to convey its independence from the Administration. The SDL tried to tell Allied Socialists that American radicals wholeheartedly supported the war effort, and that the Social-Democratic League represented American Socialists. The Allied Socialists all knew, however, that the American Socialist Party had passed a strong anti-war manifesto, and that its leaders were not allowed to travel to Europe to confer with Allied Socialists. The attempt of the SDL members to portray themselves as the legitimate representatives of American radicalism was more than inept.

The more sophisticated SDL members, especially John Spargo, staked success on their ability to help consolidate a Wilson–social democratic solidarity. Had the Wilson Administration opted for the approach taken by men like Colonel Edward M. House and William C. Bullitt, the SDL might have appeared as architects of American foreign policy. The House policy of uniting the Allied Left behind the war, under the guidance of Wilsonian anti-imperialist values, had been rejected. House desired to control the Allied Left and keep them loyal to the Entente, by putting his stress on war aims revision. Bullitt added to this approach by suggesting that the Administration could act most effectively against Bolshevism by offering support to the moderate Socialists in the Allied bloc. Such a policy had also been suggested by Ray Stannard Baker. But Wilson always came back to the policy pursued by Secretary of State Robert Lansing. From the start of his term in

[80] MacDonald to Germer, October 31, 1918, Simons MSS. See Germer to Morris Hillquit, October 11, 1918, Morris Hillquit MSS, State Historical Society of Wisconsin, Madison, Wis. Germer wrote to "forestall" any move by Spargo to have SDL members represent American Socialists at any inter-allied Socialist meetings. Word "should be sent to the comrades in the different countries," Germer wrote, "impressing upon them the fact that Spargo and his alleged Socialist organization do not represent the Socialist movement of this country." Germer saw great danger in "the Spargoes being recognized as the Socialist movement here."

office, Lansing feared any class politics and favored complete separation of Wilsonianism from all forms of Socialist anti-imperialism.

Woodrow Wilson himself feared antagonizing the Allied
governments by entering into the type of association favored by House and Bullitt. While he may have been sympathetic to the internal conditions that motivated the anti-
imperialist spirit among European masses, Wilson had
decided to avoid any direct appeals to European workers
and Socialists on behalf of his European program. He
sought to minimize—rather than exacerbate—any latent
class conflict that might arise among Allied groups that
had contact with Wilson. Under these conditions, the propaganda of the Social-Democratic League was as misleading
as that offered by Gompers and the various AFL missions.
For the SDL members were holding out the promise of a
Wilson-Socialist alliance that was never to take place. The
Administration had moved behind the rigid policy espoused by Robert Lansing, and rejected compromise with
any form of class radicalism. From this perspective, the
bitter attacks on Spargo that emanated from William English Walling become comprehensible. Walling was certainly dogmatic; his interpretation of policy, however, was
accurate. Walling's line of thought, not Spargo's, represented the tone of Administration policy.

At the same time, the Wilson Administration saw no
harm in using the services of Spargo and his associates.
While they understood that Spargo held illusory beliefs
about Administration policy, the Administration welcomed
their attempts to build up support for a pro-war policy. As
long as the SDL mission favored a policy of military victory, their efforts could be subsidized. The other pro-Socialist nuances of the mission members could be tolerated—
and ignored. The real beneficiary of the SDL work was the
Wilson Administration. Woodrow Wilson had gained the
services of a talented, if small, body of men. They would
try their best to keep the vacillating Allied Socialist groups
committed to a pro-war course. Possibly, Wilson hoped,
they would be more successful than Samuel Gompers. The

use of American Socialists by Administration officials, so common in the 1950's and '60's, had been instituted with skill by the Wilson Administration. The "responsible" anti-revolutionary Socialist, who opposes revolution and praises moderation, had become the welcome ally of conservative American administrations. Their use in the future by various American governments was a continuation of the policy instituted during the first great war.

CHAPTER

VIII

JOHN SPARGO

AND AMERICA'S RUSSIAN

POLICY [*]

Like their associates in the American Federation of Labor, the pro-war Socialists also adopted a hostile attitude toward Bolshevism. The Bolsheviks had from the start denounced the basic philosophy of the moderate Socialists. After they successfully took power in Russia, they revealed their opposition to bourgeois democracy by ruthless abrogation of the Constituent Assembly. Later, the Bolsheviks showed their contempt for the Allied struggle against Germany, when they signed a separate peace treaty with the Kaiser. Brest-Litovsk, the members of the Social-Democratic League claimed, threatened the Allies with a possible German military victory. Since victory against the Kaiser was the *raison d'être* of the pro-war Socialists, their attitude toward Bolshevism was partially conditioned by Lenin's refusal to keep Russia in the war.

With the failure of intervention, the Wilson Administration sought new means of dealing with the continued viability of Bolshevik Russia. Once again Woodrow Wilson

[*] Portions of this chapter appeared in slightly different form as "John Spargo and Wilson's Russian Policy, 1920," *Journal of American History*, LII (1965), 548–65.

saw a possible use to which the pro-war Socialists could be put. Many of the old SDL group, like William English Walling and Algie M. Simons, had severed their Socialist connections since the war's end. Walling had drawn close to Samuel Gompers, and was now functioning as the key adviser to the AFL. Only John Spargo still considered himself a Socialist. Once the war was over, Spargo saw no reason for continued restrictions on civil liberties. Woodrow Wilson's refusal to pardon Eugene V. Debs, along with dissatisfaction about the outcome of Versailles, led Spargo to share in the growing postwar disillusion. The Wilson Administration "has become reactionary," Spargo wrote in 1920, "and deserves no support from any of us."[1]

Spargo's opposition to the Wilson Administration, as sincere as it may have been, was short-lived. Wilson had arranged to convene the First Industrial Conference for the purpose of trying to reach "some common ground of agreement and action with regard to the future conduct of industry." John Spargo had proved his usefulness to Wilson during the war, and he had come to hold more influence with the government than other pro-war Socialists. Possibly hoping to prevent Spargo from becoming an opponent of his Administration, Wilson appointed Spargo to sit alongside John D. Rockefeller, Jr., Bernard Baruch, and Judge Elbert Gary as a representative of the "public" group at the Conference.

At the meeting, Spargo revealed how far he had strayed from orthodox Marxism. Calling himself a Socialist, he pointed out that "I did not for a moment indulge the hope or the thought that through this conference we could change the existing social order." Spargo pledged that he would not seek to introduce "any socialist aim, or any socialist effort." It was necessary for a Rockefeller at one end of the social order and a Spargo at the other to "unite in a common policy here and now." In the interest of stabilizing American life Spargo came to "utter here a word of regret

---

[1] Spargo to J. G. Phelps Stokes, January 29, 1920, J. G. Phelps Stokes MSS, Butler Library, Columbia University.

against class consciousness" in either the Left or the Right. The United States, he stated, could not "afford to be divided in itself if she is to prevail in the great onward march of the nations."[2]

Spargo gave adequate proof that he still opposed the type of class-conscious politics favored by the regular Socialists who had continued to function as opponents of Wilsonian liberalism. By 1920 Wilson frequently sought Spargo's advice and aid in the formulation of American policy. The alliance forged between pro-war Socialists such as Spargo and statesmen such as Robert Lansing and Bainbridge Colby flowed from a coalescence of views about the necessity of defeating foreign radicalism. Within this framework Spargo came to identify with the problems of an expanding capitalist market and to view Bolshevism not only as a moral wrong but as a threat to American prosperity.

Spargo pointed to the great Russian land mass as perhaps America's greatest potential market and asked whether the United States wanted this great "volume of trade." The answer: America was a great manufacturing nation; productive capacity had increased under pressure of wartime demand; and if America was to hold the gains made, it could not be "indifferent to such a demand as must come from Russia. Unless we can find markets capable of absorbing the vast surplus of our manufactures, we must quickly pass into a period of prolonged industrial depression."

Spargo did not view it as a contradiction for a self-proclaimed Socialist to urge the acquisition of new foreign markets for American industry. "We are a capitalist nation," he wrote, "living in a capitalist world, in an era of capitalization. Some of us believe that another form of society would be better. . . . In the meantime, however, only visionaries and addle-pated chatterers profess to be indifferent to the success or failure of our capitalist enterprises." If the Russian foreign market was closed to Amer-

[2] *Proceedings of the First Industrial Conference* (Washington, D.C., 1920), pp. 147–48.

ican trade, the result would be unemployment for American workers. Therefore trade with Russia, essential for that nation's regeneration, was a social question of immense importance for Americans. The United States could supply the machinery and manufactured goods which Russia needed in order to live as a civilized nation. Spargo spoke of Russia's reconstruction as basically an "American problem."[3]

In a memorandum on Russian policy, Spargo told Secretary of State Lansing in November 1919 that his information pointed to "the early dissolution of Bolshevist rule." He stressed that Germany was working for restoration of the economic supremacy she had enjoyed in European Russia before the Armistice, and that if she and Japan gained control of Russia's economic life, American development would be hindered. The United States had to be prudent in a situation where Japan was actively seeking control of the Bering coast and Japanese interest in Kamchatka challenged American hegemony over Alaska. More important, if the Russian market were secured, American industries would be kept going at full capacity. It was therefore desirable that the United States rather than Germany or Japan control this great volume of trade. Russia was thus an American problem, and indeed "with the exception of our domestic industrial problem, it is the greatest problem now confronting the American people." Spargo urged Lansing to give vigorous support to anti-Bolshevik forces within Russia. Even if the triumph of the armies of Deniken, Yudenitch, and Kolchak "should bring about the creation of a reactionary regime in Russia," Spargo believed it "necessary to overthrow the Bolsheviki that fact notwithstanding."[4]

[3] John Spargo, "Russia's Reconstruction as an American Problem," typewritten manuscript, February 1920, Spargo MSS, Wilbur Library, University of Vermont.

[4] Spargo to Lansing, November 4, 1919, and Spargo, "Memorandum on the Russian Situation, Political and Economic," NA, RG 59, 861.00/5577.

Correspondence in the Spargo MSS indicates that Spargo took a different position when talking to his Socialist associates. William J. Robinson asked Spargo how a "half-way decent man could for a

Spargo also emphasized the need to oppose the dismemberment of Russia, and he greeted with admiration Lansing's action in refusing to recognize the Provisional Government of Lithuania. Without the existence of a unified Russian republic, American economic enterprise would be circumscribed and subject to limitations. Opposing those "short-sighted" people who urged recognition of the independent republics, Spargo predicted that when Russia was restored to its health and power, Lansing's policy would prove to be "one of the most important acts of constructive statesmanship of this very trying and difficult period."[5]

---

moment support Kolchak, Deniken or Yudenitch. They belong to the worst of vilest murderers and cut-throats that reaction has produced." (Robinson to Spargo, March 18, 1920, Spargo MSS).

Spargo answered Robinson's criticism by claiming that various Russian liberals and Socialists had told him that Kolchak was a democrat who held no political ambition. His only concern was freedom for Russia and restoration of the Constituent Assembly. Spargo, in fact, claimed that Kolchak's instincts were with the Socialists, not the reactionaries. It was this instinct of Kolchak which led Aksentiev, a Russian Socialist leader, to ask Spargo as an American Socialist to lend Kolchak his support and to urge the Allied governments to give him assistance (Spargo to Robinson, March 23, 1920, *ibid.*).

Robinson was not convinced by Spargo's answer. He ended the short debate by telling Spargo that Kolchak's men were the worst Czarist and reactionary forces, and that it was their brutality as well as Trotsky's genius and the idealism of the Bolshevik army that led to their defeat. Robinson once again expressed disbelief that a liberal or radical could "support the counter-revolutionary movements in Russia which caused untold woe and indescribable misery" (Robinson to Spargo, March 25, 1920, *ibid.*).

Other pro-war Socialists split along the same lines. While J. G. Phelps Stokes supported intervention in Russia, Upton Sinclair took a position similar to Robinson's. "Without realizing it," he wrote Stokes, "you are allying yourself with Universal Reaction. . . . If Kolchak ever gets into Russia, he will kill twenty people for every one the Bolsheviki have killed, and he will settle complete reaction on Russia for a generation." Sinclair agreed that the social revolution in Russia did not work out "the way either you or I wanted it to do so," but he felt that it had to be let alone to "quickly correct its own errors" (Sinclair to Stokes, June 17, 1919, Stokes MSS).

[5] Spargo to Robert Lansing, February 11, 1920, NA, RG 59, 860M.01/39. For Spargo's complete view on dismemberment, see Spargo, "Russia's Dismemberment: A World Menace," typewritten manuscript, Spargo MSS.

Lansing welcomed Spargo's support. The Secretary stated that opposition to dismemberment was "the only sound and sensible policy" and that the President held the same view.[6] He wrote Spargo that no letter had given him more pleasure than the memorandum on Russian policy, and that the American people would "in the future recognize how much you did in their behalf." [7]

Spargo carried his analysis straight to Wilson, and on March 19, 1920, he asked the President to accept his aid "in the development of a policy which will, in measure, fulfill your own ideal." Spargo urged that the United States assure Russia that she would not be forced to accept a form of government against her will and that the United States desired to assist Russia and to protect her against exploiters. The organization of an expert group to formulate policy on economic relations with Russia was necessary to achieve this goal. Only trade would permit Russia's recovery, and an American commerce board would have to provide initial government loans and develop other sources of investment from private industry.

This board would buy all supplies for Russia available in the United States and sell in the market whatever Russia had to export to the United States. It would receive and hold all concessions and securities which Russia would offer on a credit basis. American manufacturers would be relieved of having to demand extortionate prices which accompany poorly secured credit, and Russia would be protected against vicious exploitation since the board would act as a "friendly trustee" holding concessions, revenues, and secured pledges to be redeemed by surplus Russian production. Spargo argued that such a policy would be met with joy by the anti-Bolshevik Russians and would demonstrate that the United States was sincerely a friend of Russia. The policy would avert economic domination of Russia by Germany and Japan and bring about

[6] Lansing to Spargo, February 23, 1920, *ibid.*
[7] Lansing to Spargo, February 21, 1920, *ibid.*

stabilization of economic conditions in Europe and the United States.[8]

By the President's direction, the memorandum was forwarded to the Department of State for consideration.[9] The new Secretary of State, Bainbridge Colby, told Spargo that he had read the memorandum to the President "with great interest," and he expressed his desire to see Spargo any time that he came to Washington.[10] Spargo's opportunity to present a policy of "constructive" action was not far away.

Upon learning of Colby's appointment, Spargo expressed his pleasure that the Department of State was in the hands of one who could "see the soul of Russia amid the weltering chaos" and had "the good-will to aid in her restoration."[11] By June Colby had read excerpts of Spargo's book, *Russia as an American Problem,* and had responded to it favorably. "Your reasoning," Colby wrote, "is as tight and close as that of a first-class lawyer, and your use of citations gives your chapters the power of a brief." Evidently Colby shared Spargo's views. He ended by requesting a conference on the question of trade with Russia.[12]

Within a month Colby had come to rely on Spargo to articulate Russian policy. On July 31 Spargo warned Colby of the threat of Japanese expansion in Siberia. This letter, along with a draft statement of policy which he enclosed, was to become Colby's famous policy note of August 10, 1920. Spargo was concerned about Japanese occupation of Russian Sakhalin and of Siberia east of Lake Baikal. He believed that large deposits of coal and oil in northern Sakhalin would sorely tempt Japan, and that it was sheer nonsense to assume that Japan's sole interest in eastern Siberia was to find an outlet for surplus population. The Japanese government's expansion was motivated by political and military desires, specifically the strategic impor-

8 Spargo to Wilson, March 19, 1920, NA, RG 59, 861.00/6610.
9 Joseph P. Tumulty to Spargo, March 22, 1920, Spargo MSS.
10 Colby to Spargo, March 22, 1920, *ibid.*
11 Spargo to Colby, February 26, 1920, *ibid.*
12 Colby to Spargo, June 8, 1920, *ibid.*

tance of territory between Lake Baikal and the Pacific. Like England and France, Japan was using Russia's weakness to extend her own economic power, and Spargo urged that the United States proclaim that such aggression against Russia's interests would be met with great disfavor. Moreover, he warned that since American and British naval bases were so far from Japan, which might become an active enemy of the United States, it was necessary to stop that country from preventing Russian-American cooperation or from prohibiting receipt of supplies from Russian ports in the Pacific.

Spargo desired that the United States make a clear statement of its entire policy toward Russia, rather than rely on fragmentary responses. It was imperative that a general statement, perhaps in the form of a letter of instruction to diplomatic and consular agents, be issued. Specifically, Spargo argued that the government must give complete information on its Russian policy or forfeit its role as a world power; that smaller nations surrounding Russia and Poland could not formulate policy until the United States had revealed its approach; and that the Lloyd George and Alexandre Millerand "intrigues" with Lenin harmed the true democratic interests of Russia and other nations. Anglo-French imperialism could sow "a vast crop of dragons' teeth for hideous harvests" unless American leadership was asserted. It was "monstrous" that the United States would not be represented in the coming international conference over Russia and Poland.

Spargo realized that the coming presidential campaign disposed the Administration to inaction. But a policy statement would both help the campaign and make it impossible for general issues to take precedence over the Russian question. Moreover, a policy statement would have the effect of placing before Senator Warren G. Harding, should he be elected, "a *fait accompli* not to be lightly or easily undone or reversed." Spargo warned that Harding meant to reverse America's policy toward the Soviets, and that if elected he would recognize the Soviet regime and adopt the Lloyd George attitude. If Wilson wanted "to place his work beyond the possibility of its undoing" it would be necessary to confront Harding with a strong, irreversible statement of policy.[13]

Before the Department of State received Spargo's plea, it had already decided to ask his help. On August 1 John A. Gade, chief of the Department's Division of Russian Affairs, wrote Spargo that "a clear definite Russian policy" had to be presented at an early date "by those best fitted to advise. And no one has a clearer judgment than you. We cannot afford to wait long after Lloyd George with Clemenceau in his pocket has come to some understanding" with the Soviets. Gade asked Spargo if he would be willing "to frame such a policy" and come first to New York for conferences and then proceed to Washington.[14]

Spargo answered that Gade's proposal gave him the greatest pleasure, especially if they were in substantial agreement regarding details. He expressed the view that it was unfortunate that there should be such little chance of a comprehensive statement coming from Washington before the new conference with the Soviet, British, French, and Italian representatives took place. A statement "*could* be made, and would have the effect of preventing commitments by the European powers concerned." In the absence of a forceful statement, other nations would ask the United States to define its position, and the Department of State would have to reply. Such a reply should take up the attitude of the United States toward Russia, Poland, and the border states in a candid and comprehensive fashion. "Unless we can exert whatever influence we may have," Spargo wrote, "we shall miss a very big opportunity," and Colby would miss his best chance to associate his name with a "great State paper and policy of epochal importance." Spargo contended that the United States should not only decline to have any relations with the Soviet government but should go farther and say that "other governments should agree to a similar course." In Spargo's eyes,

    [13] Spargo to Colby, July 31, 1920, Bainbridge Colby MSS, Library of Congress.
    [14] Gade to Spargo, August 1, 1920, Spargo MSS.

Lenin's approach and Bolshevik logic itself made Russia "an outlaw nation."

Spargo also argued that the United States should continue to oppose dismemberment of Russia and manifest sincere friendship for Poland, but it should state its opposition to any attempted Polish aggression beyond lines set by the Versailles Treaty. "Opposition to any attack against the territory of the old Russian empire," Spargo continued, "would hasten the disintegration of Bolshevism by weaning from the regime those non-Bolshevist elements which for nationalistic reasons naturally gave it support." Finally, Spargo believed that the policy paper should be a definite appeal to the non-Bolshevik Russians. The United States would recognize Russia's absolute right to choose any form of government she desired provided such a government was established by a freely elected constituent assembly. The need for equal trading opportunity would be stressed and the desire of the United States to give assistance toward economic restoration would be acknowledged. Such a program might give the anti-Bolshevik Russians something to work and hope for, and thus weaken the Bolshevist hold. Direct military attack was rejected by Spargo on the grounds that an army powerful enough to liberate Russia from the Bolsheviks could not be raised.

Thus Spargo had set before Gade suggestions for the main line of policy. He urged Gade to prepare his own draft for consideration, promised that he would independently prepare a new draft, and that both should then be considered without prejudice. Spargo was concerned that he had so defined his own views that it would be hard for Gade to make a fresh statement. He nevertheless agreed to go to Washington with both drafts. "Only one thing would I urge," Spargo concluded, "we must not delay a moment longer than is absolutely necessary."[15]

Events moved too fast for Spargo and Gade to meet. On

[15] Spargo to Gade, August 3, 1920, enclosed with Gade to Colby, Colby MSS. Gade enclosed Spargo's letter along with his own draft of a policy note, indicating that he had received Spargo's letter after writing his own statement.

August 3, the same day on which Spargo had written his reply to the Under Secretary, the Italian Ambassador at Washington, Baron Camillo Avezzano, wrote Norman H. Davis of the Department of State that the precarious situation in Europe made it of great importance that his government be informed of the point of view of the United States. Avezzano said he would be grateful for any information and would personally come to confer with Colby or Davis if so requested.[16]

When the Secretary of the Italian Embassy delivered the note to Davis, he stated that the Ambassador had requested him to inform the United States that Italy felt the moral influence of the United States would effectively clarify the situation regarding Poland and Russia if it would only "define its view." The Italian government made clear that it would not only welcome a statement of American policy but would "be glad to cooperate." Davis told the Secretary that the United States had not decided whether it would make a statement, but it had "little or no confidence in the wisdom of negotiating with the Bolshevists or the possibility of making any arrangements with them which can be depended upon."[17]

Davis' response was similar to Spargo's. Davis asked Colby to lay particular stress on the maintenance of both Polish and Russian integrity. The United States could indirectly criticize Polish aggression by stating its opposition to the extension of Polish boundaries beyond those accorded by Versailles, while making clear its equal opposition to violation of Polish integrity. Davis agreed that the United States would have to reiterate its reasons for refusing to negotiate with Russia or to recognize the Soviet regime as well as its reasons for opposing dismemberment or aggression within Russian territory, actions which would "merely crystallize the national spirit which is now bolstering Bolshevism." Davis wanted Colby to stress that Russia be allowed to establish whatever form of government the

[16] Camillo Avezzano to Norman H. Davis, August 3, 1920, *ibid.*
[17] Memorandum of a conversation with the Secretary of the Italian Embassy, Norman H. Davis, August 5, 1920, *ibid.*

majority of her people might select, and that America refused to deal with the current Soviet regime because Bolshevism was the rule of a "murderous minority" that did not represent the free will of the Russian people. Davis ruled out the possibility of any coexistence between the two systems: "It is utterly impossible for two systems based on such diametrically opposed principles to work in peace and harmony."[18]

The need for a policy statement had been made clear. Spargo had no time to compose a new draft or to confer with Gade about its contents. Gade notified Spargo that a message had to be sent immediately, and that he was forced to submit his own recommendations at once. Gade assured Spargo he had covered all the points the letter had made, and that he had passed Spargo's letter on to Colby.[19] It was up to Colby to decide whose draft he would use for the policy note.

The Gade draft was rejected; no part of it was used in the policy note.[20] As finally delivered, the Colby Note contained the bulk of Spargo's statement of July 31. Aside from the introductory and concluding paragraphs which Colby composed, another short paragraph in the middle of the text, and minor changes in grammar, the note was taken word for word from Spargo's draft.[21] The Department of State had welcomed and accepted Spargo's aid and advice precisely because his passion against Bolshe-

[18] Davis to Colby, August 7, 1920, *ibid.*

[19] Gade to Spargo, August 9, 1920, Spargo MSS.

[20] John A. Gade, "Memorandum for the Undersecretary of State, Subject: America's Russian Policy," August 9, 1920, Colby MSS.

[21] Spargo, "Memorandum on Russian Policy," deposited with envelope containing material relating to the Colby Note, Colby MSS. On separate paper Colby wrote in longhand the few paragraphs he was to insert in the final note, and crossed out sections to be deleted from Spargo's original draft. Colby eliminated one extensive section pertaining to the disadvantages of trading with the Soviet regime. While Spargo's memorandum has no date on it, it is clearly the one he submitted to Colby on July 31. The memorandum may be found in the separate envelope kept by Colby which contains all material pertaining directly to the note. The letter of July 31 is not attached to it and is in the proper chronological section of the Colby MSS.

vism was so strongly developed. Frustrated in their own
attempts to rid the world of the Bolshevik scourge, men
like Colby must have believed that the advice of one so
thoroughly schooled in Socialist politics would have more
chance of success.

The note, issued on August 10, 1920, expressed solici-
tude for the maintenance of Poland's "political independence and territorial integrity," and stated that while the
United States took no exception to the effort being made
to arrange an armistice between Poland and Russia, it
would not favor the expansion of these negotiations into
a general European conference. Such a meeting would lead
to recognition of the Bolshevik regime and a settlement of
the Russian problem on the basis of dismemberment,
events from which "this country strongly recoils."

The note also asserted that there was no common
ground upon which the United States could stand with
Russia, for the United States could not hold official relations with "the agents of a government which is determined and bound to conspire against our institutions,
whose diplomats will be the agitators of dangerous revolt."
Recognition of the Soviet regime could not lead to friendly
relations, for that regime was based "upon the negation of
every principle of honor and good faith . . . upon which it
is possible to base harmonious and trustful relations."[22]
With this note, which one historian has called "the most
comprehensive exposition of the attitude of the Wilson
Administration toward Russia," Spargo gave expression to
and codified the existing American policy toward Soviet
Russia.[23] Colby sent the final draft to President Wilson on
August 9. The note, he pointed out, had a weakness in that
it did not say what the United States would do; and it was
also quite long, "but there is a reason for saying almost
everything it contains. I hope you will not find it altogether
inadequate." Wilson returned the note the same day,

[22] These quotations are taken from the final version of the note,
signed by Colby on August 9, 1920, and released the next day.
Colby MSS.

[23] Robert Paul Browder, *The Origins of Soviet-American Diplomacy* (Princeton, N.J., 1953), pp. 16–17.

briefly inscribing: "Thank you. This seems to me excellent and sufficient."[24]

Spargo himself viewed the note "as one of the most important diplomatic documents of the post-war period." With the "great documents announcing the Monroe Doctrine and the 'open-door' policy," Spargo wrote, "the historian of America's foreign policy must henceforth include Secretary Colby's Russian note."[25] Rarely, perhaps, has the author of a policy note had the opportunity to comment on his own work in such an immodest manner. In reality Colby's note only verbalized the policy that had been followed by Wilson since the outbreak of the Bolshevik Revolution. What is of some significance is the role Spargo played in enunciating the framework of American anti-Bolshevik policy, and the consensus between former Socialists like Spargo and Administration statesmen like Colby about the nature of American policy toward the Soviets.

With tongue in cheek Spargo congratulated Colby on "how splendid I feel your Note to be" and on how admirably Colby "united a wise and just appreciation of Poland's interests to an equally wise and just appreciation of the interests of Russia."[26] When newspapers criticized the policy, Spargo took pen in hand and used his avowed Socialist views to justify and draw support for the note. To the *New York Tribune*, he wrote: "I am not a thick-and-thin supporter of the Administration. Upon many points I have criticized it without mincing words. A Socialist (though perhaps of a rather pale pink shade!) who is none the less a Socialist for being detached from the Socialist Party," Spargo urged the destruction of Bolshevism as the "supreme task of civilization." Colby's policy was the "most efficient single force recently directed" toward that end.

---

[24] Colby to Wilson, August 9, 1920; notation from Woodrow Wilson inscribed on the returned Colby letter, August 9, 1920, Colby MSS.

[25] John Spargo, "Bainbridge Colby," in Samuel Flagg Bemis, ed., *The American Secretaries of State and Their Diplomacy* (10 vols.; New York, 1927–1929), X, 200–01.

[26] Spargo to Colby, August 14, 1920, Colby MSS.

Polish aggression against Russia would result only in a
Bolshevist uprising in Poland, and Colby's statesmanship
could prevent such an occurrence.[27] With his own author-
ship of the note and his tie to the Administration a carefully guarded secret, Spargo was able to adopt the pose of
an independent Socialist who merely argued the need to
support what he felt was a correct Administration policy.

Those who knew that Spargo wrote the Colby Note expressed a candid appreciation for his efforts. Major Stanley
Washburn wrote asking Spargo to "accept my congratula-
tions for the excellent note which you wrote for Mr. Colby.
. . . It seems to me quite the most important document
which has been issued from the State Department in many
years." As if to cast aspersion on Spargo's earlier Socialist
Party activity, Washburn added that Spargo's contributions in the past two years "have more than justified all
the efforts you have made . . . for the last twenty years."[28]

Spargo and Colby were not content to let the Russian
question rest after the note was issued. No sooner was it
off the State desk than Spargo convinced Colby to take
"constructive" action to back it up. Spargo believed that a
new course of action was necessary to bring Russia back
into the family of nations. Since the Bolsheviks faced a
crisis which would force them to accommodate to the
American position, he proposed a policy to be put into
effect through the agency of the Swedish Social Democratic Premier, Hjalmar Branting. According to Spargo's

[27] Spargo to the *New York Tribune*, August 28, 1920, *ibid*.
[28] Washburn to Spargo, August 28, 1920, Spargo MSS. To Washburn, Spargo answered that he hoped "you were only joking when
you suggested that I wrote it 'for Mr. Colby.' Fortunately, the present
Secretary of State doesn't have to have anything written for him."
Adding that if his efforts had helped "to crystallize opinion and to
produce more tangible results," he would be "more than gratified,"
Spargo cautioned Washburn that "it would do our cause some harm
if that influence were much emphasized," and that "there is some
element of danger in suggesting that I wrote the document referred
to." (Spargo to Washburn, August 30, 1920, Stanley Washburn
MSS, Library of Congress.) The "danger" was that this knowledge
would detract from the authority of the message and would weaken
Spargo's pose as an independent Socialist who merely agreed with
Wilsonian policy.

plan, Branting would address both the Soviet government and the United States in a state message, offering a program for the voluntary liquidation of the Bolshevik regime and the formation of a new Russian republic. If the proposal was agreed to by Lenin, the West would offer assurance that the new Russian government would be recognized, that the principle of non-interference in their internal affairs would be honored, and that comprehensive economic assistance would be offered. Spargo was able to give Branting a pledge that Wilson would respond affirmatively to the suggestions if the Swedish Premier agreed to offer them to the world as his own policy.[29]

Spargo and Colby showed extreme naïveté in their belief that a crude American policy statement, which attempted to offer an obviously American creation as the independent view of the Swedish government, would result in voluntary liquidation of Bolshevik rule. Whether Wilson fully endorsed Spargo's plan is not known, but he did agree to send Spargo to Sweden to try to carry it out. Spargo was to tell Branting that he could frame the actual statement in his own words, with full assurance that Wilson would publicly issue a favorable response. "We had reversed the usual procedure," Spargo recalled, "here was a reply drafted prior to the request."[30]

On August 25 Spargo sent Colby a draft of the message he hoped Branting would adopt. The use of Branting, Spargo explained, "was the surest way to create a big diversion in the labor forces of Europe." Millerand, the French Socialist leader, would have to support the note because he also was demanding a constituent assembly in Russia as a prerequisite to support of the Russian government. By deferring the question of debts owed by Russia to the new constituent government, the French would gain the victory they wanted on that question. The program to be offered was meant to rally non-Bolshevik Russians and to be so democratic that domestic American liberals would find it difficult to oppose. If Branting finally refused to

[29] Spargo, "Bainbridge Colby," in Bemis, *op. cit.*, pp. 206–07.
[30] Spargo, COHC, 343.

issue the appeal, Spargo suggested that Colby draw up a
new statement and issue it in the name of the United
States government.[31]

To Ambassador Brand Whitlock in Belgium, Spargo
urged that the time was opportune to bring the Russian
situation "to a definite head" and that a possibility existed
for bringing about the final "pacification" of that "unhappy
country." Enclosing a draft of the statement he was asking
Branting to issue, Spargo informed Whitlock that upon its
issuance the United States would signify complete acceptance, while efforts would be made to gain British and
French approval in advance. Even though the Soviets had
rejected it, the note might have split their own forces and
rallied other Russian elements. Spargo asked Whitlock to
go to Stockholm and "try to persuade M. Branting to act
at once." Whitlock was to inform Branting that the only
reason the United States offered a text which was already
drawn up was to ensure a favorable world reception.
Spargo stressed, however, that Branting be forbidden to
make "serious changes in the suggested program without
reference back for further consideration."[32] In the proposed note, Spargo would have Branting support the Colby
Note as a document which opened the way for future cooperation between the United States and a democratic
Russian republic. Branting was to ask the Russians to
agree to a freely elected constituent assembly, the creation
of local assemblies, freedom for all political parties, and
acceptance of the new assembly's decisions in exchange
for the act of political recognition from the Western
nations.[33]

In late September Spargo himself departed for Sweden
to handle the negotiations with Branting. He found the
Premier in accord and enthusiastic, so he reported, but
fearful that other cabinet members would consider the
step too momentous for their country to undertake. Seeking to convince Branting that immediate American ap-

[31] Spargo to Colby, August 25, 1920, Colby MSS.
[32] Memo to Whitlock, n.d. [Summer 1920], Spargo MSS.
[33] "Proposed Draft of Letter," n.d., *ibid*.

proval robbed this consideration of its force, Spargo argued that Sweden too would enjoy an "open door for Russia without concessions or exclusive monopolistic privileges." Branting protested that the Colby Note had upset Swedish plans by making impossible the proposed recognition of Estonia, and he feared that this might color the attitude of Swedish officials toward the suggested policy statement.[34]

In early October, after reading the proposed statement, Branting wrote Spargo that he could not agree to the role assigned him. It was insane to believe that the Bolsheviks would consent to call together a constituent assembly elected by general suffrage, since such methods had been "directly repudiated by them as against their fundamental conceptions and as a bourgeois democratic prejudice." In Europe, he warned, such an appeal would be met with astonishment. The desired pronouncement was "coloured so openly by a special American point of view" that all would realize it did not originate from a statesman representing a small neutral country. It came as no surprise that Foreign Minister Erik Palmstierna sent it back with similar objections, declaring such a step as "absolutely impossible." Branting expressed sorrow at giving Spargo this answer, but he felt it better "to say the truth" without offering excuses.[35]

The fact that such an absurd policy was considered seriously by the Department of State indicates the illusory nature of the view that the Soviet government was bound to collapse. Spargo may have been one step ahead of those who still urged armed intervention against the Soviets, but his differences with that group were only tactical. Spargo's claim that the effort was "well advised" and that it "showed a clear understanding of the Russian situation" as well as holding the "elements of probable success" was unfounded.[36]

[34] Spargo to Colby, September 28, 1920, *ibid.*
[35] Branting to Spargo, October 2, 1920, *ibid.*
[36] Spargo, "Bainbridge Colby," in Bemis, *op. cit.*, p. 208.

Spargo finally claimed that Branting rejected the U.S. proposal for the sake of Swedish national interests, and that the Premier had personally approved the proposal during his first conference with Spargo. It was Social Democratic losses in recent elections that forced him to take the nationalist approach. The United States could urge the French Socialists or the Belgian leader Emil Vandervelde to issue the appeal, but Spargo advised that such a step would be undesirable. An official United States government reply to a policy note of a European Socialist party could only have a detrimental effect on the forthcoming American presidential election.[37]

Branting met once more with Spargo. He then confirmed what Spargo had appraised as his "nationalist" position. Branting reportedly expressed personal agreement with American policy and opposed recognition of the Soviet regime, and differed only in that Branting favored more trade with the Bolsheviks.[38] Spargo returned to the United States, his mission unfulfilled. Nevertheless, Colby was satisfied. He had succeeded in having a prominent Socialist articulate Administration policy in the name of socialism. "I am not too hurried to again say," Colby proclaimed, "what a delight this intellectual intimacy that I have formed with you has been and how valuable a possession and resource I regard it."[39] Of the entire group of pro-war Socialists and labor leaders, it was John Spargo who had been honored by being chosen to help formulate the tactics of official policy.

The failure of the Swedish mission did not deter Spargo from continuing to pursue the underlying objectives of that journey. His original purpose in urging Colby to prepare a policy note, it will be recalled, had been to create an irreversible "*fait accompli*" for Warren Harding,[40] should he win the election and attempt to fulfill his August campaign promise that "there will be none of the present

---

[37] Spargo to Colby, October 3, 1920, Spargo MSS.
[38] Spargo to Colby, October 4, 1920, *ibid*.
[39] Colby to Spargo, November 27, 1920, *ibid*.
[40] Spargo to Colby, July 31, 1920, Colby MSS.

foreign policy if we succeed. On the contrary, there will be a complete reversal." The Republican Party, Harding had stated on August 16, a brief six days after release of the Colby Note on Russia, would "make a very sweeping change in the foreign policies of the nation."[41] Now, with Harding actually elected, Spargo undertook new efforts to ensure the maintenance of Wilson's Russian policy.

To put pressure on the Republican President-elect, Spargo "carried on a quiet campaign which was both extensive and intensive." He first prepared a memorandum on Russian policy to submit to Harding. But before he took that step, Spargo presented his analysis to "a number of [Harding's] friends and party associates," including Nicholas Murray Butler, William Howard Taft, George Wickersham, Henry Cabot Lodge, Elihu Root, and other prominent individuals. The response was favorable, Spargo wrote to Colby. Taft had written that he was sending the memo himself to Harding along "with a note of warm commendation." Butler promised to take up the matter personally with the President. And before Charles Evans Hughes was publicly designated as the new Secretary of State, Spargo received a "cordial note of approval" from him.

As Spargo further recounted to Colby, he carried on an active speaking tour before business groups in Chicago, Cleveland, Toledo, Cincinnati, and other cities in order to "reach a good many of President Harding's personal and political friends." He always emphasized the need to maintain "unimpaired the principles laid down" in the Colby Note. The result, Spargo claimed, was "that some of the President's closest personal and political friends personally assured me that they were going to write to him, urging in the strongest possible manner, the importance of maintaining vigorously and without compromise" the Colby policy of non-recognition. Spargo boasted that he personally knew of five hundred people who as a result of

[41] *New York Times,* August 17, 1920. Cf. Spargo, "Bainbridge Colby," in Bemis, *op. cit.,* pp. 428–29.

his contact with them had written to Harding and Hughes "urging that there be no change in our policy."[42]

Spargo may have exaggerated, but he did succeed in reaching influential government and business figures. William C. Redfield wrote that he was "deeply interested" in Spargo's memorandum and that he was "surprised at the lethargy with which the people most interested treat the whole matter." Redfield informed Spargo that "the radicals will not have a cordial reception from the new administration" but nonetheless he feared that Bolshevik propaganda was far more powerful and widespread than most people realized.[43] Nicholas Murray Butler responded that he agreed with Spargo's position. If Spargo would let him have a copy of the memo, Butler noted that he might "find myself in a position to discuss it with" Harding.[44]

In addition to personal contact, Spargo had addressed the Cleveland Chamber of Commerce "on the subject of post-war conditions and our international policy." Of course the "Russian Question," Spargo wrote to Boris Bakhemeteff, "inevitably looms large in that connection." Spargo felt that the Cleveland group in particular was "an important and influential body" because so many businessmen in that city were "close to Senator Harding." Because of that, Spargo not only presented his case publicly but also arranged "informal conversations with individuals." He was confident that the Soviet regime would not be recognized. Meyer London, a Socialist congressman, was going to introduce a resolution favoring trade with Russia and *de facto* recognition of the Bolshevik government. London's Socialist ties would "inevitably have the effect," Spargo thought, "of creating a certain prejudice against it."[45]

Before submitting his memorandum to Harding, Spargo set the stage for a favorable reception by personally addressing the President-elect after his election victory. On

42 Spargo to Colby, March 22, 1921, Spargo MSS.
43 Redfield to Spargo, December 30, 1920, *ibid.*
44 Butler to Spargo, January 12, 1921, *ibid.*
45 Spargo to Bakhemeteff, December 9, 1920, *ibid.*

the 5th of November, Spargo and Boris Bakhemeteff wrote urging the necessity of developing adequate outlets to absorb the "superfluous wealth of the United States." A strong, united Russia, they pointed out, would be of decisive importance for American economic development. The growth of American foreign trade had not "taken place in the form of colonial expansion," Spargo accurately noted, but rather had occurred by means of securing an "open door" for trade and commerce. In that tradition, Spargo saw Russia as "the greatest promise for American investment." The greater and stronger she remained, Spargo warned, the bigger the investment in Russia could be. German domination of Russia would come about only if the United States followed an incorrect policy and thrust her into Germany's hands.[46]

After sending the letter, Spargo emphasized the need of tying the Russian problem to the general question of European policy. This approach, he hoped, would allow him to avoid the reproach that he was a pro-Russian propagandist. Spargo was particularly concerned with the latter charge because he was in close association with Boris Bakhemeteff, who had been the ambassador to the United States from the defunct Kerensky government. If they emphasized Europe, Spargo hoped, they could gain the support of "a very powerful element, men who will have great influence with Mr. Harding," such as Herbert Hoover and Henry Cabot Lodge.[47]

Bakhemeteff thought that whatever plan Spargo drew up should not be widely circulated, but instead should be used to give Harding the "benefit of being the author of a right policy." Taft and Root would go over the draft of Spargo's plan, Bakhemeteff wrote, and perhaps Hughes and Philander Knox would do the same. These men had to face the "question of persuading the future chief to give all his attention to the problem and to follow the lines suggested." Bakhemeteff hoped that Attorney General Harry M. Daugherty would support them, and that someone in

[46] Spargo and Bakhemeteff to Harding, November 5, 1920, *ibid.*
[47] Spargo to Bakhemeteff, December 17, 1920, *ibid.*

government would urge Harding to meet with Spargo. "The most desirable thing," Bakhemeteff suggested, "would be to have the memorandum given to Mr. Harding as the basis of a policy which he might announce as being his own" and at the same time get influential men to argue with him along the same lines.[48]

By the 28th of December, Spargo was ready to send his memorandum to Harding. He had arranged to have Oscar Straus visit the President soon after to indicate his approval of its contents. The deportation of Ludwig Martens, the Soviets' trading agent in the United States, strengthened their position. Yet strong pressure was being put on Harding to appoint some cabinet members who favored recognition of the Soviet government.[49] Harding would be glad, Spargo wrote the President, to have laid before him "such a carefully studied statement of the special problem of Russia and its relation to the general European situation." Spargo noted that he had discussed his analysis with Elihu Root, William Howard Taft, Oscar Straus, and others, and as a result he was "firmly convinced of the soundness of the constructive policy outlined in the enclosed Memorandum."[50]

In the memorandum, portions of which were also submitted to the Senate Committee on Foreign Relations in January, Spargo set forth the basis for his entire attitude toward the Bolshevik regime. There could be no European reconstruction or economic stability in the world, he argued, unless a large trade was established with Russia. Yet this posed a dilemma for the United States, because it would be disadvantageous to enter into trade relations with Soviet Russia "under existing conditions, without incurring serious risk of unprecedented economic disaster and revolutionary upheaval."

Some workers within the United States were arguing that the economic blockade of Russia had to be lifted, because it was causing domestic unemployment. "The danger of

[48] Bakhemeteff to Spargo, December 20, 1920, *ibid.*
[49] Spargo to Bakhemeteff, December 28, 1920, *ibid.*
[50] Spargo to Harding, December 28, 1920, *ibid.*

such an appeal to masses of unemployed men," Spargo emphasized, "can hardly be" overestimated. It was also false, as some industrialists argued, that the government's prevention of trade with Russia deprived industry of immense profits. The purpose of Russian trade overtures was to cajole the government into granting political recognition. Any trade with Russian firms, which were supervised by the state, would amount to *de facto* recognition of the Soviet regime. Trade, moreover, could only be carried on if the United States government officially engaged in it. This in turn would mean that the government would be asked to protect the rights of those businessmen engaging in such trade. This was a poor risk.

Concessions which the Soviets had offered to the banker Washington Vanderlip, for oil lands in Kamchatka, were meant to cause a strain in relations between Japan and the United States. Western capital would be used to further Russia's goal of world revolution. At an unannounced time, when it was least expected, the Soviets would declare that they would no longer tolerate the presence of Western capital. "I respectfully submit that while this country needs a great extension of its foreign trade," Spargo argued, such extension had to be on the "basis of long-time well-secured credit." Nothing could be "more dangerous to us than to attempt such a large volume of trade upon the basis of insecure credit, and especially to incur the risk of probable repudiation by the debtor nations." Trade with the Soviets meant an "invitation to economic bankruptcy and to revolution."

The danger of debt repudiation existed not only because of Bolshevik perfidy, but because of the patriotism of the democratic anti-Bolshevik forces. Sooner or later, Spargo thought, "the bolshevist rule will either collapse of its own rottenness or be overthrown." Any agreements made with the Soviets at that time would be abrogated. Moreover, Russia's present needs were in excess of any capital she held or could acquire. Foreign capital required security, but Bolshevism by its nature could not offer it. To ask for trade with the Soviets was "to stake our own existence upon credit no more secure than the promise of men who have already revealed their intention to default whenever and however they can." No security for credit could exist until there was a large-scale organization of Russia's productive capacity of a type which Bolshevism by its very nature precluded. To recognize Russia, Spargo argued, would mean to stamp with legality their confiscation of property and to afford them the means to promote social revolution within the United States.

Trade, moreover, was an impossibility. If, for example, Soviet hides were transferred to the United States for American manufacturers to process, the original owners from whom the Bolsheviks stole the hides could claim them. The courts would deny the legality of the transfer to the American firms. If a Soviet authority was recognized by the United States, means would exist for validation of the confiscated goods. *De jure* recognition would make it possible for traders to receive confiscated property owned by other Americans or Westerners. Only the Bolsheviks would profit from such exchanges. "So long as the Bolsheviki remain in power and maintain their present policy," Spargo concluded, "there can be no security for foreign capital invested in Russia." Since the elimination of capital was the Soviet goal, large investments in Russia would jeopardize America's economic life. Billions in goods, supplied on credit as the basis of Russian securities, would be confiscated, and economic disaster adversely affecting every American family would occur. The result, perhaps, would be insurmountable crisis.[51]

After waiting two months without hearing from the President, Spargo addressed Harding once again. Referring to the December memorandum, Spargo informed Harding on March 10 that Elihu Root and William Howard

[51] Spargo to Senator Brandegee, January 24, 1921, "The Question of Trade with Soviet Russia," in U.S., Congress, Senate, Committee on Foreign Relations, *Relations with Russia*, 66th Congress, 3rd Session, 1921, pp. 63–83. Cf. Spargo, "The Problem of Trading with Soviet Russia," *The Weekly Review*, January 12, 1921, pp. 74–83; and Spargo, "Memorandum on Russian Policy," n.d. [January, 1921], Spargo MSS.

Taft had led him to "feel that you would be glad to see it, and would not regard it as in any sense an officious intrusion." Spargo warned Harding that a policy conceived in opposition to the Bolsheviks would not apply in the changed conditions after the Bolsheviks were overthrown, and he thus asked Harding's permission to help shape a policy geared to the latter eventuality. Spargo did not know whether revolt would lead to the regime's demise, but he felt that "Bolshevik power will be so weakened in consequence of the revolt that the end of their rule will inevitably be hastened."[52]

To cope with this result, Spargo proposed a policy to deal with a new provisional Russian government. Russian demands for food and fuel, he suggested, would have to be met or the United States would see a desperate population overthrowing the new government out of disappointment at not obtaining immediate relief. But "if the new Provisional Government that is set up is immediately given large moral and material support by this country," Spargo recommended, "its success will be practically assured. If it is not given that support, its failure is practically certain." Spargo predicted that Harding's "administration will thus be confronted by one of the most serious challenges in the history of civilization." It was clear that Spargo was resting his case on the belief that the Bolshevik regime was due for imminent collapse. He therefore asked Harding to offer his sympathy and friendship at the time at which a new constituent assembly was proclaimed. Then the government could proceed to recognize the new regime in Russia. The United States would also undertake rapid relief mobilization and would send a commission to Russia to develop a plan for economic aid.[53]

To guarantee that Harding would follow the policy he recommended, Spargo continued to travel around the country gathering support. In nine days he delivered ten lectures, attended three conferences, and spoke with influ-

---

[52] Spargo to Harding, March 10, 1921, *ibid.*
[53] *Ibid.*

ential members of the Chicago Chamber of Commerce. At
a round-table session he answered the questions of forty
manufacturers and businessmen, and he urged them to
put pressure on Harding. "I think," Spargo wrote, "that
they were all thoroughly impressed with the importance of
my contention that extensive credits to the Bolshevist Government would jeopardize American industry and Business in a very serious manner." Spargo recognized that
the "serious condition of industry" made many manufacturers want to trade with Russia. Spargo agreed that it
would be desirable, but argued that the Bolshevik regime
had to be done away with as a prerequisite. Spargo also
reported to Bakhemeteff that his memorandum, according
to Attorney General Daugherty, had "knocked the bottom
out of the case of the other side, and made any further
argument superfluous." Spargo was also confident that his
policy would be accepted. Although he did not know Herbert Hoover, he was acquainted with Hoover's "right-hand"
man, George B. Baker, and Spargo believed "we can count
upon his influence being exerted on our side to the very
utmost."[54]

According to Spargo's analysis, the Bolshevik regime
was "nearing the end of its tether." Although he was not
identified with any political party, Spargo wrote to Senator
Carrol Page of Vermont, throughout the "whole period of
the conflict in Russia" he had placed himself "unreservedly
at the advice of President Wilson and the Department of
State." Spargo now offered to do the same for the new
administration. He had tried to let Harding know this, and
was waiting to receive a request for aid.[55] Page promised
to bring the matter to Harding's attention, "for I feel that
I may properly urge upon him the fact . . . that your knowledge of the Russian situation is of the very best."[56]

As part of his attempt to maintain the policy of non-
recognition, Spargo also sought to enlist the aid of the
ailing former President. Writing to Woodrow Wilson on

[54] Spargo to Bakhemeteff, March 1, 1921, *ibid.*
[55] Spargo to Page, March 9, 1921, *ibid.*
[56] Page to Spargo, March 14, 1921, *ibid.*

March 10, Spargo related that he had sent Harding a memo on Russian policy after gaining the approval of men like Taft, Root, and Butler. Spargo let Wilson know the essence of the thoughts he had addressed to Harding that same day, copying the letter to Harding verbatim.[57]

On March 17, Wilson sent the letter to the new Secretary of State, Charles Evans Hughes, and wrote: "I am handing you herewith a letter that has come to me from John Spargo, in whose information about the Russian situation I have had considerable confidence." Enclosing a digest of Spargo's views which Wilson prepared, he told Hughes: "I simply bring the matter to your attention in the belief that it contains some suggestions that are very well worthy of consideration."[58]

Spargo in actuality had little reason to worry about a possible reversal of Russian policy. The response to Spargo's analysis was sympathetic. Attached to Wilson's letter was a memorandum for Harding drawn up by Judson Welliver. After summing up Spargo's views, Welliver added that he had spoken with the Under Secretary of State, who had told him that the Department of State "is keeping in touch with Russia's affairs; he inclines to sympathize with the Spargo view; and he believes, also, that the present anti-Bolsheviki movement can hardly be expected to succeed."[59]

Within a few short months after Harding assumed the presidency, it had become clear that the Wilson non-recognition policy was to be maintained. The postwar recession had indeed motivated segments of both capital and labor to call for increased and regularized trade with Russia, and many who favored such a step saw trade as the first move in a collaboration that could bring about a *rapprochement*. But this group was not successful. "With the aid, explicit direction, and corrective advice supplied by various economic interests and Secretary of Commerce Hoover," William Appleman Williams has written, "the Secretary of

[57] Spargo to Wilson, March 10, 1921, NA, RG 59, 861.01/384.
[58] Wilson to Hughes, March 17, 1921, *ibid.*
[59] Memo for the President by Judson Welliver, *ibid.*

State sought to extend the Open Door to Russia and to use economic pressure to effect a fundamental change in the economic structure of the Soviet Union."[60] They sought, not a collaboration, but a commercial relationship strictly on their own terms and one that might be used as a political weapon.

Hughes' agreement with Spargo was made clear when on March 15, Samuel Gompers wrote to ask Hughes for help in his battle against those among organized labor who were fighting for trade with Russia. There was much propaganda, Gompers wrote, that Russia's demand for manufactured goods was so great and the purchasing power of the Soviet government so vast that "it is almost impossible to determine the actual capacity of the Russian market to absorb goods of foreign manufacture." Others were claiming that if restrictions on trade were removed it would "place in operation many mills, shops and factories now closed down and would give employment to the unemployed of America." To deal with these assertions, Gompers asked for the "widest publicity of the facts," so Americans would "not be misled by propaganda" directed to aid the Soviet government "against the interests of our people."[61]

The answer which Hughes gave pointed to the direction that the Harding Administration would take. Hughes sought to follow the approach favored by Spargo, the traditional assertion of the Open Door for trade and commerce. The Open Door meant, of course, that trade and commerce be open to American interests, not closed to them by colonial powers with traditional spheres of influence. After years of war, Hughes asserted, "Russia does not now possess important quantities of commodities which might be exported." Three years of civil warfare had left the Russian countryside paralyzed, and no evidence existed that the "unfortunate situation above described is

---

[60] William Appleman Williams, *American-Russian Relations, 1781–1947* (New York, Toronto, 1952), p. 178.
[61] Gompers to Hughes, March 15, 1921, Gompers MSS, State Historical Society of Wisconsin, Madison, Wis.

likely to be alleviated so long as the present political and economic system continues."

Other countries had been left disabled after war, Hughes asserted, but Russia had not taken any steps to re-establish confidence. She could not obtain credit and was perforce deprived of commodities necessary for consumption, purchase of raw materials, and productive equipment. Russia was free to trade, but the volume of trade was insignificant "due to the inability of Russia to pay for imports." As for the claim that if the United States recognized the Soviet government, Russia would export lumber, flax, hemp, and fur, Hughes wrote that the facts "completely refute such statements. Russia does not today have on hand for export commodities which might be made the basis of immediately profitable trade with the United States."

Finally, Hughes denied that if trade restrictions were lifted, many American mills and factories that were closed would resume operation. Even before the war, he argued, trade with Russia constituted only one and three-tenths per cent of the total trade of the United States. Since Russia's purchasing power was now greatly diminished, it was evident that "even under the most favorable circumstances the trade of Russia could have but a minor influence on the industrial and agricultural prosperity of the United States."[62]

The declaration on trade followed exactly the proposals which Spargo had set forth in his "Memorandum on Russian Policy." Spargo had written to Hughes later in March to express his "earnest hope that there will be no compromise with the Bolshevist regime." To allow any official Russian delegation into the United States, as Kalinin had offered, would allow the group to become the "center of a very dangerous agitation." Again Spargo accused the Soviets of having only political ends. These were more easily accomplished "by reason of the prevailing unemployment." Recognition of Russia would occur once trade took place, and Spargo urged a firm refusal to deal with the

[62] Hughes to Gompers, April 5, 1921, *ibid.*

Bolshevik government.[63] A few days later, Spargo once again wrote expressing his "admiration and cordial approval" of Hughes' response to the Soviet appeal for a trade mission. Hughes' reply, Spargo wrote, was "at once adequate, wise, and incontestably sound." Hughes had placed the "issue squarely where it belongs, and wisely emphasized the futility of the proposal." There could be no trade until a resumption of production took place. But "Bolshevism by its very nature," Spargo wrote, made that "impossible."[64]

After receiving Spargo's letter, Hughes informed him that he fully appreciated "the importance of what you say." Hughes referred Spargo to his answer to Gompers.[65] Two days later, he again wrote to let Spargo know that he was glad to gain Spargo's approval of "my statement on the Russian trade proposal."[66] Soon after, Spargo received confirmation that the Harding Administration had taken the course he suggested. "I am delighted to know that you had such influence with Mr. Hughes," William Howard Taft wrote Spargo, "as he reported to me you did have, in respect to his reaching a right conclusion in respect to our proper policy toward Russia."[67]

A key element of Spargo's argument was that refusing to trade with Bolshevik Russia in fact favored the interests of business, since such a stance would allow American capital to enter the new democratic Russia after a provisional government was established. At that point, the rewards for holding out could be reaped. Foreign capital would be needed to restore Russia, and the new government would have to see that the investments it attracted were guaranteed by its good faith.[68]

By this time, however, Spargo was growing "positively

[63] Spargo to Hughes, March 24, 1921, NA, RG 59, 661.115/P81/-191.
[64] Spargo to Hughes, March 28, 1921, NA, RG 59, 661.115/P81/-192.
[65] Hughes to Spargo, March 29, 1921, Spargo MSS.
[66] Hughes to Spargo, March 31, 1921, *ibid.*
[67] Taft to Spargo, April 20, 1921, *ibid.*
[68] Spargo to Alexander Kerensky, January 13, 1921, *ibid.*

sick of the task of constantly combatting Bolshevism."
Negation, "destructive criticism and bitter controversy," he
wrote to Phelps Stokes, "has me almost hag-ridden."[69] Privately, Spargo admitted that his emphasis on the creation
of a new democratic Russia was not mere rhetoric. He had,
he admitted to Bakhemeteff, lost interest "in the Socialist
phase of the problem." Although he was still opposed to
reactionary tendencies, Spargo now felt there was "no possibility of anything like Socialism in Russia, and that the
logic of reconstruction precludes anything like a Socialist
arrangement of the economic life." The best that could be
hoped for, Spargo believed, was that moderate Socialist
elements would be part of a coalition government.[70]

Spargo's emphasis on constructive action, rather than
on purely anti-Bolshevist agitation, now found new expression in the crucial issue of humane relief for Russia. It was
through suggestions on this score that Spargo saw the
opportunity to be of direct help once again in ending the
Bolshevik reign.

A great need existed within Russia for relief. Years of
civil war and foreign intervention had bled Russia badly,
and by 1921 the great working class that led the Bolsheviks
to power had largely been decimated. Throughout Russia
many were homeless, and disease and famine were ramp-
ant. To deal with the human misery produced by this situation, the Bolshevik government at the end of the 1921
summer asked foreign powers to help administer relief aid
on a non-political humane basis. The United States government responded to this plea by creating the American
Relief Administration (ARA), with Herbert Hoover in
charge. The Bolsheviks gave it official status and permission to function in Russia, and at the end of its services,
official gratitude and commendation were voiced to the
agency and to Hoover by the Soviet government.

The problem facing American leadership was how to
square the administration of Rusian relief with commitment to the Open Door for trade and commerce. The

[69] Spargo to Stokes, March 11, 1921, *ibid.*
[70] Spargo to Bakhemeteff, June 13, 1921, *ibid.*

answer was set forth by Herbert Hoover. "The relief measures," Hoover wrote to Hughes, "will build a situation
which, combined with the other factors, will enable the
Americans to undertake the leadership in the reconstruction of Russia when the proper moment arrives." The hope
"of our commerce," Hoover continued, "lies in the establishment of American firms abroad, distributing American
goods under American direction, in the building of direct
American financing and, above all, in the installation of
American technology in Russian industries." Good relations with the Russians could be established only after
"fundamental changes" were effected in their whole economic system.[71]

Before Hoover agreed to administer relief, he pointed
out, he held "a long and difficult negotiation with the Soviet
authorities." It was agreed that all American prisoners held
in Russia would be released. When the Soviets approved
that demand, Hoover then had "an agreement drawn up
providing for the independence of this administration
from any interference by the Soviet authorities." Hoover
made it perfectly clear that he thought the famine was not
caused purely by natural phenomena. Ever since Russia
had been "under the sway of the Soviet government," he
argued, it had been steadily degenerating in agriculture
and production. Relief would have one other beneficial
domestic effect. "The food supplies that we wish to take to
Russia," Hoover pointed out, "are all in surplus in the
United States, and are without a market in any quarter of
the globe." If the U.S. government went into the market
and bought a substantial amount of corn it might "give
some relief to the American farmer in disposing of his
surplus."[72]

The independence of the relief authority was a key
concern of promoters of aid. Samuel Gompers pointed out

[71] Hoover to Hughes, December 6, 1921; cited in Williams, *op.
cit.*, p. 193.
[72] U.S., Congress, House, Committee on Foreign Affairs, *For the
Relief of the distressed and starving people of Russia*, 67th Congress, 2nd Session, December 13–14, 1921, pp. 37–39.

that he had only hostility toward the "greatest autocracy existing in any civilized country on the face of the globe." He simply could not "tolerate such a condition of affairs." Since he wanted to avoid giving the Bolshevik government either moral or financial support, Gompers wanted to be certain that money expended by Congress for the ARA would not "give aid or comfort to the present Government of Russia." He wanted to be sure that the ARA "would be in absolute control" of the money so that it would "not be taken over to help the existing regime in Russia called the soviet government."[73]

Gompers had little to fear. Relief measures, ostensibly carried out for an entirely humanitarian reason, were to be conducted in such a fashion that they would contribute to overall political aims. Hoover's conception of relief aid, explained succinctly to Hughes in December 1921, was precisely that advocated by John Spargo the previous July and August, after the Bolsheviks appealed to the world community for aid.

Whatever relief aid was contemplated, it had to be administered to people throughout all of Russia. Spargo understood as early as 1919 that it would be foolish to try and raise funds just for the homeless and hungry in areas of Russia not under the control of the Bolsheviks. If they raised money for those outside of Bolshevik-controlled areas, Spargo argued with a wealthy Russian exile, they would only create a greater fund drive from the pro-Bolsheviks. If they revealed the extent of suffering in the anti-Bolshevik areas, people would say conditions were worse in the Bolshevik provinces. Moreover, the pro-Bolsheviks would with justification insist that "the misery in Russia is quite as great under the anti-Bolshevists and, therefore, Bolshevism cannot be held responsible." While they had to be critical of Bolshevism, Spargo argued, they had to support relief aid for all Russians who needed it. But Spargo cautioned that relief could be administered only after the independence of the ARA was recognized by the Bolsheviks. Mere promises were worthless, because the Bolshe-

[73] *Ibid.*, pp. 40–41.

viks might use the aid just for their own areas. Spargo was confident that the Bolsheviks would accept the American proposal. Lenin and Trotsky were too wise to refuse. Refusal would only horrify the world at their senseless brutality.[74]

Spargo did not have to appeal for acceptance of relief aid. The Bolshevik government requested such aid on its own, after economic deprivation reached an intolerable stage. Spargo saw this request as the opportunity for which he and the government had been waiting. If used rightly, he wrote to Hughes on July 25, 1921, it might lead to destruction of the Bolshevik regime. "I believe that it is well within the range of practical political possibility," Spargo believed, "that a wise and candid, and at the same time generous, statement by the American Government at this time may prove to be the decisive factor leading to a solution of the entire problem." Twenty-five million people, Spargo claimed, were suffering from famine, cholera, and general epidemics. Apart from political considerations, "we must desire to succor and relieve the innocent victims." The castastrophe had served to break the resistance of the Bolshevik leaders to accepting relief aid from the United States.

The basis for Spargo's hope that the ARA project would help destroy the Bolshevik regime was the possibility that a moderate group within Russia would be given the power to administer the aid on their side. Spargo noted that a great change had taken place in the regime; the more extreme Bolshevik leadership was being pushed to the rear. If, as now seemed feasible, moderate Russians were designated to help run the program, they could serve as a "*group actively functioning in Russia which, if it is properly and adequately supported by the generous cooperation of this and other nations, can develop into the respective government of Russia.*" Such a group could safely be guaranteed freedom of action in relief work, and would have independence in both collection and distribution of funds.

[74] Spargo to Princess Julia Cantacuzene Speransky, nee Grant, November 22, 1919, Spargo MSS.

Any group engaged in this work would "become the most important body functioning in Russia, and to which the people will turn naturally"; the allegiance of the populace would thus be given to the moderates. Although the group would scrupulously have to avoid political activity, it would still "tend to become the real government of Russia" because it would be the only body that met the people's needs. The relative importance of the Soviet regime would decline, and the moderate group would step into the breach as soon as the Bolshevik government collapsed.

Spargo closed by suggesting the very course that the United States government was to follow. Hoover had the power to take the final action that would eliminate the scourge of Bolshevism. Spargo urged that Hoover ask for the authority to assist Russia through cooperation with a a coalition of moderate Russians. Foreign intervention would be avoided, and neutral agencies such as the Red Cross could be mobilized to distribute aid. The United States government would issue a statement setting forth its appreciation of the situation and noting its willingness to help. One prerequisite to aid, Spargo suggested, would be prior release of all Americans then imprisoned in Russia.[75]

On the 26th of July, Spargo informed Hoover himself that he had "admiration and gratitude" for the Secretary's formal answer to Maxim Gorky, the Russian writer who had said Russia would decline aid from capitalist America, Spargo was under "no illusions concerning the difficulties of the task or its magnitude," but he was convinced that changes taking place in the Bolshevik government presaged "the beginning of the liquidation of the Bolshevist regime itself and the nucleus of a new Provisional Government which will save the country from complete anarchy."

The need, Spargo noted, was immense. Seven million children were famished, and twenty million adults were near starvation. Medical relief had to be arranged, technical assistance introduced, and the transportation system built up. "Understanding quite fully that there must not be

[75] Spargo to Hughes, July 25, 1921, *ibid*. (Emphasis added.)

the slightest suggestion of political interference connected
with any of our relief activities," Spargo stressed, "I can
not blind myself to the fact that, almost inevitably, political
developments of far-reaching importance will result from
a comprehensive relief program properly carried out." The
United States would have to have freedom to select personnel, in order to assure protection for non-Bolshevist elements "which have heretofore been repressed." The Bolshevist machine would be reduced in importance and local
bodies created that would be "in effect an organization
capable of providing a responsible Provisional Government
if and when the Bolshevist regime falls."

The effect of American aid, provided the Bolshevik leaders accepted Hoover's conditions, would be to strengthen
constructive Russian elements. It would help to "bring
about the peaceful and bloodless liquidation of Bolshevism." Finally, Spargo asked Hoover to forgive his writing
and offering advice. But having "consecrated my time and
energy for so long to the fight against Bolshevism," Spargo
wrote, he felt a "moral right to urge that the stage has been
reached for constructive effort to assist in the redemption
of Russia." Spargo ended by suggesting the course Hoover
would follow: he urged a Congressional appropriation for
the Russian relief.[76] Hoover's response was brief but cour-
teous. He was "most grateful" for Spargo's letter, and he
noted that he had "read with interest" Spargo's suggestions.[77]

For the time being, Spargo received some indication
that his views were again being taken into consideration.
William C. Redfield replied that he agreed with Spargo,
and that he was writing to Hughes "along the lines of your
own valuable suggestion" in order to "reinforce what you
have already so ably stated."[78] Spargo himself wrote Bakhemeteff that it was his judgment that relief work would
"be undertaken in such a manner as will be likely to aid
our program," and that they could stop devoting their en-

[76] Spargo to Hoover, July 26, 1921, *ibid.*
[77] Hoover to Spargo, July 28, 1921, *ibid.*
[78] Redfield to Spargo, July 29, 1921, *ibid.*

ergies to it.[79] On the 29th, Spargo got word from Secretary Hughes that much would depend "upon the reply received" from the Bolshevik government to Hoover's offer of assistance.[80] After Hoover demanded that American prisoners in Russia be released as a precondition for any aid, Colby took this to mean that "there may be the thought of proceeding further along lines which are suggested by your letter."[81]

Events seemed favorable for initiation of Spargo's approach. John A. Gade felt that "the Soviet authorities are in such a pickle that they will have to accept Hoover's conditions," but he feared that to demand release of American prisoners constituted "recognition of the Soviet government." Gade understood that the U.S. government could not "officially address a body which we refuse to acknowledge existent." Gade agreed that if Hoover's aides were admitted their relief organization would undermine Soviet influence and would probably "become the truly representative Russian assembly."[82]

By the 11th of August, Spargo's fears were set aside. Bakhemeteff had conferred with Hoover, and he reported that "the anxiety which we entertained is groundless." Hoover understood "the situation thoroughly" and knew that relief was only a temporary stopgap since the despair was due to the Soviet system itself. Hoover also was aware that the Soviet government sought to make political capital from the aid, and Hoover's methods and instructions to the relief workers "leave nothing to be desired." Bakhemeteff advised Spargo that they should urge all their friends to support the ARA, and that Hoover "should be the source of all initiative and action."[83] A few days later, Spargo himself left for Washington after being called there by Hoover for a conference.[84]

Spargo himself realized that Hoover was in basic agree-

[79] Spargo to Bakhemeteff, July 28, 1921, *ibid.*
[80] Hughes to Spargo, July 29, 1921, *ibid.*
[81] Colby to Spargo, August 1, 1921, *ibid.*
[82] Gade to Spargo, August 1, 1921, *ibid.*
[83] Bakhemeteff to Spargo, August 12, 1921, *ibid.*
[84] Spargo to Iassaiev, August 17, 1921, *ibid.*

ment with the goals he and Bakhemeteff favored. No movement of any kind for relief should be started, Spargo wrote, without Hoover's approval and without being set up under his auspices. If anyone else had his own favorite plan, it had to be submitted to Hoover for consideration and his judgment would be final. Spargo set out one word of caution to Bakhemeteff. While they had to be closely identified in the public mind with relief, "leaving no possible room for suspicion or accusation that we are callously indifferent to the suffering of the Russian people," they had to at the same time "pursue our political goal." They could not permit themselves "to be swamped and engulfed in the actual work of a relief movement."[85]

After conferring with Hoover, Spargo saw his role as keeping the Secretary on his toes so that the political implications were not downgraded. Point 21 of the agreement for ARA relief called upon the Soviets to acquaint the Russian people with the aims and methods of the ARA and to present the American people with non-political information as to the progress of relief work. Spargo was worried that the Russians would not keep to this. While enforcement might make Hoover's work harder, Spargo realized that it would also tend to make Hoover "more cautious" and cause him to pay "greater heed to political considerations which, in his enthusiasm, he would perhaps otherwise ignore." It would mean that the Cabinet would have to give close scrutiny "to the political aspects of the problem." An example was that Russian exiles should stress, Spargo suggested, that all manufacturing in Russia of tools and goods needed for relief work should be "directly under Mr. Hoover's direction and control," and that no "contracts of any kind should be made with the Soviet regime itself."[86]

Spargo stressed this aspect of the question with Henry Morgenthau and the banker Felix Warburg. Both agreed that unless all industrial work was done under the ARA's auspices, "the result can hardly fail to be a strengthening

85 Spargo to Bakhemeteff, August 17, 1921, *ibid.*
86 Spargo to Bakhemeteff, August 25, 1921, *ibid.*

of the tottering regime." Spargo felt confident that "this fact will be brought home to Mr. Hoover."[87]

In all respects, it had become clear that Herbert Hoover shared the outlook of John Spargo. In a pamphlet issued by the American Federation of Labor in 1922, the AFL stressed that the money given to the ARA had reached the people and did "not go into the pockets of their oppressors." The AFL cited Hoover's well-known claim that the famine had occurred because of the Bolshevik system itself, and that "radical improvement" could not take place "without a fundamental change in their whole economic system." The famine prevailed not only in areas hit by drought, but throughout all of Russia. It existed because the peasants lacked incentives to produce.

ARA aid was not given to the Soviet regime, which was "largely responsible for existing misery and disease." The AFL was particularly upset at supporters of the Bolshevik government who were asking that aid be given directly to Russian labor and government leaders. The Soviet government, the AFL claimed, was trying to make famine permanent. Even though the government was aware of famine early in 1921, they did not appeal to foreign powers for aid till the end of the summer, a time in which they sought to achieve cooperation with Western powers at a scheduled international conference. The AFL blasted American Socialists for refusing to support Hoover's ARA, in spite of official commendation of it by the Soviet government. The Socialists, the AFL commented, sought to use aid to help the Soviet government and save the Bolshevik revolution, not to feed the starving. Their slogan, in contradistinction to Hoover's, was to "give without imposing imperialistic and reactionary conditions, as do Hoover and others." Thus they favored giving supplies directly to the Soviet authorities for distribution.[88]

The Soviet government did not collapse from the effect of ARA aid. Although the United States persisted in the

[87] Spargo to Bakhemeteff, August 27, 1921, *ibid.*
[88] "Russian Famine Relief Campaign," AFL memo, April 1922, Gompers MSS.

policy of non-recognition until 1933, other Western nations, much to the disappointment of Hughes and Hoover,
followed an independent policy and extended a hand of
welcome to their former Bolshevik enemies. Once again,
however, John Spargo had entered into direct communication with top policy makers. Although in this case they
had developed a similar analysis on their own, Spargo's
proposed plan for dissolution of the Bolshevik power was
precisely that favored by Herbert Hoover and Charles
Evans Hughes. Like Hoover and Hughes, Spargo also
sought to integrate Germany into the Western community
of nations in order to prevent forging a revolutionary alliance of Germany and Russia that would undo Versailles.
Germany, Spargo had warned, would try to destroy the
Versailles Treaty and Bolshevik Russia would support her
efforts "as the best means of bringing on the world revolution they are aiming at." Since some of Germany's grievances were real, Spargo noted, it was as a "potential leader
and director of the energies" of all the "discontented peoples" that Hoover and Hughes had to "henceforth consider
Soviet Russia."[89]

Spargo's sophistication had ironic overtones. At the very
moment in which his analysis was shared and developed
as the basis for policy by Hoover and Hughes, Spargo was
vigorously attacked by dogmatic anti-Communists in the
National Civic Federation. As Spargo understood, the
Federation did untold harm to the anti-Bolshevist cause
by its close identification with conservative and reactionary elements. Most upsetting to Spargo was the Federation's argument that Menshevism and Bolshevism were
similar programs, the former differing from the Bolshevik
only in that it favored confiscation of property at a later
date. If opponents of Bolshevism viewed these two diverse
groups as the same, Spargo argued, "they might just as
well abandon their opposition to Bolshevism at once." The
basic difference was that the NCF favored military intervention against the Bolsheviks, a course that had already

[89] Spargo, "Memorandum on Russian Policy," n.d. [January
1921], Spargo MSS.

failed and had been abandoned by the State Department as well as by Spargo.

All previous interventions had "the effect of strengthening the Bolsheviki," Spargo argued, and a new intervention might very well plunge the Western nations themselves into Bolshevism. The only forces to be relied upon, as Spargo saw the picture, were the Social Revolutionaries and the Mensheviks. Spargo asked the NCF to give its support to those elements who would uphold a new constituent assembly, the negation of a proletarian dictatorship. If they did not do it, it meant that the NCF was opposing recognition of a government set up by the free will of the Russian people. "Those of us who are combatting Bolshevism," Spargo argued, "have not the slightest intention to assist in the restoration of a czarist bureaucracy." The only position for Americans to support was that outlined by Colby in his note of August 10, 1920. Any democratic government established, moreover, would be pledged to give full security to "the foreign investor as a condition *sine qua non* of the economic restoration of Russia." The approach of the Civic Federation, on the other hand, was termed "an obstacle in the path of every person who is intelligently combatting Bolshevism in this country."[90]

Spargo's arguments did not affect the Civic Federation dogmatists. Conde Pallen, chairman of that group's department on the study of revolutionary movements, claimed that they alone backed the Hoover-Hughes policy. Not realizing Spargo's close work with government authorities, the NCF spokesman accused Spargo of having a "Socialist bias" which gave a "peculiar twist" to his judgment. While admitting that Spargo had used his pen in the anti-Bolshevist cause, Pallen argued that Spargo's belligerency "has in no way cooled your ardor for Marxian Socialism." It was Spargo's desire to put Russia in the hands of Marxian Socialists who were a bit moderate, and let capitalism develop in Russia only temporarily until it would evolve into socialism.

Spargo opposed Bolshevism, Pallen claimed, because

[90] Spargo to Alton B. Parker, April 19, 1921, *ibid.*

"you think Bolshevism is in too much of a hurry," that it was a "precipitate experiment ending in disaster, and that by preserving private property a little longer Socialism will in time come to its full realization in a not wrecked capitalism . . . but in a capitalism intact and prepared for the Socialist helmsman." The ship would not be driven on the rocks as with the Bolsheviks, but would traverse a longer and more orderly voyage. Spargo's argument that it was only on moral grounds that Russia was not recognized was not the Hoover-Hughes policy. The government insisted on Russian abandonment of their present system, and it refused to trade with them or extend credit until it had certain and final evidence that Bolshevism had been given up.[91]

Spargo truly had a more sophisticated understanding of the government's tactical approach. Quoting the Colby Note, Spargo argued that non-recognition was not based on disapproval of Russia's economic plans, but rather on the non-representative character of its government and its tyrannical political practices. The United States would recognize any government that observed international law, and Spargo said he, as well as Hoover and Hughes, abided by that policy. To negotiate at present with the Soviet government would indeed be futile, but that was because it did not produce enough to make any trade possible.

To argue that if the Mensheviks took power their government would not be recognized was unsound and contrary to actual American policy, as well as "fundamentally immoral." Any representative government, just in law, should be recognized. Disapproval of economic organization could not be made the basis of refusing to recognize lawfully constituted government. According to this view, Spargo argued, it would be wrong to have recognized the Russian provisional government in March of 1917. "To state your position with precision and honesty," Spargo argued, "is to reveal its absurdity and its revolutionary character." Moreover, Spargo knew that Mensheviks, SR's, and other Socialists were the backbone of the anti-Bolshevik movement.

[91] Pallen to Spargo, May 17, 1921, *ibid.*

They had to predominate in any new coalition government with Russian conservatives. There was no doubt that such a government had to gain cooperation of foreign capitalists and governments, and that in order to establish the necessary credit it would have "to shape its economic policies with due regard to the requirements of capitalist creditors." Spargo ended by informing Pallen that there was no chance that a responsible American statesman would "commit the stupendous folly of attempting to base our foreign policy upon the dangerous and ridiculous principles which you advocate."[92]

The exchange between Spargo and Pallen provided insights into the direction Spargo had traveled since the beginning of the First World War. Spargo was correct in his technical description of the basis of non-recognition. However, Pallen was correct in that, despite the way the American policy was described, recognition was not yet to be afforded any Russian government that was not committed to private enterprise and to abandonment of a Socialist course.

When Pallen accused John Spargo of holding a Socialist bias and of preferring a moderate Marxian socialism in Russia, he did not know that Spargo had already come to feel that no chance existed for creation of socialism in Russia. Spargo had long since abandoned calling for Russian socialism, and spoke only of the need to build a democratic capitalist Russia. Spargo, who began his public career as an immigrant Socialist, ended it as a confidant of American policy makers and as a respected adviser on American policy toward Soviet Russia. He took pride in the fact that unlike many of his former Socialist colleagues, he had not deemed it necessary to "recant and repudiate the principles and ideals for which as Socialists we stood." Yet, he wrote in May of 1921, he had "materially modified my position." Theories which Spargo formerly advocated now seemed untenable. "Whether I can henceforth fairly and consistently call myself a Socialist," Spargo admitted to Phelps Stokes, "I must frankly admit that I do not know."

[92] Spargo to Pallen, May 27, 1921, *ibid.*

Spargo was thus particularly upset at the attacks on him
issued by the Civic Federation. An "honest struggle to
emancipate oneself from the errors and illusions of past
affiliations" was difficult enough, he wrote, and no "right-
eous purpose" could be served by compounding it with
"poisonous prejudice and intoleration [sic]."[93]

Despite these hesitations, Spargo for the time being
allowed himself to be referred to as a Socialist. After a few
years, however, Spargo began to admit that his lifelong
belief in socialism had definitely been an error. "Today I
am thoroughly convinced," he wrote sometime in 1927 or
1928, "that the Socialist philosophy is unsound, the Socialist program dangerous and reactionary, and the Socialist movement a mischievous illusion." With all its imper-
fections, Spargo admitted that the capitalist system "now
seemed to me to hold the greatest hope for mankind."[94]

The former Socialist leader had abandoned his once
cherished Socialist beliefs. Having accepted Woodrow
Wilson's rhetoric regarding America's war aims, Spargo
placed himself at Wilson's disposal in carrying out Administration policy. Later, Spargo offered his services to
Warren G. Harding in his attempt to unseat the Bolshevik
regime. At the beginning, Spargo and the pro-war Socialists believed that their acceptance of the war would enable
them to advance socialism by achieving representation of
labor on all boards and governing bodies formed during
the war. This representation was obtained, but cooperation
with the government did not increase the real power of the
Socialists. Rather, their activity enabled the Wilson Administration to undertake programs which would have
been difficult to execute had the Socialists refused to participate in pro-war activity.

Both the Wilson and Harding administrations had
gained from Spargo the advice of a man whose contact
with the European Socialist movements could hopefully
aid them in formulation of a successful anti-Bolshevik

[93] Spargo to Stokes, May 24, 1921, Stokes MSS.
[94] Spargo, "A Confession of Faith," n.d. [1927 or 1928], Spargo
MSS.

policy. More than any of the other pro-war Socialists, Spargo had moved to the position where he actually took part in the formulation, as well as articulation, of American foreign policy. Unlike Samuel Gompers, who used the AFL as a pressure group fighting for a militant anti-Bolshevik posture, Spargo sat with the policy makers as they tried to decide on the course to be charted. When Spargo did this, the two administrations had the satisfaction of seeing an avowed Socialist pursue administration policy in the name of socialism.

In reality, John Spargo had simply allowed himself to be used as an agent of a conservative foreign policy, aimed at non-recognition of Russia and restoration of a capitalist economic system. Spargo's opposition to the use of troops in Russia was only a tactical difference based on previous failure. Spargo eventually advocated restoration of a democratic capitalist government, claiming that Russian Socialism had become an impossibility. This demand put him in line with all those who sought such an end for eminently conservative purposes. Every position Spargo took slowly undermined his original Socialist ideology until there was nothing left but the shadow of a former belief. Spargo opposed what he as a Socialist should have supported, and he supported what as a radical he should have opposed. Acting as an agent of Wilson and later of Hoover and Hughes, Spargo did everything but serve the interests of the socialism in whose name he often spoke.

Toward the end of his public career, Spargo had realized that his activity had not led in the direction of socialism. He could repudiate the work he engaged in during the war years and thereafter, or disavow his belief in a Socialist vision. Spargo took the latter course. No longer would he have to answer the criticism of former associates by arguing that policies he espoused were Socialist in content. John Spargo, interpreter of American anti-Bolshevik policy, could now admit that he was proud he was not a Socialist.

CHAPTER

IX

AMERICAN LABOR,
ALLIED SOCIALISM, AND
THE VERSAILLES
PEACE CONFERENCE

Throughout the duration of the War, Woodrow Wilson's main allies in Europe were the moderate Socialists in Britain and France. With the achievement of a decisive military defeat of Germany and the Central Powers, the forces of the Allied Right had been strengthened. The Allied Left now sought to use whatever political power they had to gain adherence to a Wilsonian peace. Such a peace, they believed, was a prerequisite for a policy of social reconstruction at home which would be based on new recognition of the strength and role of Allied labor and socialism.

Once again, the Allied Left looked to Woodrow Wilson for political leadership. By forging an alliance with Wilson, they thought that they would be able to prevent imposition of an extremist Old World peace treaty. But the Allied Left had underestimated the extent to which Wilson remained committed to a centrist, anti-revolutionary politics, as well as to inter-Allied governmental unity against the newly defeated Germany. The Left did not realize the extent to which Wilson viewed a peace conference in conventional diplomatic terms; that is, as a meeting of victorious powers that would impose a just but nevertheless severe peace on a defeated criminal enemy. Despite the hopes of the European social democrats, Wilson did not want to risk inter-Allied unity or the Entente's political control over Germany in his effort to soften the extreme proposals of the French and British governments. Wilson was not about to launch an anti-imperialist assault on the stable Allied powers. The rhetoric he had engaged in during the war was, to a large degree, aimed at the imperialism of the Kaiser's Germany. Wilson preferred to moderate Allied demands and then to consolidate the Allies' control over European politics, rather than to achieve a solidarity with the European Socialists in the postwar world.[1]

While Wilson responded to the fact that the Socialists looked to him for leadership, he tried to make sure he would not become the captive of those he led. He understood that they were too radical. Their desire for vast changes in capitalist economies only scared away liberal conservatives. The Socialists, for their part, were equally wary of becoming Wilson's prisoners, since the President was too moderate. Wilson's extensive concern with the Socialists was dictated largely by an exaggerated fear of their importance. He also thought the possibility existed of using the Socialists to force a more moderate policy on the part of the Allied premiers—but Wilson desired to secure this end without increasing the power and authority of the Socialists in the process. As for the Allied Socialists, they "had no alternative but to remain loyal even to an overly cautious and compromising Wilson: Lenin was too far away, the Right and the incumbent governments were all powerful, the Socialist leaders were irresolute, and the immediate postwar crisis was considerably short of revolutionary in the victor nations."[2]

The forthcoming peace conference, as far as Allied labor

[1] N. Gordon Levin, Jr., *Woodrow Wilson and World Politics* (New York, 1968), pp. 162–63.
[2] Arno J. Mayer, *Politics and Diplomacy of Peacemaking* (New York, 1967), p. 170.

was concerned, would reval whether their confidence in the American President had been well placed. Here, at a conference at which Woodrow Wilson would play a major role, the moderate Socialists and labor leaders would be able to judge whether their wartime goals would be realized. They would see, finally, whether Wilson would stand with them, even if it meant a firm opposition to policies espoused by their own Allied governments.

The Allied Socialists, the Wilson Administration, and the American Federation of Labor all looked at postwar developments with caution. The Old World was in disarray, and extreme demands from the Allied governments might work to nourish sentiment and social forces that favored social revolution. The old conservative labor movements might enter a period of decline, might take false steps that would produce the growth of a powerful revolutionary labor movement. Conditions germinating within Europe, John P. Frey believed, were "almost as dangerous to stable civilization as the war itself." Frey understood that "the problems of peace and reconstruction present obstacles almost as insurmountable as those of a military character." It was necessary for the most able and unselfish men to "stabilize the reconstruction period if we are to save ourselves from upheavals and chaotic conditions of such a serious character that the mind hesitates to consider them. All the movements of men," Frey predicted, "political, social, industrial—are to undergo a profound change."[3]

Woodrow Wilson surveyed the postwar era with similar caution. During the war, Wilson had stood with those European conservatives who did not want Allied labor to act independently of their own existing governments. Wilson opposed the Stockholm Conference, backed Gompers in his opposition to an inter-belligerent labor-Socialist meeting, and arranged to send both AFL and pro-war Socialist groups to Europe for the purpose of gathering

[3] Frey to William B. Rubin, November 7, 1918, Rubin MSS, State Historical Society of Wisconsin, Madison, Wis.

support for Administration policy. Despite his recognition of the Wilsonian orientation of moderate Socialists like Henderson, Wilson never seemed willing to risk entering into a formal alliance with these centrist groups.

At the war's end, Woodrow Wilson again acted to avoid encouragement of class politics—even of the moderate Socialist variety. Wilson's actions eased the fears of many European conservatives, who believed that the President would seek the kind of direct contact with European masses that would amount to a Wilson-Socialist alliance. As a moderate follower of Edmund Burke and as a believer in evolutionary, ordered progress, Wilson was personally opposed to any form of socio-political radicalism. Holding that one transcended the past only by a purely evolutionary process, Wilson opposed not only the Jacobin-like Bolsheviks, but the regular class politics engaged in by the moderate European social democrats.

Wilson's views were consistently reinforced by the advice given the President by Secretary of State Robert Lansing. Both Lansing and Wilson had been urged by William Bullitt, among others, to make careful distinctions between reformist and revolutionary socialism. Since the reformists were the worst enemies of the Bolsheviks, Bullitt had urged that the Bolsheviks be broken "by cooperation with the moderate socialist and labor leaders of Europe: Henderson, Webb, Albert Thomas, Renaudel, Scheidemann, David, Victor Adler, etc."[4] Rejecting Bullitt's view, Lansing argued that:

While there is a certain force in the reasoning as to the peril from extreme radicalism under the leadership of such men as Liebknecht and the Independent Socialists, who affiliate with the Bolsheviks, the danger of compromise with any form of radicalism and the unwisdom of giving special recognition to a particular class of society as if it possessed exceptional rights impress me as strong reasons for rejecting such a proposal.

[4] "The Bolshevist Movement in Europe," November 2, 1918; cited in Mayer, *op. cit.*, p. 66.

Kerensky's experience in compromise and the results which
have followed the exaltation of class at the expense of the rest
of society (whether the class be aristocratic, land owning or
labor), are not encouraging to adopting the course suggested.[5]

Wilson did not reply to Lansing's letter, but he clearly
shared his Secretary's views about the dangers of giving
special recognition to any form of working class or radical
politics. At Paris, Wilson would prefer to work with Gompers and the AFL, bypassing any solidarity with the Wilson-oriented Socialists. Even Colonel House, who recognized the need to keep Allied labor and socialism on a
moderate course, proved unwilling to advise Wilson to
present direct appeals to the moderate Socialists over the
heads of established Allied governments. No matter how
much they desired to curb Allied imperialism, Wilson and
his aides were not about to give up traditional diplomacy
for class-oriented and radical measures. To "act in that
way would have meant revolution," Austin Van Der Slice
perceptively commented, and Wilson "had neither the in-
clination nor intention of risking that."[6]

Following the Armistice, the Allied Socialists and labor
leaders continued to try to use their power to attain a just,
or a Wilsonian peace. The same Socialists who had endorsed the Stockholm Conference during the war now
spoke of holding a postwar international Socialist conference that could rebuild the International while it also
exerted pressure on the official Peace Conference. During
the war, the Socialists and union leaders had invoked two
major proposals: that each nation have at least one labor
representative on the official conference delegation, and
that an international labor-Socialist conference be held
concurrently with the Peace Conference.

While the moderate Socialists desired such a conference,

[5] Lansing to Wilson, November 9, 1918, Wilson MSS, Library of
Congress.

[6] Austin Van Der Slice, *International Labor, Diplomacy and the
Peace, 1914–1919* (Philadelphia, London, 1941), pp. 298, 368; cf.
Levin, *op. cit.*, pp. 165–67.

they sought to gain the approval of their own Allied governments before issuing a formal call. On Armistice Day, Arthur Henderson had presented a memorandum to Lloyd George, in which the British Socialist had presented his reasons for desiring such a conference. Henderson went out of his way to point out that the proposal had originated with Gompers and the AFL in 1914, and that the AFL had reached agreement with Allied labor and socialism during the September 1918 Inter-Allied Conference. Not only would the labor-Socialist conference "mark the responsibilities of Allied Labour in the highest degree," Henderson wrote, it would also expedite the Peace Conference's job of determining an international standard for conditions of labor.[7]

In attempting to show how they would be of service to the Peace Commissioners, Henderson revealed that his comrades in the moderate Socialist movement did not favor international subversion or civil disobedience. They did favor a Wilsonian peace, which they saw as a prerequisite for the growth of moderate socialism in Europe. At the same time, they sought to break with the more radical forces and enter into a closer relationship with the Social Patriots and with Samuel Gompers. Again, as during the war, Henderson still hoped to win Gompers to stand behind rebuilding of the Second International.

Henderson's request for a concurrent congress was subsequently taken up by the Allied premiers at the beginning of December 1918, before Wilson's arrival in Europe. Previously, Clemenceau had already rejected the idea of holding a labor-Socialist meeting in Paris, because he felt that undesirable public demonstrations would take place if German delegates appeared in the French capital. But Clemenceau offered no objections to holding such a meeting outside Paris. The other Allied delegates agreed no

---

[7] "Memorandum on the World Labour and Socialist Peace Conference to be held during the Peace Negotiations: Presented to the Prime Minister on behalf of the Parliamentary Committee of the T.U.C. and the National Executive of the L.P., November 11, 1918"; cited in Mayer, *op. cit.*, p. 377.

obstacles would be placed in the way of any groups holding an international conference, provided that it was to be held in a neutral nation.[8]

While Henderson and the Socialists were getting ready to convene an international conference, Gompers and his AFL aides were deciding what steps of their own to take. Gompers' key adviser, William English Walling, was especially hopeful that Gompers would personally travel to Europe. "The great danger," Walling warned, "is the revival of the Socialist International" and revolutionary upheaval in France and Italy. In fact, thought Walling, the entire "European situation" was "dangerous to the very last degree." Walling stressed the importance of Gompers' personally "being on the ground," and hoped that the French and British governments "will not be given any excuse to discourage your effective action in Europe."[9]

Since Walling and Gompers from the start opposed any effort to rebuild the International, they had no reason to fear opposition to Gompers' presence from the Allied governments. Lansing had already informed Woodrow Wilson in late November that the French government had "expressed a desire to have Mr. Samuel Gompers return to France to be in Paris at the time of peace negotiations." The French government believed that Gompers might "exercise a steadying influence" on French labor. Many in Britain as well agreed "that it would be helpful to have Mr. Gompers in Europe at this time."[10]

Assistant Secretary of State Polk was even more explicit. The French government, he informed Lansing, was anxious "to have Gompers go over as soon as possible." They believed his "presence in France would be helpful in holding the French labor party in line."[11] These feelings were

[8] Notes of an Allied Conversation held in the Cabinet Room, 10 Downing Street, December 3, 1918, Imperial War Cabinet 41; cited in *ibid.*, p. 378.

[9] Walling to Gompers, December 4, 1918, Samuel Gompers MSS, State Historical Society of Wisconsin, Madison, Wis.

[10] Lansing to Wilson, November 29, 1918, Wilson MSS; C.F. NA, RG 59, 763.72110 So/42a.

[11] Polk to Lansing, December 2, 1918, Wilson MSS.

reinforced by W. H. Buckler. Pointing out that German delegates to the Peace Conference were likely to be Socialists and labor men, Buckler wrote House that "Gompers and co. could best checkmate or modify their possible extravagances—*on the spot,* i.e. in Paris."[12]

Gompers not only opposed any resurrection of the Socialist International, he favored holding an exclusive inter-Allied labor conference that would meet only in Paris. Before making any moves, however, Gompers asked the President for official approval. Wilson replied that he "saw no objection" to such a meeting, and that he "thought it advisable for Gompers to be present in Paris at any event."[13] Wilson desired the labor chieftain's presence. However, he carefully revealed his aversion to class politics by refusing to appoint Gompers as a member of the official United States Peace Commission.

The omission of Gompers from the Peace Commission was a great disappointment to the AFL president, as well as to his closest advisers. Gompers, Ralph M. Easley argued, was more than a representative of labor. "Employers who two years ago would have sneered at such an idea," he told Wilson's personal secretary, "are today loud in their praises of Mr. Gompers' statesman qualities." Moreover, his omission would be a severe disappointment for labor, and the reaction among workers if he was not appointed "might have unpleasant consequences in this country." Reactionaries might conclude that because the war was over, the President no longer looked to Gompers. Since delegates from Italian, French, and German labor would all be Socialists, it was necessary that labor be represented by the one "man who is more responsible for making their forces negligible than any other man."[14]

If the President did not wish to appoint Gompers, Easley

[12] Buckler to House, December 17, 1918, W. H. Buckler Collection, Edward M. House MSS, Yale University Library.

[13] Gompers to Wilson, November 30, 1918, Gompers MSS; Lansing to Polk, December 5, 1918, NA, RG 236, 185.161/1; RG 59, 555 B1/4.

[14] Easley to Joseph P. Tumulty, November 26, 1918, National Civic Federation MSS, New York Public Library.

suggested announcing that he had been invited to be a commission member, but could not accept because of domestic labor responsibilities. "The point is," Easley emphasized, "at this particular time when the Bolsheviki are making considerable headway, it will be a great aid to them to have Mr. Gompers appear to be slapped in the face, and his face must be saved . . . on account of the labor situation at large." The imprisonment of Tom Mooney, irritation due to postwar wage reductions, and curtailment of overtime work all were "producing an ugly spirit." Everything possible had to be done "to keep Mr. Gompers's hand strengthened."[15]

Gompers appreciated the President's desire to use him to curb the more extreme elements among Allied labor. But the labor chieftain was frankly disturbed that "labor was not represented on [the official U.S.] Peace Mission." He let it be known that he was not willing to travel to Paris "unless he had some reason for being there." Moreover, Gompers felt strongly that any labor conference had to take place in Paris and meet concurrently with the official Peace Conference.[16] Wilson was now torn between satisfying Gompers and the Allied premiers, who accepted a labor conference only in neutral territory. Wilson realized that a purely Allied labor conference, dominated by Social Patriots and the AFL, would not advance Wilsonianism in Europe. But at the same time, he understood the dangers of demanding another type of meeting. Thus Wilson, who wanted the support of all European internationalists, acquiesced in Lloyd George's and Clemenceau's decision to approve only a neutral site. Gompers should be told, Lansing informed Polk, that the President agreed "a labor conference might very properly be held in Paris or in any other place at any time that the leaders of labor deemed it wise." The labor leaders should simply "do what they conceived best."[17]

After it was clear that Wilson had accepted the Allied

[15] Easley to Tumulty, November 27, 1918, *ibid.*
[16] Polk to Lansing, December 16, 1918, NA, RG 236, 185.161/3.
[17] Lansing to Polk, December 18, 1918, *ibid.*

premiers' decision. Arthur Henderson contacted his associates on the labor organizing committee. "I should like you
to inform Gompers," Henderson wrote, "that while we
should prefer the conference to be held in Paris, we are
advised by Vandervelde, Huysmans and others that the
personal liberty of the Austrian German delegates could
not be guaranteed there." Henderson desired that the conference occur in Lausanne, French Switzerland. He also
reminded Gompers that the conference call would be issued under the name of the group chosen by the September
1918 Inter-Allied Conference, of which Gompers was a
member.[18]

The conference was not to take place in Lausanne. Officials from French Switzerland preferred Berne as the
meeting place. Acting on their suggestion, Henderson
proceeded to ask the Second International executive to
give him authority to have the inter-Allied organizing
committee extend invitations for the tenth congress of the
International, also scheduled for Berne. Branting gave
Henderson the authority, and Camille Huysmans also
agreed to cooperate. Instead of an Allied labor conference,
Henderson had sent out invitations to a purely Socialist
conference that would meet in Berne.

In calling the meeting, Henderson was not about to
rebuild a militant left international. Instead, he wanted to
win Gompers' support, reassure the Social Patriots, and
gain the confidence of the Allied governments. Therefore,
despite the sponsorship of Berne by the Second International, Henderson asked that the meeting be termed "an
International Labour and Socialist Conference, in order
to meet the prejudices of the A.F. of L." Moreover, Henderson announced that the American Socialist Party would
not be invited to send representatives to the conference. It
was more important, he argued, "that the A.F. of L. should
be represented." Henderson noted that they met in order

[18] Henderson to Vandervelde, Thomas, and Frossard, December
19, 1918; cited in John W. Davis to Lansing, December 20, 1918,
NA, RG 59, 555 B1/1; telegram 4470. Cf. Henderson to Gompers,
December 19, 1918, *1919 AFL Convention*, pp. 13–14.

to "sustain the demand for a Wilson Peace." But the American Socialist Party opposed America's participation in the war, although it was America's war action "which alone has made a Wilson Peace and even the victory of the Allies possible." He also asked that delegates "appreciate the intensity of the bitterness which marks the relations between the Trades Union and the Socialist Movement in America."[19]

Henderson's moderate stance had no effect on Gompers. The AFL president firmly rejected any alliance with Henderson, whose policies he believed to be one step away from Bolshevism. Gompers continued to oppose any labor meeting in a neutral nation, and he showed anger at Allied leaders who feared to let labor confer in Paris. Nations holding such a position, Gompers complained to Wilson, acted in an unjust and foolish manner. If an international Allied labor conference was not held in Paris, European and American radicals would "be given a seeming justification to demonstrate that freedom of assemblage and speech is denied by the governments claiming to be democratic." Moreover, Gompers asserted, they would charge the AFL with deceiving world labor into believing that after victory it would have the opportunity to meet and discuss world labor problems. If American labor was prevented from traveling to Paris, the AFL would "be humiliated and made the laughing stock of the world." If objections were removed, on the other hand, the AFL delegation could leave for Paris and remain until the Peace Conference began. It could then meet with other labor groups and help "to guide the [labor] conference aright."[20]

For a brief moment, Wilson seemed to have second thoughts. He asked Lansing to "have frank conversation with the French authorities and representatives of English government in order to straighten the matter out." The

[19] Henderson to Vandervelde and Frossard, December 19, 1918, Labour Party Archives, Correspondence 1918–20, file Peace Conference and International Meetings; cited in Mayer, op. cit., p. 381.

[20] Gompers to Wilson, December 21, 1918, NA, RG 59, 555 B1/3a.

only "wise and prudent" as well as "expedient course," Wilson understood, was to allow labor to hold its international conference. Wilson favored such a course, despite the truth that if they were forced to "sit in a neutral country, their discussions and conclusions will certainly be dominated by dangerous radical elements."[21]

Woodrow Wilson had not used his influence to urge cancellation of Berne. Gompers, however, vigorously continued to protest the scheduled Socialist conference. Arriving in Britain, Gompers met with the Parliamentary Committee of the TUC on January 20. Not only did Gompers firmly oppose "any conference with enemy representatives at the present time," he now made the alternative proposal "that an Inter-Allied Trades Union Congress, which might later become a revised " 'Internationale' should be held." Just as Lenin threatened the unity of world socialism with his call for a new Third International, Gompers threatened it from the right, with a call for a purely trade union international. This meeting, he told the TUC, would serve as a substitute "for an International Labor Congress in a neutral country, such as the one now proposed." The meeting favored by Henderson "might easily fall too much under the influence of extremist elements."[22]

The AFL, Gompers explained to the British labor leaders, could not be "placed in the very questionable position of being free and independent of political domination in the United States and then subject itself to domination of a political party in Europe." Henderson had also proposed that an international trade union congress meet alongside the labor and Socialist conference in Berne. Gompers "deplored the fact that the proposed trade union conference was apparently looked upon as of secondary importance and in the nature of a 'side-show' to the political conference." The AFL would meet only with union groups at an inter-Allied labor conference. They would not sit with representatives of enemy nations "in a conference in which

[21] Wilson to Lansing, December 24, 1918, NA, RG 236, 185.161/7.
[22] Davis to Lansing, January 21, 1919, NA, RG 59, 032. G58–.

the aims and purpose of organized labor would be subordinate to those of any political party."[23]

Gompers maintained the same arrogant posture toward Allied labor leaders that he had shown during the war. James H. Thomas, general secretary of the National Union of Railwaymen, attempted to explain the position of British labor to Gompers. Thomas emphasized that British labor leaders were " 'sitting on a safety valve' and felt that opposition to proposals for hastening the coming of peace and so expediting the release from arms of British soldiers, might give rise to serious trouble in Great Britain, particularly in view of the grave labor unrest which now prevails." British labor leaders felt bound by resolutions passed by the TUC Congress, which had approved convocation of an international labor conference. Thomas himself "believed that these [resolutions] were conclusive regarding the admission of enemy delegates." Although Thomas expressed sentiments held by the majority of British labor leaders, John W. Davis reported that Gompers' "visit to London has been beneficial in bringing forth an expression of Inter-Allied Trades Union opinion, which might formulate proposals for submission to the Peace Conference for International Labor legislation." Generally the British unionists had been reasonable and agreed that both British and American union leaders "should present a united front" on these demands.[24]

After meeting with British leaders, Gompers and his delegation crossed the channel to France. They began their stay by conferences with leaders of the General Confederation of Trade Unions (CGT). Léon Jouhaux told Gompers that while they would participate in an informal conference between Allied labor groups, the Berne conference was the meeting to which the CGT looked as an official expression of labor's demands. Gompers again responded by arguing that Allied labor could not meet with enemy delegates before a peace treaty was completed. Jouhaux

---

[23] Minutes of the meetings of the AFL Delegation to the Peace Conference, n.d. Gompers MSS.

[24] Davis to Lansing, January 21, 1919, NA, RG 59, 032/G58–.

claimed that the war was practically over, and that representatives of all the world's workers had to have a voice in formulating peace terms.[25]

Having closed their first meeting on such an unsatisfactory note, the CGT leaders and the Gompers delegation met one week later. This time Gompers told Jouhaux that he had never given his permission to have his name used on a call for a labor conference anywhere but in Paris. Jouhaux was adamant. He replied that responsibility for the war was on the German leaders and not on the people. "The whole trend of the statement" he read, according to the AFL delegation, "was to the effect that no harm could come from meeting the German Labor representatives at Berne." On the first day of February, Gompers formally told the CGT leaders that the AFL opposed the Berne conference, and would only agree to an international labor conference after the peace treaty was signed. Gompers then lectured Jouhaux that the French labor leaders would "regret their action later." The CGT leaders then implored Gompers not to make public the AFL's opposition to Berne.[26]

In the meantime, the position taken by the Allied governments towards the Berne meeting had shifted. The Allied premiers, and Wilson, presumably now desired that Gompers attend Berne to act as a moderating influence. They had already decided to allow the conference to take place in a neutral country. It was too late to go back on this decision. More to their liking, the conservative Social Patriots had decided to endorse Berne in order to give the meeting an anti-German as well as anti-Bolshevik orientation. If Gompers was to attend at the side of Albert Thomas, the Social Patriot forces would easily be able to dominate and control the proceedings. Not only did the Berne sponsors—including Henderson and Huysmans—agree to a debate on war responsibility and guilt, they also agreed to an overt anti-Bolshevik position. When the Social

---

[25] Minutes of the meetings of the AFL Delegation, Paris, January 23, 1919, Gompers MSS.

[26] *Ibid.*, January 31, 1919; February 1, 1919.

Patriots let it be known that they would ask for an explicit
condemnation of Bolshevism, Henderson acquiesced. Anti-
Bolshevism would appeal to both majoritarians and cen-
trists in the Central Powers as well as those from the
Allied camp, while it also would meet the satisfaction of
the Allied premiers and Gompers. Henderson went out of
his way to point out that neither the Bolsheviks nor the
German Spartacists would be represented and that the
Bolsheviks throughout Europe were the most opposed to
Berne.[27]

The position taken by Henderson led the extreme Left
to formally boycott the conference. Henderson had made
notable concessions to the Social Patriots, for the purpose
of gathering broad backing for a Wilson peace. This tactic
only put his own centrists on the defensive. It was clear,
as Arno Mayer explains, that "under the pretext of condemning Bolshevism the Social Patriots of all nations
planned a basic overhaul of the Second International.
Whereas before the war the International at least paid lip
service to the class struggle and to the revolutionary sei-
zure of power, in the post-Armistice world there would be
no pretense." Extreme conservatives continued to attack
Henderson and Thomas. In reality, the Allied cabinets had
no fears. Passports were issued and the premiers offered no
opposition to Socialist delegates' attending the meeting.[28]

The evidence suggests that the Wilson Administration
also sought to use the Berne meeting as a force that would
promote a Wilsonian peace. Special efforts were made to
have Gompers attend the conference. Buckler, who had
earlier accompanied Gompers in Europe, now urged the
AFL president "to go to Berne and act with Branting and
with the Germans in opposing Bolshevism and supporting
the 14 Points." Like Colonel House, Buckler believed that
the British Cabinet was dominated by reactionaries, and
that they would work with similar groups in France and
Italy to "neutralize so far as possible the President's ideal

27 Mayer, *op. cit.*, pp. 382–83.
28 *Ibid.*, pp. 383–84.

of a clean peace." Buckler thought that international labor had to come to Wilson's rescue.[29]

Sharing the same judgment, William C. Bullitt sought to advise the Wilson Administration on the proper policy to take towards the Berne conference. Noting that Gompers had formally asked for advice on the subject, Bullitt argued that a "direct reply" from Wilson would "influence vitally the relations between our government and the labor movement of Europe." Bullitt's memorandum synthesized the views of those who argued that Wilson should make use of Gompers at Berne to draw support for the President's own aims. Bullitt wrote:

1. It is impossible for Mr. Gompers to split the trades union movement and the political labor movement of Europe. The leaders of these movements are working in perfect accord and all of them regard Mr. Gompers without sympathy.

2. It is undesirable for us to urge Mr. Gompers to follow a course of disruption.

Today the President has an enormous prestige with European labor. His proposal in regard to Russia and his address on the League of Nations completed his hold on the leaders of the labor movement. . . .

The leaders of French and British Labor plan at Berne to draw up resolutions on three things: (a) League of Nations (b) Territorial settlements (c) International Labor legislation. *They intend to follow definitely the lines the President has laid down. It is possible, therefore, to steer the conference at Berne so that it will be an enormous support to the President in his work here.*

3. It is respectfully suggested, therefore, that the President should advise Mr. Gompers to go to Berne in a spirit of cooperation and not of hostility: That the President should explain to Mr. Gompers the broad outline of his policy in regard to Germany, Russia and the League of Nations: That the President should advise Mr. Gompers to use his efforts to obtain the

[29] Buckler to Georgina Buckler, February 1, 1919; Buckler to House, December 18, 1918; Buckler Collection, House MSS.

passage of resolutions at Berne of the same sort as the terms for which we are working in Paris.[30]

Gompers was not to be swayed by Bullitt's Wilsonian arguments. He was particularly piqued to find that newspaper reports had leaked out claiming that Wilson approved the Berne conference, and had rebuked Gompers for opposing it. "Even if W. C. Bullitt or any other person correctly represented the view of the American Commissioners," Gompers was to write, their views were opposed to the entire course taken by the AFL. "If these men represented American labor," Gompers argued, "there was no further use for the A. F. of L. commission to remain in Paris."[31]

Acting to curb Bullitt's influence, Gompers and Walling prepared a memorandum to be presented to the Peace Commissioners. Addressing Colonel House, Gompers argued that "a group of men principally interested in their several political parties arranged for a conference at Berne, Switzerland." They then called "without authority" for that meeting to be held concurrently with the Peace Conference. Gompers added that he had tried his best to arrange a purely labor conference in Paris that would constructively influence the Peace Commissioners to include its recommendations in their own reports.[32]

Nevertheless, Gompers continued, the British and French labor leaders had "concluded to attend the Berne conference . . . although admitting the irregular course pursued in calling it." Berne was convened "for the purpose of arranging Socialist procedure of an international character," and that site had been chosen because it was not diplomatically proper for German, Austrian, and Bul-

---

[30] Bullitt to House, January 27, 1919, House MSS. The complete memo is printed in Mayer, *op. cit.*, pp. 386–87. Bullitt also suggested that Buckler be sent to Berne to guide labor leaders along Wilsonian lines; and that American Socialist Party delegates be granted passports to attend.

[31] Gompers, *Seventy Years of Life and Labor*, II (New York, 1925), 483–84.

[32] Gompers, "The Position of American Labor," n.d. [1919], House MSS, File drawer 34.

garian delegates to meet in Paris before the signing of a peace treaty. Gompers argued that Henderson's desire to have Berne influence the Peace Commissioners "might largely be hampered if labor conditions and provisions were submitted to them in which labor delegates" from the Central Powers participated, because their proposals would be "German-made."[33]

As far as Gompers was concerned, the war was not over. The original intention of holding a labor conference had been "covertly altered" to include delegates from nations with which "our countries were and technically are still at war." By sitting with such men and calling them "comrades" the labor delegates would be publicly condoning "the hideous and unforgettable crimes against humanity" that the Germans had committed. Only at Paris could Allied labor present its demands. Labor delegates from the Central Powers could meet and let their views be known only after the victorious Allied nations had agreed on peace terms. "We declare," Gompers told House, "the Berne conference to be irregular in conception and we can conceive of no good which would result from our attendance."[34]

When put under pressure, Woodrow Wilson refrained from taking Bullitt's advice. He probably hoped that Gompers would on his own see the sound nature of the advice presented by men like Buckler and Bullitt. But when he found that this was not the case, Wilson did not wish to challenge publicly the views of the AFL president. Gompers and the AFL mission conferred with Wilson on the 28th of January. They discussed Berne with the President in "a spirit, not of antagonism, but of deep interest" in attaining "mutual and common helpfulness." After leaving the meeting, Gompers announced his formal opposition to Berne, which he claimed would meet in order to exonerate Germany of responsibility for the war. Wilson had told him, Gompers asserted, that "there was absolutely no foundation" to stories that the Administration had criticized the AFL chief for opposing the conference. Wilson, Gom-

[33] *Ibid.*
[34] *Ibid.*

pers claimed, was "in full accord with the action we had taken."[35]

Since the Wilson Administration actually desired to use the Berne conference for its own ends, Gompers' refusal to attend did not end their efforts to influence the meeting's outcome. Wilson chose to send Bullitt himself as their observer, since this choice might indicate to Henderson that the Administration did not support Gompers. Like House, Bullitt was a frightened radical who wanted the moderate Socialists to help Wilson against both Clemenceau and Lenin.[36]

In seeking groups to attend Berne in order to steer the conference to Wilsonian anti-revolutionary ends, the Wilson Administration had more willing pupils among members of the Social-Democratic League. J. I. Sheppard, who had helped arrange the SDL's wartime mission to Europe, argued that socialism had increased by the war's end, and hence it would "have to be met and dealt with squarely by the Peace Conference." Sheppard favored the appointment of a pro-Allied American Socialist to the official Peace Commission, so that the Administration would have on hand a "loyal and well tried socialist" that could bring the Commission expertise on the general problem of socialism.[37] While Wilson would not make such an appointment, which would give formal recognition to socialism, a passport was granted to William English Walling, so that the leading pro-war Socialist could accompany Gompers as his chief adviser.[38]

When the American Peace Commission received reports that Frank Bohn and Charles E. Russell were both in Paris and wished to attend Berne, they assisted them in getting passports issued. Lansing confirmed that Russell was "a very reliable and loyal American whose opinion on the Conference at Berne would be very valuable." Bohn was

[35] Memorandum No. 1, January 30, 1919, Gompers MSS.

[36] Mayer, *op. cit.*, p. 387.

[37] Sheppard to Lansing, November 19, 1918, NA, RG 59, 763.-72110 So/80.

[38] Walling to Gompers, December 4, 1918; Gompers to U.S. Passport Agency, July 11, 1919; Gompers MSS.

also held to be reliable. The Commission decided to "facilitate the journey" of these two SDL members to Berne. But their actions at the conference had to be strictly "informal and verbal."[39]

While the American Commission allowed these two pro-Allied Socialists to attend Berne, their decision was dictated by the ideological position taken by Bohn and Russell. These men were of the type who could use their influence to curtail domination by extremists. Russell recalled that when he met Ray Stannard Baker in Paris, Wilson's representative had told him that the President was "greatly interested in the Berne meeting."[40] Russell's own view of Berne was akin to that taken by Gompers and the Social Patriots. The conference, Russell believed, was a "trick to rehabilitate the old control of the International and to embarrass the Peace Conference by exhibiting labor in the act of condoning the German betrayal of democracy." Berne was dominated by the "same old Socialist leaders" who supported the Kaiser in 1914 and who now endorsed the Bolsheviks.[41]

The Administration action on Russell was in marked contrast to the attitude it took toward participation by the regular American Socialists. Backing Bullitt, Wilson realized that his Administration could no longer refuse to permit American Socialists to attend international gatherings as they had during the war. Wilson therefore approved issuing passports to Socialists who desired to attend Berne. "It would be very unfortunate," he explained to Lansing, "to make a blunder by treating our Socialists differently from the way in which the Socialists of other countries are being handled."[42]

The other Allied leaders, however, had decided to allow Berne to go on precisely because they viewed the confer-

---

[39] Minutes of the Daily Meetings, January 21, 1919, of the Commissioners Plenipotentiary (Lansing, White, Bliss, House, Herter), NA, RG 256, 184.00101/33.

[40] Charles E. Russell Diary, February 5, 1919, Charles Edward Russell MSS, Library of Congress.

[41] *Ibid.*, January 23, 29, 1919.

[42] Wilson to Lansing, February 1, 1919, NA, RG 256, 185.161/22.

ence as a potential fiasco in which the Allied Socialists
would reveal their disunity and total failure as an opposition force. Therefore the State Department had changed
its earlier policy that any discussion of international affairs
by Socialists would embarrass the Allied governments.
State had previously held that it would be unwise to permit
unauthorized meetings conducted by representatives of
minority political parties.[43]

Despite this decision, the Administration practiced se-
lectivity in the granting of passports. John M. Work did
not receive one because "his record was extremely bad."
Socialist leader Algernon Lee did, but Polk admitted that
State had made a "mistake in granting passport to Lee
as he was connected with many disloyal movements."
Once it was granted, however, the Administration was
forced to allow Lee to attend.[44]

The Social-Democratic League found itself in a confused situation. The Wilson Administration consciously
sought to obtain the services of Administration Socialists
at Berne, for the purpose of guiding the conference in an
anti-revolutionary Wilsonian direction. The SDL, however,
was highly conscious of the need to maintain its wartime
alliance with Gompers and the AFL. This was particularly
so because the League was under the political control of
Walling and Simons, both of whom shared Gompers' general perspective. Yet Gompers had rejected the Administration's request that he attend Berne. From the start, the
League announced that joint action with the AFL "proved
to be considerable upon arrival" of their own mission in
Paris. Action between the two groups was coordinated by
Chester M. Wright, a former pro-war Socialist who had
become AFL publicity director. The SDL saw its job as
dealing with Allied Socialists whom Gompers could not
reach, because of his separation "from any political organization."[45]

[43] Lansing to Sharp, March 19, 1918, NA, RG 59, 763.72119 So.
[44] Polk to Lansing, February 20, 1919, NA, RG 59, 763.72119
So/44.
[45] Social-Democratic League of America—*One Year's Activity
of the Newly Reorganized Society*, 11–15.

The SDL delegation arranged a meeting between Gompers, Albert Thomas, and Emil Vandervelde. As a result, the League claimed, Vandervelde backed out of attending the conference. Although Thomas decided to attend, he went "solely for the purpose of fighting the Bolsheviki and German Socialists." The League reported that since so many European Socialists were to attend, "pressure was brought directly to bear by high officials of the American Government both on the Gompers Mission" and the SDL "to attend the Conference." The League escaped their predicament of divided loyalties by formally endorsing Gompers' opposition to Berne, while permitting their members to attend the conference in an individual capacity. Like Gompers, the Social-Democratic League attacked Berne as being incapable of firmly standing against Bolshevism. By giving a voice to the German Socialists, they argued, the conference automatically condoned German war crimes. Berne, according to the official SDL statement, had betrayed "democratic socialism into the hands of imperialism and reaction" by failing to oppose "anti-socialistic Bolshevism which overturned so ruthlessly . . . the promise and chance of genuine socialism in Russia."[46]

When the SDL members arrived at Berne, they quickly learned that they were not welcome. The Berne delegates refused to recognize Bohn's credentials. They preferred to seat only members of the Socialist Party as the legitimate official representatives of American socialism. The British delegation let it be known that if the SDL members were seated, they would "have to consider whether they will remain any longer in the Conference." If the SDL members sat as representatives of American socialism, the British delegates claimed, the Berne conference could only be considered as "a laughing stock."[47]

In retrospect, the deep fear of radicalism emerging from

[46] *Ibid.*
[47] "Official Bulletin of the International Labour and Socialist Conference," Berne, Switzerland, February 9, 1919, I. No. 6, morning session of Febraury 6, 1919; enclosed in Stovall to the American Commission to Negotiate Peace, NA, RG 256, 185.161/35.

the Berne conference appears naive. Berne's extremism,
Mayer points out, was of "Radical rather than Socialist
vintage: peace of reconciliation, popular representation,
pacifism, arbitration, free trade, open door, and labor legislation. Only the international controls of food and raw
materials carried collectivist overtones; and these controls
were conceived—in terms of Fabian efficiency—as an
extension of wartime institutions into the postwar world."
In addition, Berne moved fervently in the direction of anti-
Bolshevism. Not only the Social Patriots, but independents
and revisionists like Ramsay MacDonald and Karl Kautsky
supported a rededication to civil liberties, universal suffrage, and parliamentarism. These themes were implicitly
meant to be an anti-Bolshevik manifesto that would give
the Socialists a ground of solidarity with anti-radical
Wilsonians. The Berne conference had "confirmed the
moderate tempers and internal fragility of the Second International, its distrust of the German Majority, and its
readiness to participate in the struggle against Bolshevism." The fears originally expressed by the Allied premiers had been mitigated. The Berne conference actually
confirmed the worst fears held by the Russian Bolsheviks.
"European Socialism," Mayer writes, "was fast becoming
an integral part of the bourgeois, capitalist, and counter-
revolutionary amalgam which, frightened by Bolshevism,
proposed to fight it."[48]

The moderate posture taken by the Berne delegates had
been reassuring to the Wilson Administration. Returning
to Paris, William C. Bullitt accurately summed up the
compromising stance taken by the Allied Socialists:

The Conference was composed of the moderate Socialist elements of 26 countries. There was not one Bolshevist in attendance, and numerous speakers condemned the antidemocratic
standpoint of the Bolsheviks. Indeed, during the five days I sat
in the conference hall I heard not one word of "revolution."

---

[48] Mayer, *op. cit.*, pp. 395, 403, 407, 409. For a complete account
of what transpired during all the sessions of the Berne conference,
see Chapter 12 of Mayer's work: "The Stillborn Berne Conference,"
pp. 373–409.

The entire conference showed an almost pathetic confidence in President Wilson. Speaker after speaker praised the President and insisted that the masses of Europe must stand behind him in his fight for the League of Nations.[49]

The Administration's satisfaction was matched by the dissatisfaction of the more militant Socialists. Typical was the response shown by Victor Berger, the anti-war Socialist congressman from Milwaukee. Berne, Berger informed Morris Hillquit, was "cowed by the war patriots and completely dominated by English laborites." Most of them, "were 'weak sisters' and dull. The Berne aggregation was just as impossibly reactionary as the Spartacans [German Spartacists] were crazy revolutionary."[50]

That European socialism had revealed its truly conservative nature at Berne escaped Samuel Gompers. The AFL chieftain failed to distinguish between the Wilsonian doctrines of the majority at Berne, and the revolutionary socialism of the Leninists. Gompers was particularly disturbed to hear reports of Bullitt's evaluation. Gompers was confused because Wilson had approved the AFL position of rejecting Berne, but had asked pro-Allied Socialists and Wilsonians to attend.

Once again, Gompers appeared before the American Peace Commissioners. Because the AFL stood behind its own government, Gompers argued, American labor had not joined "certain other labor movements of Europe which favored . . . a negotiated peace." Now that unrest was "seething in the ranks of the people," Gompers urged that the Commissioners allow labor to find in the final "peace treaty a real recognition of its needs and demands."[51]

[49] Memorandum for Colonel House, February 9, 1919, in David Hunter Miller, *My Diary at the Conference of Paris*, V (New York, 1924), 240.

[50] Berger to Hillquit, August 20, 1919, Morris Hillquit MSS, State Historical Society of Wisconsin, Madison, Wis.

[51] Minutes of the Daily Meetings of the Commissioners Plenipotentiary, February 22, 1919; NA, RG 256, 184.00101/33. AFL participants at this session included Gompers, James Duncan, John R. Alpine, Frank Duffy, and William Green. Commissioners included Lansing, House, White, Bliss, and John Foster Dulles.

Turning to the Berne conference, Gompers expressed concern that certain "faddist parlor socialists were more agreeable to the Commission than the representatives of American labor." The Peace Commission, he was disturbed to hear, "had supported the Berne Conference and sent representatives there." Secretary Lansing then explained that Bullitt had gone as "an observer to report the doings," and that he could in no way be considered a "representative."[52]

Gompers' reply to Lansing again revealed the inflexible nature of the AFL's position. He still failed to see why the Wilson Administration desired the presence of its supporters at Berne. Bullitt, Gompers told Lansing, was considered by many to be in sympathy with the Bolsheviks. Lansing denied the allegation, and assured Gompers that the Commissioners considered labor's participation in the postwar world to be of utmost importance. Lansing further sought to put Gompers at rest. The Secretary revealed a fear he shared with the AFL leader, that radicalism was leading toward the supplanting of the nation-state by class as the basic unit in political structures. Lansing referred "to what appeared to be the significant fact of the present time—a breakdown of nationalism and an increased emphasis on class against class cutting across national lines. The Commissioners, he said, were alive to the seriousness of the problem."[53]

Gompers was undoubtedly satisfied by Lansing's concern. A short while later, however, he became incensed by further rumors that reached him. Bullitt had purportedly told Frank Bohn that he had been sent to Berne by the American Commission "in order to give his approval to the activities of the International Socialist Conference." Lansing again assured Gompers that the report was an unsubstantiated charge. Gompers insisted on putting his views in writing for future discussion.[54]

[52] *Ibid.*
[53] *Ibid.*
[54] Minutes of the Daily Meetings of the Commissioners Plenipotentiary, March 13, 1919, NA, RG 256, 184.00101/33. Cf. Mar-

In order to satisfy Gompers, and to give him a positive role in Paris, Wilson appointed the AFL president American representative to the international labor commission. Subsequently, Gompers was elected chairman of the commission as well. The creation of the commission was closely related to the Allied government's fear of radicalism. Wilson himself favored including a provision in the League of Nations Covenant that urged raising the general standards of labor's working conditions on a worldwide basis. But he did not want such a declaration to imply radicalism. Rather, Wilson desired to minimize and curb labor unrest. He would gain this end on a worldwide basis by instituting the same type of labor-management cooperation that he sought to build in the United States. For this purpose, Wilson would convene an industrial conference in 1919. The meeting was to build management-labor links and "close cooperation" so that a "practicable method of association based upon a real community of interest" could be developed. Class-oriented radicalism was to be avoided. Wilson sought to unite labor and capital in one corporate consensus.[55]

Holding a similar goal, the Allied Peace Commissioners specified in Article XX of the draft covenant (League of Nations) that the Allied powers would try to secure fair and humane labor standards. To gain this, the Supreme Allied Council established the Commission on International Labor Legislation. This body would prepare a labor charter and create an agency to supervise its administration.

The labor charter was favored by the Allied governments as a device to pacify their own working classes, who had been agitating for a voice in determining peacetime condi-

---

garet Hardy, *The Influence of Organized Labor on the Foreign Policy of the United States*, Liege, Belgium, 1936, p. 75; and Van Der Slice, *International Labor, Diplomacy and the Peace*, p. 310.

[55] Wilson to Gompers, September 3, 1919, Gompers MSS. Cf. Ronald Radosh, "The Development of the Corporate Ideology of American Labor Leaders, 1914–1933" (unpublished doctoral dissertation, University of Wisconsin, 1967), pp. 35–69, 70–79. Cf. also Levin, *Woodrow Wilson and World Politics*, pp. 166–67.

tions. The Allied governments, Van Der Slice writes, were "seeking ways in which to divert labor attention from too critical or independent actions." The creation of an international labor commission "was a device on the part of the governments to guide labor into less embarrassing channels of activity." The Allies did not want labor leaders to interfere in solving the political and national problems of the peace. But in labor's demand for labor legislation, "they saw a chance to divert labor's attention from the large political aspects of the peace 'to more constructive channels.' "[56]

Allied fears were visibly demonstrated from many sources. In a memorandum distributed to the British delegates by Lloyd George on March 25, the British Premier informed his members that "the whole of Europe is filled with the spirit of revolution. There is a deep sense not only of discontent, but of anger and revolt, amongst the work men, against pre-war conditions. The whole existing order," Lloyd George realized, "in its political, social and economic aspects is questioned by the masses . . . from one end of Europe to the other." Much of this unrest was healthy, Lloyd George argued, and showed that pre-war conditions could not be restored. But danger existed that the masses might be thrown into the "arms of the extremists" who wanted to "destroy utterly the whole existing fabric of society." Particularly dangerous was the possibility that Germany would move toward the Spartacists and that Eastern Europe would be "swept into the orbit of the Bolshevik Revolution."[57]

To deal with this situation, the Council of Ten recommended creation of the international labor commission. Major Van S. Merle-Smith, an American officer who served as the Peace Conference secretary, urged that the body serve as a sounding board for labor's opinions. The League

56 Van Der Slice, *International Labor, Diplomacy and the Peace,* pp. 306–07. My account of the International Labor Commission is heavily indebted to Van Der Slice's pioneering discussion.

57 Memo circulated by the Prime Minister on March 25, 1919; cited in *ibid.,* p. 307.

of Nations, he wrote, would have to "give expression in world affairs to the various elements of political opinion and to offer a normal rather than a dangerous channel for the development of the broad community of ideas." It would have to gather the support "of the Socialistic elements of the world for the League." If it did not, "socialistic unrest will find its expression intentionally through abnormal channels" with the consequent "possible danger of revolution." But the League could develop and mold "common and sane action."[58]

The motivation was made explicit by Edward J. Phelan, British Minister of Labor. At a luncheon meeting with David Hunter Miller and James Shotwell, Phelan asked for "some agreements for the benefit of labor." They were necessary in order to "block the effect of the projected international socialist conference, by turning labor toward constructive channels rather than merely critical ones."[59] The international labor commission, therefore, would serve as well to counter the Allied Socialists' meager efforts at independent organization and resurrection of the weak Second International.

To aid the process, Shotwell introduced a memorandum on labor organization for discussion. "The unreconciled rebellious section of the population," Wilson's aide stressed, "will turn to anarchism if we do not move honestly along the lines of social legislation." Many international Socialist congresses had been held, Shotwell conceded, but their programs were "so thoroughgoing and revolutionary that they carry us too far." The Socialists raised the question of the internal social structure of member nations, of the people's right to settle political problems, and these "dreams" blocked "the path to practical progress."[60]

But precisely because the Allied governments desired a labor commission for a negative purpose—that of chan-

---

[58] Miller, *My Diary at the Conference of Paris,* VI, Document No. 537.

[59] *Ibid.,* I, 68–69.

[60] James Shotwell, *At the Paris Peace Conference* (New York, 1937), p. 104 (Memorandum on Labor Legislation, introduced at Paris, January 3, 1919).

neling labor's actions into conservative paths—the League
meetings on labor were relatively uninspired. The first plenary session on labor, held 'in April, was "a terribly dull
meeting in fetid air in a dirty room." Worse than that, Ray
Stannard Baker commented, "the entire proceedings gave
one an unhappy sense of unreality, perfunctoriness. It *was
staged for a purpose,* to show the labor of the world—the
unrestful proletariat—that the Peace Conference had not
forgotten it." Attention "was pathetically called to the fact
that this was the first time labor had figured at a Peace
Conference, but the speeches were laborious and dull. The
main presentation was made by [George] Barnes, a labor
leader without following in his own country, and his subject was a report gathered by Gompers—regarded by labor
all over the world as a representative of extinct issues."[61]

The labor commission, in fact, presented many difficult
problems for Gompers. Each of the five nations represented
were to name two members. Five smaller nations were to
appoint one delegate. The commission, with Gompers as
its chairman, met four days a week for seven weeks. Gompers emerged as the only purely labor representative on
the body. Barnes represented Great Britain, but as a member of the War Cabinet, he also sat on Britain's Peace Commission as a government spokesman.

Most of the commission members saw their job as creation of an international labor parliament that would have
the power to make laws in the form of international treaties. Such a proposal, James Shotwell explained, was "in
contradiction with Mr. Gompers' philosophy that Labor
should abstain from taking direct part in the making of
legislation, but should use the existing political parties to
that end." Shotwell worried that European labor "was in a
very restive and critical state of mind." Therefore the commission members had to build quickly "an international
organization for labor that would be non-revolutionary and
work through governments themselves to build up the

[61] Ray Stannard Baker, "My Mission to Europe, 1918–1919,"
unpublished manuscript, Ray Stannard Baker MSS, Box 171, Series
2, p. 415 (April 11, 1919), Library of Congress.

safeguards of labor the world over."[62] Gompers had a hard task, Shotwell commented. He had first to assure "himself that all was right in the day's work at the Commission" and then satisfy his AFL colleagues, "some of whom were afraid that he might be carried away by the novel situation."[63]

The commission began by acting to institute an international labor organization and a labor conference that would develop laws which League member nations would then ratify. Failure of approval by member nations would subject the dissident powers to League penalties. Each nation's delegation to the labor conference was to consist of one government representative who would have two votes, one employer delegate, and one labor delegate. Gompers immediately objected to this formula, since it ensured a government-employer bloc against labor. Gompers could not understand why the delegates believed that employer and labor delegates would ever vote together against the government representatives. The truth was that many employers opposed labor legislation, and only struggle and "the danger of revolutions" had allowed them to secure advantages. "Did not the Commission agree," Gompers asked, "that since no convention could be adopted unless it had obtained a majority of ⅔ it had already taken sufficient precautions against the adoption of too bold measures?"[64]

Once again, Gompers found himself in the position of opposing the suggestions emanating from moderate Socialist quarters. "I am presumed to be a conservative," he admitted to the other delegates, "but save me from such radicalism as would put the workers in such a predicament and in such a minority." The program favored by the Belgian Socialist Emil Vandervelde, Gompers argued, meant increasing the power of the employers over labor. "This world is now seething," Gompers stated, and labor had to

[62] Shotwell, *op. cit.*, pp. 199–200 (notes of March 20, 1919).

[63] *Ibid.*, pp. 220–21.

[64] Minutes of the Proceedings of the Commission on International Labor Legislation, fifth meeting, February 17, 1919, NA, RG 256, 181.1401/9.

have an adequate means of expressing itself. Gompers favored giving labor delegates two votes and the employer and government representatives one vote each. He refused to support giving each group equal representation and voting power. The commission refused to accept Gompers' position. They compromised by voting to give each delegate one vote.[65]

Gompers' disagreement extended to more basic issues than voting power. He opposed the majority view that conventions developed by the commission would then be ratified and put into effect by League member nations. Certain matters, Gompers held, should not be the domain of legislative bodies. Such an issue was the working hours of adult men. Any legislation on such a social issue amounted to a Socialist scheme meant to build up the authority of government. The result would be a lowering of living standards in those nations which had a higher living standard than the International Labor Organization would establish as a base. The minimum standard set by the ILO would then become the maximum attainable by labor in the advanced nations. The delegates met this objection by passing a resolution that the establishment of standards did not give any nation the mandate to lower the standards that had already been achieved.[66]

Finally, Gompers was concerned that the American constitutional system would be subverted by the proposed plan. The Supreme Court held that labor legislation lay within the jurisdiction of the independent states of the union, not within the domain of the federal government. To approve the ILO plan meant to violate the autonomy of the states. Since each state had internal police powers, the President of the United States could not legislate on internal affairs by citing international treaties. The Senate would not carry out penalties for violation of measures of which it did not approve. It would be impossible for American delegates to agree to a labor convention that contradicted the Constitution—a "true declaration of the rights

---

[65] *Ibid.*, February 27, 28, 1918, NA, RG 256, 181.1401/17.
[66] *Ibid.*

of man." As a citizen, Gompers stressed that "he would be the first to have grave misgivings if any international convention would be regarded as binding on his own country."[67]

At the commission meetings, Gompers worked to oppose the efforts of those delegates who had sought to use the existing League machinery to gain solid benefits for labor. Socialists like Vandervelde were no longer asking for internal transformation of the capitalist states as a prerequisite for change; they now asked only that the workers influence the League to gain benefits that would curb the self-interested actions of the Allied governments. But Gompers still saw the moderate proposals of the Socialists as contrary to his own beliefs. Any stress on government action was *per se* socialistic to Gompers.

Gompers presented his own declaration to counter the one offered by Vandervelde. Any convention passed by the labor conference which was inconsistent with the constitution of a member nation, Gompers argued, only obliged that nation to make its best efforts to create appropriate labor legislation. Gompers also wanted each of the forty-eight American states to have a formal representative at the labor conference, since they were sovereign agents when it came to labor legislation. Gompers' objection was met by a new British proposal. In the case of federal governments, the national government would be obligated to communicate ILO conventions to each separate state; the states would then arrange to give their own separate approval. The American delegates continued to oppose issuance of any penalties for non-compliance. Gompers desired issuance of recommendations alone. Member nations would simply be required to submit their ILO programs to the properly constituted authorities. When the commission concluded its meetings on March 24, it submitted its draft labor convention and program to the official Peace Conference. The Conference adopted them with an additional clause that the nations should endeavor to apply the labor

[67] *Ibid.*

planks "so far as their specific circumstances will permit."[68]

When Gompers returned home, he launched a campaign to secure labor support for the peace treaty, the International Labor Organization, and American membership in the League of Nations. At the AFL's June convention, Gompers defended the peace treaty as an affirmation of AFL principles. Seaman leader Andrew Furuseth objected, arguing that the League was a super-parliament that would fix labor laws throughout the whole world. Furuseth was critical because the labor charter did not prohibit involuntary servitude, nor did it assert the right of seamen to leave their ships when in harbor. "There isn't a solid thing here," Furuseth told the convention, "that leaves any of the American ideals in this document." Gompers angrily replied that some people were handed Paradise and still managed to "find some fault with it." Although perfection may not have been actually obtained, Gompers stated, at least they had realized international labor unity.[69]

Privately, Gompers had developed some doubts about the outcome of the labor commission's deliberations. He had received reports that after he had left Paris, the ILO provisions had been so weakened "as to practically nullify effectiveness." Gompers was wary of asking "the rank and file of labor to endorse propositions which have been or may be made valueless."[70]

Woodrow Wilson assured Gompers that only technical changes had been made. Differences in climate, habit, customs, and economic opportunity made strict uniformity in codes difficult to obtain. But since the statement of principles asserted "that labor should not be regarded merely as an article of commerce," the President noted, and that ILO standards should be accepted throughout the world, the results were progressive and would mean lasting benefits for the world's wage earners. Each convention would have to be submitted to the United States government for

[68] Bernard Mandel, *Samuel Gompers* (Yellow Springs, Ohio, 1963), p. 424.

[69] *1919 AFL Convention*, pp. 83, 399–416.

[70] Gompers to Polk, June 16, 1919, NA, RG 59, 763.72110/5338.

ratification. Acceptance or rejection, Wilson assured Gompers, "lies in our own hands irrespective of the constitution of the general conference." The President closed by letting Gompers know that he depended on the AFL leader to give the Administration continued support.[71]

Wilson must have known that he had no reason to fear the loss of Gompers' allegiance. Throughout the war years, Gompers had proved his willingness to use American organized labor in the service of Administration foreign policy. As an American labor leader in a nation where the Administration sought acceptance for labor as part of a corporate consensus, Gompers shared both Wilson's and Lansing's aversion to any form of class politics—moderate Socialist or revolutionary. When he functioned in the international arena, therefore, Gompers permitted no alliances to be forged with the representatives of moderate centrist parties.

Gompers' position, ironically, interfered with the achievement of united action and solidarity between Wilson's European followers and the American Wilsonians. Gompers' views and obstinacy often weakened Wilson's hold on European affairs and strengthened the Allied Right and the wartime Social Patriots. But since Wilson himself viewed the League as part of an effort to achieve a "road away from revolution," Gompers and the AFL were naturally valued allies of the conservative Administration leaders. Although Wilson may have presented an idealist program for the postwar world, when he toured Europe at the war's end he urged a moderate course. Wilson consistently remained loyal to the ideal of class harmony, and he avoided making any direct appeals to workers and Socialists. The President made no attempt to gain support for his program by suggesting an alliance with the moderate social democrats in Europe. Gompers' rejection of these Socialist groups only parallelled the policy of the Administration.

Gompers' differences with the Administration were

[71] Wilson to Gompers, June 21, 1919, NA, RG 59, 763.72119/5571a.

purely tactical. While Wilson saw the advantages of having a sympathetic observer at the Berne Conference—in order, hopefully, to steer the meeting along Wilsonian anti-revolutionary lines—Gompers' ideological position did not allow the AFL president even to consider attending. Had Gompers attended, his mere presence would have indicated support to his most important opponents in the international labor movement. Gompers would have appeared to be endorsing the validity of political rather than business unionism, and he did not wish to permit his opponents to make such a spurious claim. In some cases, therefore, Gompers' position appeared as more militantly conservative than the policy espoused by the Wilson Administration. Yet both he and Woodrow Wilson sought the same long-range goals.

Like the Wilson Administration, and the subsequent Republican administrations of the 1920's, Samuel Gompers favored an interventionist—rather than an isolationist—course abroad.[72] In many respects, Gompers shared the same Protestant missionary zeal for which Woodrow Wilson was so famous. While a "progressive spirit" had been manifest in domestic affairs, Gompers wrote in 1923, "it still slumbers where the affairs of the world are concerned." There could be no claim for any "living mandate from the people to play the part of 'splendid isolation,' which would be better called the art of blind hermitage." The door was open to "intelligent and constructive participation in the affairs of the world." One's soul could not be inspired nor could it achieve a sense of righteousness "until we stand forth to the world as a nation of people unafraid to go to the help of those who are afflicted." Americans who favored isolation, Gompers claimed, had "buried their heads in old documents from which they have quoted what seemed to suit their needs." Actually, Gompers argued, the Founding Fathers had not counseled isolation. "Pious words have cloaked many a detestable cause,

[72] For the view that the AFL followed an isolationist course in foreign policy, see James O. Morris, *Conflict within the AFL* (Ithaca, N.Y., 1958) pp. 81–82.

but they were never used to less credit than in holding America back from her manifest duty." Like Wilson, Gompers wanted public assertion of "America's determination to help the world to right itself and save itself."[73]

In loudly proclaiming the right and manifest duty of the United States to help and eventually save the world, Samuel Gompers had shown that organized labor shared the same values and aspirations as American businessmen, statesmen, and government leaders. Gompers also left a legacy of labor opposition to those Americans who sought a more limited and circumspect role for the United States abroad. From the 1930's to the present, the majority of American labor leaders subscribed to an interventionist doctrine. This appeared most acceptable and reasonable during World War II—when most Americans supported the war effort against the leaders of Nazi Germany and Imperial Japan. But in the postwar era, new international problems arose as the Cold War began. Once again, the leadership of organized labor showed that they had learned the lessons taught them by Samuel Gompers. In exchange for acceptance by government and private groups, the labor leaders became the most militant advocates of the new Cold War policy. The ranks of organized labor produced the most dependable advocates of a hard-line policy. Eventually, labor leaders would even be willing to work with the Central Intelligence Agency to accelerate their mutually shared program of anti-communism. How the era of Lovestone diplomacy developed is the concern of the rest of this book.

[73] Gompers, "Progressives, Be Leaders," *American Federationist*, XXX (1923), 66. For other examples of Gompers' rejection of isolationism, see William C. Redfield, "America's World" (speech of December 9, 1922, with introduction by Gompers), *ibid.*, 122–27; Gompers, "The World's Choice—League of Nations or League of Financiers," *ibid.*, XXXI (1924), 17–41; Gompers, "American Labor in Peace, War and International Relations," *ibid.*, 385–91; Gompers, "Avoid Spurious Dollar Diplomacy," *ibid.*, 820–21.

CHAPTER

X

LOVESTONE DIPLOMACY—

1945-1950

After the Versailles Peace Conference, the AFL refused to build new ties with European labor, unless it could establish its own terms. Allied labor moved in the postwar era to build a new international trade union federation, the International Federation of Trade Unions. This body was created in July 1919 at a conference held in Amsterdam. Samuel Gompers had originally planned to affiliate with the group, but the socialistically oriented program of moderate European unions led the AFL leaders to stay out. The IFTU had called for socialization of the means of production and approved of unions taking stands on political issues. When the question of formal affiliation to the body was taken up by the AFL Executive Council in 1921, the majority of AFL leaders firmly rejected such a course. In addition to the IFTU's political orientation, the AFL leaders opposed the failure of the IFTU to support complete autonomy for all national union centers.[1]

The AFL maintained its course throughout the 1920's. The rise of Hitler and the birth of fascism, however, pro-

[1] Unless otherwise indicated, material from this brief introductory section is based upon: Philip Taft, *Organized Labor in American History* (New York, 1965) 591–606; Philip Taft, *The A.F. of L. in the Time of Gompers* (New York, 1957), 433–40; and Philip Taft, *The A.F. of L. from the death of Gompers to the Merger* (New York, 1959), 204–17, 342–44.

duced a need for re-evaluation of AFL policy. In early 1933, AFL President William Green urged a boycott of German goods until trade union freedom was restored in Germany and repression of Jews was ended. The AFL also endorsed Lend-Lease aid to Great Britain, which it termed an instrumentality of the national defense of the United States. At the same time, AFL leaders stressed that they wanted the United States to maintain a policy of neutrality and to avoid involvement in another European war.

The changed European situation led the AFL to increase its contacts with the IFTU. The British Trades Union Congress wanted the AFL to enter the international body, and negotiations for that purpose began in 1935. The AFL finally decided to enter, but its associaiton with the IFTU was to be relatively short. In the same period, IFTU officials had approached Soviet unions about the prospects of affiliation. Soviet Russia had become a major enemy of Nazi Germany, and was pursuing the policy of a "united front" against fascism. Green opposed overtures to the Soviets, arguing that the Soviet unions were the equivalent of the Nazi labor front in Germany.

Another area in which the unions grew closer to the position taken by the State Department was foreign economic policy. The basic policy of the United States was the program of reciprocity treaties developed by Cordell Hull. Conceived by the New Dealers as a vehicle for domestic recovery as well as a vital part of U.S. foreign policy, the achievement of reciprocity was said to mean employment of labor at high wages. Great support for reciprocity came after export-minded steel, auto, electrical, and machine industries were unionized by the CIO, but in the early 1930's some key AFL leaders, such as John P. Frey of the Metal Trades Department, approved the program. Other AFL unions opposed the Hullian doctrine, arguing that imports would lead to reduction in wages and jobs in their industries.[2]

[2] Henry W. Berger, "Union Diplomacy," 138–52. Berger presents a complete account of the fight between Franklin D. Roosevelt and AFL Vice-President Matthew Woll on this issue.

The Administration continued to argue that the road to prosperity lay through increased production, which meant a sustained search for foreign markets. While the newer CIO unions were most favorable to export-minded arguments, it was the growing opposition of United Mine Workers chieftain John L. Lewis to Administration policy that received a great deal of attention.

Lewis has often been accused by his detractors of being an isolationist, and of holding a short-sighted policy toward European affairs before Pearl Harbor. The complete story of Lewis' evolving position awaits publication of Henry W. Berger's careful study. Berger points out that Lewis certainly opposed involvement in a European war, but he did not favor the Axis powers. Rather, Lewis hoped for a solution of domestic problems through extended trade with Latin America, which became for him the key to a peacetime policy as well as to a defensive strategy for the United States. Believing that German, Japanese, and British traders were sucessfully challenging American exporters in the European market, Lewis "advocated a developed, balanced and integrated economy for Latin America in order to provide a stable and prosperous market for American goods."[3]

Lewis saw success and neutrality guaranteed if Latin America was reserved as a bastion for American commercial enterprise. Lewis won support for his opposition to the conscription bill, but as European hostilities increased many CIO unions began to move in an opposite direction. Unions such as International Ladies Garment Workers Union, which had a predominantly Jewish membership, called for aid to the Allies "short of war." By 1940, many labor leaders had joined the Committee to Defend America by Aiding the Allies. Included in this group were Louis Hollander, Vice-President of the Amalgamated Clothing Workers; Alex Rose, President of the United Hat, Cap and Millinery Workers; Robert J. Watt, Vice-President of the International Ladies Garment Workers Union; A. Philip

[3] *Ibid.*, 156–73. Quotation is on p. 163.

Randolph, President of the Sleeping Car Porters, and ILGWU President David Dubinsky.

From their perspective, the AFL continued to move in a similar direction. Their 1940 convention declared in favor of extension of all aid to Britain, short of war, and William Green came out publicly for Lend-Lease aid. He favored, however, a Congressional limit on the time during which the President could make use of powers given him under the Act. The AFL also established a committee for national defense, a move which was followed by CIO endorsement of Administration defense measures.

Both labor federations had entered into an Administration consensus on U.S. foreign policy. But the AFL primarily kept its sights on the need to oppose European communism. In 1944, the AFL convention endorsed creation of the Free Trade Union Committee (FTUC), a group that would play a major role in the postwar period. The FTUC was empowered to raise one million dollars to assure assistance to workers from liberated nations and to laborers in South and Central America. But its main *raison d'être*, as Philip Taft candidly explains, was "the growth of Communism as a world force," which had brought "a new and alien element into the international labor movement." Since the AFL leaders believed that the war had destroyed moderate labor movements, the AFL "saw the need to support a labor movement devoted to freedom and democracy."[4]

The FTUC became the official foreign policy arm of the AFL in the latter days of the War. While it worked to aid trade unionists who were part of the anti-Nazi underground, it tried to move against those who were sympathetic to the Communists. Hence its leaders worked closely with Socialists who were opponents of both the Nazis and Communists, and who were not cooperating with Communist-led resistance groups in France and Italy.

The history of AFL foreign policy since 1945 is in many ways tied up with the personal history of Jay Lovestone,

[4] Philip Taft, *The A.F. of L. from the Death of Gompers to the Merger,* 343.

the relatively anonymous and somewhat mysterious archi-
tect of labor's foreign policy. No other non-governmental
figure, associated with a private institution, wields as
much power in the making of foreign policy. The AFL-CIO
currently uses twenty per cent of its annual two-million-
dollar budget for foreign affairs. Lovestone, as chairman
of the AFL-CIO International Affairs Department, is in
charge of its disbursement.

Jay Lovestone is particularly equipped to handle the
AFL-CIO's international anti-Communist program. In his
youth, Lovestone had himself been the top American Communist leader. Lovestone, who is now in his seventies, had
left his native Lithuania at the age of ten. Settling in New
York City, he attended and graduated from the City College of New York. He grew up in the left-wing atmosphere
of New York's large immigrant Jewish community, and
became one of the founders of the American Communist
Party in 1919.

As editor of *The Communist*, the Party's theoretical
journal, Lovestone revolved in the highest party echelons.
In a short time, he was elected General Secretary of the
Communist Party of the United States, that organization's
highest position. His downfall came after the 1928 congress of the Communist International in Russia. Lovestone
had the misfortune of supporting the position espoused by
Nikolai Bukharin, who was soon to be ousted from the
world Communist movement by Stalin. Rather than join
in the repudiation of Bukharin, Lovestone stuck to his
guns, and was himself soon expelled from the Party. Although Lovestone had been found guilty of the heresies of
"American exceptionalism" and "revisionism," he refused
to give up his allegiance to communism. He rapidly formed
an opposition group of Communists, and throughout the
1930's Lovestone and his followers continually sought re-
admission to the American Communist Party.

Considering himself a Marxist, and an enemy of the
Stalinists, Lovestone offered his services to labor leaders
who were busy fighting the tightly organized Communist
bloc in their unions. Lovestone first found a niche in the

United Auto Workers, where along with his friend Irving Brown, he supported the faction led by UAW President Homer Martin. Martin lost control of the UAW leadership, and Lovestone lost his position with the auto workers. Lovestone's fight against the Stalinists, however, now brought him to the attention of David Dubinsky. Dubinsky, head of the powerful International Ladies Garment Workers Union, was faced with a militant pro-Communist minority that threatened to disrupt his control of the union. Lovestone personally knew most of the Communists in the New York clothing industry, and was able effectively to aid Dubinsky in combatting and isolating his opposition. By 1940, Lovestone disbanded his own Communist opposition group. He now took a position with a labor group created by Dubinsky for the purpose of drumming up labor support for intervention against the Axis powers. Dubinsky next appointed Lovestone to head the ILGWU's International Relations Department. When Dubinsky, William Green, and George Meany formed the Free Trade Union Committee in 1944, Lovestone was their immediate choice as its executive secretary.

Working closely with Lovestone at the war's end was Irving Brown, his old associate from the factional fight in the United Auto Workers. Brown had already been working in Europe as director of the Labor and Manpower Division of the Foreign Economic Administration, serving on this job from April through September of 1945. Brown shared Lovestone's concern with the growth of Communist strength among European labor. When Brown had finished his stint with the FEA, Lovestone asked him to do some work for the FTUC in Europe. Brown agreed immediately, and stayed on the job for seventeen years. Brown became Jay Lovestone's most important European operative, and administered AFL foreign policy throughout Western Europe. Wherever Lovestone and Brown saw a threat of Communist strength, they moved into action. Their aim was to help build AFL-type unions that would not only guide trade unionism in a stable craft direction, but would work to gather support for U.S. foreign policy

objectives among European workers. To do this, Brown
and Lovestone had to work to free European unionism
from any association with communism. The definition of
this task led Irving Brown to work primarily in France,
Germany, and Greece. It is the Free Trade Union Committee efforts to which we must now turn our attention.

I. *The AFL in France*

A few months after leaving the FEA, Irving Brown arrived in Paris. Observing the workings of the postwar
coalition government, Brown predicted a crisis. The government was composed of a working coalition made up of
the Mouvement Républicain Populaire (MRP), the Communists, and the Socialists. The Communists held a slim
parliamentary majority, and were fighting for an important cabinet seat. While the Communists desired to aid
in the reconstruction of the French economy, Brown reported, they did not want to take on too much responsibility for operation of the government. This would leave
them freedom to criticize and build their own strength.
The Socialists agreed to form a government based on a
coalition between the three leading parties, but insisted
that the Communists take responsibility. Because of the
poor economic situation, the lack of coal and basic raw
materials, Brown saw future paralysis for the radical parties. "I am beginning to lay the groundwork," he wrote to
AFL headquarters, "for our relationship with the non CP
and CGTers."[5]

[5] Irving Brown, memo, November 18, 1945, Florence Thorne
MSS, State Historical Society of Wisconsin, Madison, Wis. Florence Thorne, whose papers are filed as part of the massive AFL
collection at the State Historical Society of Wisconsin, was the
original secretary to and confidant of Samuel Gompers. As the
"grand old lady" of the AFL in the late 1940's and 1950's, Miss
Thorne received copies of many of the confidential reports and
papers of Irving Brown and Jay Lovestone. These are enclosed
among her own papers. Undoubtedly, the reticent Brown and

The major problem facing Brown was the strength of the General Confederation of Labor (CGT). Because of Communist strength within the CGT, Brown found the French situation to be "not very encouraging." The CP, he frankly admitted, had "a terrific hold on the CGT. They control whatever is important to control. The opposition forces are weak, lack program and are divided in their strategy." To deal with this problem, Brown began to make preparations for the April 1946 CGT Convention. He already had "made contact with some of the opposition forces," Brown reported, "and this may develop into something in the near future." Strict "caution and watchful waiting," he warned, "must be practiced or one can spill the beans." Brown advised staying "close to the French situation" since he viewed it as the "key to Western European labor developments "[6]

The Communists were strong among labor, Brown argued, because of their record with the Resistance. They claimed seventy-five thousand martyrs, they had a large propaganda machine, and the dire economic circumstances allowed the Party to appear "before the masses as their only savior." Their forces had grown to such an extent that due to political and electoral successes a "conspiracy of silence" reigned about the "true nature of communism." No longer did opposition leaders dare mention the role played by the French CP before the invasion of the Soviet Union.

The mass of the CGT was non-Communist, Brown claimed, and only voted for the Party because its leaders appeared as "dynamic trade unionists" and "very dynamic fighters." At present their aim was to defend the national interest of France and to build a Popular Front. Their ef-

---

Lovestone are unaware that these files are open to inspection in a public manuscript collection. The Richard Deverall Papers at Catholic University, Washington, D.C., contain many Lovestone letters that are particularly rich. This collection was only recently opened to scholars, too late for use in this book.

[6] Irving Brown to Abraham Bluestein, November, 22, 1945, *ibid.*

fort to control Western European labor through the CGT was aided by the World Federation of Trade Unions, to which the unions of the USSR, the British Trades Union Congress, and the American CIO also belonged. "The British and the Americans," Brown wrote, "have contributed to the construction of such a world-wide CP controlled Frankenstein by their acceptance of the World Federation."

A further problem faced Brown. Many former non-Communist CGT leaders had become collaborationists during the wartime Vichy regime. Because they were so anti-Communist, they felt justified in continuing to function as CGT leaders even under the Nazi occupation of France. Some of these men had been close to Léon Jouhaux, the aging Socialist CGT chieftain, and had been identified with his period of active leadership in the union movement. Their wartime activity compromised them, and the Communists used these facts to their own advantage. Jouhaux, however, was still undoubtedly the CGT's outstanding personality. While he was not in the CP camp, Brown judged that he did not carry on "a fight against the Communist Party" and instead held "a very cautious cooperative attitude." The Communists could isolate him and still hold enough votes to maintain their control of the CGT.

The major group of committed anti-Communists was gathered around *Résistance Ouvrière,* a small newspaper put out by the anti-CP Force Ouvrière. Brown singled out its leader, Robert Bothereau, as "the most hopeful in understanding the struggle ahead." Bothereau planned to expand his paper before the April CGT Convention. His group, moreover, was "*secretly sending people all over the country building up their fences and preparing for the election of delegates.*" Most important was that Bothereau's group was "interested in help from us." They had to discuss the situation with Jouhaux, "without whom they could not do anything." Their goal was to unite the opposition forces within the CGT so that they could attend the April convention "with [a] fighting bloc against the Communist Party's forces." There was no doubt, Brown wrote, "that it is an almost unbelievably difficult job but it must be done and even if victory cannot be achieved by April the basis will have been laid for the future."

Brown was frank to observe that the Communist forces within the CGT could not be defeated at the April convention. The real danger was that the Communists would move on their own against the CGT minority and reduce them to impotency. The only reason the Communists were strong, Brown reasoned, was because they could out-maneuver and out-finance their opponents. Yet Bothereau's group was "the most hopeful . . . around which the non-communist forces can build a stable opposition." Brown's goal was clear: to work toward splitting the CGT and creating a dual union. Such a policy, however, would leave him and the AFL open to severe condemnation from any good trade unionist, and on traditional union grounds.

They could not publicly give funds to the opposition, Brown understood, because that would expose the AFL to criticism from the Communists. Such a step was "unworkable and dangerous." Nevertheless, Brown stressed, *the best possible way to assist is to work with the Bothereau group.* This, however, meant "working with an opposition rather than with official unions." The paradox and challenge was to operate in such a way "that neither the AF of L nor the comrades in the CGT will be open to justifiable criticism." Pledging to give thought to the problem, Brown hoped "to come up with a method and a proposal very soon." One thing was clear. France was "the number one country in Europe from the point of view of saving the western labor movement from totalitarian control." Brown requested that Matthew Woll and David Dubinsky take up the question of "putting some money at our disposal over here."[7]

The same dilemma that faced Brown—to split the CGT, while avoiding reproach for his activities—faced the anti-

[7] Brown to Bluestein, November 27, 1945, *ibid.* (Emphasis in original.)

Communist opposition among French labor. Bothereau
and his group wanted to accept AFL funds, but were "reluctant to accept aid that will compromise them in their
internal struggle in the CGT." Brown preferred to wait until they had devised an appropriate formula for securing
AFL money. Meanwhile, Brown had already made contact
with another reliable unionist, Largentier, "who has developed a group of non-Communist forces within the
CGT." This man, Brown felt, "could go places if he had
sufficient financial aid." While he was not part of Bothereau's group, he had "more freedom of action and movement not being tied down to a functionary's job." Until
Jouhaux was ready to break with the CGT, Brown thought
it best to give aid to this member of the printer's union.
Needed immediately were 600,000 francs to finance three
months' work. Brown asked that the money be deposited
in the account of the Jewish Labor Committee in New
York. The Committee would serve as a front, and the funds
would be secretly transferred to the opposition group in
France. "There is no great hope that the CP will be defeated," Brown admitted, "but a crystallization and con-
solidation of the true trade union forces can begin."[8] That
Irving Brown was determining for French workers what
the "true trade union forces" were, and working against
the majority of the French working class, did not seem to
faze him.

Irving Brown was clearly urging that the AFL finance
an otherwise impotent and miniscule opposition force. A
few days later, Brown wrote again to state how badly the
opposition desired AFL funds. Even reformist unions were
under Communist influence, he reported. The Communists pushed through their candidates and would be able
to control the April CGT Convention. They controlled most
of the strategic unions. The metal workers had an executive committee of twenty-five, only four members of which
were not Communists. Brown proposed building an AFL
base among Socialist groups, disillusioned Communists,
and intellectuals. An opposition, he hoped, was "in the

[8] Brown to Matthew Woll, December 5, 1945, *ibid.*

process of materializing and beginning to take shape." That is why it was urgent "to put at my disposal the funds suggested in my previous report."[9]

Brown became more insistent upon learning of the Communist Party's tactics for the April convention. The Party was proposing that the CGT Secretariat be reduced from nine to four members—Franchon, Louis Saillant, Pierre Reynaud, and Léon Jouhaux. This step would eliminate five anti-Communists, and put Jouhaux in a weaker position, leaving "the commies completely in control." The CP also wanted to reorganize national unions to end their control by "reformist" elements, and were proposing amalgamation. The metal workers union would then encompass white-collar clerical workers, for instance, which would break the hold of Socialist groups on unions of governmental employees.

Because of this CP plan, Brown argued that a long-range program to build an opposition required a great deal of money. He now revised his financial estimate to at least $100,000 for six months' work. "It would pay to aid in the entire job," Brown advised, "or not at all." It was a "desperate situation, but the stakes are high and are worth the fight for free trade unionism." Referring to his plan of backing a dual union, Brown observed that "it is not a nice way of doing business." The European national unions, however, could not "be treated with in the same open, direct fashion as in the U.S.A." It was simply "necessary to work with the opposition groups." Largentier and his followers in the printers' union were judged to be "good, reliable, trustworthy union men" and Brown had great "faith in their possibilities." He still hoped for "a split at the next convention."[10]

When the CGT Convention finally took place in April, Brown regretfully reported that it was completely dominated by the Communists. "It is almost safe to say," he advised, "that the CGT no longer exists as a trade union." But since it was so obviously a Stalinist organization, many

[9] Brown to Woll, December 10, 1945, *ibid.*
[10] Brown to Woll, December 14, 1945, *ibid.*

hesitant members of the opposition were now prepared
"for the eventual and inevitable split." At the convention,
eighty-two per cent of the delegates voted for changes proposed by the CP. The CGT was reorganized according to
the CP's plans, and a majority of the delegates approved
the amalgamation scheme. Six federations controlled by
the CP now ran the CGT, and the power of the smaller
non-Communist unions had been eliminated. The pretense
that the CGT was apolitical could no longer be maintained,
and to Brown, the CGT stood "today as a direct instrument
of Communist Party policy." The reformists had voluntarily submitted to "complete imprisonment."

The Communists had won, Brown believed, because they
were able to use their role in the Resistance as a spring-
board for capturing strategic positions in the unions. Elements opposed to their domination were smeared, and union militants who opposed decrees issued by the Communist Minister of Labor were dismissed. Yet the habit of
preserving trade union solidarity was so ingrained that
even Jouhaux did not wish to fight the Communists. The
Party, in the meantime, had built up a single-purpose bloc
with a clear line, while its opposition was divided and had
not even a minimum program around which to unite. Finally, the Communists never allowed the workers to forget
that many CGT leaders had gone over to the regime of
Marshal Pétain in 1940.

Brown shrewdly moved to use the Communists' conservative postwar policy to try and discredit both the Party
and the CGT. As part of the government of reconstruction,
the French Communists supported piecework and speedup,
and developed the slogan of "produce, always produce."
Because the Party favored sacrifices by the workers, the
opposition of the rank-and-file to bad conditions and to the
high cost of living produced no response from Party leadership. "The Communists," Brown correctly observed, "are
acting as a brake on the economic demands of the workers." Government control of wages froze the average laborer's income, while prices rose and food shortages created a thriving black market. The Communist Minister

of Labor, Croizat, had to assume responsibility for wage practices. His endorsement of piecework was particularly embarrassing to CP members in the CGT, and Brown thought it could serve to "strengthen opposition forces."[11]

Brown's estimate of Communist policy was accurate. The Communists did not advocate a revolutionary course. They entered the government, historian Gabriel Kolko writes, "on the basis of a United Front strategy and a desire to see French power restored at home and abroad. Given their relationship to the working class, only they could extract the indispensable precondition for the restoration of the Old Order—production. The Communists became the party of production, even the party of speedup." The French Communists ironically played "a critical role in disciplining the working class and ultimately making it possible for capitalism as an institution to survive and profit in France. Above all the Communists were the advocates of production, for they above all others could make the workers toil."[12]

The adoption by the French Communist Party of a basically capitalist course played into the AFL's hands. It provided Irving Brown with a solid ground for his splitting policy. If Brown had trouble, it was due to the lack of "central direction," a "unifying program" and a "strong, dynamic leadership" in the Bothereau and Jouhaux groups. Despite all the factors that should have made it easy for them, the opposition had not united its forces behind a clear program. The result was that it moved in a leftist direction, permitting the CP to characterize the opposition as a " 'Trotskyite' movement." Brown, of course, preferred that discontent be channeled into a "constructive" path—not toward the Left.

The CGT could not be reformed, Brown advised, because of its "Stalinite" nature. The future of the French union movement lay "in the eventual split which will leave the

[11] Brown, "The C.G.T. Convention," n.d. [1946], *ibid.*
[12] Gabriel Kolko, *The Politics of War: The World and United States Foreign Policy, 1943–1945* (New York, 1969), pp. 439, 443.

CGT as a pure, unadulterated CP organization about which the workers will have no illusions." Believing that the "truly militant elements" were moving in this direction, Brown hoped that the "catastrophic defeat" suffered by the opposition in the April CGT Convention would lead them to "weld together a common front . . . without any illusions and without any false hopes about what can be done under the false banner of unity." It was necessary, Brown warned, to "handle this issue with great care and preparation so that the split becomes a logical necessity in the eyes of the workers and not something which they fear will reinforce the interests of the employers." It was a "question of setting out the objectives" and "planning carefully and tactfully how to mature the struggle so that the CP cannot use the issue of unity falsely against the democratic elements."

Brown had met during the convention with every opposition delegate, both individually and in small groups. The new leaders showed a fighting character and had a sound base in the provinces. Brown began to see some chance that Jouhaux and Bothereau would split from the CGT, since by now they too recognized this development as "inevitable." Bothereau had even desired to resign his CGT executive post during the convention, but Jouhaux restrained him. The time was obviously ripe, Brown suggested, for the opposition to "consolidate itself around a minimum program" and to wage a fight for "free" trade unionism. In this struggle, he pointed out, the AFL could "be of infinite assistance in a multiplicity of ways."[13]

The AFL's first opportunity to assist arose in May 1947, when labor walkouts took place for wage increases. The Communists were now trying to stir up trouble, and the Socialists were pointing out that the strikes were politically inspired. Brown asked that the AFL use pressure to have the State Department keep Ambassador Jefferson Caffrey in France. Caffrey, Brown stressed, "has been a bulwark for the right side in this struggle." Brown also had

[13] Brown, "The C.G.T. Convention," n.d. [1946], Thorne MMS.

succeeded in forging links with the Socialist Party, which had "begun to make some moves on the trade union side in France that are encouraging." Vouching for the "soundness and ability" of Socialists in the union movement, Brown pledged to "work with them very closely." Any AFL aid could now "be strategically used." Brown noted that when "requests [for money] come they are urgent."[14]

Brown's tireless efforts had finally borne fruit. To Brown, the AFL was participating in a vast international struggle against communism. Meeting in New York City with Matthew Woll, William Green, George Meany, David Dubinsky, and Jay Lovestone, Brown reported that the AFL had "penetrated every country of Europe." The AFL was a "world force in conflict with a world organization in every field affecting international labor." It was defined by Brown as the "focal point around which the struggle for freedom is now waging in every part of the world." Those opposed to communism were looking toward the AFL for encouragement, support, and assistance. Brown recommended that the AFL increase its efforts to have American unions affiliated with the World Federation of Trade Unions withdraw from that organization. One alternative that could be stressed was membership in the International Trade Secretariats, organizations of workers in different trades, with a potential role in international labor developments. Secondly, Brown suggested holding an international conference on the Marshall Plan, which would serve as a pretext for withdrawal from the WFTU.

It was in France and Italy that the AFL was "engaged in our most immediate and critical activity to advance free trade unionism." Because of Communist influence in union federations, Brown claimed, "these countries are in danger of going communist." If this occurred, the result would be to "push America off the continent." The AFL could prevent this by working with the French railway unions, the miners, and the postal, telephone, and telegraph workers. All of these unions were outside of the CGT. But

---

[14] Brown, "Report on Englasd and France," May 1947, *ibid.*

above all, Brown stressed the printers as the major "source of aid and leaders."[15]

By December, Brown had convinced some of the groups with which he was working to break from the CGT. The French Communists were now opposed to Marshall Plan aid for the reconstruction of France. Twenty unions affiliated with the CGT had declared a general strike and had formed a National Strike Committee, controlled by CP members. "The Force Ouvrière [Bothereau] group has declared itself against the strike," Brown reported, "but has not been too well organized." Even Jouhaux was being pushed into fighting the Communists, although he still refrained "from the necessary organizational steps to guarantee success." But Brown felt confident enough to report that the AFL's "friends are . . . beginning to develop their organization throughout France." There would definitely be another national trade union movement.[16] One of the reasons the Force Ouvrière was able to organize was because it received heavy financial assistance from the AFL. In October, the AFL leaders in New York agreed to send the FO five thousand dollars every three weeks, and to extend their payments into January of 1948.[17]

Results of the kind envisioned by Brown were produced. Reporting for the leadership of the CIO, John Brophy remarked that the failure of the general strike "marked a break in the power of the unions. That strike, political in purpose, resulted in a split in the Communist controlled CGT. Led by Jouhaux and Bothereau, one fifth of the membership seceded and organized the anti-CGT Force Ouvrière. This break was an indication of considerable dissatisfaction among the workers with the political strike method." However, Brophy honestly noted, "the CGT still has the bulk of the organized industrial workers." As late

[15] Minutes, Meeting of the International Labor Relations Committee of the AFL, November 11, 1947, *ibid.*

[16] Confidential Report of Irving Brown, December 17, 1947, *ibid.* October 19, 1947, *ibid.*

[17] Minutes of the AFL International Labor Relations Committee, October 19, 1948, *ibid.*

as 1949, when CGT membership had dropped from six to three million, and the FO had gained 800,000 members, Brophy realized that it "still has to prove itself." Even though the International Confederation of Free Trade Unions (ICFTU) now existed as an international anti-Communist trade union center, Brophy admitted that in France the CGT "still has sufficient numbers and experience to be a considerable force."[18]

Brophy, if anything, had overstated the case for the FO. The bulk of industrial workers remained within the CGT, and only a few small white collar unions made up the ineffective Force Ouvrière. Nevertheless, Brown's success in creating even this kind of split led to a briefing session for the Department of State. In a private meeting held in Washington, D.C., Brown explained that "the Russians and the Communists have never fundamentally believed that they could take power in France, at least within this time period." They did, however, use their power to prevent economic and political stability. But their attempt to stage a general strike proved advantageous for the "possibility of defeating the Communists."

Since the liberation the CP had controlled the trade union apparatus, Brown told State, and they were now trying to "prevent any kind of government in France . . . from operating." They used the unions to keep France from playing its proper role in the reconstruction of Europe. Before German industry could realize its industrial potential, Brown stressed, the "French situation must be resolved." France was the "area where we must fight." Brown explained that the strike effort of 1947 was a political act aimed "against the successful conclusion and successful application of the Marshall Plan." The Communists desired to bring on an inflationary situation and to increase the problems of the French economy.

The CP's "political" strike, however, appeared to offer

[18] John Brophy, "European Trade Unions and Related Matters," n.d. [1949], John Brophy MSS, Catholic University, Washington, D.C.

"the major basis for the creation of a new trade union movement in France outside of the CGT, which was anti-Communist." The creation of the FO marked for Brown "the real defeat of the Communists," because the top leadership of the FO group had originally "fundamentally opposed the creation of a new trade union movement." Referring specifically to Léon Jouhaux, Brown admitted that an important element among the union leaders still opposed creation of a new movement. But the CP had "so incensed and so angered the non-Communist trade unionists" that the FO was formed "against the decision and the policy of the Jouhaux leadership."

Brown was realistic enough to acknowledge the limited nature of his success. The developing economic situation bode ill for the future of the FO. Between January and October of 1948, "the general economic situation in France deteriorated completely, from the standpoint of the workers." Wage increases were completely wiped out by inflation. The FO and other non-Communist unions that identified with the government's program were harmed. The workers "no longer believed in the efficacy of a price cut program . . . in the Force Ouvrière position."

Unless the FO position changed, Brown asserted, Communist demands for wage increases "would win the overwhelming percentage of the working class to the C. P. banner." The main argument used by the CGT was that the FO tied itself to price cuts and "to American imperialist intervention" in Europe. Brown admitted that if he was a coal miner, he would have voted in favor of a strike called by the Communists, even though its real purpose was to prevent French coal from being used for the reconstruction of Western Europe. The French Communists, Brown argued, wanted Charles de Gaulle to come to power in France, because both they and he opposed the reconstruction of West Germany. The French masses also felt that if de Gaulle led France, "there remains a hope for stabilizing the French political situation." In the meantime, Brown saw a slight chance of gain for the FO if it acquired "sufficient facilities and sufficient means to build the organization."[19]

Brown's talk before the State Department revealed the close liaison between the AFL and State. But Brown failed to talk about his work with the Central Intelligence Agency. Large amounts of money were provided the AFL by the CIA. Information regarding CIA subsidies to the AFL was offered by Thomas W. Braden, who directed the program of grants to anti-Communist fronts for the CIA from 1950 through 1954. Referring to a receipt for fifteen thousand dollars in his possession, signed by Brown in 1947, Braden explained that Brown

needed it to pay off strongarm squads in Mediterranean ports, so that American supplies could be unloaded against the opposition of communist dock workers. In 1947 the Communist CGT led a strike in Paris which came near to paralyzing the French economy. A takeover of the government was feared. Into this crisis stepped Lovestone and his assistant Irving Brown. With funds from Dubinsky's union, they organised Force Ouvrière, a non-Communist union. When they ran out of money they appealed to the CIA. Thus began the secret subsidy of free trade unions. . . . Without that subsidy postwar history might have gone very differently.[20]

The only thing wrong with Braden's account is his dates. While the CIA undoubtedly gave money to help build the FO in 1947, the dock worker strike took place in 1949–1950. Brown supported Pierre Ferri-Pisani, who formed the Mediterranean Committee. That group hired Italian laborers to unload American arms at Marseilles and other ports. With CIA funds, which Braden claimed amounted to two million dollars per year, Brown received enough to

[19] Brown, "The Fight Against Communism in Western European Countries," Restricted Meeting at the Department of State, November 9, 1948, International Labor Relations File, AFL-CIO Headquarters Library, Washington, D.C.

[20] Thomas W. Braden, "I'm Glad the CIA Is 'Immoral'," *The Saturday Evening Post*, May 20, 1967, 10–12.

pay the salaries of the Italian workers who broke the strike of the French CGT.

By the 1950's, it had become apparent that the CGT still had the allegiance of most French laborers. It still provided "the Cominform with 50,000 cadres," Brown claimed, "entrenched in the most strategic industries of France." Although they were unable to bring even sixty or seventy per cent of French workers out on political strikes to retard rearmament, a danger existed "if and when 'Der Tag' of [Soviet] military aggression should come." The strength of the Communists had little to do with poverty. The Party's hard corps would not be swayed by improvements in the economic position of the working class. At any rate, Brown admitted, it would be "some time before any real profound changes take place in the French workers' standards."

Speaking in 1951, Brown proposed a new approach to break the power of the CGT. The free unions suffered from a lack of leadership. This was due, Brown claimed, to the 1945 purge of pro-Vichy union leaders from the CGT. The purge was "done unjustly under Communist instigation," Brown argued, and contributed to "lack of manpower on the non-Communist side." Former union leaders who supported the Vichy government during the Nazi occupation of France were now "black-listed."

What Brown advised was that French supporters of the Vichy occupation regime be allowed to hold positions in the CGT, and that Communists be removed from CGT leadership. Could the French union movement, Brown asked, condemn "eternally people who out of mistaken patriotism supported the Vichy regime although they were mortal enemies of the Nazi occupation"? As a way of strengthening the anti-Communist movement, French labor had to ask "whether many who are labelled ex-Vichyites are not eligible to be accepted back into the free labor movement."

On the other hand, Brown suggested that Communists who held CGT posts in 1939–40 should be excluded from the union movement. At that time, the Communists were supporting an alliance with Nazi Germany and opposed

any moves that might produce a military conflict with
Germany. "Both the government and the labor movement,"
Brown recommended, "should allow the rehabilitation of
all trade unionists blacklisted at Communist instigation"
from 1944 to 1947. At the same time, the government
should take "measures . . . against the CP's goon squads,"
employers should refuse to negotiate with the CGT, and
the right of trade union representation should be withdrawn from "those who were traitors to France during the
Nazi-Soviet Pact of 1939–1940."

Brown's call to rehabilitate Vichyites and dismiss Communists, even to take away the CGT's collective bargaining
rights, alarmed many French laborers. Brown's proposed
policy also reflected the extension of American McCarthy-
ism to the European scene. What Brown was demanding
was an alliance with the proto-fascists in order to beat the
Communists. Representation rights had to be denied the
CGT, Brown argued, because it was "an organization which
is not 'independent'" and was actually "an agency of a
foreign power." The CGT, in other words, had to be out-
lawed. But since the French CGT, by his own admission,
was still the organized representative of French labor,
Brown was asking that the French working class be deprived of a channel of expression. Had such a policy been
followed, it would have undoubtedly worked only to further strengthen the control of the CGT by the Communist
Party.[21]

II. *The AFL in Germany*

The AFL faced a different problem in postwar Germany.
The older social democratic leaders of the pre-war union
movement had been persecuted by Hitler, and a great void
in union leadership and organization existed. Germany
had been divided into four zones, each controlled by the

[21] Irving Brown, speech to the American Club at Brussels, December 13, 1951; from the files of *Ramparts*, courtesy of Michael
Ansara.

various Allied occupation armies. In this context, the AFL saw its duty as a struggle to eliminate "pro-Communists" from leadership positions of unions formed in the zone supervised by the American Military Government (AMG).

Efforts to rebuild the old German unions were begun by former union leaders in most cities of the American, British, and French zones. In Frankfurt, which was occupied by the American army at the end of March 1945, thirty-five former union officials set up a provisional organizing committee, and requested permission to hold meetings and enroll members as early as April 10. All the principal unions from the pre-1933 period were represented, Irving Brown reported to George Meany, including the social democratic and Christian unions. Their new organization was called the Free German Trade Union League.

These German unions wished to act as a central organizing committee that would rebuild unionism on a democratic basis. They were determined "to make the unions independent of control by any political party." In the Russian zone, on the other hand, trade union organization was guaranteed to establish Communist control. The Russians had announced an eight-man executive board uniting eighteen Berlin unions, and already claimed a membership of 200,000. Yet the policy of the AMG, Brown complained, was one that discouraged and even prohibited union organization. Although the Potsdam Conference declaration stated that formation of unions would be permitted, subject to military security, the interpretation of that policy in the American zone was producing severe handicaps to union organization.

The American policy was to permit shop steward elections to be held in single factories. This meant, the AMG authorities argued, assurance that new unions would be completely democratic and would represent the actual work force. But since all former union officials had been blacklisted by the Nazis, and were not employed in existing factories, "the most experienced trade unionists" found themselves "shut out from even this limited form of union organization." The effect was, Irving Brown argued, "to give an advantage to Communists in gaining control of the local plant organizations. In the absence of experienced leadership and advice," it was not "difficult for a small Communist nucleus to take control." This was made even easier by the infiltration of Communists into policy-making branches of the AMG, particularly its Manpower Division.

These elements, Brown claimed, opposed "any revival of trade union organization at this time, even on a local scale." In Frankfurt, Lieutenant Ed Fruchtman of the Wages and Hours Administration in Washington, ordered the thirty-five trade union leaders "to cease all trade union activity." This "go slow" policy occurred while unionism was being "vigorously promoted in the Russian zone and in Berlin." When unionism finally developed, the "Russian fostered groups" would have gained "a substantial advantage over the organizations in the other zones."

Most responsible for this disastrous policy, Brown claimed, were General Lucius D. Clay and Brigadier General Frank J. McSherry, head of the Manpower Division of the AMG. According to Brown, the "Party-liners in the Manpower Division were already there" when McSherry took charge. McSherry himself was a "man of honesty and uprightness," sympathetic to organized labor. But he was "also somewhat naive." The labor division of his branch was led by Newman Jeffrey, a UAW member who was part of Walter Reuther's group. Acknowledging that Jeffrey was also "strongly opposed to Communists," Brown argued that he nevertheless was forced to abide by a policy initiated before he had arrived on the scene. The Communists, moreover, had made him the object of a "malicious whispering campaign" within the CIO.

One of McSherry's deputy directors in Frankfurt was Lieutenant Colonel George Cassidy, who believed "that unions need to be carefully regulated to make them democratic." He also backed a "go-slow" policy. Chief of labor standards and relations under McSherry and Cassidy was Henry Rutz, an Army captain and a former executive of the International Typographical Union. Rutz, who later would represent Brown and the AFL in Germany, believed that "the opportunity for the rebuilding of a democratic German trade union Movement is being pretty well lost."[22]

Brown's analysis was confirmed by other AFL leaders two months later. At a Heidelberg meeting, Henry Rutz and David Saposs, a former Communist and a noted labor economist, explained that the Communist Party had "the inside track with General McSherry and have managed to control labor policy in Bavaria." The Communists wanted to prevent old Socialist leaders from taking union positions. Hence they urged a policy of democracy from the bottom up, "a slogan on which they have completely sold McSherry."[23]

The effects of AMG policy were compounded by an influx of German émigrés who were members of Free Germany, a group tied to the French CGT and viewed as Communist by the AFL. Emigré Socialists had organized a counter-group, but the financial superiority of the Communists allowed many of them to return illegally to Germany. The AFL received pleas that it help the Socialist activists return to Germany, by providing a three-month budget of 250,000 francs. "If the Socialist sector of the newly forming German trade union movement is not strengthened," an AFL confidant reported, "the influence of the Communists for the immediate future remains overwhelming."[24]

To the AFL leaders, American policy was clearly following a pro-Communist direction. AFL leaders never seemed to indicate any need for caution to avoid using the services of Nazi sympathizers. Instead, their attention was constantly riveted on the anti-Communist struggle. In December, Abraham Bluestein reported that Newman Jeffrey had been discharged from the Manpower Division because of

[22] Memorandum for Mr. Meany, "Trade Union Developments in Germany since German Defeat," September 21, 1945; Thorne MSS. There is no name given on the report, but it was most likely written by Irving Brown.
[23] Alfred Bingham to [blank] Murray, November 18, 1945, *ibid.*
[24] Report by G. Marksheffel, Paris, November 25, 1945, *ibid.*

"his violent disagreement with prevailing policies being followed in Germany by U.S. group control." Local plant unions were company outfits, according to Bluestein, and were forbidden to affiliate with other unions in the same industry or to federate into a central labor union.

In the Russian zone, to the contrary, an apparatus had been set up under state control. There was no doubt in Bluestein's mind that American policy was "formulated by a group of Communists and Fellow Travelers in the Army." Jeffrey had told him that the "American group of Communists" were working with German Communists for the "deliberate purpose of creating utter chaos and confusion in the American zone so that the German Communists shall be able to take over at an opportune time." McSherry's pro-Communist policy, Bluestein claimed, was abetted by Sidney Hillman, Franklin D. Roosevelt's close associate and president of the Amalgamated Clothing Workers. When Jeffrey was dismissed, his replacement was Mortimer B. Wolf, an Amalgamated lawyer who was with the legal division of the Department of Labor. The AFL considered Wolf to be a pro-Communist. Also working on McSherry's staff was Captain Joe Gould, who had been with the CIO Office Workers. In the eyes of the AFL, the various CIO staff members on the AMG were evidence of Communist penetration. Bluestein reported that Jeffrey hoped to "stir up non-Communist elements in the CIO" and get them to "tackle this problem."[25]

The seriousness of the situation led the AFL to send Irving Brown to Germany. In the beginning of 1946, Brown met representatives of German unions in Great Britain. After speaking to a delegation headed by Erich Ollenhauer, Brown reported that the union group had published a sound pamphlet, but needed an additional amount of money to print twenty thousand copies that would be sent into Germany "through their own channels since all external publications are forbidden in Germany by the authorities." They wanted only two hundred dollars at the

---

[25] Bluestein to Matthew Woll, December 12, 1945, *ibid*.

start, which, Brown noted, "is not very much and could aid the free trade union movement."[26]

In order to build anti-Communist unions, the AFL began a campaign to have the AMG return to the old Socialist unions the funds, printing presses, and buildings which the Nazis had confiscated during the war. Soviet representatives had cars, office equipment, paper, and printing presses. To prevent pro-Western unionists from gaining access to the same kind of equipment meant abandoning the German workers to communism. Printing presses, paper, and mimeograph machines were a key priority. Furthermore, the AFL told Secretary of State James F. Byrnes, American policy had to be changed to permit friends of German families to send gift food packages.[27]

A great opportunity for the growth of trade unionism existed, Joseph Keenan reported, if the AFL developed "a practical program of helping the free trade unions of Germany." As General Clay's labor secretary and as an AFL member, Keenan worked to that end. Germany needed raw materials and dollar credits. Its future depended on getting industry operating, and on defeating the Communists. Keenan requested that the AFL send food to trade union leaders so they could carry on physically. He also suggested assigning Henry Rutz to Germany and Irving Brown to Europe as the general AFL representative.[28]

Pursuing Keenan's suggestions, the AFL argued that the "revival of free trade unions should be a basic provision in the democratization of Nazi Germany." AFL representatives throughout Europe, AFL economist Boris Shiskin reported, had prepared lists of items needed by unions. Noting that European unions had no central organization to appeal to for advice and aid since the liquidation of the old International Federation of Trade Unions, Shiskin commented that "Soviet domination of Europe would be a return to the Dark Ages." The only agency for rehabilitating

[26] Brown to Woll, January 1, 1946, *ibid.*

[27] Woll to Brynes, June 3, 1946, *ibid.*

[28] Minutes of the meeting on International Labor Relations, July, 19, 1946, *ibid.*

former Axis nations was the free trade unions. "These are the considerations," Shiskin explained, "that convinced us we should maintain a representative in Europe."[29]

A year of hard work by the AFL agents in Germany produced some results. By August of 1946 General Clay had responded to their pleas. The AFL reported that union organization was moving at a better pace, and that new unions resembled some of the older ones led by the German Socialists. In new zonal amalgamations, the Communists controlled less than ten per cent of the unions. Clay had ordered a return of union property, and had stipulated that cars, tires, and gasoline be made available to union executives. Keenan was able to report that three hundred food packages a month had been sent to German union leaders, at a cost of three thousand dollars.[30]

Toward the end of 1946, AFL policy began to be criticized by some CIO officials. The CIO was still a member of the World Federation of Trade Unions, a world labor organization to which the USSR unions were also affiliated. Frank Rosenblum of the Amalgamated Clothing Workers and CIO Vice-President Adolph Germer accused the AFL of "planning all sorts of splitting tactics such as keeping the German trade unions out of the WFTU." Brown, of course, firmly opposed affiliation of German unions with the WFTU, and the American AFL had refused to affiliate. Brown, for the first time, proposed building a new anti-Communist international union organization. Such a group, he emphasized, would also provide him with "an excellent official function for my presence in Europe."[31]

Berlin union elections in 1947, however, revealed that the pro-Communist Einheit union had won recognition by a vote of 300 to 75. The victory was due, Brown claimed, to the pro-Communist policy of the AMG Manpower Division.

[29] Boris Shiskin, "AF of L Educational Activities Among 'Unions Abroad'," August 1946, Boris Shiskin MSS, State Historical Society of Wisconsin, Madison, Wis.

[30] Minutes of the International Labor Relations Committee, August 7, 1946.

[31] Brown, Report No. 2, December 23, 1946, *ibid.*

The CP had made progress as well in coal, transportation, and the metal industry. It was no longer enough to oppose the WFTU. The AFL had to give its active support to the International Trade Secretariats as an alternative. While the AMG was slowly moving toward freedom for union organization, the economic situation was worse than ever and unions were torn by political fights. The long-range answer was integration of West Germany into the European economy. Until this was achieved, Brown predicted, AFL-style unionism would be doomed.[32]

In the meantime, the Communists were charging that the AFL was influencing the AMG. As a result, Henry Rutz claimed, the AMG "faltered and agreed to a compromise." Membership of the Berlin union executive board was increased from thirty to forty-five members, making Communist maneuvering easier. The anti-Communist groups still lacked newsprint. Only one hundred thousand copies of union publications had to serve over one million unionists.[33]

To cope with these problems, Rutz presented the AFL with a German program. In the past year, Rutz reported, he had at General Clay's suggestion requested a military entry permit, since Clay also "wanted to prevent the WFTU and the CIO from requesting office" space in Germany. Rutz received his permit, and was able to set up an office in Stuttgart and to gain freedom of travel throughout Germany with AMG privileges. Because the WFTU had an office in the Russian sector of Berlin, Rutz wanted the AFL to make a formal request for establishment of an AFL office in the American zone of that city.

In addition, he urged that the AFL distribute a propaganda paper in the Russian zone which could "be smuggled easily and be easily disposed of in case of necessity." The German Socialists had underground channels and would let the AFL use their facilities "for the dissemination of our message in return for American paper." They needed forty thousand leaflet sheets and 10,000 sheets of regular

[32] Brown, "Report on England and Germany," April 7, 1947, *ibid*.
[33] Henry Rutz, "Report on Germany," n.d. [1947], *ibid*.

paper monthly. Rutz also suggested an extended program of CARE packages so that full-time union functionaries, approved by the AFL, would not have to worry about food. Four hundred forty-seven had already received aid from CARE, but there were twice as many functionaries as CARE packages.[34]

Rutz's request was approved by Jay Lovestone. "The underground German organization," Lovestone reported to his AFL associates, "was now set for an active campaign in the Soviet Zone. They had been unable to obtain the type of thin paper needed for their work, and the needed monthly supplies of 10,000 9 x 9 sheets." These would be provided by the AFL. Irving Brown confirmed that the AFL had been directly "aiding the reconstruction of the destroyed labor movement," and had "acted as adviser, guide and critic of Military Government on general economic and political policy, as well as on trade union matters; and worked with the German trade unionists to prevent WFTU intervention and eventual domination of the German trade unions." Brown again suggested immediate affiliation of German unions with the International Trade Secretariats, and urged that an underground struggle against the Soviets in the Eastern zone be conducted. In conjunction with the general secretary of the metal workers, Brown reported, "the AFL can assist materially in keeping this opposition network alive."[35]

Lovestone and Brown gained some support from elements within the AMG. Sol D. Oser, an economic adviser to the Manpower Division, wrote his superior that the United States "must give all possible support to democratic trade unionism in Germany." The government, Oser claimed, had "been too neutral." Unions were just not another institution; they were the "most important," and if lost to the West, U.S. efforts to promote democracy "may never come to fruition." The problem was that if extensive formal aid was given to the pro-Western unions, it might

[34] Rutz to Woll, November 5, 1947, *ibid.*
[35] Meeting of International Labor Relations Committee, November 11, 1947, *ibid.*

look as if they were serving "in fact as agents and stooges of a foreign nation." Oser recommended that aid be dispensed directly from the AFL to German unions, as a way of getting around the problem of U.S. government sponsorship. Regarding the unions as the "democratic bulwark against dictatorship," Oser suggested a vast program in which AFL leaders would be put on the U.S. payroll, to work on propaganda, labor libraries, material aid, and technical assistance.[36]

With the formulation of the Marshall Plan and establishment of the European Recovery Program, Jay Lovestone himself led a delegation of German unionists to see the Secretary of the United States Army in October 1948. His purpose was to offer "former German war pilots to fly the airlift into Berlin."[37] Lovestone, evidently, did not shy away from working with former Nazi air pilots, as long as they were opposed to the Communists.

Lovestone had traveled to Germany for the purpose of conferring with General Clay. Russian control of Berlin labor, he argued, would lead to Bolshevik hegemony in Western Europe and would ruin the plans for European recovery. After meeting with Clay, Lovestone received assurance that AFL demands for a labor voice in European Recovery Program activity would be taken into account. Allocation proposals would be made after consultation with employers' associations and unionists. Lovestone asked Clay that all remaining union property seized by the Nazis be returned to the unions.

Lovestone revealed his sophistication when he told Clay that the AFL supported the demand for socialization of basic industries. The entire trade union movement, he informed the General, wanted both basic industries and public utilities to be socialized. To turn over natural resources to magnates who had financed Hitler would only breed the

[36] Sol D. Oser to Leo Werts, Director, Manpower Division, Office of Military Government, "American Aid to German Trade Unions," March 31, 1948, *ibid*.

[37] *New York Times*, October 26, 1948, quoted in Sidney Lens, "Lovestone Diplomacy," *The Nation*, July 5, 1965, p. 14.

revival of Nazism. "Clay said that as the military representative of a government devoted to the private enterprise
system," Lovestone reported, "he could not be expected to
order or promote socialization in Germany."

Clay preferred that the unions rely on their own independent strength rather than on military law, and he
criticized the unions for a lack of militancy. William Richter, head of the Hesse Federation of Labor, told Lovestone
that Clay "considered the unions as a sort of necessary
evil while fostering the interests of private property." The
only reason why German unions did not fight harder "for
the economic interests of their members," Richter argued,
"was that they feared that such struggles would play into
the hands of Russia and its Communist supporters in
Germany." After negotiating with the union leaders, Lovestone got them to rescind demands on socialization pend-
ing a vote on the issue before the Constituent Assembly.
Lovestone appropriated another thousand dollars from the
Free Trade Union Committee to aid the Berlin unions with
office supplies, paper, and CARE parcels.[38]

After Lovestone's visit, the AFL and West German unions put great pressure on Clay's office. By the start of the
new year, Clay assured Matthew Woll that the military's
policy had always been "to encourage the growth of trade
unions in Germany." While the military did not always
agree in all particulars with the unions, they did recognize
that the growth of democracy depended upon the establishment of "democratic" unions. "We have been impressed," Clay wrote, "with the way in which the German
trade unions have gradually reduced the number of Communists in positions of responsibility." Clay admitted that
some time had passed before the unions received back all
of their confiscated property, but this was due entirely to
a legal problem of corporate rights. Unions had to be re-
cruited into new legal bodies. Clay readily acknowledged
the right of German labor to have some say in European
Recovery Program operations. Finally, he admitted to up-

[38] Report on Germany by Jay Lovestone, on behalf of George
Harrison and David Dubinsky, n.d. [1948]. Thorne MSS.

holding the right of the "advantages of free enterprise in restoring a normal economy." It was because so many union leaders were Socialists, Clay argued, that they felt "that we are not in full sympathy" with their aims.[39]

The AFL was still not completely satisfied. Insisting that all old union property be returned, Woll argued that the new unions were the legitimate successors to the pre-1933 unions, and only differed in form. They must not be compelled to go to court to establish their claims. Secondly, Woll disapproved of the fact that major posts in the German government were filled by leading Nazis. This was repugnant to public opinion and was gratifying to Communist propagandists. Thirdly, Woll claimed that the AMG still rejected union participation in industrial groups. As for socialization, Woll argued that Clay's position played into the hands of the Russians. It was "the Russian demagogues who have been making such accusations against the Government and the Marshall Plan." ERP could not depend upon asking a nation to abandon private ownership of industry. Yet, Woll emphasized, the United States had to support unionists who were Socialist as well as anti-Nazi, and it had to stop backing employers who were pro-Nazi.[40]

The AFL leaders concluded that their pressure and work had been successful. David Dubinsky was probably correct when he wrote in January 1949 that "had it not been for the extensive educational activities of the Free Trade Union Committee of the AFL . . . the Communists . . . might by now have seized control of the reviving German trade unions." Such an outcome might "have been unfortunate," Sidney Lens has commented, "but it is odd that Dubinsky never asked himself whether the German workers had a right to make their own choice without 'educational activities' from the outside. Had the help been given to *all* union leaders, or even to all non-Communist leaders, it is possible that a different movement might have evolved."[41]

[39] General Lucius Clay to Woll, January 5, 1949, *ibid*.
[40] Woll to Clay, February 14, 1949, *ibid*.
[41] Quoted in Sidney Lens, *op. cit*., p. 14.

Lens' judgment is well taken. The AFL had engaged in more than "educational" efforts. Lovestone and Brown never seemed to question the legitimacy of American union leaders choosing which Germans would receive funds, printing presses, paper, and CARE packages. Anti-communism was the criterion, and as long as the chosen German union leaders pledged to operate in this framework, the AFL leaders would do their best to give them help.

III. *The AFL in Greece*

"In the years after the Second World War," writes the historian of Greek trade unionism, "the reconstruction of the trade union movement was of primary importance to the social and economic recovery of Greece." But such efforts required "the full cooperation of all the political and social forces of the country and especially of the trade unions themselves—a cooperation which in this case was found almost impossible to achieve." Divisions in the movement, as well as the Greek civil war, made such a reconstruction effort extremely difficult. "The postwar development of Greek trade unionism experienced many setbacks," and a limited reconstruction was not achieved until 1950. Even then, Christos Jecchinis writes, "the progress that followed was not very impressive."[42]

As in other European nations, the Greek Communists had come to play a major part in the growth of organized labor. Most older Greek unionists, including non-Communists, were affiliated with the EAM—the National Liberation Front—which had been created by the Left in the early days of Nazi occupation and in which Communists and other left-wing political groups participated.

Greek labor was united in the Greek Confederation of Labor—the GSEE—to which four separate groups belonged. One group was headed by a former Nazi collaborator. One small group was led by two men who had left

[42] Christos Jecchinis, *Trade Unionism in Greece* (Chicago, 1967), Introduction, n.p.

the EAM after December 1944. The largest group, in which the Communists were active, "and one which has received an overwhelming majority of votes in almost every Trade Union election, was led by Theos, and known as the ERGAS group, or the Workers' Anti-Fascist Coalition. Its close association with EAM," explained a British M.P., "explains its wide mass support." The other large group was headed by "a declared supporter of the Monarchists," Fotis Makris. But at first the monarchists refused to participate in the GSEE Congress, and had been excluded with the agreement of WFTU representatives. In the March 1946 union elections for the GSEE executive board, ERGAS won four out of the available seven seats, and its candidates received the four highest vote totals.[43]

The rapid growth and popular appeal of the Greek Left was highly upsetting to the American Federation of Labor. But the electoral victory scored by ERGAS in the March 1946 union elections did not allow the Left to consolidate its position or to solve the problem of creating a viable and representative Greek union movement. The general postwar government elections, the first held in Greece since the war, took place in late March. Success at the polls came to the parties of the Right, and this counterbalanced the success gained by the Left in the unions. Having won the election, the Right did not "intend to allow the trade unions to remain in the hands of the communist dominated ERGAS. . . . They claimed that a series of hard-hitting and well-organized strikes, with political motives, could wreck the efforts at economic reconstruction."[44]

The Greek government decided to move against ERGAS by throwing its support to the minority of Greek "reformists" in the labor movement, who were organized in a faction called EREP. It was with this group that Fotis Makris emerged as a young and dynamic anti-Communist leader. Makris began his ascent by joining the right-wing Populist Party, and obtaining a nomination for candidacy to Parlia-

[43] Leslie J. Solley, M.P., *Greece: The Facts* (London, League for Democracy in Greece, 1946), pp. 9–10.

[44] Jecchinis, *op. cit.*, p. 96.

ment. After winning the election, Makris pushed through
legislation that changed the nature of union representation. One result was that Makris was promoted to the post
of GSEE general secretary. By August of 1946, a British
parliamentary delegation reported, the new right-wing
government had "taken exceedingly drastic measures in
connection with the trade unions." Following a judicial
decision obtained by Makris, the elected executive committee of the GSEE was displaced, "and the elected executives of many trade unions and trade councils" were
removed from office. In their place were put "Government
nominees" like Makris. The government also "seized trade
union offices and records and arrested many of the leaders."[45]

The Greek Council of State had invalidated the March
1946 GSEE elections, and the Minister of Labor asked the
elected ERGAS leaders to resign their posts. When they
refused, the government took possession of GSEE offices,
arrested members of its executive board and appointed a
new provisional executive board composed of twenty-one
members, and made up of a disproportionate number of
reformists and right-wingers, and only five members of
the ERGAS group.

As a result of these political maneuvers, the Greek union movement fell into chaos. Protests from the ousted
ERGAS leadership produced a visit to Greece from Léon
Jouhaux. The British government also tried to resolve the
crisis. Foreign Secretary Ernest Bevin traveled to Greece,
and dispatched W. Braine, the British labor attaché in
Rome, to handle matters. Braine had signed an agreement
with the Greek Prime Minister, Tsaldaris, on November 2.
Their treaty stipulated that the government would restore
the position of former elected members of the GSEE executive board, and would also appoint reformists as part
of a new provisional executive. The new provisional ex-

[45] *British Parliamentary Delegation to Greece: A Report* (London, His Majesty's Stationery Office, 1947) p. 6. The delegation
visited Greece in August 1946, and was made up of Seymour Cocks,
E. R. Bowen, Leslie Hale, John Maude, W. Monslow, W. R. Vane,
and Evelyn Walkden.

ecutive, meant to be a compromise between ERGAS and EREP desires, was to include seven ERGAS members and five EREP members.

No sooner was the agreement signed, however, than the Makris group worked to sabotage the treaty. The government released only a small number of arrested union leaders, thereby violating their pledge to Braine. Further negotiations went on through the last months of 1946 and the beginning of 1947. For the first time, other foreign representatives entered the picture. Truman Doctrine aid had given new importance to the role played by Americans. Now Irving Brown, along with the U.S. labor attaché in London, Sam Berger, began to work with Makris and his followers. After persistent negotiations, Berger, Braine, and Brown arranged a new agreement. A new provisional executive board was to be set up for the GSEE. This time it would be composed of seven EREP reformists, four members of a right-wing labor group called EME, six members of ERGAS, and four assorted Socialists. The agreement went into effect without ERGAS, however. The Greek civil war had entered a new phase, and ERGAS ordered its members to leave the GSEE.[46]

In helping to set up an executive board for the Greek Confederation of Labor, Brown was seeking to keep ERGAS representation at a minimum. Again he was using his position to defeat the Communist "enemy" in yet another European nation. Greek workers were in despair, Brown reported back to the AFL. They had a low standard of living, and the average wage did not cover one-fourth of the necessities of life. Society was not democratically organized, wages were controlled by the government, and the unions had no real collective bargaining power.

Greece was a problem, Brown asserted, because the Communists wanted to control it as a means of gaining entry to the entire Middle East. The Communist drive had produced a reaction that brought victory to the monarchy and checked any hopes for creation of a democratic center government. "The responsibility for the present Greek gov-

---

[46] Jecchinis, *op. cit.*, pp. 101–04.

ernment not being more democratic," Brown argued, lay
at the door of the Communists. They had produced such
fear that workers turned to the monarchy for stability and
protection against totalitarians of the Left.

This situation, however, gave Brown a context within
which to work. GSEE leaders appointed by the government
were refusing to deal with ERGAS and were looking to the
AFL for support. Smaller "center" groupings, while agree-
ing that ERGAS was Communist, objected to Makris and
the EREP reformists accepting positions handed to them
by the Greek authorities, believing that EREP had "become
a tool of the government."

"The economic situation," Brown believed, was "the
horrible breeding ground for the partial successes of the
Communist Party movement in the trade unions and
amongst the workers," who were forced to spend forty per
cent of their wages just for bread. It was Soviet insistence
on a Greek government that would approve Russian foreign policy which made "impossible any atmosphere of
compromise or conciliation." Since the unions were the key
to possible Russian control of Greece, Brown saw a need to
fight ERGAS, although it had admittedly gathered a majority of working class support.

ERGAS, Brown stressed, was an out-and-out CP instrument, "acting in complete support of Russian goals in
Greece." If its leaders won power, *"this Communist group
would destroy free trade unionism."* (Brown seemed to
ignore his earlier observation, that free trade unionism in
fact did not exist in postwar Greece.) The problem was
that "good militant workers and trade union leaders" were
to be found "in the ranks of ERGAS." They could be won
over *"not on the basis of negative proposals, but only in
terms of the material alleviation of the conditions of the
masses."*

Brown admitted that the EREP-Makris group now controlled the GSEE purely as a result of government action,
including the receipt of a government-enforced check-off
of union dues, and the forcible ousting of ERGAS leaders
from union positions. *"In spite of their too ready accept-*

ance of State intervention," Brown nevertheless emphasized, *"the 'appointed' group united with the larger part of
the center independent groups . . . can become the basis
for a real trade union movement, free of Communist domination."* Brown objected to unionists relying for their
positions on government appointments. But it would be
suicide to regard ERGAS as merely another legitimate union tendency, and he opposed the 1946 Braine-Tsaldaris
compromise because it would have given ERGAS too much
power. ERGAS was Russia's instrument for capturing
Greece, and to support a united union movement meant
acceptance of Communist penetration of Greece.

Again Brown's method of operation had been made
clear. Anything was justifiable when seeking to oppose
Communists in the trade union movement, including cooperation with a government-appointed group that did not
have the support of Greek workers. To be sure, he did
recommend that the state end its intervention in unions
and act to raise living standards, and also that American
economic aid, loans, credits, and materials should "be
conditioned on greater guarantees of democratization of
the government." But he again paused to note that "compared to Russia and its dominated spheres the present
Greek society is a model of democracy." And he urged a
strenuous objection against the efforts of the WFTU to
intervene in Greek union affairs—although he saw nothing unusual about his own activity on behalf of the Free
Trade Union Committee.

Finally, Brown proposed that a labor attaché should be
sent to the U.S. Embassy who had knowledge of world
communism and who could keep the U.S. government
informed on Greek labor affairs. The AFL had a responsibility to help Greek workers establish a "free" union
movement—which Brown defined as one free of both
Communist domination and government control. For the
time being, Brown threw his support to the government-
backed EREP-Makris group. "Until . . . unity can be
achieved by the reformist forces," he wrote, the AFL had
to "assist in every way possible every move to have the

Greek government carry out the . . . basic reforms suggested."[47]

Having worked out the most satisfactory agreement to date, Brown believed that he had succeeded in blocking the attempt of the WFTU to create support abroad for ERGAS. Communist Party attempts to control Greek labor had been blocked. Brown, however, was not sure how long the new compromise agreement would work. AFL operatives were needed to give "constant advice and guidance" to the "inexperienced Greek" union leaders, as well as to direct the State Department in its work with unions.[48]

The Makris group's endorsement of the agreement did not lead to permanent stability for Greek trade unionism. The Communists had been eliminated from the GSEE, but this only led to a new series of fights between divergent anti-Communist factions. The Greek government had shifted further to the right, as the civil war had renewed itself. A newcomer in the GSEE, Patsanjis, now challenged Makris for control of the Federation. The Ninth GSEE Congress was scheduled for March 1948. Patsanjis now worked to gain the support of a majority of GSEE members.

Fotis Makris lost no time in trying to strike back. His opportunity came after a new collective wage agreement was signed with the Greek government on November 4, 1947. Minimum wages were to be increased up to thirty per cent and the workers were pledged to increase productivity and improve workmanship by a corresponding amount. At first the agreement, negotiated by Patsanjis, built up his prestige within the GSEE. It soon became apparent, however, that the wage increase would be highly inadequate. Makris then accused those who had negotiated the agreement of being "stooges" of the government. Finally, Makris took the extreme step of calling a general strike to protest the inadequacy of the scheduled wage boosts.[49]

[47] Brown, "Report and Recommendations on the Crisis in Greece," May 13, 1947, Thorne MSS.
[48] Meeting of the International Labor Relations Committee of the AFL, November 11, 1947.
[49] Jecchinis, *op. cit.*, pp. 112–14.

By the time the ninth GSEE Congress took place, the main order of business was factional struggle for control of the GSEE executive board. The two major contenders were the groups led by Patsanjis and Makris. Balancing off these two opponents was a new figure, A. Dimitratos, a former GSEE secretary-general who had been Minister of Labor during the Metaxas dictatorship from 1936 to 1940. Dimitratos appeared as a neutral figure, and early balloting revealed that he, rather than Patsanjis or Makris, might actually win the position of secretary-general of the GSEE.

This possibility was repugnant to the Greek government, the Allied powers, and Irving Brown. "A victory for a former Metaxas official who was considered a semi-Fascist in many international political and trade union circles," Jecchinis explains, "could become very embarrassing to the trade union movement and the Greek Government, both of which were already being labelled 'monarcho-fascist' by the Communists." To avoid this possibility, the Minister of Labor pushed a law through Parliament introducing a new scheme of proportional representation for elections to the GSEE executive. New balloting was held on April 10. The results gave the Makris-EREP group 577 votes, and the Patsanjis group 545. Negotiations were held. Makris was appointed secretary-general and Patsanjis treasurer. This was considered a victory "for the Populist Party" and thus "afforded still another example of political intervention in the affairs of Greek trade unionism."[50]

Observing this Ninth GSEE Congress, Irving Brown reported that the united anti-Communist front "which we organized fell apart last December." Expressing his anger at Makris' failure to put the unity of anti-Communist forces ahead of his own personal ambition, Brown stated that "we have the purse strings in Greece and we could have accomplished much in forcing Makris and his crowd to play ball with the united-front set-up." As the convention balloting got under way, Brown blamed the turmoil on Makris' behavior. After witnessing a sharp attack by Makris on his opponent, Brown vowed to "bring about unity" and to wrap

[50] *Ibid.*, pp. 117–18.

up the GSEE Congress. Unless it was brought together, he reported, "there would be no central trade union or it would become the plaything of politicians and demagogues."

To deal with this division, Brown proposed that the sessions end, and that compromises be worked out among the proposed executive board members. Brown volunteered to arbitrate all issues on which both factions disagreed. After learning that Patsanjis was negotiating with Dimitratos and scheming against Makris, Brown argued that the AFL "would have nothing to do with such a character and that any organization in which he played an important role would be exactly what the Communists desired. The Communists would be given some substance to add to their propaganda about the 'fascist' nature of the Greek Trade unions." Dimitratos' participation in the congress was partially their own error. They should have insisted that AFL and CIO observers supervise delegate credentials.

The problem, according to Brown, was that an inadequate union tradition, inexperience, and obsession with civil war, had been compounded by American failure to give "forceful direction to Greek trade unionists." Brown now recommended that they not give "a penny for the Greek trade unions" and that he personally "did not propose to do so." Yet Brown admitted that a time might arrive when he would again have to visit Greece, "to see what can be done to pull this out of the fire." It was necessary in the long run that the AFL "do everything in our power to justify and maintain the Greek policy."[51]

As Brown predicted, the Ninth GSEE Congress was not the last time that he participated in Greek union affairs. His role in the 1950's, however, lost him the support of his old social democratic collaborators. By that time, Jecchinis writes, Brown had "already acquired the reputation . . . of being much more interested in the anti-Communist fight than in the social and economic problems confronting the working class." This dovetailed with the policy of the U.S. Embassy, when Ambassador John F. Peurifoy boycotted

[51] Brown, Report on the Greek Labor Convention, April 20, 1948, Thorne MSS.

center and left parties in favor of the Right, and criticized the center groups for being too soft on the Communists.[52]

The policy pursued by the Greek government in the 1950's and early '60's was to weaken labor and deprive wage earners of their ability to resist the government's wage-restraining policies. Under F. Gonis and later Dimi-tratos, the Ministry of Labor put harsh restrictions on trade union activity. Irving Brown now ditched Makris, who had become a critic of the far Right, and shifted his support to a faction led by Theodorou-Triandafilakis. In October 1961, Brown "promised support and possibly gave some financial assistance to their campaign against Makris and the GSEE Executive." As a result, the GSEE declared Brown *persona non grata* in Greece. "The important question," Jecchinis writes, "is not the form or the degree of assistance or support that Brown had promised to an opposition group in the Greek trade union movement nor the comparison of factions and personalities . . . but whether it was either right or wise for the representative of a foreign trade organization to intervene in the internal affairs" of the GSEE.

Jecchinis is correct, but it must be mentioned that neither Makris nor Jecchinis objected when Irving Brown was giving his assistance and money to the Populist Party group headed by Makris. By the early 1960's, Makris took a position similar to that held by Walter Reuther in the United States. While George Meany and Jay Lovestone saw no changes taking place in world communism, Reuther supported the moderate efforts towards a *modus vivendi* and growing cultural contacts with the Eastern European bloc. Brown and Lovestone were still completely motivated by fear of communism, and Brown was "now interested in the establishment of a new anti-communist front under new leadership because he probably felt that Makris and his collaborators were on the way out and a new GSEE leadership had to be pushed quickly to the top." The Makris group now argued that Brown was trying to "establish con-

52 Jecchinis, *op. cit.*, pp. 151–52.

spiratorial anti-communist organizations under the guise of trade unionism."[53]

The characterization of Irving Brown's rigid attitude toward communism was correct. But the explanation for Brown's activity missed the mark. The activities carried out by the AFL Free Trade Union Committee in Germany, France, and Greece were indeed dedicated to the establishment of solidly based trade unions. But in Lovestone's and Brown's eyes, a solid union movement by definition had to be anti-Communist. The model for European unionism was the American Federation of Labor, a body of conservative craft unions whose leadership endorsed the fundamental policies of the United States government. To beat the Communists, Brown and Lovestone were willing to compromise their own professed principles of independent unionism, and to work with state-controlled unions, and even with unions whose leadership was semi-Fascist. An end result was the elimination of the very AFL-type unionism that Lovestone and Brown professed to support.

[53] *Ibid.*, pp. 165–68. After the Greek government shifted further to the right, it attacked the Makris GSEE leadership. The Communists, in true Popular Front style, asked their followers to "support Makris" against the government, and urged the "many noncommunist trade unions to withstand the onslaught." Jecchinis explains that the Communist dependency on Makris turned "Brown, the old 'protector' of Makris, against him." Makris, of course, was not any less anti-Communist than before. That Brown viewed him as having shifted reveals that Irving Brown's policies were in many ways simply a reverse image of the policy advanced by the Soviet government.

CHAPTER

XI

AMERICAN LABOR
IN LATIN AMERICA
1898–1950

The roots of American labor policy toward Latin America
go back to the period of the Spanish-American War. Even
before President William McKinley opted for war in order
to pacify Cuba, the Cigarmakers' Union demanded intervention by the United States on behalf of Cuban independence.[1] These unionists feared competition from non-
union Cuban cigarmakers, as well as from Cubans who
had migrated to Florida. Samuel Gompers, as president of
the AFL and as former chieftain of the Cigarmakers, also
argued that "Cuban independence must be obtained before
the Cuban proletariat can be organized."[2]

At the war's end, Gompers opposed annexation of formerly Spanish possessions by the United States. Gompers
joined the Anti-Imperialist League, and gave many
speeches attacking what he called incipient colonialism.
But while he opposed territorial annexation, Gompers en-

[1] John C. Appel, "The Unionization of Florida Cigarmakers and
the Coming of the War with Spain," *Hispanic American Historical
Review*, 25 (1956), 38. For early AFL policy, see John C. Appel,
"The Relationship of American Labor to United States Imperialism,
1895–1905" (unpublished doctoral dissertation, University of Wisconsin, 1960).

[2] *1896 AFL Convention*, pp. 53–54.

dorsed extension of United States commerce, power, and influence over the earth by peaceful means. A powerful United States, he argued, could control the markets of the world without territorial annexation. "The nation which dominates the markets of the world," he told the Anti-Imperialist League, "will surely control its destinies." Gompers asked whether to attain this end, "the acquirement of the Philippine Islands, with their semi-savage population," was necessary. His answer was that it was "surely not," for "neither its gates nor those of any other country of the globe can long be closed against our constantly growing industrial supremacy."[3] The victories for American commerce—and labor—could be won without annexation. It was simply unnecessary "to subjugate by the force of arms any other people in order to obtain that expansion of trade."[4]

A small group of unionists did advocate traditional colonialism. Samuel Donnelly of the International Typographical Union supported acquisition of Hawaii and the Philippines. The first newspaper printed in the newly acquired territory was put out by ITU members, an ITU chapter already existed in Hawaii, and one was being organized in Havana. Only the cigarmakers, Donnelly claimed, faced and feared competition from cheap native labor. A colonial policy, he argued, could only help the AFL.[5]

The majority of AFL members opposed this analysis, and cited the threat of competition from cheap native labor that would accompany annexation. The average unionist feared, with Gompers, that American workers would be dragged down to the level of the "semi-barbarians" who inhabited the colonies. Yet these workers were not opposed to American expansion. As S. J. Kent of the Carpenters told delegates to the 1898 AFL Convention, "I am not in

[3] Speech to the Saratoga Conference, N.Y., August 20, 1898, *American Federationist*, V (1898), 139.
[4] Gompers to F. B. Thurber, November 25, 1898, *American Federationist*, V (1898), 206–07.
[5] *1898 AFL Convention*, p. 94.

favor of the English policy of colonization." Kent believed in expansion, but "not the kind in vogue on the other side." [6]

The Anti-Imperialist League lost its fight. Once they did, however, the AFL leaders immediately accepted the new reality. They began at once to work toward reform for labor in the new territories, as well as taking first steps toward the establishment of "an organized labor movement within the territories."[7] In 1901, Gompers sent Ed Rosenberg of the Central Labor Union of San Francisco to the Philippines and Hawaii, and Santiago Iglesias as AFL representative to Puerto Rico. Their job was to organize trade unions that would be "affiliated to the American trade union movement under the auspices of the American Federation of Labor."[8] Gompers himself visited Puerto Rico in 1904, in order to aid the AFL affiliate in a fight against an indigenous labor group that existed prior to the AFL's entry.[9]

Having decided to proceed by building AFL-type unions in Latin America, the AFL moved in the direction of developing a new inter-American labor organization. The new body would be devoted to fostering the growth of trade unions while at the same time encouraging opposition to revolutionary ideologies current among Latin American laborers. The Pan-American Federation of Labor—or PAFL—was formed by Gompers in 1918, and became the model on which all contemporary inter-American trade union groups were based.

One of the motivating factors behind formation of the PAFL was the influence of the revolutionary syndicalist Industrial Workers of the World in Latin America and Mexico. The IWW advocated industrial unionism, building

[6] *Ibid.*, p. 95. For further discussion of Gompers' views of imperialism, see Ronald Radosh, "American Labor and the Anti-Imperialist Movement," *Science and Society,* VIII (1964), 91–100.

[7] Samuel Gompers, *Seventy Years of Life and Labor,* II (New York, 1925), 328.

[8] Gompers to Governor William B. Hunt, October 14, 1901, Samuel Gompers MSS, State Historical Society of Wisconsin, Madison, Wis.

[9] Gompers to Enrique Pacheco, March 12, 1904; Gompers to S. Morales, March 12, 1904, *ibid.*

of "one big union," and revolutionary anti-capitalist action. Because of its militancy and strength where businessmen refused to recognize workers' rights, the IWW threatened the craft basis and conservative approach of the "business unionism" supported by Gompers. The IWW had already had some success in leading striking Mexican miners in 1906, and their growth challenged Gompers' ability to extend AFL influence in Mexico.

Gompers took a firm position toward political developments in Mexico. He opposed the dictatorship of Porfirio Diaz, and backed the reformists led by Francisco Madero. The Diaz regime not only opposed trade unionism within Mexico, but its policy of permitting Mexican laborers to cross the border into the United States interfered greatly with AFL efforts at organization. When Madero took power in November 1912, the AFL immediately gave him its support. Madero, however, was murdered four months later, and was replaced by Victoriano Huerta. Gompers feared that Huerta led a dictatorial regime, and that foreign nations would be tempted to intervene in Mexico. The result would be that "our Monroe Doctrine with all that implies will be destroyed and thrown to the four winds of the heaven."[10]

Gompers was most concerned with creating a base for development of a conservative union movement in Mexico. He appointed John Murray, a member of the International Typographical Union, to be his adviser on Mexican problems. Murray tried to establish contact with groups hostile toward Huerta, and to pressure Woodrow Wilson to support the Constitutionalists led by Venustiano Carranza. Gompers personally established liaison with Carranza's representatives in the United States, and widely publicized this development.[11]

Once Carranza successfully replaced Huerta, the way was open to build a new labor movement in Mexico. Unity

[10] Transcript of discussion by Gompers on Resolution 163, for the 1913 AFL Convention, November 21, 1913, *ibid.*

[11] Gompers to R. Zubaran, American representative of the Constitutionalists, July 1914, *1914 AFL Convention*, pp. 50–51.

in the Mexican labor movement had fallen apart in 1917, when revolutionary syndicalists formed their own labor association. Conservative workers were led by Luis N. Morones, and formed the Regional Confederation of Mexican Workers (CROM). Gompers established contact with Morones, and the Mexican labor leader would from that time on be the AFL contact in Mexico.

Working with CROM and Morones, Gompers moved to build the PAFL as an inter-American labor organization. A joint conference of Mexican and American labor leaders held in May 1918 spelled out PAFL objectives. These included gaining economic, political, and social improvement for the workers through economic action and cooperative administration; establishment of a permanent PAFL and its growth through all of Latin America; gaining cooperation in meeting these goals from both the Mexican and U.S. governments, and the safeguarding of "autonomous independence" from "insidious attempts of autocratic forms of government."[12]

Since the AFL was building the PAFL during wartime, they were almost assured of support from the Wilson Administration. Having gained Gompers' valuable services in Europe, Wilson could not afford to work against the AFL in Latin America. Support of the PAFL was interpreted by the Administration as another contribution to keeping organized labor loyal to the war effort. On July 17, 1918, AFL leaders met with Secretary of Labor William B. Wilson, Felix Frankfurter of the War Labor Policies Board, Edgar Sisson of the Committee on Public Information, and Chester M. Wright of the American Alliance for Labor and Democracy. The Administration leaders approved the PAFL and allocated government funds for its establishment.[13]

The procedure used in funding the PAFL was exactly the same as that developed for the AALD. Since any gov-

---

[12] Sinclair Snow, "Samuel Gompers and the Pan-American Federation of Labor" (unpublished doctoral dissertation, University of Virginia, 1960), pp. 56–57.

[13] *Ibid.*, pp. 63–67.

ernment subsidy of the PAFL was likely to be attacked by its opponents, the Committee on Public Information provided the PAFL with fifty thousand dollars from the President's special fund. The PAFL was also given a free permit for mailing. Money was to be handled through the CPI and American Alliance offices. The AALD then took care of funding the *Pan-American Labor Press,* the official PAFL publication. Permission to publish was granted by Bernard Baruch, acting in his capacity as chairman of the War Industries Board.[14]

Despite these Administration efforts, the PAFL declined after Gompers' death in 1924. Because the organization was dominated by the AFL, it was continually led into conflicts with the anarcho-syndicalist unions in Latin America. Santiago Iglesias, who in addition to his AFL post in Puerto Rico was an officer of the PAFL, explained that the organization stood "on a declaration of policy squarely in harmony with the policies of the American Federation of Labor." The organization was termed the "instrumentality through which constructive trade unionism can gain the ascendancy in Latin America, thus saving the American trade union movement from a continuing battle at its back door with a most destructive and revolutionary labor movement."[15]

Throughout the 1920's, the Latin American nations developed the economic pattern of dependency on one-crop cultures. To deal with this economic imbalance, the AFL leaders supported the growth of liberal capitalism— the kind of economic development that was in fact not to take place in Latin America. American corporations continually developed new investments in Latin American extractive industries. Raw materials were taken out at low cost, and U.S. manufactured goods were sold back at high prices. The AFL not only refused to condemn this economic relationship, it offered its endorsement. The AFL leaders echoed the arguments of American exporters,

[14] *Ibid.,* pp. 68–71.
[15] Santiago Iglesias, "The Child of the A.F. of L.," *American Federationist,* XXXII (1925), 928.

claiming that "our business relations with Europe, Canada, Mexico, and to a lesser degree other countries, are essential to the maintenance of stable business operations and prosperity."[16]

Since the AFL supported traditional corporate goals in Latin America, during the 1930's its leaders attacked "agents of radical and revolutionary European organizations," who they argued were "seeking to destroy the confidence which Latin American workers have" in the AFL. "In Brazil, Cuba, Colombia, Uruguay and other countries, their propaganda is carried on in a subversive manner."[17] Because the AFL unions faced severe internal economic problems, their concern with Latin America was mainly in the realm of rhetoric.

Only in Cuba, where the administration of Gerard Machado sponsored a campaign of assassination against labor leaders in the late 1920's, did the AFL issue vigorous protests to both Havana and Washington. Soon afterward, however, leaders of the Cuban Federation of Labor informed the AFL that they supported Machado in his efforts to break the large and radical National Confederation of Labor. Since their group was the local affiliate of the PAFL, the American Federation backtracked on its original protests.[18]

In 1934, the new Cuban administration of Carlos Mendieta replaced the more liberal government of Ramón Grau San Martín. Grau had been forced out of office by a military coup led by Fulgencio Batista, who had the backing of the United States government. Mendieta turned against Cuban labor, which he rightfully considered to be his enemy, and he suspended all constitutional guarantees of labor's rights. The Cuban army was employed by Mendieta "to break strikes, thousands of suspected terrorists were jailed, and a semblance of order was restored." A

---

[16] *American Federationist*, XXXIX (1932), 379.

[17] *1934 AFL Convention*, p. 170.

[18] William Green, February 26, 1927; John A. Beck to W. C. Roberts, April 14, 1927, William Green MSS, State Historical Society of Wisconsin, Madison, Wis.; *The American Labor Yearbook, 1927* (New York, 1928), pp. 228–29.

general strike was called to protest Mendieta's labor policy. The AFL remained oblivious, and continued to support Franklin D. Roosevelt's approval of Mendieta. Rather than condemn Mendieta, the AFL concentrated on attacking radical activists in Cuba who were accused of spreading subversive propaganda.[19]

With the birth of the CIO in 1935, the internal political battle between it and the AFL was transferred to Latin America. Both federations were active in Latin America, but their leaders pursued different policies. The AFL worked through Morones' CROM in Mexico, and through the PAFL, which was revived after 1936. The CIO, on the other hand, offered its support to the nationalist regime of Lázaro Cárdenas, President of Mexico after 1934. John L. Lewis and the CIO backed Cárdenas' expropriation of British and American oil companies carried out during March of 1938. The CIO desired to organize Mexican workers in the southwestern United States, and believed that its efforts could be furthered by fraternal relations with the radical Mexican union, the CTM, headed by the Marxist labor leader, Vicente Lombardo Toledano. The CIO also gave its blessings to the Confederation of Latin American Workers—the CTAL—which Toledano formed as an inter-American union body meant to counter the conservative PAFL.

The AFL leaders charged that the CTAL marked the extension of communism to Latin America, echoing the Communist smear with which they greeted organization of the CIO at home. AFL leaders also opposed the Cárdenas nationalization program as interference with private property. Instead, the AFL supported Cordell Hull's demand for immediate compensation for expropriated American property. In late 1938, Matthew Woll and Chester M. Wright met with State Department representatives. Wright informed State that the AFL intended to work exclusively through Morones' CROM, and that their "tendencies were along reasonably conservative lines in labor matters."

---

[19] Wayatt Macgaffey and Clifford R. Barnett, *Twentieth Century Cuba* (New York, 1965), p. 27.

When State officials warned the AFL leaders that they
would face pressure from Mexican officials to accept the
expropriation decrees, Wright "said that he was very much
opposed to the present activities of the Mexican government in this respect and that he would, of course, say
nothing endorsing them." Wright then asked whether
State was "seeking to build up Lombardo Toledano" and
the CTAL. The answer was negative, but it was noted that
State could not endorse the AFL's counteroffensive. Yet
the State Department aides made clear their agreement
with the AFL, and their hope that "labor in Mexico would
be less drastic in its demands."[20]

AFL efforts to revive the PAFL, however, were to no
avail. Toledano's CTM was closely allied with the Party of
the Mexican Revolution (PRM), the official organization
of the Cárdenas faction. Since the CTM was the major
body of Mexican organized labor, it was able to block any
steps to build up the CROM and PAFL. When the United
States settled its disputes with Mexico in 1941, because of
fear that blocking exports to Mexico would force the Mexi-
cans to deal with the Axis, the final agreement further
strengthened the CTM and hence the policy pursued by the
CIO.

The pattern of government-labor cooperation in Latin
America was institutionalized in the work of the Office of
Inter-American Affairs, headed by Nelson Rockefeller

[20] Herbert S. Bursley, Assistant Chief, Division of American
Republics, September 28, 1938, memo of meeting with Chester
M. Wright, Oliver Hoyem, and Thomas L. Burke, Chief of the
Division of International Communications, NA, RG 59, 812.504/
1805. Quoted in Henry W. Berger, "Union Diplomacy: American
Labor's Foreign Policy in Latin America, 1932–1955" (unpublished
doctoral dissertation, University of Wisconsin, 1966), pp. 102–03.
For a complete account of the Mexican crisis and American labor,
see pp. 79–114 of the Berger study.

Professor Berger is currently revising his study and preparing
it for publication. The complete story of American labor and Latin
America during the 1930's and 1940's awaits publication of his
excellent text. This writer is highly indebted to Professor Berger.
Much of the presentation in this chapter is based on his work; and
he was kind enough to share some of his research notes and writings with this author.

from 1940. Working with Rockefeller on his staff were labor men like John Herling fróm the AFL, as well as the labor economist David Saposs. A key area of concern for the OIAA was unsettled labor conditions in Brazil, Bolivia, and Chile, and the need to deal with them in order to further "the war effort among workers of all the Americas."[21]

As in World War I, the U.S. government sought to build pro-American groups in Latin America. In 1943, the OIAA, in conjunction with James Carey and Philip Murray of the CIO, and William Green and George Meany of the AFL, arranged a visit of Latin American labor leaders to the United States. Noticeably absent from the group was Lombardo Toledano, the Marxist labor leader from Mexico. But the group did include Bernardo Ibáñez, secretary general of the Chilean Confederation of Labor, and a major rival of Toledano. Ibáñez was backed by the AFL as a labor leader who could potentially undermine Toledano's position in Latin America and thereby increase AFL influence in labor circles. CIO unions, on the other hand, preferred to work through unions affiliated with Toledano's CTAL, and they kept close contacts with Toledano himself. The CIO established a Latin American committee, and brought Toledano to the United States for a meeting with the CIO executive board.[22]

Unity with the CTAL was to end, however, toward the end of World War II and the dissolution of the Left-center alliance. At a meeting held at the Chapultepec castle in Mexico City during February 1945, Assistant Secretary of State William Clayton presented an argument for the lowering of tariff barriers by Latin American nations, in exchange for extensive entry of American industrial exports to Latin America. Clayton also supported heavy investments by United States firms in agricultural and extractive industries. The investment capital would come from the private, rather than the public, sector of the American

[21] *1942 AFL Convention*, 222; quoted in Berger, *ibid.*, p. 199.
[22] *CIO News*, February 15, 1943, 5; cited in Berger, *ibid.*, pp. 200–01.

economy. In his speech—which came to be termed the
"Clayton Plan"—the Assistant Secretary called for unin-
hibited investment of foreign capital throughout Latin
America.[23]

Clayton's plan received a poor reception from Latin
American labor leaders. They viewed it as an attempt to
keep Latin America as a source of raw materials for American manufacturers, while guaranteeing it as a great market for industrial exports and capital investments. The
Mexican labor Left attacked the Clayton Plan as a scheme
for "uncontrolled foreign capital investment in Latin America [which] will cause the deterioration of programs which
look to the industrialization of the countries of Latin America, aggravating their great dependence on one crop cul-
ture and exports."[24] Both the AFL and CIO, on the other
hand, defended Clayton's approach. Both union federations supported the negotiation of reciprocal trade treaties,
which were meant to develop new markets for American
products in Latin America.

The CIO leaders argued that increased trade with Latin
America would aid unionized American industries in the
export trade. "Several of our basic industries are dependent
upon exports to sustain their high levels of production,"
United Electrical Workers chief James Carey told Congress. "In refined copper, cotton, machine tools, sewing
machines and tractors, for example, sales range from one-
fifth to over one-half of the total. Many such concerns find
that their export business carries them beyond the break-
even point into the profit side of the ledger and means full
employment of otherwise unutilized facilities and manpower. Larger volume means lower costs and opportunity
for lower prices in this country to consumers on the farms
and in the cities. Thus the value of exports as a spur to the
whole economy greatly exceeds any measurement based
solely on the volume of exports. There seems to be," Carey

[23] Howard F. Cline, *The United States and Mexico* (Cambridge,
Mass., 1953), pp. 280–81.
[24] *CTAL News,* August 14, 1945, 1; cited in Berger, *op. cit.*, p.
242.

argued, "a direct correlation between domestic prosperity and foreign trade."[25]

In taking this line of argument, Carey was revealing a basic consensus held by labor leaders, government spokesmen, and members of the large corporation community—a consensus that viewed extension of the export market as the *sine qua non* for achieving domestic prosperity. Carey was also reasserting the position put forward by Samuel Gompers in the post Spanish-American War period. Labor's advance, Gompers had argued, would occur as a byproduct of American foreign expansion. Under Gompers' leadership, the old AFL had formed the Pan-American Federation of Labor to block the advance of revolutionary syndicalism of the IWW variety. In the post-World War II era, the American unions now found themselves moving into opposition to the Latin American Left and labor movement, whose members desired to advance industrialization and to limit foreign investments. By necessity, the Latin American unions opposed the Clayton Plan, which did not seriously envision independent industrialization at the expense of United States business.

As in Europe, the American Federation of Labor leadership was most taken up with fighting Communist influence in the latter days of World War II. The man whom Jay Lovestone would choose to represent the Free Trade Union Committee in Latin America was Serafino Romualdi. An Italian émigré from Fascist Italy, Romualdi had obtained a job with David Dubinsky's ILGWU. Working out of ILGWU offices, Romualdi began to organize Latin Americans of Italian extraction as an anti-Mussolini opposition. In the process of carrying out his wartime duties, Romualdi forged many new contacts with Latin American labor leaders. He was eventually placed on the payroll of the Office of Inter-American Affairs as part of Nelson Rockefeller's staff, where he worked to consolidate the position of the United States in Latin America. At the war's end,

[25] U.S., House, Committee on Ways and Means, *Hearings on the Extension of Reciprocal Agreements Act,* 79th Congress, 1st Session, 1945, II, p. 2378; cited in Berger, *op. cit.,* p. 251.

Romualdi decided to stay on as the chief AFL and FTUC
representative in Latin America.

If not for his own efforts on behalf of the AFL, Romualdi
has written, most of Latin America would today be Communist. "Had not organized labor and the peasants of Latin
America actually opposed the subversive program of the
Communists, the political map of our hemisphere today
would be quite different. Venezuela, Colombia, Guatemala,
Peru and above all Brazil," according to Romualdi, "also
would probably be another Communist nation."[26]

Romualdi's claim is highly overstated. What is accurate
is his account of AFL attempts to split Latin American
labor and to build pro-United States unions in the Western
Hemisphere. The AFL effort was carried on in the context
of the developing split between Western (i.e., British and
American) and European organized labor. The World
Federation of Trade Unions, to which the British TUC and
CIO originally belonged, collapsed after Russian opposition to the Marshall Plan was made clear.

Romualdi sought a similar split in Latin America. As his
assignment with the OIAA ended, Romualdi prepared a
memo for Matthew Woll, chairman of the FTUC. Submitted as early as December 18, 1943, it urged creation of
a new inter-American trade union federation to replace the
Left-led CTAL, and to destroy Toledano's leadership of
Latin American labor. The existence of the CTAL was a
particularly bitter pill for the AFL leaders to swallow. Because the Communist parties supported the Allied war
effort, the State Department was forced to subdue its criticism of the CTAL. Their delegates, moreover, were fra-
ternally received by CIO unions, and were even "recognized

---

[26] Serafino Romualdi, *Presidents and Peons: Recollections of a
Labor Ambassador in Latin America* (New York, 1967), p. 2.
    The material contained in Romualdi's book is of great signifi-
cance to those seeking to understand AFL–CIO foreign policy. Romualdi composed the book by using his private papers. Often he
inserted verbatim texts of private reports and other key documents.
The book may therefore be used as a substitute for Romualdi's
complete papers, which have not been made available to scholars.
One must, of course, take into account that Romualdi himself chose
what material to include, and more important, what to omit.

as the legitimate spokesmen for Latin American labor even in our own State Department."

While the majority of Latin American organized labor was affiliated with the CTAL, Romualdi argued, "it is not to be assumed that all of the CTAL's components agree" with Toledano's Marxist position. In Argentina, Uruguay, Chile, Mexico, and Cuba, he asserted, many unionists desired "to come to closer contact with the American Federation of Labor, in spite of Toledano's antagonistic stand against it." Romualdi realized that the AFL could not form "any new inter-American labor body" in 1943, because "this would necessarily resolve into an anti-CTAL move and our friends in Latin America are not yet ready for it." Nevertheless, Romualdi opted to take the first step on such a path: a program of education and publicity which would seek to popularize AFL and anti-Communist positions among Latin American labor. "From this exchange of information, to be eventually supplemented by exchange of visits," Romualdi predicted, would "result a meeting of minds," the basis for "eventual organization of an inter-American labor body, composed of free, independent, democratic unions."[27]

As part of this effort, a meeting took place between the AFL leaders and Bernardo Ibáñez, head of the Chilean Confederation of Labor. Ibáñez explained how difficult it would be to force a split in the CTAL. Toledano approved of anti-Fascist wartime goals, and his group had great strength among the workers. Ibáñez himself only controlled Chilean labor by a small majority, and he was understandably hesitant to break publicly with Toledano.

The problems did not deter the AFL leaders. George Meany traveled to Mexico in December 1944. The purpose of his trip was to establish contact with factions in the CTM that opposed Toledano's leadership. The State Department ostensibly had no connections with Meany's efforts. Actually, as Professor Henry W. Berger points out, "it in fact gave assistance and encouragement." Meany reported to Ambassador George S. Messersmith that he was "deeply

[27] Romualdi to Woll, December 18, 1943, quoted in *ibid.*, pp. 7–8.

impressed by the intelligence and progressivism of Mexican labor leaders and . . . was pleased to discover that they are not the 'wild men' that they are generally thought to be in the United States."[28]

In the following year, the AFL continued to try to work toward building a new organization that would destroy the CTAL. The opportunity arose in late 1945, when Ibáñez and Arturo Sabroso, General-Secretary of the Confederation of Labor of Peru (CTP), stopped in the United States on their return from an ILO Conference in Paris. Traveling with Albino Barra, the men established contact with Romualdi. Although their own unions were affiliated with the CTAL and the WFTU, the leaders expressed their desire to revive, under new conditions and with a different name, the old tie with the AFL that existed in the days of the Pan American Federation.

The visiting Latin American labor leaders met with Matthew Woll, serving in his capacity of FTUC chairman. They agreed that Ibáñez, Sabroso, and Barra would form a committee "to seek advice and exchange views with leaders of the AFL and labor people of other American countries." Ibáñez and his associates had clearly committed themselves to the AFL camp. Before returning to Chile, Ibáñez arranged to stop first in Venezuela and Brazil, while Barra arranged to travel to Mexico and Guatemala.[29]

Their efforts were aided by an AFL announcement that Romualdi had been officially put in charge of Latin American labor affairs, and would soon head an AFL mission to Latin America. This news brought forth strong opposition from the CTAL. "The Latin American labor movement," Lombardo Toledano declared, "will have to proceed to the immediate expulsion of each and every one of the agents

[28] W. K. Alishie, Second Secretary of the Mexican Embassy; Report for the Ambassador, Mexico City, December 13, 1944, to Secretary of State Edward Stettinius, 032 George Meany/12–1344, NA, RG 59; Decimal File 1944; quoted in Henry W. Berger, "Union Diplomacy," 276.

[29] Romualdi, *op. cit.*, p. 37; memo of a meeting at Matthew Woll's office, December 5, 1945, Florence Thorne MSS, State Historical Society of Wisconsin, Madison, Wis.

of William Green and of the foreign monopolists who may attempt to interfere in the domestic affairs of our countries." Claiming that most Latin nations had laws prohibiting political activity by foreigners, Toledano argued that it would constitute political activity "if the AFL attempts to organize a rival to the CTAL." As for Romualdi's scheduled visit, Toledano vowed that he would be treated as an "agent provocateur," as an advocate of dual unionism who had thereby issued a "declaration of war."[30]

As a result of his work with Romualdi and the AFL, Ibáñez was expelled from the Chilean Confederation of Labor in February 1946. Rather than give up, Ibáñez organized a second Chilean labor federation, which immediately received the aid and endorsement of the AFL. AFL leaders now felt that the time had arrived to announce their plans to create a new inter-American labor federation, sorely needed to build support in what Romualdi called the AFL's "war against the Communists." Splitting the CTAL, however, was not a simple task. Even anti-Communist unionists were still pledged to the concept of Latin American labor unity, which meant continuing to work within the existing CTAL. The CIO unions, moreover, were still affiliated to the World Federation of Trade Unions, and hence approved the affiliation of Latin American labor unions with the CTAL. The first step in the plan, therefore, was to gain unity around an attack on Toledano's personal leadership of the CTAL.

In April 1946, a regional conference of American states belonging to the International Labor Organization was held in Mexico City. The meeting gave AFL delegates the opportunity to confer with others about establishment of "working relationships on a permanent organizational basis" with the AFL. CIO leaders Michael Ross and Willard Townsend attended the conference, but unlike the AFL men, they did not "participate in any of our behind-the-scenes maneuvers to win converts to our project."[31]

[30] *Hoy* (Havana, Cuba) February 13, 1945, p. 1; cited in Romualdi, *op. cit.*, p. 38.
[31] *Ibid.*, pp. 39–40.

Romualdi won the cooperation of labor delegates from Chile, Canada, Peru, and Venezuela. The most prominent "convert" was Father Benjamin Nuñez of Costa Rica, a popular priest who was head of the Costa Rican Confederation of Labor. Delegates from Bolivia, Colombia, Cuba, and the Dominican Republic, on the other hand, felt it was impossible to split from the CTAL at that time. When a secret ballot was taken at the conference to elect leadership for the Workers Group of the ILO governing body, only six delegates present voted against Toledano.

The AFL had suffered an important defeat. This led them, however, to decide to work outside of the Mexican Confederation of Labor. Although Romualdi acknowledged that the CTM was "the largest and most influential" labor organization in Mexico, and even admitted that it "was not under actual Communist control or even Communist oriented," he vowed to break its power because it supported the CTAL. George Meany and Romualdi made contact with a small and now discredited dual union, the old CROM headed by Luis Morones, who had served as head of the Pan-American Federation during the Gompers era. Together with a group of small unions in different industries, the AFL created a National Labor Council "whose combined strength . . . was less than that of CTM." Despite its clearly unrepresentative character, Romualdi and Meany saw their creation as an instrument with which they could break the CTAL. They had won the cooperation of leaders of "some legitimate Mexican trade unions," men who were "allies in the very seat of the CTAL."[32] At a dinner given by Meany in these delegates' honor, the final decision was made to move ahead toward creating a new inter-American labor organization. The initiative would come from the Latin American labor leaders; the policy, direction, and funds would come from the AFL.[33]

To proceed with their work, the FTUC sent Romualdi on a tour of South America. Leaving in June 1946, Romualdi

---

[32] *Ibid.*, p. 41.
[33] Report of Serafino Romualdi, May 5, 1946, to the AFL Committee on International Relations, Thorne MSS.

armed himself with letters of introduction from Nelson Rockefeller, Max Ascoli, Adolf A. Berle, Jr., and Galo Plaza, Ecuadorian Ambassador to the United States. His travels to Venezuela, Brazil, Uruguay, Argentina, Chile, Bolivia, Peru, Ecuador, Colombia, and Mexico were assisted informally by the Department of State. Secretary of State James Byrnes sent a circular to American embassies asking their "informal assistance to Romualdi." Instructing the embassies how to deal with him, Byrnes stressed that it was "important, of course, for the Embassy to avoid any formal sponsorship of Mr. Romualdi's activities which might give rise to charges that the State Department is favoring the A.F. of L. over the Congress of Industrial Organizations which has ties with the CTAL."[34] But State's approval was clear.

The journey itself brought Romualdi many valuable new contacts. In Peru he met Victor Raúl Haya de la Torre, and in Venezuela he met Rómulo Betancourt, two men with whom he and the AFL would work closely throughout the 1950's and '60's. In Chile, Romualdi again met with Bernardo Ibáñez. Reporting to Matthew Woll, Romualdi related that Ibáñez was now ready to take the formal leadership of a new inter-American labor group. Ibáñez only desired "definite assurances" that the new body "would not lack the necessary financial support to combat the opposition, and to carry out its own program of concrete trade union activities." Promising the necessary funds, Romualdi suggested that a meeting of Latin American labor leaders and AFL heads take place at the forthcoming September 1946 ILO Conference in Montreal.[35]

Romualdi's luck in getting associates varied according to local conditions. In Ecuador, he met with the Socialist labor leaders headed by Juan Isaac Lovato. Lovato at that time shared leadership of the Confederation of Labor of

---

[34] Secretary of State James Byrnes, June 11, 1946, to American embassies at Caracas, Rio de Janeiro, Sao Paulo, Montevideo, Buenos Aires, La Paz, Lima, Quito, Bogotá, Panama City, and Mexico City; NA, RG 59, Decimal File 1946, 810.504/61146; cited in Berger, *op. cit.*, p. 280.

[35] Romualdi, *op. cit.*, p. 42.

Ecuador (CTE) with the Communists. He favored affiliation of the CTE with the new inter-American group formed
by the AFL, but hedged on severing his group's ties with
the CTAL. Fearing for their own leadership positions
within the CTE, the Socialists did not want to be held
responsible for forcing a split in CTE ranks. They agreed
to set up a regular chain of correspondence with the AFL,
and even asked for "technical assistance and trade union
counsel." But they kept their ties strictly "confidential,"
Romualdi complained, and the CTE remained within the
CTAL.

In Colombia, Romualdi had better luck. A split had already taken place in the Colombian Confederation of Labor
(CTC) convention in August. All the non-Communist
delegates had walked out of the meeting, Romualdi wired
Jay Lovestone. They were exasperated by "Communist
dictation, fraud, multiplication of paper locals, political
interference." The group that walked out composed a majority of bona fide CTC members and claimed rights to the
CTC name and union funds. Romualdi met with the leaders of the anti-Communist opposition and pledged "AFL
assistance without going into specifics."[36]

Romualdi's last stop was in Mexico, where he again met
with the AFL-created National Labor Council. Its members
had planned to build a preparatory committee for the new
inter-American organization. While attending the Montreal ILO Conference, they intended to issue a formal call
for a new inter-American labor organization, to list organizations invited to participate, and to draft rules that would
assure the group's success. Upon his return to the United
States, Romualdi met with the AFL International Labor
Relations Committee. On September 13, they decided to
invite the fifteen Latin American delegates to the ILO
meeting to travel on to attend the Chicago convention of
the AFL.[37]

Romualdi's efforts to split the CTAL coincided with the

[36] Romualdi to Matthew Woll, August 19, 1946, quoted in *ibid.*,
p. 43.
[37] *Ibid.*, p. 45.

direction taken in Latin America by the administration of
Harry S. Truman. In May, Truman had asked Congress for
legislation establishing military collaboration with Latin
American nations and providing for the training, organization, and equipment of these nations' armed forces.[38] The
Administration could only regard the organization of a
new anti-Communist labor federation as a mechanism that
would strengthen the Truman Doctrine in Latin America.

Romualdi's job could not be accomplished as quickly as
he had first hoped. It was not until June 1947, at an annual
ILO conference in Geneva, that the Latin American delegates again had a chance to meet to bring their plans up
to date. At that session, and at meetings held in New York
after its conclusion, they scheduled the first meeting of the
new group for Lima, Peru, in January 1948. In the meantime, Romualdi kept traveling, trying to gain definite commitments from ambivalent union leaders, and working to
gather new supporters. He traveled to Mexico, Peru, Colombia, Venezuela, Bolivia, and Brazil, making new contacts and working to gather support for a split from the
CTAL.

A major problem confronting Romualdi on his travels
was the official attitude of the United States toward AFL
plans. Without official State Department approval, many
Latin American government leaders feared repercussions
if they openly endorsed Romualdi's mission. In Brazil,
national union federations could not affiliate with any international group except by an act of the Brazilian Congress and by recommendation of Brazil's President. Unions, moreover, could not spend money for travel expenses
of delegates to meetings without the approval of the Minister of Labor.

Brazil's leaders therefore wanted to know the position
taken by the United States government toward the projected Lima conference. "Although I could not speak for
the State Department," Romualdi recollected, "I assured
the Brazilians that my demarche was favored by Washing-

[38] *Public Papers of the Presidents of the United States: Harry
S. Truman, II, 1946* (Washington, D.C., 1952), 233–35.

ton." Romualdi had set the stage for State approval at the
AFL's 1946 convention, where he had issued a strong criticism of State Department hesitancy. Those responsible
for Latin American policy, he had argued, "have for too
long a time remained silent. . . . If not openly allied, they
are definitely supporting groups in Latin America who are
enemies of the American way of life and who are followers
of the Communist Party line."[39]

State feared to show partiality to Romualdi's work, out
of a concern that such endorsement would offend the CIO,
whose leaders approved Latin American affiliation with
both the CTAL and the WFTU. Romualdi complained that
the AFL had also not gained support of State's International Labor Division. State Department neutrality between AFL and CIO, Romualdi complained, hindered their
operations in Latin America. If a Latin labor movement
depended on their local government, and that government
did not want to provoke the wrath or displeasure of the
United States, it would not encourage a split from the
CTAL. Ibáñez, moreover, protested that the State Department failed to prevent the Communist takeover of the
Chilean Confederation of Labor.

The reasons for Romualdi's dissatisfaction disappeared
with the advent of the Truman Administration. In April
of 1947, Romualdi and Ibáñez met with Spruille Braden,
Assistant Secretary of State for Latin American Affairs,
and Daniel Horowitz, head of the State Department International Labor Division. Ibáñez criticized American diplomats who "still regard Communists as democratic types"
and who viewed anti-Communist elements with suspicion.
Braden's reply assured Romualdi "that the attitude of the
State Department toward our efforts to combat Communist
and other totalitarian influences in Latin American labor
will from now on be not only sympathetic but cooperative.
He informed us that the International Labor Division of
the Department had undergone a radical change and that
in the future it will be guided by different policies." Braden
"went even further by pledging to me and to Ibáñez what-

[39] Romualdi, *op. cit.*, p. 72.

ever assistance (compatible with the obvious limitations of nondirect government interference and diplomatic propriety) we may require in our work in preparation of the forthcoming inter-American labor conference." Romualdi was delighted since Braden had "never expressed himself so completely in agreement with our plans."[40]

Braden's eventual departure from the State Department did not lead to a change in the new policy. Norman Armour, a former career diplomat who inherited Braden's post, let Romualdi know in July that he shared the same analysis. Since Armour favored "active cooperation" between State and the AFL leaders, he assigned John Dreier, a staff member, to instruct the American embassies in nations which Romualdi planned to visit that the AFL should be given "all possible assistance" in building the inter-American trade union organization. Romualdi, at Armour's suggestion, met with the entire State Department labor section and the chief of all labor attachés to work out the details of labor policy. The results of this meeting, Romualdi reported, were "most satisfactory."[41]

Having gained the overt cooperation of the State Department, Romualdi next sought endorsements from leading public figures influential in Latin America. Positive responses were gathered from such old Latin American hands as Nelson Rockefeller, Spruille Braden, Sumner Welles, and A. A. Berle, Jr. Most welcomed by Romualdi, however, was the letter of endorsement presented by the Socialist Party's most prominent leader, Norman Thomas. Thomas wrote:

It will be a tragedy which may contribute to a catastrophe if in this world the workers are given no choice except allegiance to regional and divided labor unions, or no unions, on the one hand; and, on the other, allegiance to a federation dominated by fifth column labor organizations of communist

[40] Romualdi to Woll, Meany, and Dubinsky, April 15, 1947; cited in *ibid.*, p. 73; confidential memorandum, Romualdi to Florence Thorne, April 15, 1947, Thorne MSS.

[41] Confidential memorandum, Romualdi to Woll, July 10, 1947, *ibid.*; Berger, *op. cit.*, p. 290; Romualdi, *op. cit.*, p. 73.

totalitarian states. Even in a democratic socialist world, there will be a place for independent labor unions. They will be functionally necessary and they will constitute a protection against the omnipotent and omni-competent state. . . . It is perhaps the bitterest irony of our times that we should see a numerically powerful federation of trade unions which is in its fundamentals, the creature of a dictatorship and the apologist for slave labor.[42]

That Thomas was giving his approval to a new labor organization that was the creature of the State Department and the Free Trade Union Committee seemed to escape the old Socialist leader's attention. Thomas saw no contradiction in tying the Socialist Party to such an effort, since he conceived of the AFL (and the State Department) as worthwhile allies in a worldwide anti-Communist struggle. Thomas had become, since the end of World War II, the contemporary prototype of a State Department Socialist; the up-to-date equivalent of the World War I John Spargo.

Romualdi's work finally began to bear fruit. In early 1948, the scheduled Lima conference took place. In attendance were such Latin American labor luminaries as Arturo Sabroso of Peru, Bernardo Ibáñez of Chile, Victor Raúl Haya de la Torre, Benjamin Nuñez of Costa Rica, and Juan Arévalo of Guatemala. In all, 156 delegates from seventeen nations attended, although many represented only minority factions of their own labor movements.

On January 12, 1948, Romualdi was able to announce formation of the Inter-American Confederation of Labor, the CIT. The group had hardly started to function when developments in the European labor movements began to work to its advantage. By 1949, the CIO and the British TUC had withdrawn from the World Federation of Trade Unions. This action provided a green light for the similar withdrawal of moderate Latin American unions from the CTAL. Because of political conflicts between the CIO and AFL unions, the leaders of the CIT believed that new conditions demanded formation of yet another new interna-

[42] *Ibid.*, pp. 74–75.

tional labor body. When the International Confederation of Free Trade Unions was established as an anti-Communist counter to the WFTU, the CIT leaders decided that their organization should become the regional arm of the ICFTU. Since the old CIO unions had entered the ICFTU after its formation in December 1949, it was felt that in Latin America a new inter-American federation was needed, one with a new name and new structure. The result was formation of the Inter-American Regional Organization of Workers, the ORIT, which until the early 1960's, functioned as the principal anti-Communist institution through which both the AFL and CIO worked in Latin America.[43]

[43] Carroll Hawkins, "The ORIT and the American Trade Unions —Conflicting Perspectives," in William H. Form and Albert A. Blum, *Industrial Relations and Social Change in Latin America* (Gainesville, Fla., 1965), pp. 87–104. ORIT was created in January 1951.

XII

AMERICAN LABOR
IN LATIN AMERICA
1951–1968

The formation of the Inter-American Confederation of Labor (CIT), and later the Inter-American Regional Organization of Workers (ORIT), provided the first mechanism for anti-Communist operations among the labor force in Latin America. The existence of the new organizations, however, did not guarantee easy success for the American Federation of Labor. The problem confronting the AFL leaders was clearly expressed by George C. Lodge, former Assistant Secretary of Labor for International Affairs (1958–1960). Because Latin Americans have to fight "the threat of military dictatorship from the right and the continuing exploitative oligarchy of rich landowners and businessmen," Lodge wrote, "the class struggle is very much alive in Latin American society and it works against collective bargaining. . . . To many Latin American trade unionists, even those who are not Communists, the employer is the enemy. . . . Mutuality of interest between management and labor is not an easy concept for the Latin American laborer."[1]

Community of interest between worker and employer,

---

[1] George C. Lodge, *Spearheads of Democracy: Labor in the Developing Countries* (New York, 1962), p. 23.

however, is precisely the doctrine preached by American labor leaders working through ORIT and, since 1962, through the American Institute for Free Labor Development (AIFLD). American labor unionists operate in Latin America, according to Carroll Hawkins, "committed to the free enterprise mystique." Having won high status within the United States, "Big Labor and Big Management often deal with each other as affluent fellow corporate groups. There is nothing of the 'class war' sentiment in their collective bargaining. . . . In many cases markedly friendly relations exist between the rival leaderships as between fellow members of a power elite. The close cooperation of certain business interests with labor in the American Institute for Free Labor Development is a reflection of this 'partnership.' "[2]

Recognizing the insurmountable problems such an approach creates, writers like Hawkins urge American union chiefs to accommodate themselves to the forces of social revolution and nationalism, to give their support to Latin American independence movements, and to appreciate the resentment of imperialism and the desire of many Latin Americans to use collectivist methods. Union leaders, who Hawkins correctly argues have "the appearance of a corporate power group indistinguishable from American business executives," must make this accommodation if they are to give the lie to those Marxists "who say that the Alliance for Progress is a façade for Yankee capitalism which cannot be an instrumentality of a needed revolution."[3]

The problem is that such an accommodation is out of the question. American union leaders work in Latin America explicitly for the purpose of building institutions that can forestall social revolution. The unions they build are meant to serve as a means by which the State Department

[2] Carroll Hawkins, "The ORIT and the American Trade Unions —Conflicting Perspectives," in William H. Form and Albert A. Blum, *Industrial Relations and Social Change in Latin America* (Gainesville, Fla., 1965), p. 94.

[3] *Ibid.*, p. 102.

can neutralize Latin American working classes who otherwise might work for revolutionary movements. It is precisely because American unions play this role in Latin America that leading corporate spokesmen favor their future growth. "Businessmen in Latin America have become convinced," writes an author in the official publication of the Standard Oil Company, "that free labor unions are essential to free enterprise and that part of management's job today is encouraging the development of such unions." The corporations approve of the unions since their leaders have the same goals as the corporation executives. The unions "do not generate the waste of wildcat strikes; they are opposed to expropriation; and they are solid bulwarks against extremism in the ranks of labor."[4]

Because the American-led unions play such a conservative role in Latin America, the major organizations through which they work have fallen into disrepute. This point was recently made in a study prepared for the Committee on Foreign Relations (U.S. Senate) by Robert H. Dockery. ORIT has declined, the staff report noted, because of its "tendency . . . to support U.S. Government policy in Latin America. ORIT endorsed the overthrow of the Arbenz regime in Guatemala and of the Goulart regime in Brazil. It supported [Forbes] Burnham over Cheddi Jagan in Guyana, and it approved the U.S. intervention in the Dominican Republic. To many Latin Americans, this looks like ORIT is an instrument of the U.S. State Department."[5]

Since the Fulbright Committee's staff report singles out some key areas in which American labor unions have blindly pursued the path taken by the State Department, it would serve our purposes to take a closer look at the details of American labor policy in these same Latin American nations. Only thus can we develop criteria by

[4] Enno Hobbing, "Doing Business in Latin America," *The Lamp* (Standard Oil Company of New Jersey), Spring 1967.

[5] U.S. Senate, Committee on Foreign Relations, Subcommittee on American Republics Affairs, *Survey of the Alliance for Progress, Labor Policies and Programs,* 90th Congress, 2nd Session, July 15, 1968, p. 9.

which to judge the carefully understated critique presented by the Foreign Relations Committee staff report.

I. *Cuba and American Labor* ✓

ORIT, and the AFL leaders, were quite ready to condemn Latin American dictatorships that did not allow freedom for AFL-style unions, and whose leaders insisted upon maintaining complete control over their own nation's labor movement. Serafino Romualdi was one of the earliest critics of Juan Perón's regime in Argentina from 1946 until its collapse in 1955.[6] But in other cases, when right-wing dictatorships were welcomed by the United States, the position taken by the labor leaders was quite different.

In Cuba, the labor movement was originally composed of many Communists, organized since 1938 in the massive Confederación de Trabajadores de Cuba, the CTC. But in May of 1947, labor leaders close to President Grau San Martín's Auténtico Party moved to gain control of the federation. As a result of formal intervention by the Ministry of Labor, then under control of the Auténticos, CTC leadership was in the hands of Cuba's ruling political group. Carlos P. Socarras, the Minister of Labor, gave formal recognition to the Auténtico faction as the legitimate CTC leaders, and the Communist group was reduced to the position of a small rump organization.[7]

By 1949, leadership of the CTC was in the hands of Eusebio Mujal, the new secretary-general of the union movement. Mujal had been the leading labor representative of the Auténtico Party, and had been primarily responsible for engineering the 1947 CTC split with the Communists. Although he had been a Communist himself

---

[6] The most complete account of AFL and CIO responses to Perón is in Henry W. Berger, "Union Diplomacy: American Labor's Foreign Policy in Latin America, 1932–1955" (unpublished doctoral dissertation, University of Wisconsin, 1966), pp. 299–318.

[7] Robert J. Alexander, *Organized Labor in Latin America* (New York, 1965), pp. 160–61.

in his early years, Mujal had been subsequently elected to the Cuban House of Representatives and later the Cuban Senate as a candidate of the Auténtico Party. During the years of the pro-labor Grau government, both the Auténticos and the CTC gained a good deal of political strength.

All this was to end on March 10, 1952, when young army officers on Havana's outskirts seized the power of government under the direction of Fulgencio Batista. The surprising coup created a major crisis for the Cuban labor movement. Batista had overthrown a government led by the Auténtico Party, the same group whose leaders controlled the Cuban CTC. The possibility existed that the CTC would immediately move into opposition to the new Batista regime. Rather than adopt such a course, the CTC leadership decided to strike a bargain with the new dictator. Batista agreed to leave the CTC alone, if its leaders agreed not to use the Cuban labor movement as an instrument of opposition to his government.

The rationale for this policy was set forth in a memorandum sent out by CTC leaders on March 18, 1952. The CTC leadership, which had reacted to the coup at first by issuing a poorly distributed call for a general strike, moved next to initiate a meeting between Eusebio Mujal and Batista's new Minister of Labor. According to the CTC, this Minister had on the night of March 10 "offered guarantees that all the present trade union officers would be respected, that all the labor gains would be protected, and that the government would strongly oppose Communist as well as reactionary forces . . . he guaranteed that the government would not interfere in any way with the union's activities." The CTC Executive Board approved the offer. To show its faith, the Batista government returned union quarters occupied by the army to the CTC, and ORIT was allowed full freedom to function. The CTC leaders agreed to "continue our normal trade union activities within the limits accorded by the law."[8]

The AFL Free Trade Union Committee, however, took

[8] Serafino Romualdi, *Presidents and Peons: Recollections of a Labor Ambassador in Latin America* (New York, 1967), pp. 181–82.

a different stand from that adopted by the CTC leaders.
While they offered a mild criticism of the new government,
however, they did not take a position of firm opposition
such as typified their response to Perón in Argentina. "We
disagree with the estimate of the situation given by our
Cuban friends," declared Jay Lovestone. Lovestone was not
seeking to give advice to the Cuban CTC, but could not
"keep quiet about a situation where force and violence
were used in a military putsch to overthrow a legally constituted, democratically elected government."[9] Despite this
rhetoric, neither Lovestone, Romualdi, nor the FTUC ever
moved to wage a campaign against either the Batista government or the CTC which had accepted the dictator's
protection.

As Batista consolidated his rule of Cuba, he was soon
faced with the efforts of a small but determined band of
revolutionaries. After Fidel Castro led his famous attack
on the Moncada military barracks in Santiago, Serafino
Romualdi asked that the AFL back the efforts of a few
prominent Cubans to get Batista to meet with the *legal*
opposition and work out a schedule for return to a constitutional situation. Romualdi took care to point out that
strengthening this opposition would not enhance the position of the Communists:

> The present political opposition to Batista is aiming to re-
> gain power, the latest by 1958 when a new president is elected,
> or possibly before as the result of general elections which may
> be called in order to appease the opposition and divert it from
> resorting to violence. This opposition is led by people like
> Carlos Prio, Raul Chibas, Grau San Martin . . . who are strongly
> opposed to Communism—perhaps even more than Batista
> himself. . . . Since the opposition to Mujal leadership in the
> labor movement is made up largely of those who are against
> Batista . . . there is no reason for the time being to worry about
> the possibility that a change of government may enhance the
> prestige and strength of the Communists.

As to the relationship of the Opposition leaders with the

9 *Ibid.*, p. 182.

United States . . . most of them can be counted on to follow
the present policy of friendship and cooperation with our
country.[10]

Such an opposition group did not get the desired aid,
and Fidel Castro's revolutionary movement began to gain
the support of a growing number of Cubans. As a result
of the warfare initiated by Castro after his return to Cuba
on the *Granma,* after December 1956, the Batista government became more brutal in a desperate effort to maintain
its hold on Cuba. Despite the evident brutality of the regime, the relationship between the CTC and the Batista
government grew more firm. Castro favored a general
strike by Cuban labor, for the purpose of toppling the regime. Batista feared such a strike, but so did the CTC
leadership. If a general strike collapsed, and the CTC had
endorsed it, the union leadership worried that Batista
would then crush the CTC. Thus both Batista and Mujal
worked "to prevent any general movement of the workers
against the regime."[11]

For these reasons, the CTC leaders declared that a general strike would not be in the interests of Cuba. "We do
not need an insurrection," the CTC told Castro, "to achieve
the triumph of our program." Denying that conditions in
Cuba warranted calling a general strike, the CTC leaders
argued that "trade union rights have not been infringed,
nor have the unions been closed down."[12] This pro-Batista
policy was supported by Serafino Romualdi. The CTC position, he wrote, "was correct. Every competent observer
of the Cuban trade union scene at that time could reach
no other conclusion than that it would have been suicide
for the CTC to go along with a call for a general strike."[13]

The result of CTC inaction was the development of a
strong opposition within the union movement itself. To

[10] Romualdi to the AFL-CIO Executive Council, April 4, 1956, in
ibid., pp. 183–84.
[11] Alexander, *op. cit.,* p. 164.
[12] CTC statement of September 3, 1956, in Romualdi, *op. cit.,*
pp. 185–86.
[13] *Ibid.,* p. 186.

deal with this, the Mujal leadership suspended union elections, removed opposition leaders from office, and declared many strikes illegal. Mujal also got Batista to agree to a compulsory check-off system for payment of union dues, so that the national CTC rather than local chapters received the workers' payments. These actions strengthened the CTC's immediate position, and Fidel Castro's appeals for a general strike failed in both August 1957 and April 1958.

Mujal may have held the reins of power within Cuban organized labor, but his policies drew attack from AFL affiliates. Growing pressure was put on ORIT to have its leaders condemn the Batista government. Such a step would have followed the precedent set by ORIT's strong condemnation of Juan Perón and of the Peronista labor organization in Argentina. Louis Alberto Monge, the Costa Rican labor leader who was secretary-general of ORIT, was personally sympathetic to Fidel Castro's movement and favored giving ORIT's support to the 26th of July Movement. Romualdi opposed Monge's desire. The Cuban CTC was an original founder of ORIT, and a CTC officer was its president, while another was a vice-president of the International Confederation of Free Trade Unions. To preserve unity, Monge carefully refrained from attacking the CTC. Yet its leaders felt that Monge had rebuked them and Mujal accused him of interfering with the internal affairs of Cuban labor.

One of the results of Monge's disapproval of Batista was an official ICFTU mission to Cuba. Charles Millard, ICFTU director of organization, visited Cuba in August 1957 to investigate labor conditions. In his November report Millard praised the Cuban CTC and defended it as a non-political organization. Trade union freedom existed, the Millard report stated, and union rights were fully respected by the Batista government. Monge, as ORIT secretary-general, rejected Millard's conclusions. But ORIT's president, himself a leader of the Cuban CTC, accepted the report's findings. Mujal then accused Monge of permitting Communist penetration of ORIT.

Monge's opposition to Batista, and his refusal to accept
a whitewash of the Cuban CTC, created a crisis within
ORIT. A special executive board meeting held on January
13–15, 1958, was called to discuss the Cuban situation.
Mujal cabled the session that he had just met with Cuban government leaders, and had obtained from them
the promise of "restoration of constitutional guarantees,
elimination of press censorship, and reestablishment of
freedom of political activities for four government and
four opposition parties in preparation for June 1 general
election."

The ORIT Executive Board, after discussing Mujal's
cable and the Cuban problem, voted to accept a resolution that rationalized the CTC's course. Cuba was "undoubtedly a military dictatorship," ORIT's Executive
Board admitted, but Cuba was "passing through difficult
and turbulent times, which demand great diplomacy,
strength and tact on the part of the CTC." Rather than
criticize Mujal or the CTC, the ORIT Board voted 8–3 to
express "our sympathetic understanding of the problems
of our affiliate, the CTC, and we reaffirm our historic
policy of opposition to all forms of oppression and dictatorship." ORIT's leaders then added that scheduled
elections in Cuba must "be freely conducted along democratic lines."[14]

This meeting marked the last time when ORIT could
have broken away from its conservative course. But
rather than follow the path defended by their own secretary-general, ORIT remained loyal to Romualdi and the
United States Department of State. Overt criticism of the
CTC was eliminated, and a mild rebuke issued to Batista.
Mujal's course, in fact, had been charted for the CTC by
Romualdi. The previous October, the Free Trade Union
Committee had suggested that Mujal issue a memo appealing to Cubans "to stop all civil war and to activate
all political parties for strengthening the democratic in-
stitutions of the country." Both Romualdi and Lovestone

[14] ORIT Executive Board Resolution, January 1958, in *ibid.*, p.
191.

proposed that Batista assure that free elections would be held at an announced date. Furthermore, they warned Mujal that Cuban labor's image was being tarnished. Romualdi naively believed that issuance of this memorandum showed that the CTC was truly "an independent, bona-fide free trade union organization."[15]

Since the CTC statement and the ORIT endorsement did not solve the Cuban dilemma, Romualdi himself journeyed to Cuba in March. His visit was ostensibly for the purpose of attending the inauguration ceremonies of the Havana Hilton Hotel, built by the Cuban Hotel and Restaurant Workers' Union retirement fund.[16] According to *Washington Post* reporter Dan Kurzman, the real purpose of Romualdi's mission was to seek out Fidel Castro to arrange a deal. Mujal, who by now could foresee the eventual collapse of the Batista government, would offer Castro CTC support. In exchange, Castro would allow the CTC to function with its same leadership and with AFL-CIO connections.[17] Castro wisely did not accept this offer. The AFL-CIO continued to back Mujal. On April 11, George Meany once again defended the Cuban CTC:

> The CTC of Cuba is an affiliate in good standing of the International Confederation of Free Trade Unions (ICFTU) and its Inter-American Organization (ORIT). Like all other affiliates, it enjoys a high degree of autonomy, especially in matters affecting national affairs and its internal policy. Therefore the AFL-CIO is reluctant to pass individual judgement and to assume that it knows better than the CTC how to protect the interests of the Cuban workers and their organizations.[18]

The AFL-CIO had put its faith in Batista and Mujal, just at the moment when Castro was preparing for his final march into Havana. On January 1, 1959, Fulgencio

---

[15] AFL-CIO Free Trade Union Committee, "For Democracy and Peace for the Cuban People," October 22, 1957, in *ibid.*, p. 192.

[16] *Ibid.*, p. 197.

[17] Dan Kurzman, "Lovestone's Cold War," *The New Republic*, June 25, 1966, p. 21.

[18] George Meany, statement of April 11, 1958, in Romualdi, *op. cit.*, p. 198.

Batista fled and Fidel Castro and his rebel army seized
control of the island. As part of their revolutionary policy, the rebels took over union headquarters, cut CTC ties
with the AFL-CIO, and appointed a pro-Castro labor
leader, David Salvador, as new head of the CTC. Eusebio
Mujal fled from Cuba, and took with him other CTC leaders, who received new positions from AFL-CIO affiliates
elsewhere in Latin America. Mujal became head of the
Central Cuban Workers in Exile, and operated out of
Mexico City. Jose A. Carbénel, former CTC treasurer,
represented the American Institute for Free Labor Development in Central America; and Estebán Rustán, secretary-general of the Confederation of Bank Employees,
became an ORIT executive in Costa Rica.

While Batista ran Cuba, Romualdi, Lovestone, and the
Free Trade Union Committee were capable of offering
only mild rebuke to the Batista regime. They rationalized
the support given Batista by the Cuban CTC, and fought
the moderate opponents of Batista within ORIT. Once
Castro established his revolutionary government, however, they became the first advocates of a firm opposition
to the new government. As early as April 1959 Romualdi
opposed Castro for "purging" anti-Batista union leaders
who had been active in the CTC with Mujal. Romualdi
was particularly bitter since the new CTC leadership tried
to get Latin American labor to withdraw from ORIT and
break all ties with the AFL-CIO. "This is," he wrote
George Meany, "precisely the current Communist line."[19]
By May 4, 1960, the AFL-CIO Executive Council officially
declared that Castro's policies were part of "a well-
planned strategy designed to make Cuba an advanced
outpost of the Soviet Union's drive to infiltrate the New
World." By February 28, 1961, they proclaimed that
"Cuba has become a Soviet satellite," and recommended
breaking off diplomatic relations with Cuba and the imposition of economic sanctions against the Castro regime.[20]

[19] *Ibid.*, p. 206.
[20] *Ibid.*, pp. 222–23.

II. *Guatemala and American Labor: 1954* √

Guatemala serves as an example of the problems which are faced by the leadership of small underdeveloped nations, when they begin moving to lift their nations from the conditions which keep them in a state of subordination. The lower classes compose from seventy to eighty per cent of the population of three million people, and the annual per capita income was $150 in 1957.[21] Despite the misery suffered by its population, Guatemala received a considerable amount of investment from United States economic interests. The Guatemalan economy was particularly dependent on the production of the United Fruit Company. United Fruit controlled Guatemala's second greatest export industry, banana production. They also owned the only steamship service in the nation, as well as seaport facilities at Puerto Barrios on the Atlantic, and held majority control of the International Railways of Central America, the only railroad running from Puerto Barrios to the capital. Their great power had enabled United Fruit and other foreign corporations to gain concessions from earlier governments, meant to maximize returns on 108 million dollars of holdings. Thus United Fruit was exempt from taxes on business profits, except those resulting from the sale of consumer goods in company stores.[22]

Until 1944, Guatemala had been ruled by a military dictatorship headed by General Jorge Ubico. The military regime was overthrown in that year, and was replaced by a revolutionary junta headed by Jorge Toriello, a businessman, Javier Araña, a tank commander, and Jacobo Arbenz, an army captain and large landowner. The junta set up elections, which were won in December by a social democratic schoolteacher, Juan

[21] Nathan L. Whitten, *Guatemala: The Land and the People* (New Haven, Conn., 1961), p. 87.
[22] United Nations Department of Economic and Social Affairs, *Foreign Capital in Latin America* (New York, 1955), pp. 97-99.

José Arévalo. Arévalo immediately instituted a series of social reforms and steps towards industrialization, meant to decrease Guatemala's dependency on coffee and bananas. Arévalo also moved to legalize labor organization. A new Labor Code was issued, providing for legal recognition of trade unions, a new minimum wage of twenty-six cents per day, an eight-hour day, and establishment of labor courts to hear workers' complaints. A social security system was instituted, and the nation's first central labor organization, the Confederación de Trabajadores de Guatemala was created as a CTAL affiliate in 1945.[23]

The Arévalo laws comprised the first steps toward reform; the laws were a moderate response to an extreme system of deprivation. Yet they brought forth a pronounced opposition. "It is a mute testimony to the stagnation and backwardness of Guatemala under Ubico," State Department political analyst Ronald Schneider writes, "that as essentially moderate a program as that supported by Arévalo should be thought of as radical or even 'Communistic' by the Guatemalan employers." Yet some twenty-four "abortive attempts to overthrow the government occurred in the first four years of his terms, as well as several more serious ones in 1949–1950."[24]

The assassination of Colonel Francisco Araña on July 18, 1949, moved his followers to stage an attempt to seize power. The Arévalo government asked the unions to help them defend themselves. The new unions not only declared a general strike, but provided volunteers who were given arms. It was their military effort, alongside loyal army troops, that was responsible for defeating the attempted coup. As a result of the union activity, the political Left strengthened its position within Guatemala. The 1950 presidential election was won by Jacobo Arbenz, a left-of-center politician who was willing to work with Communists in the trade union movement.

The eventual justification for overthrow of Arbenz's

23 Alexander, op. cit., p. 203.
24 Ronald M. Schneider, Communism in Guatemala (Philadelphia, Pa., 1959), p. 21 n.

democratically elected government was that he permitted international communism to gain a political base in the Western Hemisphere. Shortly after his election, the charge was often heard that Communists had consolidated their position and had infiltrated the government with Arbenz's permission.[25] This charge was highly exaggerated. The Communist Party had only three to four thousand members, held only four of the fifty-six seats in Congress, and did not receive any cabinet positions. Political power, as elsewhere in Latin America, remained in the hands of the army. Yet the Communists *were* given important posts in government administrative bodies, particularly in administration of the agrarian reform program and in the trade union movement. Secretary-general of the newly merged central labor movement, the Confederación General de Trabajadores de Guatemala, was Victor Manuel Gutierrez, Communist member of the Chamber of Deputies and the leading congressional exponent of agrarian reform. Arbenz faced pressure from many landowners when he moved forward with agrarian reform in 1953, and because of Communist support for his own program, "the stock of the Communists rose in Arbenz' eyes. Through their control of the labor movement they held out to him an efficient arm for the implementation of agrarian reform and mobilization of *campesino* support."[26]

But the Communists were in no sense ready to make any serious bid for power, and they had not been able to develop a successful popular movement. They had influence through key positions in the political structure, but had not "found sufficient time to build a broad base or to sink their roots deeply."[27] The Communist issue enabled Arbenz's opponents, including the Eisenhower Administration, to mask their real reason for opposing the social

[25] *New York Times*, June 5, 1951, p. 6.
[26] Schneider, *op. cit.*, pp. 36–37.
[27] *Ibid.*, pp. 317–18. For an extensive discussion of communism in Guatemala and an evaluation of the entire 1954 crisis, see David Horowitz, *The Free World Colossus* (New York, 1965), pp. 163–86.

democratic regime. This was, indeed, the ambitious program of agrarian reform which the Guatemalan Communists supported.

Prior to the reform, two per cent of the landowners owned seventy per cent of the arable land, while two-thirds of all landowners held only ten per cent of the cultivated land area. The purpose of Arbenz's law was to "liquidate feudal property . . . in order to develop . . . capitalist methods of production in agriculture and prepare the road for the industrialization of Guatemala."[28] It was the land reform program that produced the friction between Guatemala and the United States government. In March 1953, Arbenz expropriated 234,000 out of 295,000 uncultivated acres owned by United Fruit in the Tiquiaste area. Compensation offered ($600,000 in three per cent, twenty-five year bonds) was based on values set on the property by United Fruit itself. Now United Fruit termed the compensation offer unacceptable. The United States intervened diplomatically on behalf of United Fruit, arguing that the compensation offered did not conform to the "minimum standards of just compensation prescribed by international law."[29]

In April, the United States filed a claim of sixteen million dollars against Guatemala for the expropriated properties, claiming nine million covered damages to properties not expropriated, but which were harmed as a result of expropriation of the other acres. By August, Arbenz began proceedings to expropriate 173,000 out of 273,000 other United Fruit acres at Bananera, on the Atlantic coast. Despite official disclaimers, it was this vigorous program of reform that led to the charge of communism which was leveled against the Arbenz government.

While the charge of communism emanated from John Foster Dulles and other representatives of the Eisenhower Administration, the representatives of the AFL were not

[28] Bernard Rosen, "Counter-revolution: Guatemala's Tragedy," *The Nation*, July 31, 1954, pp. 87–89.
[29] *Foreign Capital in Latin America*, p. 98.

slow to join the chorus. As early as 1951, Serafino
Romualdi had told delegates to the AFL Convention that
although United States business interests in Guatemala
opposed the union movement's economic demands, the
real issue in that nation was that Communists "dominate
the labor movement and seem to enjoy the favors of the
government."[30]

AFL opinion was crystallized by 1954. In February,
George Meany addressed Arbenz in a public letter. While
the AFL supported social reform and Arbenz's labor code,
Meany claimed, it was "concerned over the growing in-
fluence of Communist elements in Guatemala." Three
pieces of evidence revealed to Meany that Guatemala had
become a Communist state. Newspaper attacks on the
United States, support by government leaders of international Communist organizations, and patronage of
Communist-dominated labor groups were offered as proof.
Meany was especially upset at Arbenz's opposition to the
AFL attempt to organize a dual union in Guatemala. In
1953, ORIT and the AFL funded the National Union of
Free Workers of Guatemala, the UNTL. Their leaders
were arrested, and Arbenz deported UNTL's president to
Mexico. "Were it not for the continuous Government
support of the Communists' control of the organized labor
movement," Meany wrote to Arbenz, "many workers'
groups would be willing and anxious to break the shackles
of Communist domination."[31]

Arbenz's evident dedication to his chosen path of agrarian reform led to increased diplomatic pressure from the
United States. At the Caracas conference of the Organization of American States in March 1954, the United States
urged adoption of an anti-Communist resolution aimed
at Guatemala. By a 17–1 vote, with Mexico and Argentina
abstaining, the OAS voted to ban communism from the
hemisphere, whether its source was armed intervention

[30] *1951 AFL Convention*, pp. 317–18.
[31] Meany to Arbenz, February 5, 1954, in Romualdi, *op. cit.*, pp.
267–68. The letter was originally published in the *Inter-American
Labor Bulletin*.

from without or revolution from within.[32] These measures were approved heartily by Meany. Writing in the official AFL publication, Meany announced that the United States had revealed "its intention to lay the cards on the table and come to a showdown."[33]

The showdown was to take place during the third week of June 1954. A "Liberation Army," in which members of the AFL-ORIT dual union took part, crossed the border from neighboring Honduras and invaded Guatemala. Under the leadership of Colonel Carlos Castillo Armas, the invading force fought for ten days, until it had successfully toppled the Arbenz government. The coup was planned, financed, and equipped by the United States government, and carried out under the direction of the Central Intelligence Agency. While the scheduled purchase of Czechoslovakian arms by the Arbenz government served as a pretext for the invasion, the coup had been planned and prepared carefully for quite some time. Years later former President Eisenhower admitted that economic aid was given Armas by the United States, as well as the crucial support of American bombers. Without the dispatch of these planes to replace those destroyed in conflict during the first days of the invasion, Eisenhower reported, Armas would have most likely been unable to seize power in Guatemala.[34]

To their credit, some of the minority leaders of the CIO privately made known their opposition to the Armas invasion. O. A. Knight, president of the Oil Workers Union and chairman of the CIO Subcommittee on Latin American Affairs, opposed Administration policy. "Communist infiltration in Guatemala," Knight told the CIO Executive Committee, "may have been greatly exaggerated." Knight argued that State Department policy was motivated by their desire "to give aid and comfort to the United Fruit

[32] John R. Beal, *John Foster Dulles* (New York, 1957), p. 230.

[33] George Meany, "On Latin-American Policy," *American Federationist*, vol. 61, no. 3 (March 1954), p. 17.

[34] Dwight D. Eisenhower, *Mandate for Change, 1953–1956* (Garden City, N.Y., 1963), pp. 422–24; cf. Horowitz, *op. cit.*, pp. 163–64, 175–82.

company which was doing all it could to set aside . . . some
of the decent legislation that has been passed down there
recently."[35]

Emil Mazey, secretary-treasury of the United Auto
Workers, was even more outspoken. Addressing the Michi-
gan CIO Convention, Mazey charged that "we have been
supporting the wrong people." Mazey blamed both the
State Department and "the United Fruit Company for the
difficulties that we have in Guatemala at the present time
. . . the State Department and the United Fruit Company
have been manipulating the politics of that country. They
have organized revolutions in the past against the best interests of the people. They have opposed land reform. They
have opposed any special progress for the people of Guatemala and then we wonder why the Communists who make
promises of land reform, who makes promises of social
security and other necessary gains for the people, wind up
on top. I say we have to change this foreign policy of ours.
We have got to stop measuring our foreign policy on what's
good for American business that has money invested in
South America and elsewhere in the world."[36]

The CIO critics were a small minority among the leadership of organized labor. "The American Federation of
Labor," George Meany announced, "*rejoices* over the downfall of the Communist-controlled regime in Guatemala,
brought about by the refusal of the Army to serve any
longer a Government that had betrayed the democratic
aspirations of the people and had transformed the country
into a beachhead of Soviet Russia in the Western Hemisphere." Meany continued to offer his hope that the new
Provisional Government would "restore as quickly as possible absolute respect for civil liberties and human rights
and will preserve the social gains codified in the Guatemalan labor and agrarian legislation." Meany also offered
Castillo Armas the aid of formerly exiled anti-Communist
trade union leaders, who were "now returning to their

---

[35] Minutes, CIO Executive Board meeting, June 29, 1954, pp.
95–105; cited in Berger, *op. cit.*, p. 357.
[36] *Latin America Today* (New York: June–July 1964), 6.

country determined to rebuild the labor movement." The AFL, he pledged, would "assist them in this difficult task of reorganization." Citing his opposition to the efforts of "reactionary, pro-Fascist forces to turn the clock back to the pre-1944 feudalistic dictatorship," Meany warned that such a development would be extremely harmful. "Serious repercussions" would occur if the overthrow of the "first Communist controlled regime in the Western Hemisphere were not to be followed by the establishment of a strong democratic regime."[37]

Meany, like Herbert Hoover in the 1920's, nominally favored the growth of a stable, international capitalist liberal order that avoided the growth of either a revolutionary Left or an old-world-style extreme Right. Yet in fact, while Meany disavowed the activities of old-world reactionaries, he refused to back any meaningful measures to curb the political and economic power of local oligarchies in Guatemala. To endorse such a move toward the Left meant a danger of intensifying the internal class struggle and thereby threatening the hegemony of American corporations in Latin America. Meany's warnings about the restoration of conservatism amounted to pure rhetoric. The policy he had the AFL pursue was based on support of the very elements whose Fascist tendencies he warned about. Meany verbally cited his identification with the social gains of the Guatemalan labor legislation; but it was this very legislation that was opposed by the men who invaded Guatemala. Those who favored extending and building upon the post-1944 reforms were working through the Arbenz government that had just been deposed.

A short ten days after Castillo Armas had taken power, Romualdi, Daniel Benedict of the CIO, Raul Valdivia of the Cuban CTC, and Otero Borlaff of ORIT arrived in Guatemala. The men arrived to help the unions "reorganize their forces" and to advise Armas on labor policy. Romualdi spent the full months of July and August in Guatemala, and his work there led him to express a positive view of the Armas policy, a view which he expressed in the September

[37] Romualdi, *op. cit.*, pp. 240, 267 n.

1954 *American Federationist* and which he heartily endorsed again in his own book in 1967.

"The people of Guatemala," Romualdi told union workers, "were solidly behind Castillo Armas and a strong wave of anti-Communism was sweeping the country." The problem, however, was that "this wave of anti-Communism threatened to sweep away the labor movement itself." Because of previous Communist domination of the union movement, unionism had become synonymous with Communism. Romualdi had the job of persuading people that "free trade unionism was the means of preventing the resurgency of the Communist danger." Romualdi used ORIT and AFL funds to bring together young people from twenty unions to form a National Committee for Trade Union Reorganization. Romualdi saw two opposite currents operating in the Armas government; "one that would like to reduce [unionism] to a minimum if not to suppress it altogether, and another that believes in organized labor's usefulness and constructive possibilities." Armas, he believed, "himself favors the development of free trade unionism."[38]

The reality of the AFL policy was that Romualdi and his associates had contributed to the resurgence of the most autocratic type of government possible. Almost immediately, Armas removed all the anti-Communist labor leaders from office. For the unions to exist, they had to choose leaders accepted first by Armas. Working conditions declined drastically, as government commissions struck "down labor's most respectful pleas as Communist agitation," and as landowners began "seizing the property of the peasants by burning them out."[39] The new regime, Charles O. Porter and Robert J. Alexander wrote, "in spite of the good intentions [*sic*] of the President was a brutal dictatorship. Hundreds and perhaps thousands of peasants and workers were killed in a wave of revenge on the part

[38] *Ibid.*, pp. 244–45.
[39] David Graham, "Liberated Guatemala," *The Nation*, July 17, 1956, pp. 34–37.

of employers and landlords, who felt that they had been mistreated during the Arévalo-Arbenz period."[40]

Even Romualdi was forced to admit the "reactionary forces eventually gained the upper hand." In February 1956, Armas amended the reform Labor Code so that it became, to cite Romualdi's gross understatement, "much more difficult for a trade union to operate and exist." The employers, Romualdi had learned, with "the connivance of the governmental authorities, had resorted to wholesale dismissals of every active trade unionist whom they classified as agitators. Agricultural workers were brought back to conditions of servitude if not actual slavery."[41]

Romualdi was shedding crocodile tears. The AFL had consistently opposed the Arévalo-Arbenz government and its social reforms as having opened the door to communism. By the time of Arbenz's agrarian reform, George Meany viewed Guatemala as a part of the Communist camp. The problem was that anti-communism had always been "relatively meaningless to the Guatemalan masses, who were interested primarily in a fuller and more satisfying life." Noting that Guatemala enjoyed new freedom between 1944 and 1954, Ronald Schneider added that "the working class had particular reason to feel loyal to the revolutionary regime. For the first time in Guatemalan history labor enjoyed the right to organize freely, bargain collectively and strike. Never before had they felt free to speak out openly and voice their feelings without restraint, much less be confident of gaining a sympathetic hearing from the government. The lower classes enjoyed the novelty of living in a new atmosphere, officially fostered, in which they were treated with a measure of respect and dignity."[42]

Rather than give their support to the first government to gain the loyalty of the working classes, the AFL leaders joined those who branded this government as Communist.

---

[40] Charles O. Porter and Robert J. Alexander, *The Struggle for Democracy in Latin America* (New York, 1961), p. 70.

[41] Romualdi, *op. cit.*, p. 245.

[42] Schneider, *op. cit.*, pp. 302–03.

Because the trade union movement was led by Communists, and was certified as the official bargaining agent for the workers by the government, the AFL tried to build a dual union federation. The AFL implemented a counter-revolutionary policy, the logical end of which was support to the CIA-financed Armas invasion. During the Arévalo-Arbenz years, the AFL had used anti-communism to help bring down the pro-labor government. After the Armas victory, the AFL leaders came to resent the use to which this same anti-communism was being put. For Armas was now using it to prevent organization of pro-United States, AFL-type unions in Guatemala. Armas, however, had paid his debts. He recognized the regimes of Trujillo and Franco, dissolved Congress, restored all lands expropriated from United Fruit, abolished all taxes on interest, dividends, and profits payable to investors living outside of the country, and made it possible for petroleum to be extracted by any firms and exported in its crude state, later to be resold to Guatemala as gasoline. The corporations benefited, and the United States contributed ninety million dollars in loans, arms, and subsidies in two years. All of this had been accomplished by Armas, while the employers had simply "failed to realize the absolute need of a free, independent, strong democratic labor movement."[43] What Serafino Romualdi did not go on to say is that part of the blame for this lay with the American Federation of Labor.

III. *British Guiana and American Labor*

The crown colony of British Guiana (now the independent nation of Guyana) is a small country in South America, in which the Indian and black descendants of imported slaves formed two distinct, submerged elements. The colony remained in a dormant stage until 1943. In that year an East Indian dentist, Cheddi Jagan, returned to British Guiana with his new American wife, Janet. They formed the People's Progressive Party, dedicated to achieving inde-

[43] Romualdi, *op. cit.*, p. 246.

pendence on the basis of an anti-colonialist and Socialist
program.

After years of effort, Jagan's radical party won a majority of parliamentary seats in the 1953 general elections.
One of the major opponents of Jagan's PPP was Lionel
Luckhoo, a wealthy politician who served as president of
the Man-Power Citizens' Association, a conservative central union that represented sugar workers on the great
plantations. Luckhoo, and other older politicians associated with him, lost their bids for seats on the Guianese
Council. The PPP won a majority of votes cast, and obtained eighteen out of the twenty-five elected seats.

Having won a majority of votes, Cheddi Jagan became
premier of the new government. Almost immediately, the
PPP introduced and passed a Labor Relations Bill, providing for union recognition and for settling questions of
union representation by tallying the votes of workers at the
production point. At stake was whether sugar workers
would continue to be represented by Luckhoo's MPCA, the
body favored by the large Booker's Company, or whether
they would choose the more radical Guiana Industrial
Workers Union (GIWU), the body favored by the PPP and
the union which was leading a long strike at the Enmore
factory. When the Labor Relations Bill was passed, the
GIWU members had already been on strike for twenty-five
days. Upon hearing that the bill was now law, the union
called off the strike, since they now expected to receive
union recognition according to the provisions of the bill.
Their basic demand could now be met through electoral
action, since it was expected that a majority of workers
would vote for the GIWU.[44]

The Labor Relations Bill provided for the holding of
elections under procedures to be established by the Minister of Labor. This position was an appointed cabinet post.
Since the PPP would appoint an individual from its own

[44] The account of the strike, and general details about British
Guiana and Cheddi Jagan, are based on Philip Reno, "The Ordeal
of British Guiana," *Monthly Review*, XVI, No. 3 (July–August
1964), 17–19.

ranks, Jagan's opposition charged him with trying to use the labor bill as a means of controlling the trade unions. Sugar companies particularly feared the outcome of the scheduled elections. Luckhoo had run for office as a candidate of the National Democratic Party, and all of their candidates, who campaigned in opposition to the PPP program, had been defeated. Even worse, returns from sugar areas indicated heavy PPP majorities. Only two legislative seats were won by NDP candidates, and they were *not* from a sugar worker constituency.

Jagan never got a chance to put the labor bill into effect. While the measure was being debated, the British government sent its gunboats to Georgetown. British troops were sent into Guiana, the local constitution was suspended, and Jagan and the other elected ministers were all dismissed. "The constitution of British Guiana must be suspended," the government of Great Britain announced, "to prevent Communist subversion of the government. . . . The faction in power has shown by their acts and their speeches that they are prepared to go to any length, including violence, to turn British Guiana into a Communist state."

The opinion of the British government was shared by the Free Trade Union Committee. As a result of the growth of Jagan's radical party, Serafino Romualdi had become involved in Guianese affairs as early as 1951. "Having become convinced of Dr. Jagan's subservience to the Communist movement since my first visit to British Guiana in 1951," Romualdi wrote, "I did everything in my power to strengthen the democratic trade union forces opposed to him and to expose Jagan's pro-Communist activities from the day he was elected Prime Minister, following the general elections of April 27, 1953."[45]

In Guiana there was no need to support a dual union; the conservative Man-Power Citizens' Association already existed. Luckhoo's union was already affiliated with both the ICFTU and ORIT, and Romualdi backed them up in the internal struggle with the GIWU, which was affiliated

[45] Romualdi, *op. cit.*, p. 346.

with the WFTU. As Romualdi saw it, the purpose of the PPP Labor Relations Bill was not to give organized labor legal recognition, but to "destroy the MPCA with every means at its disposal." Cabinet members, including the Minister of Health and Housing, who was also president of the GIWU, "spent most of their time visiting the sugar estates, arousing the workers . . . and preparing them for a general strike." Romualdi tried to make this activity sound unusual and suspicious. What he neglected to explain was that ministers of government were chosen by the majority party, and the sugar workers had cast their ballots for candidates on the side of the GIWU. Luckhoo, as head of the MPCA, had also run for office. Had his party won a majority of seats, he would have formed a government and appointed ministers from his own group.

Romualdi opposed the strike on the sugar estates called by the GIWU in September 1953. The goal of the strike, he claimed, was to force "the employers to break the contract with the MPCA and recognize the Communist-controlled union." Romualdi backed up the contention of the MPCA, that the labor bill was meant "to collar the workers into a government union." When the issue was settled by the landing of British troops, Romualdi defended their intervention as a necessary step in the prevention of communism. Destruction of the democratically elected government, and the ejection of members of the majority party, was summed up by Romualdi in the nondescript statement that "every Communist Minister was fired." Once Jagan's government was removed, Romualdi again traveled to Guiana. This time he went "to lend moral support to the democratic labor movement." In both the *AFL News Reporter* of October 30, and the *International Free Trade Union News* for December 1953, Romualdi published the following estimate of the situation in Guiana:

Every fair-minded person interested in the preservation of democracy in the Western Hemisphere, who has followed events in British Guiana . . . must agree that the suspension of the constitution, decided upon by the British government . . .

was the only recourse left to prevent the setting up of a Communist totalitarian state.

Only those who believe, or pretend to believe, that the Communists' only interest in British Guiana was to promote "agrarian reform" and that their trained and tested leaders were nothing more than "left-wing democrats" may have ground to deplore the strong action taken by the British government. But these people would then be . . . dupes for the latest action of the international Communist conspiracy.[46]

Jagan, by his own acknowledgment, was a self-proclaimed Marxist. But he was a Marxist who formed a government as a result of winning a majority of votes cast in a democratic election. Jagan and his party were so popular, in fact, that he was able to repeat his electoral victory four years later, in the next general elections. Once again, Jagan formed a new Guianese government, despite the vast propaganda campaign that had been waged against the PPP. Referring to this achievement, President John F. Kennedy told *Izvestia* editor Alexei Adzhubei in 1961 that "Mr. Jagan, who was recently elected Prime Minister in British Guiana, is a Marxist, but the U.S. doesn't object because that choice was made by an honest election which he won."

Despite Kennedy's words, many did object. Among these were the leaders of the AFL-CIO. After Jagan's 1957 electoral victory, Harry H. Pollak, AFL-CIO Associate Inter-American Representative, visited Guiana on behalf of the Trade Union Council, a small group affiliated with the MPCA. Pollak warned that Jagan still wanted to transform Guiana into a Communist state, although he was now "prepared to act much more subtly and carefully." Now attempts were being made, according to Pollak, "to dominate the free trade union movement." These failed because the MPCA "had improved its position with a significant increase in membership and the right of checkoff, together with other benefits."[47]

[46] *Ibid.*, pp. 348–49.
[47] *Inter-American Labor Bulletin*, September 19, 1958, in *ibid.*, p. 349.

MPCA had gained a system of check-off of union dues. But this was granted because the Sugar Producers' Association favored the MPCA as a bargaining agent over the GIWU. Two major strikes in 1948 and 1953 were led by the more radical union federation. After the PPP's 1953 electoral victory, the sugar corporations tried to aid the MPCA, whose leaders were also the PPP's major political opponents, by instituting a system of check-off of dues on the basis of authorizations submitted by MPCA. The only way a worker could withdraw the authorization was by coming into the company office and signing a withdrawal form. If he wanted to stay employed, he would not do this. It was the backing of the sugar companies, especially Booker's, that kept the MPCA alive.[48]

The internal Guianese opposition to the PPP continued to build its strength. Jagan's party had split into two factions after 1957. Forbes Burnham, a former PPP leader, now was head of the People's National Congress. The PNC became the major electoral opposition to Jagan's PPP. Composed mainly of Negro laborers from Georgetown, urban dwellers, and middle-class businessmen, the PNC assumed the character of a group dominated by black urbanites whose interests were different from those of the poorer Indian sugar workers who remained loyal to the PPP. On the far right stood Peter D'Augiar's United Force, a conservative group that was opposed to Guianese independence. In the August 1961 general elections, the PPP still won twenty out of thirty-five legislative seats. But the PNC gained eleven and the United Force four. The PPP, because of a weak standing in some election districts, did not enter candidates for office in six areas. This gave them only 42.7 per cent of the total vote cast, while Burnham's PNC obtained 41 per cent.

Cheddi Jagan once again formed a new government. This time he traveled around the world in search of development capital—to the United Nations, to the White House to confer with John F. Kennedy, and to Canada. Within British Guiana, Richard Ishmael became the new president of the MPCA as well as head of the Trade Union Council. In the fall of 1961, Ishmael sent a memo to the ICFTU, attacking Jagan for praising Fidel Castro as "the greatest liberator of the Western Hemisphere." Ishmael reported that many Cuban ministers had visited British Guiana, and that PPP members had gone to Cuba "and behind the Iron Curtain for training, presumably." Ishmael also noted that printing machinery from Eastern Europe had arrived in Guiana via Cuba, and was to be used by the PPP "to commence their daily newspaper." Ishmael appealed to both ORIT and the ICFTU to help his union "avoid the unfortunate situation which the Movement faced in Cuba." The unions, he insisted, did "not intend to be dominated by Government . . . and will never permit itself to be Castroized."[49]

The main help offered was to affiliate the anti-Jagan unions with the International Trade Secretariats. The function of the ITS was explained by George Lodge. On the surface, the ITS appear merely to be federations of national trade unions operating in the same or related trades or industries. But because of their flexibility, cohesion, and independence, they are "especially effective anti-Communist organizations in the so-called neutralist areas."[50]

Singled out by Lodge was the Public Services International. Arnold Zander, president of the American Federation of State, County and Municipal Employees, a PSI affiliate—Lodge wrote—"has taken an active part in the work of the Secretariat and expects the ITS to increase its activity." The PSI, noted Lodge, "has also done effective work in Latin-America."[51] Forty American unions belong to seventeen ITS's, and they had become the preferred mechanism through which to work for the State Department. "All organizing activity and all direct assistance for the strengthening of individual worker organizations in the

---

[49] Ishmael to the ICFTU, October 15, 1961, in Romualdi, *op. cit.*, pp. 350–51.
[50] Lodge, *op. cit.*, p. 74.
[51] *Ibid.*, pp. 76–77.

newly developing world," Lodge argued, "should be channeled through the International Trade Secretariats." Direct
aid could be given national trade union federations
through the ITS, which would concentrate on aiding "individual unions in the underdeveloped countries." The
controversial ICFTU could keep its hands off, functioning
only as a service agency for the ITS.[52] The AFL-CIO could
apply anti-Communist policies "decisively and quickly . . .
through its affiliates in the Trade Secretariats."[53]

The ITS worked in just this manner in British Guiana.
Arnold Zander used his PSI secretariat as a cover agency
for the Central Intelligence Agency in Guiana. The AFL,
working through Zander's outfit, began to mobilize against
Jagan's final attempt to weaken the MPCA and to build a
radical sugar worker's union. In 1963, Jagan introduced a
new bill in the legislature. The act would permit the Minister of Labor to certify unions as agents for specific groups
of workers. The Trade Union Council and the businessmen's association argued that the board chosen to administer the law would be made up of government leaders,
which meant that Jagan would gain control over the unions. Jagan, in turn, argued that a board controlled by the
TUC and the business leaders would prevent workers from
freely changing the union which represented them to one
which they had come to favor.

What began in February as rioting in opposition to
Jagan's new proposed labor bill, ended in April with a general strike staged by the MPCA leaders. The day before the
strike began, two American labor leaders flew into Guiana
and held an all-night meeting with MPCA head Richard
Ishmael. One increasingly prominent American was Howard McCabe, who represented Arnold Zander's PSI Trade
Secretariat. The PSI formally paid the salaries of some of
British Guiana's leading civil service union leaders.

The American Institute for Free Labor Development
also was involved in the anti-Jagan effort. With Romualdi
as AIFLD's full-time director, the salary of the MPCA full-

time staff was met. Cheddi Jagan subsequently charged that "local trade unionists known to be hostile to the Government—and none others—have been trained by the American Institute for Free Labor Development to overthrow my government. Serafino Romualdi, head of the Institute, has declared his opposition to my government." Romualdi, as he himself put it, "never tried to deny Dr. Jagan's charges." Claiming to have played only a "minor" role in the general strike, Romualdi nevertheless admitted to having "put at the disposal of the strike committee the services of six graduates of the American Institute . . . who were working as interns with various local unions."[54]

Romualdi did not tell the entire story. He conveniently forgot to elaborate about the role played by the CIA. The strike lasted a full eighty days. Despite the MPCA's attempts to get all sugar workers out, only 2,000 out of the 20,000 members of the labor force responded. But the two major companies, Booker's and the Demerara Company, locked out their workers. Because of the vehemence of the different groups, massive violence occurred. British soldiers were called into patrol duty in Georgetown, where native blacks committed acts of violence against members of the Indian population, whom they considered to be automatically pro-Jagan and pro-PPP. On June 13 United Press reported that "anti-communist labor leaders vowed today to continue their general strike until it topples the government of Marxist Prime Minister Cheddi Jagan." To gain this goal, some thirty to fifty thousand dollars per week was spent at first, and later about $130,000 per week—to force Jagan to retreat and capitulate.[55]

The reason for the strike was accurately described by Washington columnist Drew Pearson on March 21, 1964. Stating that John F. Kennedy had traveled to Britain because of a "haunting worry that British Guiana would get its independence from England in July 1963 and set up a socialist form of government," Pearson added that Britain

[54] Romualdi, *op. cit.*, pp. 345–46, 352.
[55] Stanley Meisler, "Dubious Role of AFL-CIO Meddling in Latin America," *The Nation*, February 10, 1964, pp. 133–138.

could now refuse to grant independence because of the "general strike run by [Jagan's] political enemies." That strike, Pearson wrote, "was secretly inspired by a combination of U.S. Central Intelligence money and British intelligence. It gave London the excuse it wanted."[56]

Pearson was correct. The well-known "Insight" team from the London *Times* reported in a detailed series that the overthrow of Jagan's government "was engineered largely by the C.I.A." The cover used, they reported, was "a London-based international trades union secretariat, the Public Services International." As coups go, the article continued, "it was not expensive: over five years the CIA paid out something over 250,000 pounds." "For the colony . . . the result was about 170 dead, untold hundreds wounded, roughly 10 million pounds worth of damage to the economy and a legacy of racial bitterness." But the tool for unseating Jagan's government was "the Guyanese trade union movement."

To the CIA, "the local TUC was an admirable ready-made opposition." The MPCA worked with Jagan's opponents, and supported Forbes Burnham's opposition party. Civil servants were already anti-Jagan. Noting that the PSI had been in contact with the Guyana Civil Service Union since the early 1950's, the report added that it had several British affiliates. Yet the British branches were in a poor financial state. The crisis of financing was resolved by PSI's major "American affiliate union, the Federation of State, County and Municipal Employees." Under the direction of Arnold Zander, a PSI "recruiting drive" was carried out.

In 1959, Zander told the PSI "that his union was opening a full-time Latin-American section on the PSI's behalf." Its representative was one Howard McCabe, a man with "no previous union history." Although they were opening an expensive and large operation, Zander's small union had only 210,000 members and a tiny monthly income, "barely enough to cover its own expenses." Yet their Latin-American work cost a minimum of thirty thousand pounds each

[56] Quoted in Reno, *op. cit.*, pp. 58–59.

year. According to the London *Times*, Jagan had believed
that the striking Guianese unions could not hold out longer
than one month.

He had overlooked the help which McCabe could give
his opponents. McCabe came up with money for distress
funds, for purchase of radio time, and for union leaders'
traveling expenses. It had not come from the London PSI
office, which sent less than two thousand pounds to the
strikers. An unnamed donor put up "at least 150,000
pounds which reached McCabe from Zander's office." This
money enabled the unions to erect new demands each time
that Jagan gave in on their original ones. The strike, impartial British mediator Robert Willis had explained, "was
wholly political." Colonial Secretary Duncan Sandys used
it as proof that Jagan was unable to govern, and the British
wrote a new constitution that created a voting system of
proportional representation, which meant that Jagan's
vote would be split and he could no longer form a government.

Proof that the funds to keep the strike going had come
from the CIA was offered in 1964. At that time, Jerry Wurf
ousted Zander as president of the American union. Wurf
looked over the Federation's books, finding that Zander
had spent more than one hundred thousand dollars per
year on his Latin American operations. "I went into the
offices in Washington," Wurf recalled, "and there was this
whole floor crawling with clerks and translators and all
manner of people." Wurf proceeded to have the locks on
the doors changed overnight, and his "International Department" disappeared, along with Howard McCabe. In
February of 1967, Zander finally admitted publicly that
his small union was heavily financed by the CIA from 1958
through 1964. The money came from one of the leading
CIA conduits—the so-called Gotham Foundation in New
York.[57]

One week after the original report appeared, the London-
based PSI secretariat confirmed that in 1959–60, its Amer-

---

[57] "How the CIA Got Rid of Jagan," by Insight, *Sunday Times*
(London), April 16, 1967, pp. 1, 3.

ican affiliate had offered to set up a Guianese division on
its behalf. The London branch, however, pleaded ignorance of CIA penetration and financing. The office was
formally for "educational activities in underdeveloped
countries," although they knew Howard McCabe disbursed
thousands of dollars during the 1963 strike in their name.
The mysterious McCabe, the report indicated, was not
really a union leader, but "appears in fact to have been a
CIA operative."[58]

Not only did Arnold Zander get CIA money for his
Guianese operations, the New York Times added, but the
CIA, "operating under cover of the American union, helped
pro-Burnham dike and public employees unions organize
strikes" in 1962 and 1963. "The agents gave advice to local
union leaders on how to organize and sustain the strikes,"
and also provided "funds and food supplies to keep the
strikes going and medical supplies for pro-Burnham workers injured during the turmoil. At one point, one of the
agents even served as a member of a bargaining committee from a Guiana workers union that was negotiating
with Dr. Jagan." The Times estimated that Zander received sixty thousand dollars annually from the CIA until
May 1964.[59]

The work of the CIA, through the ITS and the American
unions, vindicates Jagan's original charges. Jagan had
claimed that the Kennedy Administration had pressured
the British into setting up a form of proportional representation in the colony, and had used AIFLD and the unions
as a vehicle for seeking the overthrow of his government.
Preaching a doctrine of independent trade unionism, the
AFL-CIO under Serafino Romualdi's guidance in fact practiced subordination to the policies of the United States
Department of State, the CIA, and other agencies of American foreign policy. The AFL leaders had attacked the entire concept of political strikes, and had even criticized

58 "Macmillan, Sandys Backed CIA's Anti-Jagan Plot," by Insight,
Sunday Times (London), April 23, 1967.
59 Neil Sheehan, "CIA Men Aided Strikes in Guiana," New York
Times, February 23, 1967.

Cheddi Jagan for supposedly carrying on such a political strike in the 1950's for the purpose of breaking the MPCA. Yet in 1963, the AFL-CIO encouraged a purely political strike—meant to help the United States government overthrow a democratically elected Socialist administration. In working to defeat Cheddi Jagan, the AFL-CIO leaders revealed that they were pursuing a path that led them to espouse a cause totally removed from the interests of American or Guianese workers. They were guiding nascent union movements in underdeveloped societies into becoming pawns of the anti-Communist forces, and chiefly of the U.S. Central Intelligence Agency.

IV. *American Labor and the Dominican Crisis*

Of all the examples in this chapter, the activities of American-backed unions in the Dominican Republic serve as the clearest evidence of how American unions have been used by the State Department, the CIA, and American corporations for their own chosen purposes. For thirty years, the Dominican union movement was controlled by General Rafael Leonidas Trujillo, who had formulated a working arrangement with the Dominican Confederation of Labor (CDT). After Trujillo was assassinated in May 1961, a new labor organization was created.

The new union federation was composed of unionists who had been part of various anti-Trujillo groups. The new federation—FOUPSA (United Workers' Front for Free Unions)—received immediate advice from two AFL-CIO representatives, Andrew McLellan and Fred Sommerford. Miguel Soto, FOUPSA secretary-general from 1961 to 1965, related that McLellan offered him thirty thousand dollars to call off a general strike scheduled for 1961–1962. When Soto refused, McLellan accused him of being a Communist. Since it had become clear that FOUPSA was not under the control of United States union leaders, McLellan used the same technique perfected by Irving Brown in postwar France; he used American funds and services to build an anti-Communist dual union. McLellan and Sommerford got some of the other FOUPSA executives to withdraw from their union federation. On February 11, 1962, the dissident group formed Bloque FOUPSA Libre-BFL, which later became known as CONATRAL.[60]

This second union federation had been created by representatives of the AFL-CIO. It came as no surprise that the BFL affiliated with ORIT, and received financial aid and technical advice from the United States. Aid was given the BFL by ORIT, the AFL-CIO, the ITS, and AIFLD. Working closely with the anti-Communist labor federation were a group of anti-Castro Cuban exiles. ORIT's representative in the Dominican Republic was Rolando Leonard, a labor leader who had worked closely with Eusebio Mujal in the old Cuban CTC.

In late 1962, Juan Bosch was elected President of the Dominican Republic. Bosch would only last in office for a brief seven-month term, to be ousted by the activity of a military junta. After winning his position as the chief executive of the Dominican Republic, Bosch met in Washington, D.C., with George Meany, Jay Lovestone, and Andrew McLellan. Bosch complained to the AFL-CIO foreign policy makers about disunity among Dominican labor, and urged that one united labor federation be created. The labor leaders vetoed Bosch's suggestion, preferring to keep their control over the anti-Communist CONATRAL. "We teach the principles of democratic trade unionism," McLellan explained in a press interview. "We also teach defense tactics—how to recognize Communist penetration and defeat it."

As part of this campaign, BFL-CONATRAL and ORIT became engaged in a major struggle with the other union groups in the Dominican Republic. Charging that the latter were Communist-dominated, the AFL-CIO affiliates used

[60] American labor's role in the Dominican Republic is developed thoroughly in Susanne Bodenheimer, "The AFL-CIO in Latin America: The Dominican Republic—A Case Study," *Viet-Report*, III, No. 4 (September–October 1967), 17–19, 27–28. Unless otherwise indicated, material in this section is based on the Bodenheimer article.

their strength to oppose strikes which they argued were called by the "Communist" labor groups. As a result, bitter street fighting broke out in Santo Domingo in 1962, and members of the original FOUPSA burned effigies of Mc-Lellan and Sommerford.

As in the rest of Latin America, the type of unionism sponsored by the AFL-CIO was totally unsuited for effective social action. This was particularly true, Susanne Bodenheimer has written, for a nation like the Dominican Republic. Any decent conditions for labor "presuppose basic social change and a redistribution of resources and income. In addition, in a country where the government sets the labor codes which regulate wages, strikes and collective bargaining, it becomes necessary for the workers' rights to be guaranteed by a constitutional political leadership which is representative of labor and mindful of its interests." Yet the CONATRAL leadership refused to cooperate with the moderate Juan Bosch, although he presided over the only Dominican government that had ever recognized the majority union in each factory as a legal bargaining agent for the workers.

CONATRAL preferred to support the Cabral regime which replaced Bosch, as well as the Balaguer regime after 1966. These military governments endorsed austerity programs, froze wages, and declared strikes illegal, as well as arrested militant labor leaders and fired workers from jobs. Because its leaders supported policies opposed by the rank-and-file, CONATRAL rapidly began to decline in numbers and to lose support. Before 1965, CONATRAL claimed a membership of one hundred thousand. After the 1965 revolt, its membership fell to twenty-five thousand.

CONATRAL's opposition to reform elements in the Dominican Republic was a matter of public record. Robinson Ruiz Lopez, secretary-general of CONATRAL, actively campaigned against Bosch before the 1962 presidential election. In July 1963, when military plots against Bosch's government were underway, Lopez made a radio speech praising the Ecuadorian armed forces for ousting their nation's president, and urging that the Dominican army follow their example. This speech was answered by a full-page advertisement in leading newspapers, defending the Republic and the Bosch Administration. The ad was signed by labor leaders from all the existing unions *except* CONATRAL, whose leaders criticized Bosch for not being sufficiently anti-Communist.

After the Army succeeded in ousting Bosch in the coup of September 1963, CONATRAL hailed "unconditionally the heroic gesture which our armed forces have made in defense of liberty, democracy and justice [by removing] the pro-Communist government." In a declaration published on September 27, CONATRAL greeted "the new junta" and recognized "the patriotic gesture of the armed forces." Despite an official AFL-CIO statement "deeply" regretting the coup, Andrew McLellan attacked Bosch for being too lenient with the Left, and praised General Wessín y Wessín for overthrowing Bosch "when it became obvious that the Bosch Administration was unable to control the lawlessness which had enveloped the nation."

CONATRAL gained its greatest influence and numerical strength during the military government of Donald Reid Cabral. The Cabral regime raided the offices of other unions, including CASC (Autonomous Confederation of Christian Trade Unionists) and FOUPSA-CESITRADA (FOC) and arrested its leadership. CONATRAL was granted immunity from prosecution and a working relationship was established with the military dictatorship. At the CONATRAL National Congress in December 1964, Cabral praised the major union federation as a responsible group.

Official recognition of the role played by the AFL-CIO was given on April 12, 1965, when "Serafino Romualdi . . . received from the hands of Dr. Donald J. Reid Cabral . . . the decoration of the Order of Duarte, Sanchez y Mella with the grade of Knight Commander." The ceremony took place at the National Palace, and was attended by U.S. Ambassador William Tapley Bennett, Jr. and by ORIT representatives. Cabral told Romualdi that "the government of the Dominican Republic wishes to reward, with the highest decoration at its command, your lifetime services on behalf of the free trade union movement." Cabral praised Romualdi for helping "to transform into free democratic trade unions what had been a slave labor movement." Romualdi accepted the reward as a "recognition of what the labor movement of the United States . . . has done in defense of freedom in the Dominican Republic."[61]

An example of what the Cabral government meant by "free" trade unionism was provided when POASI, an independent union of port workers in Santo Domingo, struck the ports in 1964. The government placed the army in charge and broke the strike. A parallel dual union, STAPI, was set up by the regime. It comprised army veterans and active members of both the police and armed forces. After the April 1965 revolution, the Provisional Government refused to recognize STAPI, pointing out that only five hundred legitimate workers belonged to it. CONATRAL formally protested this decision. ORIT denounced the government for "authorizing the legal recognition of undemocratic workers' groups while denying the recognition to the worker's organizations of a known democratic orientation." Although STAPI was the artificial creation of a despotic military regime, ORIT considered it "democratic" because of its leadership's anti-communism. When Bosch was again ousted and the Balaguer regime resumed control of the Dominican Republic in June 1966, STAPI was again recognized and a pact signed with POASI was renounced.

The true nature of CONATRAL was to be revealed during the April 1965 revolt. The rebellion was not allowed to take its natural course. Massive intervention by the United

[61] *El Caribe* (Santo Domingo) April 13, 1965, in Romualdi, *op. cit.*, pp. 402–03. It is interesting to observe that Romualdi ends his entire discussion of the Dominican Republic with the overthrow of Trujillo in 1961. Evidently the subsequent role played by the AFL-CIO, in defense of military regimes, is too obvious and disquieting to be whitewashed. Therefore Romualdi merely left this period out of his account. The citation of the medal awarded by Cabral is the *only* exception, the sole allusion to an event occurring after 1961. Romualdi could simply not resist mentioning the award presented to him by Cabral.

States Marines prevented the rebels from winning control of the Dominican Republic away from the Cabral government. The official rationale for the intervention was provided by Lyndon B. Johnson. What started as a "popular democratic revolution," the President announced, "committed to democracy and social justice," had been taken over by Communists. The subsequent intervention allowed the old-line Dominican generals, headed by Elias Wessín y Wessín, to achieve success. Backing up the junta was the U.S. Embassy, whose administrators argued that the return of Juan Bosch to power meant a Communist regime. U.S. troops, the Embassy believed, would have to be used to back up Wessín's domestic forces. By April 28, 1965, the Johnson Administration sent in the Marines, on the pretext that it had become necessary to save the lives of American citizens in the Republic.[62]

When the democratic revolt against Cabral first broke out, CONATRAL issued a mild statement supporting the Constitutionalist rebels, as long as they pledged to remain "democratic." But CONATRAL leaders refrained from taking any part in the rebellion. Four days after the Johnson Administration had sent in the Marines, and on the same day in which Lyndon B. Johnson had first claimed that the movement had been taken over by Communists, CONATRAL's secretary-general, Dieto Diaz, also denounced the revolt for being captured by Communists. Diaz told Susanne Bodenheimer that "for the sake of democracy we will accept anything—even the intervention." CONATRAL argued that U.S. military intervention was needed to prevent another Cuba—precisely the same position taken by the Department of State.

CONATRAL's pro-intervention policy may have been appreciated by the AFL-CIO leaders, but it lost labor support at home. Replacing CONATRAL as the most representative trade union body was the local affiliate of the

[62] The best critique of the Dominican intervention and Johnson's policy in Latin America is Theodore Draper, "The Dominican Crisis," *Commentary*, XL, No. 6 (December 1965), pp. 33–68. Events leading up to the use of the Marines are covered on pp. 38–39.

Latin American Confederation of Christian Trade Unionists (CLASC). This group, first formed in 1954, was affiliated with the International Federation of Christian Trade
Unions, with headquarters in Brussels.

CLASC officials developed a third force position. Its
leaders rejected affiliation with both the anti-Communist
ORIT and the Left-led CTAL. As CLASC grew, its leaders
developed an independent position which blended nationalism with anti-imperialism. In a position paper delivered
to the 1967 Punta del Este summit meeting, CLASC's leaders formulated their purpose and program:

> We believe in and uphold the necessity for Latin America's
> economic, social, cultural and political integration, but carried
> out by Latin Americans . . . and we categorically reject every
> kind of Pan-American integration scheme because it would be
> the same thing as putting a fox in a chicken coop. . . . It serves
> no purpose to denounce international Communist intervention,
> if one falls in the hypocrisy and the conformism of tolerating,
> accepting, and even helping North American intervention in
> the Latin American trade union movement, at both the national
> and regional levels. Such intervention certainly has been made
> evident with the recent denunciation of the CIA's massive
> penetrations of the Latin American Labor movement.[63]

Taking such a stand, CLASC appears as a new revolutionary force whose leaders espouse neutralism rather than
communism. Yet they base their program on the insistence
that Latin American trade unions become part of a broad
revolutionary movement for fundamental social change.
"Influenced by United States labor leaders," CLASC secretary-general Emilo Maspero wrote, "various Latin American trade unions appear to operate on the belief that by
negotiating collectively agreed upon contracts . . . they
can achieve a higher standard of living for the laboring
masses and effect meaningful reform. There is no basis in
reality to justify this assumption. The only feasible goal

[63] CLASC, Manifesto de los Trabajadores de America Latina a
Los Presidentes Reunidos en la Cumbre en Punta del Este, 12
de abril de 1967.

for labor in Latin America is to organize the working forces in a decisive manner as an instrument for affecting social revolution."[64]

CLASC leaders therefore reject working through the Organization of American States, which they regard as a vehicle for U.S. control over Latin American social and economic development. They are also equally critical of the Alliance for Progress, which they judge to have raised great hopes but to have accomplished little. Most firm is their rejection of U.S.-style business unionism, which they accurately point out is of little value in the backward political structure of most Latin American nations. CLASC is especially critical of AFL-CIO cooperation with U.S. business interests through AIFLD, and it views the AFL-CIO as an agency carrying out the work of both the State Department and the CIA.

Because CONATRAL backed the U.S. military intervention in the Dominican Republic, CASC (Autonomous Confederation of Christian Trade Unionists), the local CLASC affiliate, became the principal national trade union federation. Its dominant position was "in direct contrast to the position held 1 year prior to the 1965 outbreak of hostilities in Santo Domingo, at which the National Confederation of Free Workers (CONATRAL), an ORIT affiliate, was the country's major trade union confederation."

CASC grew in strength because of its support of the rebellion. "CASC vociferously supported the constitutionalists while CONATRAL remained neutral." However, the Foreign Relations Committee 1968 *Survey of the Alliance for Progress, Labor Policies and Programs* adds, "ORIT'S avowed acceptance of U.S. intervention was interpreted, rightly or wrongly, as expressing CONATRAL's sentiments, and at one point during the crisis, CONATRAL's headquarters were looted and sacked by elements of the rebel forces." The Senate staff study reached the conclusion that CASC's "sudden rise to power in the Dominican Republic resulted less from direct trade union issues" than

[64] Quoted in Sidney Lens, "Labor Between Bread and Revolution," *The Nation,* September 19, 1966, p. 251.

from "political circumstances during that period of up-heaval and violence. More specifically, the CLASC affiliate in the Dominican Republic was viewed apparently as championing reform and social democracy while the CONATRAL (through ORIT) maintained a status quo image."[65]

The guarded language employed by the Senate com-mittee staff amounts to great understatement. Actually, the AFL-CIO Executive Council, as well as CONATRAL, had declared its "unequivocal support" for the Johnson policy in the Dominican Republic and for the U.S. military intervention. Andrew McLellan went so far as to praise General Wessín y Wessín as "one of the few incorruptible top elements in the Dominican Army." And when the 1966 election campaign was held, CONATRAL announced its support of "the candidate of peace," Balaguer, and hailed his subsequent victory as a "clear mandate for his program of peace and tranquility."

The policy followed by the AFL-CIO in the Dominican Republic serves as a good illustration of the reactionary path taken by American labor leaders. After the end of Trujillo's thirty-year reign, AFL-CIO union affiliates con-tinued to support the military elements, and to oppose the moderate social democracy favored by Juan Bosch. When a popular revolution finally broke out in 1965, for the pur-pose of overthrowing Cabral and restoring Bosch's party to power, the AFL-CIO accused Bosch's supporters of com-munism, without supplying a bit of evidence.

It is no wonder that to many Dominicans, CONATRAL is viewed as a vehicle through which the United States works to intervene in Dominican politics and to gain sup-port for American foreign policy objectives. The AFL-CIO, Susanne Bodenheimer has accurately charged, "has served American interests at the expense of Dominican workers. For one thing, American labor, which is dedicated to the preservation of the capitalist system, has done much to further U.S. business interests in Latin America by weak-ening the principal obstacle: a labor movement sufficiently

[65] Senate Committee on Foreign Relations, *op. cit.*, p. 18.

united and militant enough to exert pressure for fulfill-
ment of its demands."

To gain his goals, Lyndon B. Johnson used anti-communism as a smokescreen for destruction of a non-Communist revolutionary movement, which was seeking to restore
democracy to the Dominican Republic. Paralleling his tactics, the AFL-CIO and its affiliates, CONATRAL and ORIT,
fought the revolutionary nationalists in CASC as their major enemy in the Dominican Republic. Again, the charge
of communism was leveled at all anti-imperialist trade
union leaders. Military juntas were supported as long as
their leaders formed a working relationship with the conservative U.S.-oriented CONATRAL. This emphasis on
anti-communism, and the failure to struggle for social
change and redistribution of wealth, or to oppose the political control of the Dominican Republic by local elite
groups and the military, has, in Susanne Bodenheimer's
words, "permitted the AFL-CIO to create a docile segment
of labor which is not only willing to accept American intervention but also to collaborate with 'stable'—if grossly
unrepresentative—Dominican regimes." The AFL-CIO
has also worked closely, if secretly, with the State Department and the CIA. But the remarkable growth of CASC in
one year has revealed that one distinct group has moved
away from participation in AFL-CIO-backed unions. The
Dominican Republic's working class, supposedly the basic
constituency of a trade union movement, has liberated
itself from domination by the AFL-CIO. The choice was
a wise one. For the policies pursued by the AFL-CIO in
Latin America reveal that the American trade union movement works as one of the main pillars of the status quo in
the underdeveloped world.

XIII

AMERICAN LABOR
IN LATIN AMERICA:
THE AIFLD,
THE STATE DEPARTMENT,
AND THE AFL-CIO

Since 1961, the basic instrument for penetration of Latin American organized labor movements has been the AFL-CIO-sponsored American Institute for Free Labor Development. The AIFLD was founded, a 1968 Foreign Relations Committee staff report points out, "primarily in response to the threat of Castroite infiltration and eventual control of major labor movements within Latin America." After the Bay of Pigs fiasco, President John F. Kennedy endorsed the idea of a new Latin American labor program "through which the talents and experience of the U.S. labor movement could be brought to bear on the danger that Castro . . . might undermine the Latin American labor movement." Since labor was regarded as potentially the "most explosive sector" in a still underdeveloped region, worry existed that the Inter-American Regional Organization of Workers (ORIT) was not strong enough to meet the challenge of Castroism. Therefore President Kennedy encouraged a "labor program for Latin America that would di-

rectly involve the U.S. Labor movement." In August of
1961, the AFL-CIO chartered AIFLD as a private non-
profit corporation.[1]

By 1967, the fiscal yearly budget for AIFLD was over
six million dollars, some ninety-five per cent of which was
supplied from "public" funds. AIFLD's basic objectives are
listed as "assisting in the development of free, democratic
trade union structures in Latin America through labor
leader training centers and social development programs
in such fields as housing, workers' banks, credit unions,
consumer and producer cooperatives and related socio-
economic activities."[2]

This rather innocuous statement of purpose, however,
masks the reality of AIFLD's varied activities. As a former
AIFLD staff member has recently argued, AIFLD has been
involved in constant controversy due to "its covert Central
Intelligence Agency affiliation," its "capacity to exaggerate
the reality of its accomplishments to date," and the "smol-
dering resentment of numerous and important Latin
American trade union leaders" who have found that
AIFLD fails to fulfill promises of material aid made
through its most prominent leaders.[3]

The charges made by Joseph Palisi are damning, but
the record indicates the basic validity of his critique.
AIFLD is much more than an independent labor operation.
Rather, it is a structure around which has been built an
alliance among the United States government, the trade
union leadership, and major elements of the large corporation community. Much more exists than a simple diplo-

[1] U.S. Senate, Committee on Foreign Relations, Subcommittee on
American Republics Affairs, *Survey of the Alliance for Progress,
Labor Policies and Programs*, 90th Congress, 2nd Session, July
15, 1968, p. 9. A solid critique of the Senate staff report is:
Henry W. Berger, "What's Good for Latin America," *The Nation*,
January 13, 1969, pp. 46–48.

[2] American Council of Voluntary Agencies for Foreign Service,
Inc., Technical Assistance Information Clearing House, *U.S. Non-
Profit Organizations in Technical Assistance Abroad, Supplement,
1965*, ed. Binne Schroyer (New York, 1965), p. 7.

[3] Joseph J. Palisi, American Labor's Chosen Instrument for
Latin America, Unpublished MSS, February 9, 1967, 1. Courtesy
of *Ramparts*.

matic liaison between the Administration and the union leaders. A formal political and financial relationship exists between the Agency for International Development (AID) and the AFL-CIO. "Through AID contracts," the Senate study points out, "the AIFLD has become the principal instrument of the U.S. Government for supplying technical assistance—education and training and social projects—to Latin American trade unions."[4]

AIFLD boasts of this tie, claiming that it "reflects the unique pluralism and consensus in American society: Labor-Government-Business."[5] The financing of AIFLD, however, does not reflect the equality between the different members of the consensus. Most of AIFLD's income derives from the government, which has increased its support of AIFLD from an original 62 per cent in 1962 to 92 per cent by 1967. Through AID, the U.S. government contributed 15.4 million dollars, or 89 per cent of AIFLD's total income for the entire period of its existence. This amount comprises a heavy 67 per cent of AID's total budget for aid to labor under the Alliance for Progress.[6]

The corporate contribution to AIFLD has been less substantial than that of the government or the AFL-CIO, amounting only to 175,000 dollars by 1967. Despite a minimum monetary investment, AIFLD's Board of Directors has equal representation from members of the large corporation community. Chairman of the board is J. Peter Grace, president of W. R. Grace and Company. The role played in AIFLD by corporate interests produced some opposition from former CIO leaders, who feared that too close an association with American business interests would hinder the growth of unionism in Latin America. Victor Reuther, director of the UAW's International Affairs Department, argued that the participation of businessmen "on AIFLD's Board seriously compromises its trade-union training and educational role. Its structure exposes it to

[4] Senate Committee on Foreign Relations, *loc. cit.*
[5] AIFLD, "Progress Report to the President's Labor Advisory Committee on Foreign Assistance," March 1967, inside front cover.
[6] Senate Committee on Foreign Relations, *op. cit.*, p. 10.

the charge of conflict of interest and is a propaganda gift
to the enemies of free trade unions who effectively characterize these businessmen as symbols of Yankee imperialism and enemies of social progress in Latin America."[7]

The majority position is espoused by AIFLD's present
director, William C. Doherty, Jr. The presence of business
leaders on AIFLD's Board, he argues, sets a good example
to employers and workers about the desirability of cooperation. The result is that hostility toward U.S. business interests in Latin America and toward the United States in
general is dispelled. Conversely, business participation
also encourages U.S. corporations abroad to accept the
existence of "free" trade unions.[8]

Doherty inadvertently puts his finger on the actual purpose of AIFLD—to dispel hostility of Latin American
workers toward U.S. corporations. Corporate leaders like
Grace back AIFLD because of their general fear that social
revolution would sweep away the prerogatives of U.S. investors. "Very high stakes are at issue," Grace emphasized,
"because the political, military and economic interests of
the United States are affected. Furthermore, the communist campaign has broadened beyond the stage of attacking American companies alone; it is now concentrating on
the very basic system of private enterprise to which the
American republics are dedicated."[9]

Grace, and the other AIFLD leaders, believe that democracy and capitalism are synonymous. These two themes
were singled out by Grace in a recent statement:

Through the AIFLD business, labor and government have
come together to work toward a common goal in Latin America,

[7] Victor Reuther, "The International Activities of American
Trade Unions," in William Haber, ed., *Labor in a Changing America*
(New York, 1966), pp. 304–05. As a result of Reuther's objections,
Grace resigned as president of AIFLD, and George Meany, formerly
vice-chairman, assumed the presidency in September 1962.

[8] William C. Doherty, Jr., "AIFLD and Latin Labor Building a
Modern Society," *AFL-CIO Free Trade Union News*, July 1966, p. 3.

[9] J. Peter Grace, "Latin America's Nationalistic Revolutions,"
Annals of the American Academy of Political and Social Science,
vol. 334 (March 1961), p. 145.

namely supporting the democratic form of government, the capitalistic system and general well-being of the individual. It is an outstanding example of a national consensus effectively at work for the national interest of the United States and for the best interests of the people of Latin America.[10]

Business, labor, and government, Grace argues, have a mutual interest working for "defense of American interests abroad." There is more to be gained working together on behalf of common goals than working separately. Since all three units believe both "in the democratic form of government, and in the capitalistic system," it is better that they should "all work together along common lines."[11]

This ideology is shared by the nation's foremost labor leaders. In a speech delivered to the Council on Latin America on April 2, 1965, George Meany stressed that labor believes "in the capitalist system, and we are members of the capitalist society. We are dedicated to the preservation of this system, which rewards the workers, which is one in which management also has such a great stake." Meany added, undoubtedly to the satisfaction of his audience, that labor understood that "the investors of risk capital also must be rewarded."[12]

Meany's view was underscored by Joseph A. Beirne, president of the AFL-CIO Communications Workers of America; and member of the Postal, Telephone, and Telegraph International, a major International Trade Secretariat which had received extensive CIA subsidies. Beirne was the first labor leader to suggest formation of what eventually became AIFLD. American institutions, Beirne argued, had to be developed throughout the world. "If we are going to export the concepts of our society," he asserted,

[10] J. Peter Grace, "Labor Boosts Living Standards," *Journal of Commerce*, April 14, 1966; quoted in Senate Committee on Foreign Relations, *op. cit.*, p. 15.
[11] J. Peter Grace, speech at International Trade Week, Houston, Tex., September 16, 1965, Serafino Romualdi, *Presidents and Peons: Recollections of a Labor Ambassador in Latin America* (New York, 1967), p. 418.
[12] *Ibid.*

"all of the elements of that society must be represented."[13]

What Grace, Meany, and Beirne were arguing was clear: American capital investment in Latin America was to be encouraged, since it would benefit both Latin American workers and capitalists. The AFL-CIO would work to build the type of union movement whose members did not challenge the hegemony of American corporations in Latin America. Rather, they would demand a fair return on investments for all investors. The major assumption of Grace, Meany, and Beirne is that both American political institutions and corporate capitalism are highly beneficial to Latin America. The truth is, however, that protecting the rights of investment capitalists means assured failure to realize social progress. The Latin American nations are underdeveloped economies, tightly controlled by foreign— that is, United States—corporations and local elite groups. Any meaningful social change necessitates curbs on the economic power wielded by U.S. corporations. Even when AIFLD leaders sincerely advocate certain reforms, their programs have no teeth in them. They avoid tampering with the distribution of wealth, or with landholding and income patterns, the only course of action which would produce a real change in the lives of Latin American workers and *campesinos*.

The AIFLD Board of Directors, however, is composed of men who could never tolerate any real steps being taken toward a radical redistribution of wealth. The Board includes Charles Brinckerhoof, chairman of the Board of the Anaconda Company; William M. Hickey, president of the United Corporation; Robert C. Hill, director, Merck and Company; Juan C. Trippe, chairman of the board, Pan American World Airways; Henry S. Woodbridge, chairman of the board, Tru-Temper Copper Corporation; and J. Peter Grace. These men tend to view advocates of extreme measures of social action as "Communist," and a major concern of theirs is the type of social action that will help stem the tide of social revolution within Latin America.

[13] *Ibid.*, p. 419.

Because of this concern, a major part of AIFLD's program is dedicated to opposing the growth of "communism." Basic to this purpose is AIFLD's extensive system of training schools for Latin American labor union leaders. AIFLD's main school is centered at the Front Royal, Virginia, training institute near Washington, D.C. To this school Latin American union officials are brought for three months of training, "with particular emphasis on the theme of democracy versus totalitarianism." Since 1962, the Front Royal Institute has graduated over five hundred students. Some thirty thousand others have received similar training in the fourteen Latin American field offices. At the end of their course, the AIFLD graduates return to their native countries under a nine-month, salaried internship program.[14]

When these AIFLD graduates return home, they engage in *political* work meant to advance the interests of both U.S. foreign policy and the AFL-CIO. In many cases, such effort has no relationship to their own labor movement's needs. The political nature of AIFLD education has been stated by Paul K. Reed, former International Representative of the United Mine Workers. In a letter requesting a leave of absence for a Colombian trade unionist, Reed wrote the worker's employer that "we feel strongly that through the education of the workers, it will be possible to halt the wave of Communism sweeping through Latin America, and trust you will find it possible to look favorably on the above request."[15] It is no accident that the typical curriculum of the AIFLD training program is geared to teaching students about the virtues of American corporate capitalism. A student takes an average of eighteen hours training in "democracy and totalitarianism," compared to only five hours in collective bargaining and problems of labor in rural areas. No instruction is given

[14] Senate Committee on Foreign Relations, *op. cit.*, p. 11.
[15] Paul K. Reed to Dr. Julian Moreno Mejia (president, Empresa Acerias Paz del Rio Banco Colombia, Bogotá, Colombia), July 23, 1962, Paul K. Reed MSS, Miners' International Federation Headquarters; London, England. From the notes of Henry W. Berger.

in profit sharing, workers' education, or labor legislation.
These union leaders function as a corps of salaried anti-Communist activists, ready to do the bidding of the Department of State. They work primarily to impose AFL-CIO-style unionism upon Latin American workers, and to destroy existing unions outside of the conservative orbit. U.S. business interests, therefore, now realize "that responsible unions, even though harder to bargain with, are nonetheless easier to live with than irresponsible ones." In Colombia, the local union at Celanese Colombiana SAA (a subsidiary of Celanese Corporation of America, an AIFLD contributor) "had been debilitated by its Castroite orientation. Within a few months several illegal work stoppages had taken place, plus a sympathy strike in favor of Castro. The company retaliated with mass firings." At that point AIFLD graduates "were able to gain control of the union." They had functioned, in other words, as company-supported strikebreakers. The union then affiliated with the UTC, the major Colombian anti-Communist union federation, and according to AIFLD, "achieved some of the best collective contracts in Colombia."[16]

AIFLD tends to brand its opponents as Castroite or Communist, as in the above example. Actually, any opposition to U.S. economic penetration and informal control of Latin America is described in these terms. That is why AIFLD views CLASC, the Latin American Confederation of Christian Trade Unionists, as one of its major enemies. CLASC is anti-Communist, but its main emphasis is opposition to Pan-Americanism, which it regards as a vehicle for economic domination of Latin America by U.S. corporations. While rejecting Communist attempts to infiltrate Latin American labor, CLASC leaders point to the AFL-CIO and AIFLD "as an agent for the State Department (and more recently, the CIA)." CLASC is still weak in comparison to ORIT, the Inter-American Regional Organization of Workers. The Senate staff report warns, however, that this may soon change. Because of ORIT's close identification with unpopular U.S. policies, CLASC may

16 Senate Committee on Foreign Relations, *op. cit.*, p. 15.

be given "the opportunity of developing into a major regional labor movement, particularly in the rural sector." Since CLASC "is not congenial to many traditional U.S. points of view," the staff report predicts that the United States may fall "out of touch with increasingly important sectors of Latin American society."[17]

AIFLD has not stopped at a general political opposition to anti-imperialist labor unions. It has used its trained graduates as a source of supply for the CIA. This activity has often embarrassed the AFL-CIO, especially since it contradicts their own leaders' stated adherence to democratic principles. This stance, however, is explicable within the context of anti-communism. William Doherty has explained that the "key question of our times is the future road of their revolution: Toward Communist totalitarianism or toward democracy. For the American labor movement this is one of the paramount, pivotal issues; all other questions . . . must remain secondary."[18]

Doherty, by his own admission, puts the fight against communism ahead of concern with poor wages, lack of union recognition, substandard living conditions, and exploitation of Latin American labor. He reveals no awareness of any possible dangers from local oligarchies, the military, or economic domination by foreign corporations. It is this preoccupation with communism which has "tended to give AIFLD the appearance of being little more than an instrument of the cold war." The effect is "a polarized view of the political spectrum in Latin American labor," as well as involvement of the AFL-CIO "in some awkward contradictions of its principle that trade unions should not be tied to political parties." In effect, AIFLD has only opposed political involvement when it was the type of involvement which the AFL-CIO does not favor. Because CLASC is part of the labor wing of the Christian Democratic political parties, the AFL-CIO has even refused to arrange field trips for CLASC officials who received United States Information Service leadership grants

[17] *Ibid.*, pp. 18–19.
[18] Town Hall speech of June 1966, *ibid.*, p. 13.

to visit the United States. CLASC's appeal is steadily growing among Latin American labor; yet ORIT has officially
called these Social Christian unions "allies of communism."[19]

A logical outcome of a single-minded concern with communism was the direct participation of AIFLD-trained
labor leaders in the overthrow of Latin American governments. Serafino Romualdi, AIFLD's first full-time director,
explained that the main purpose of the internship program
was to enable financially weak unions to utilize the service
of Washington graduates for administrative duties. But
these AIFLD graduates soon found "that they had to fight"
communism "if they were going to continue to work for
the development of the free labor movement. . . . the
graduates not only held their own but eliminated totalitarian elements from a number of important unions."[20]

The key example of how they accomplished this feat
lies in labor's role in the Brazilian military coup of 1964.
From 1955 through 1961, during the Kubitschek-Goulart
regime, Brazilian labor "enjoyed unequaled freedom. The
government intervened in virtually no unions; the Ministry of Labor did not interfere with union elections. Collective bargaining became more widespread than it had been
before."[21] Despite these good conditions, AFL leaders were
critical of growing Communist strength in the organized
labor movement. Romualdi accused the Communists of
establishing a Popular Front with the Kubitschek government. Working with labor attaché Irving Salert and U.S.
Ambassador James C. Dunn, Romualdi arranged in 1956
to have Brazilian labor leaders visit the United States. The
goal was to develop "a corps of labor leaders who, by com-
manding the enthusiastic support of the rank and file,
could turn back Communist attempts to capture the Brazilian labor movement."[22]

Romualdi worked to influence Brazilian labor leaders,

[19] *Ibid.*, pp. 13–14.
[20] Romualdi, *op. cit.*, pp. 428–29.
[21] Robert J. Alexander, *Organized Labor in Latin America* (New
York, 1965), p. 81.
[22] Romualdi, *op. cit.*, p. 278.

but he did not advocate a course of opposition to the pro-labor Brazilian government. Jay Lovestone and Charles Zimmerman disagreed, preferring head-on opposition. Romualdi thought it best to urge Goulart to "make a clean break with the Communists." Romualdi won the support of George Meany, as well as the American Embassy in Brazil and representatives of the State Department.

After Kubitschek's regime ended, Janio Quadros served as President of Brazil for seven months, resigning from office in August 1961. Goulart, who had been elected Vice-President, was opposed by the military. Leading officers tried to prevent Goulart from ascending to the presidency, but mobilization of the working class prevented the staging of a military coup. During the new Goulart Administration, Communist strength in the union movement increased. Conservative trade union leaders were removed from office, and a new left-wing trade union federation was created. Goulart himself continued to steer a moderate course, and appointed a Christian Democrat as Minister of Labor.

Goulart's regime soon suffered because of the steady decline of living conditions. Between 1958 and 1963, inflation produced a six hundred per cent increase in the cost of living. "Industry, commerce, the military and the Church," Romualdi explained, "became alarmed at the direction in which Jango was leading Brazil. He began to rely more and more on the support of the Communists." The steps were now taken to have the military oust Goulart. Romualdi aided them in these efforts.

In the fall of 1963, Romualdi met with one of Goulart's chief opponents, Adhemar de Barros, Governor of São Paulo. De Barros informed Romualdi of plans "to mobilize military and police contingents" against Goulart. Arguing that "a substantial sector of labor's rank and file" was against Goulart, Romualdi and the AIFLD during the first three months of 1963 "trained in Washington a special all-Brazilian class of thirty-three participants." Ten traveled to Western Europe and Israel. Upon return to Brazil, some were sent to the interior and others to Rio, São Paulo, and other industrial centers. When Goulart acted, on March 13, 1964, to nationalize petroleum refineries and to expropriate land, and then met with a group of mutinous non-commissioned officers, the military coup staged by De Barros and Carlos Lacerda began.[23]

AIFLD's trainees played their part in creating the coup. Their role was described frankly by William Doherty, then AIFLD Director of Social Projects. On a radio panel with Harry Conn and Tad Szulc, Doherty made the following statement:

Well, very frankly, within the limits placed upon them by the administration of João Goulart, when they returned to their respective countries, they were very active in organizing workers, and helping unions introduce systems of collective bargaining, and modern concepts of labor-management relations. As a matter of fact, some of them were so active that they became intimately involved in some of the clandestine operations of the revolution before it took place on April 1. What happened in Brazil . . . did not just happen—it was planned—and planned months in advance. Many of the trade union leaders—some of whom were actually trained in our institute—were involved in the revolution, and in the overthrow of the Goulart regime.[24]

AIFLD may have "succeeded thereby in delivering the Brazilian labor movement" from Communist leadership, the Foreign Relations Committee staff report observed, but it had not succeeded as late as four "years later, in creating an independent labor movement."[25] As in other cases, the AFL-CIO had again contributed to the birth of a regime whose leaders immediately arrested "thousands of Communists and followers of Goulart, many of whom were in the labor movement. Even many Catholic trade unionists were jailed, since there were elements in the new adminis-

---

[23] *Ibid.*, pp. 288–90.
[24] AFL-CIO, Labor News Conference, Washington, D.C., press release of July 13, 1964, p. 3 (text of panel broadcast on the Mutual Broadcasting System, July 12, 1964).
[25] Senate Committee on Foreign Relations, *op. cit.*, p. 14.

tration who regarded any militant labor leaders as a 'Communist.' "[26]

Long after the coup and at a time that the authoritarian direction taken by the Brazilian military was clear, AIFLD leaders continued to support the Brazilian government and to provide rationales for its policies. By December 1965, the AFL-CIO was forced to admit that the "Castello Branco administration has recently become an authoritarian regime. It has curtailed civil and political rights and liberties, and the Brazilian labor movement has again been forced back to its original status—an integral part of the state."[27] Yet on April 1, 1966, Branco appeared on the platform with William Doherty, to help lay the cornerstone for an AIFLD housing development in São Paulo. In his brief speech, Doherty "declared it appropriate that the ceremonies were taking place on the second anniversary of Brazil's democratic Revolution."[28]

AIFLD trainees also played their part in working against Juan Bosch in the Dominican Republic. Like the other AFL-CIO affiliates, ORIT and CONATRAL, AIFLD opposed the Constitutionalists and supported the military junta during the April 1965 rebellion. AIFLD tried to develop new programs that would restore the appeal of CONATRAL to the Dominican Republic's working class.

Their problem, a private AIFLD staff report notes, was that the "political chaos" in the Dominican Republic had both "weakened the effectiveness of the CONATRAL" and had also "permitted the forces of the extreme left to endanger the very existence" of AIFLD. Unnamed "subversive forces" had created "havoc by submitting the labor unions to extreme economic and political pressure." Since the civil war and the U.S. military intervention, CONATRAL had "been identified as a Yankee-sponsored organization" and had become "ineffective." Rank-and-file workers had been urged to stop payment of union dues. The Left had become

---

[26] Alexander, *op. cit.*, p. 83.
[27] Romualdi, *op. cit.*, p. 291.
[28] *AIFLD Report* (Washington, D.C.) IV, No. 5 (May 1966), 6–7.

quite active, and in fact had "increased its activity in all
fields."[29]

To deal with these developments, AIFLD tried to create
an emergency program. After meetings with the U.S. Ambassador, the AID Mission director, and the U.S. labor
attaché, AIFLD developed a "plan of immediate action"
which they hoped would correct "a very grave situation in
the labor movement of the Dominican Republic." The
Ambassador pledged his support of an AIFLD request for
an additional fifty thousand dollars to handle the situation.
The country would be divided into new regions, they would
establish new labor education programs, purchase new
jeeps for transportation of union leaders, and begin a new
audio-visual program. Most important would be new
"organizing campaigns" run by men who were "educator-
organizers" and who would be supplemented "by a spe-
cially-trained mobile group" that would "confront and
battle the 'goon squads' of the extreme left forces."

In addition to providing "goon squads" of its own, the
AIFLD would try to create a "new image of the CONATRAL
as a just, impartial and honest organization created to best
serve the needs of its membership, to advance the standard
of living." AIFLD, according to theory, is a non-political
institution. Yet its administrators had chosen to identify
the agency with a discredited union federation, whose
appeal had been eclipsed by that of the more militant
CASC. AIFLD would seek to restore CONATRAL's appeal
by dealing with the fact that its leaders had been accused
of "favoritism, mishandling of funds" and "political involvement with its membership rather than the servicing
of its people." These problems of reputation, AIFLD naively
believed, could be handled by a mere "strengthening" and
renovation of CONATRAL leadership.[30]

The minutes of the AIFLD Board of Trustees 1965 Annual Meeting provide further evidence of how the AIFLD
leadership rivets its attention on the internal fight against

[29] AIFLD Report, "Emergency Plan for the Dominican Republic,"
November 15, 1965.
[30] *Ibid.*

"communism." Presenting a review of AIFLD programs in 1964, Serafino Romualdi stressed that in April AIFLD was to open a branch center in Recife, an area in the impoverished Brazilian northeast. This center would serve as a *campesino* training school, and as competition for a similar center already established by the non-Communist opposition to the AFL-CIO.

In Porto Alegre, Brazil, the home of both Goulart and his radical brother-in-law Brizola, it was reported, "new seminar programs are being conducted to reorient workers who had been under Communist domination." In British Guiana, AIFLD was also developing a new "special program" for shop stewards in the sugar industry, described by Romualdi as "the traditional stronghold of former pro-Communist Premier Cheddi Jagan." Romualdi concluded his report by "pointing out that almost all AIFLD graduates have returned to their own unions and are working to strengthen free labor by . . . combatting Communist encroachments." To substantiate this claim, Romualdi pointed to "a number of outstanding examples of AIFLD graduate effectiveness" in fighting communism.[31]

In addition to local anti-Communist efforts, AIFLD puts money into social projects, particularly the development of low-cost workers' housing projects. The massive claims made on behalf of these programs by AIFLD representatives, however, have been highly exaggerated. Joseph A. Beirne, for example, bragged in May 1966 that "worker's housing sponsored by the AIFLD has been started or completed in seven different countries." AIFLD reported that of "fifteen housing projects now under preparation, eight either have financing committed or are under construction." AIFLD cited 488 being built in Brazil, 30 in the Dominican Republic and 288 in Colombia.[32]

These figures obscure the limited nature of the existing housing developments. In Costa Rica, for example, AIFLD announced support of a new 1.2-million-dollar housing

[31] Minutes of meeting of the Board of Trustees of AIFLD, March 10, 1965, AFL-CIO Building, Washington, D.C.

[32] *AIFLD Report* (Washington, D.C.), IV, No. 5 (May 1966), 7.

project. Local Costa Rican residents, however, were highly
critical of AIFLD's insistence that they would determine
who was eligible to live in the apartments, and they were
angry at the establishment of a 5.5 per cent interest rate
on the provided loan. AIFLD also insisted that U.S. engineers be hired to design the houses. A similar situation
existed in the Dominican Republic. The Inter-American
Development Bank argued that builders should be selected
by open bidding. Yet AIFLD insisted upon closed bidding.
Later it insisted that a firm run by Louis Berger, a New
Jersey consulting engineer, be the only agency used for
the project. Derish Wolff, an executive in Berger's firm,
was also offered the position of director of AIFLD social
projects.[33]

In the Dominican Republic, AIFLD had announced support of a three-million-dollar housing project for sugar
workers. AIFLD spoke of building some 700–900 units, to
be financed by loans from the Inter-American Development Bank and the AFL-CIO, to be guaranteed by AID.
Only 110 units were actually built, and these were directly
financed entirely by AID. Local Dominicans protested that
AIFLD had violated Dominican law. AIFLD specified that
contracts channeled through Dominican agencies be
awarded through closed meetings, that only CONATRAL
unions be employed for construction work, and that *only
CONATRAL members* be allowed to live in the completed
development. AIFLD had revealed that their housing program in the Dominican Republic was meant as a further
"reward" for workers who refused to join CASC. These
families would be given a limited supply of decent housing.[34]

Many of the AIFLD projects, even when completed,
have turned out to be a poor bargain. The most publicized

[33] Dan Kurzman, "Lovestone's Aid Program Bolsters U.S. Foreign
Policy," *Washington Post,* January 2, 1966.

[34] Susanne Bodenheimer, "The AFL-CIO in Latin America: The
Dominican Republic—A Case Study," *Viet-Report* III, No. 4 (September–October 1967), 19, 27.

project is the ten-million-dollar, 3,100-unit workers' development in Mexico City. Named after John F. Kennedy, this project was to serve as the prototype for all AIFLD social projects. Yet the cost of these homes ranges from $2600 to $5700 per family unit—figures far out of line with a Latin American laborer's salary. The truth is that AIFLD has scaled its costs to unions whose members are among the most well-to-do elite groups of organized labor. The Kennedy Project in Mexico was built for the Graphic Arts Workers Union, a group composed of the highest-paid skilled workers in Mexico.[35]

In centering their attention on the needs of upper income workers, AIFLD leaders have rejected a broader social role and have not been concerned to build any housing that could even begin to benefit unorganized rural workers throughout Latin America. William Doherty publicly acknowledged this policy when he explained that "rural workers are so poor they can't afford to buy even the type of minimum housing, $2,000 to $5,000 housing, in which we are engaged"—thus inadvertently testifying to the built-in deficiencies of AIFLD's reform programs and to their limited nature.[36]

Perhaps the most controversial aspect of AIFLD's policy has been its covert ties with the Central Intelligence Agency. These ties are not confined to the use of AIFLD trainees as cadres in CIA-sponsored coups. The CIA desires to continue working through existing unions, as a means of counteracting the Latin American revolutionaries who are the major focal point of opposition to U.S. penetration of Latin America. In Brazil, the CIA gave funds to the International Federation of Petroleum and Chemical Workers. IFPCW financial reports showed receipt of thirty thousand dollars from the Andrew Hamilton

[35] *AIFLD Report* (Washington, D.C.), IV No. 8 (September–October 1966), 7.
[36] U.S. Congress, House, Committee on Foreign Affairs, *Hearings on the Foreign Assistance Act of 1965*, March 31, 1965, p. 1087; cited in Joseph Palisi, *op. cit.*, p. 21.

Foundation, a CIA conduit. Since 1965, both AIFLD and the IFPCW have been working to get Brazil's petro-chemical unions to affiliate with the anti-Communist IFPCW counterpart in North America.

Because of CIA-financed IFPCW activity, sixteen major Brazilian petroleum unions did not unite into a National Federation of Petroleum Workers, a step opposed by the U.S. unions and the CIA. Instead, AIFLD worked to get the Brazilian unions to affiliate with the conservative craft-oriented IFPCW, and awarded financial aid to unions taking such a course. A São Paulo union leader, Egisto Demonicali, revealed a list of payoffs prepared for Alberto Ramos, the IFPCW representative in Brazil. Typical was the following short note sent from Ramos to one A. Nogueria, from the IFPCW office at São Paulo:

I have with me 45,000,000 cruzeiros ($16,666.67) for you to distribute to the unions for campaigns in accordance with our plans. If you are not available before tomorrow, then arrange to be here on Wednesday, since I will be in Rio conversing with Velasquez about other trips to the U.S.

Sent with the note was an itemized expense sheet, covering such fees as $875 to Dr. Jorge Filho of the Ministry of Labor; a bonus of $312.50 to a reporter for favorable newspaper coverage; and $140.63 to two labor leaders for helping the IFPCW defeat an opposition candidate for union office. As a result of these revelations, the IFPCW was forced to end its Brazilian organizing efforts.[37]

Perhaps it is its close liaison with the CIA that has produced the most dramatic opposition to the AIFLD. Yet, CIA connections only serve to illustrate the basic deficiency in the entire U.S. labor policy in Latin America. Theoretically, AIFLD "allows for a minimum of direct involvement in the Latin American situation on the part of State and AID officials, and thereby lessens the chances of State and AID officials becoming embroiled in the politics of Latin American labor. . . . The design is to insure 'clean' techni-

[37] Ernest Garvey, "Meddling in Brazil: The CIA Bungles On," *Commonweal*, February 9, 1968, pp. 553–54.

cal assistance for the entire democratic segment of the Latin American labor movement."[38]

In reality, a close working relationship exists between the State Department, AID, the CIA and the AFL-CIO. AID relies primarily on AIFLD as the agency to carry out AID programs. Two-thirds of the 15.4 million dollars which comprise AID's total labor expenditures are channeled through AIFLD. AIFLD also gets eighty-nine per cent of its own funds from AID, the agency through which the "governmental" sector contributes to AIFLD. Therefore, many Latin Americans doubt that AIFLD is actually independent of the U.S. government, and "view it instead as the chosen instrument of the U.S. Government" in Latin America. This charge is countered by the assertion of some critics that the State Department lacks sufficient control of AIFLD, and that Latin American labor policy is made entirely by leaders of the AFL-CIO.[39]

This question, to which the Foreign Relations Committee staff report gives much attention, is largely irrelevant. George Meany, J. Peter Grace, and the leaders of the United States government share the same ideological assumptions, and hold similar goals for Latin America. The trade union leaders agree with corporation chiefs and the State Department that the hegemony of U.S. corporations in Latin America must be maintained. To achieve this end, a certain amount of limited social reform is held to be a necessity.

Because the AFL-CIO leaders and corporation heads believe in the validity of corporate capitalism, they both define any revolutionary or nationalist movements that challenge their prerogatives as part of the "Communist enemy." The attention paid to anti-communism is based on this essential belief, and they know the need to stop short of advocating programs that would interfere with the present distribution of wealth and power in Latin America. The conservative consensus to which J. Peter Grace refers does actually exist. But it is the assumption behind this

[38] Senate Committee on Foreign Relations, *op. cit.*, pp. 5–6.
[39] *Ibid.*, p. 6.

"consensus" that has produced the widespread dissatisfaction with AFL-CIO policy in Latin America. Until it is recognized that extending U.S. corporate capitalism to Latin America does not mean progressive change for Latin Americans, no amount of tampering with AIFLD's administrative structure will even begin to solve the problems confronting American labor leaders in Latin America. The future should indeed reveal a growth of the radical and non-Communist CLASC, and a continuing decline of ORIT, the AFL-CIO, and AIFLD throughout Latin America.[40]

[40] *Ibid.*, p. 20. The Foreign Relations Committee report reaches the conclusion that AIFLD problems will be solved if "decisions relating to official United States–Latin American labor policy and programs" are put "under the firm control of the Department of State" rather than "delegated to a private institution or contracted out." What this would do would be to change AIFLD's *structure* while continuing the same *policy*, guided by the same assumptions, but now conducted under the auspices of the State Department. While Latin Americans could no longer accuse AIFLD of fronting for the State Department under this arrangement, the suggestion misses the point that Latin American workers are opposed to AIFLD's direction and policy—not to the agency which carries the conservative policy out.

XIV

LABOR'S COLD WAR:

AN EVALUATION

Since World War I, American presidents have come to depend on the cooperation of the organized labor movement in the carrying out of United States foreign policy. The present stance of American unions goes back to the period of the Marshall Plan. In 1948 and 1949, Communists within the CIO opposed this scheme for reconstruction of postwar Europe, while Joseph Curran (National Maritime Union), Walter Reuther (United Automobile Workers), and James Carey (United Electrical Workers) led a fight to support it. These same union leaders led the fight within the CIO on behalf of withdrawal from the Communist-led World Federation of Trade Unions.

Had the CIO moved into action against the Truman Administration's plan for reintegration of Western Europe into a revived liberal international capitalist order, it might have assumed what the State Department would regard as a disruptive role. The Truman Administration feared the victory of the Left within the CIO, and it used its power to help defeat opponents of the Marshall Plan. Secretary of State George Marshall was glad to respond to Philip Murray's invitation to address the 1947 CIO Convention. At that meeting, Marshall urged CIO support for his plan. Because the Communists still had strength within the CIO, Marshall did not receive the desired support. A compromise resolution was passed which supported Marshall's ideas but which did not endorse his plan by name.[1]

The years 1947 and 1948 saw prolonged struggles within the CIO which ended with the resounding defeat of Communist leadership within many CIO affiliates. Walter Reuther won control of the UAW in 1946. Shortly after, both Joseph Curran of the NMU and Michael Quill, volatile chieftain of the New York–based Transport Workers Union, broke with the Communist Party and purged their union's leadership of pro-Communist functionaries. The balance of power within the CIO shifted to the right. Philip Murray ceased to function as a neutral conciliator between Left and Right. With Murray's approval, the 1948 CIO Convention voted to support the United Nations, to condemn the Soviet Union's use of the veto power in the Security Council, and to endorse the Marshall Plan openly and attack its opponents.[2]

By the next year, the anti-Communist majority acted to curb remaining Communist influence. At the Cleveland CIO Convention in 1949, the majority acted to end all Communist influence. The convention changed the CIO constitution to make Communists or those following Communist policy ineligible for CIO national office, including membership on the CIO Executive Board. Finally, the convention voted to expel the Communist-led United Electrical Workers, claiming that it was only "the Communist Party masquerading as a labor union." The CIO constitution was further changed to allow a two-thirds majority on the board to expel any union whose policies "are consistently directed toward the achievement of the program or purposes of the Communist Party."[3]

The expulsion of the UEW was the first step in a concerted drive against Communist-led CIO unions. The Truman Administration considered it highly important that

[1] 1947 CIO Convention, pp. 260–63, 290; cf. Henry W. Berger, "Union Diplomacy," p. 294.

[2] 1948 CIO Convention, pp. 228–50.

[3] David A. Shannon, *The Decline of American Communism* (New York, 1959), p. 216.

the anti-Communist group within the UEW, the faction led by James Carey, be successful. Carey, who controlled some of the largest UEW locals, received a charter from the CIO to build a new union, the International Union of Electrical Workers (IUE). This body would seek to raid the expelled UEW and win over the former union's membership. "An action rare in the history of the presidency," Louis Koenig has written, was taken when Truman sent a letter to the 1949 CIO Convention urging CIO support for Carey and his dual union.[4] By the 1950 convention, the CIO had expelled seven other unions: the Mine, Mill and Smelter Workers; the Fur and Leather Workers; the Food, Tobacco and Allied Workers; the Marine Cooks and Stewards'; the Fishermen's union; the International Longshoremen's and Warehousemen's Union; and the American Communications Association.[5]

The purge of Communist-led CIO unions was highly appreciated by the Truman Administration. It enabled the CIO leaders to enter the AFL–State Department coalition in foreign affairs. James Carey, who was also the main CIO delegate to the World Federation of Trade Unions, walked out of that group's meeting on January 19, 1949. In May, the CIO Executive Board supported him, and voted to withdraw from the WFTU. In Carey's view, the WFTU had "fallen completely under Communist control and had therefore become bankrupt."[6] As a result of this action, the CIO asked to hold meetings with the AFL "to explore international labor problems."[7]

Carey's walkout and joint AFL-CIO negotiations eventually led to formation of a new anti-Communist world labor federation, the International Confederation of Free Trade Unions. Differences still existed between union leaders from the AFL and CIO, but these became more and more a matter of tactics rather than principles. The CIO leaders

---

[4] Louis Koenig, ed., *The Truman Administration: Its Principles and Practices* (New York, 1956), p. 248.

[5] Shannon, *op. cit.*, pp. 102–03.

[6] Quoted in Berger, *op. cit.*, p. 296.

[7] James Carey to Matthew Woll, March 10, 1949, Florence Thorne MSS, State Historical Society of Wisconsin, Madison, Wis.

disliked the negative obsession of the AFL men with anti-communism, preferring to fight communism by support of social reform abroad. Men like Walter Reuther disliked as well the conspiratorial activities of Jay Lovestone and Irving Brown. But these were divisions of style, not overall purpose. The only immediate tension was a conflict over which union federation—AFL or CIO—would have preponderant strength within the new ICFTU. William Green argued that the AFL had the right to dominate because it had led the fight against communism. "We need to protect our position" within the ICFTU, Green explained, "against the CIO."[8]

Green's fear was ill founded. Consensus on the overall aims of American foreign policy existed within the ranks of the labor leadership. CIO leaders enrolled themselves in the battle originally fought by Matthew Woll, David Dubinsky, and Jay Lovestone. Because they so completely accepted the aims of U.S. foreign policy, CIO leaders proved as willing to accept economic aid from the Central Intelligence Agency as did the old AFL leaders. Thomas Braden, the CIA director of "cultural" activities, revealed in his famous 1967 *Saturday Evening Post* article that not only had he financially supported Irving Brown, but he had also given Victor Reuther of the UAW some fifty thousand dollars in fifty-dollar bills, to help him build anti-Communist unions in Germany.[9]

Braden's revelations embarrassed UAW leaders. Walter Reuther could not deny the charge, though he described it as "incomplete and misleading." At the end of World War II, Reuther sought to explain, "the American labor movement made a great effort to assist in the rebuilding of the free labor movement in Europe." Reuther did not realize that his subsequent explanation further revealed his agreement with the Cold War consensus. Since this movement was "weak and without resources and . . . especially vulner-

[8] International Labor Relations Committee Meeting, April 7, 1949, *ibid.*

[9] Thomas W. Braden, "I'm Glad the CIA Is 'Immoral,' " *Saturday Evening Post*, May 20, 1967, pp. 10–12.

able to communist subversion," Reuther judged that an "emergency situation" existed. Therefore his union reluctantly agreed "on one occasion to the request to transmit Government funds to supplement the inadequate funds being made available by the U.S. labor movement."[10]

Reuther justified the receipt of CIA funds by his own union. In doing so, he revealed that his own conception of European labor's postwar needs squared closely with that of Jay Lovestone and the CIA. Reuther went on to explain that "these monies were merely added to the trade union funds" already being used in Europe to build "education and organizational programs." He did not discuss the nature of this work, nor mention that the funds were made available to only one type of trade union—the acceptable anti-Communist variety.[11]

The CIA had actually tried, through Braden, to make a recruit out of Victor Reuther. According to Braden, he asked Reuther to operate as a CIA agent in Europe, using the cover of UAW international representative. Reuther refused this offer, and CIO president Philip Murray backed him up. But Braden did succeed in gaining the services of Michael Ross, the official CIO International Labor Representative. The whole episode came to light only as a result of Braden's published exposé. Had Walter Reuther firmly opposed CIA policy, he could have made the affair public on his own, especially after becoming a CIO vice-president in 1952. Reuther could have used CIA interference with independent American unions as a basis for waging a strong counteroffensive. But like George Meany, Reuther completely accepted the premises of Cold War foreign policy. The CIA was viewed as merely another institution which extended funds for legitimate purposes. The goal was extension of American-style corporate unionism abroad. Reuther shared this goal along with his AFL colleagues.

Reuther's essential conservatism was further revealed

[10] UAW press release, "Reuther Explains Use of U.S. Funds to Aid Free Labor Movement in Europe," May 7, 1967.
[11] *Ibid.*

in the 1960's, when the AFL-CIO announced creation of a new body that would do for Africa what American Institute for Free Labor Development had done for Latin America. Director of the new African-American Labor Center since January 1965 was Irving Brown, Lovestone's former chief agent in postwar Europe. Although the AALC would clearly follow a Lovestoneite policy in Africa, Reuther agreed to become a member of its board of directors. Reuther had objected to the presence of corporation leaders on AIFLD's board. Since none sat on the AALC board, he had no complaints. Reuther evidently did not object to AALC's explicit support of African labor leaders whom Irving Brown had selected as safe anti-Communist figures. Indeed, the purpose of the AALC, as recent observers have pointed out, is to support selectively African "unions on the basis of their hostility to communism."[12]

The CIO leaders had joined with the AFL executives as part of the Cold War consensus. It was not until 1966, a year in which—as John P. Windmuller accurately notes—"foreign policy issues and overseas operations overshadowed almost all others that came before the governing bodies of the AFL-CIO," that minor differences began to emerge between the Reuther and Meany camps.

In that year, the AFL-CIO endorsed the boycott staged by the American delegate to the International Labor Organization Conference in Geneva. Leon Chajn, Polish government delegate to the ILO, surprisingly gained chairmanship of the organization by a delegate vote of 184 to 183. At that moment, AFL-CIO worker delegate Rudy Faupl walked out of the ILO meeting. Faupl explained:

After the election, I called President Meany and reported what had happened. I advised him that I could not, in good conscience, sit in the Conference presided over by a representa-

---

[12] William H. Friedland and Dorothy Nelkin, "American Labor: Differences and Policies toward Africa," *Africa Today,* December 1966, pp. 13–16; Stanley Meisler, "New Mission to Africa," *The Nation,* January 13, 1969, pp. 48–49. Reuther resigned from his board membership on February 3, 1967, at which time he also resigned from the AFL-CIO Executive Council.

tive of a totalitarian country and that 'I am withdrawing the delegation.' President Meany told me, 'You are the Delegate, you are in a position to weigh the situation. If I were in your position I would do the same thing, but don't do anything that would commit the AFL-CIO to withdrawing from the Organization which is a decision that neither you nor I can make but only the Executive Council.[13]

Meany failed to inform his colleagues of this action. Reuther only learned of the walkout in the *New York Times* one day later. Ignoring his associates on the AFL-CIO Executive Council, Meany went straight to the White House. After talking to Faupl, he immediately "called President Johnson and told him what had happened and then went to see him the next day and went into great detail on the deterioration of the ILO." Meany then took up the affair with Secretary of State Dean Rusk, who suggested that Faupl remain at the conference to stand for election as a member of the ILO governing board. The Secretary did not advocate AFL-CIO withdrawal from the ILO. Meany informed Rusk that he would "convey that to Faupl" and added, "I advised Faupl that I thought that he should try to hold his seat."[14]

Reuther's reaction to Faupl's walkout exemplified his growing differences with Meany. The nature of Reuther's criticism matched remarkably the type of attack leveled by John Spargo against William E. Walling during World War I. Walling, in his vehemence against Bolshevism, had branded all moderate Socialists and European labor leaders as pro-Bolshevik pacifists. Spargo had a more sophisticated understanding of the policy advocated by the European union leaders. He knew that their support of a Socialist conference across belligerent lines was meant as a tactical step against the German propaganda machine. He also realized that the moderate Socialists in Europe were Woodrow Wilson's most committed allies. But Wil-

---

[13] Quoted in John P. Windmuller, "The Foreign Policy Conflict in American Labor," *Political Science Quarterly*, LXXXII, no. 2 (June 1967), 205–08.

[14] *Ibid.*, 211–12.

son's hesitancy to work with these moderates, and his decision to align himself with the existing Allied governments, undercut the men who were his own closest ideological compatriots. Wilson had to turn to Gompers, who supported the rigidly conservative foreign policy of the AFL, and who worked with Wilson's avowed enemies on the European right.

✓ Like John Spargo, Reuther took a more flexible position. It was similarly undercut by the State Department's support of traditional conservative elements between 1963 and 1968. Reuther, however, carped at Faupl's walkout. In the strongest terms, he expressed his objection "to and . . . disagreement with the action of the AFL-CIO delegates in walking out of the current ILO Conference in Geneva." He criticized such a step's having been taken without thorough review by the entire AFL-CIO Executive Board, and he attacked the walkout as "unwise, undemocratic . . . and unauthorized by any AFL-CIO body."[15]

As a result, George Meany convened the AFL-CIO Executive Board. All eighteen members from the former AFL unions voted for the walkout. Six out of nine presidents of the former CIO unions voted against it, but the remaining three voted with George Meany. The Executive Board, on Reuther's request, agreed to hold a special meeting at which they would review all foreign policy questions.[16]

Such a meeting was convened during August 1966. One of the major issues was the AFL-CIO policy in Latin America. Victor Reuther had recently objected that the presence of business leaders on AIFLD's board compromised its trade union role. Later, in a May 1966 interview, he implied that both the AFL-CIO International Affairs Department and AIFLD were involved with the CIA. Reuther then commented that Jay Lovestone "seems to have brought into the labor movement the working habits and undercover techniques which he learned when he was in the highest

---

[15] *John Herling's Labor Letter,* June 11, 1966, pp. 3–4.
[16] Windmuller, *op. cit.,* 213.

echelons of the Communist Party."[17] Victor Reuther's objections to Lovestone diplomacy, however, were only tactical. He argued that Lovestone's technique harmed the fight against communism.

Nevertheless, Victor Reuther's attack met with serious opposition from the Lovestone-dominated Executive Council. A resolution was introduced praising AIFLD for carrying out AFL-CIO policy, and rejecting "out of hand the vilification that has been conducted against the AIFLD." The *Christian Science Monitor* reported that Walter Reuther "expressed personal high regard for AIFLD's work." According to their report, " 'Walter admitted Victor went too far' in criticizing the AIFLD," but he also argued that the AFL-CIO policy statement likewise "went too far in its condemnation of honest criticism and serious doubts of the AIFLD."[18] The policy statement passed the board by a vote of 23–2, with only Reuther and Curran voting in the negative. Most leaders of the former CIO unions voted with Meany, and Reuther was more isolated than ever.

Reuther also differed with Meany on the war in Vietnam. Again, his differences were mainly tactical. At the December 1965 AFL-CIO Convention, the draft resolution on Vietnam was modified at Reuther's request to stress labor's support of negotiations. But the resolution argued that negotiations were the policy of President Lyndon B. Johnson, and thus the AFL-CIO endorsed "all measures the Administration might deem necessary to halt Communist aggression and secure a just and lasting peace."[19] Under the guise of advocating peace negotiations, Reuther had permitted the AFL-CIO to give the Johnson Administration labor's own version of the Tonkin Gulf resolution.

Open convention debate preceding the resolution indicated that differences between Meany and Reuther were slight, if they actually existed at all. Both men rejected

[17] Harry Bernstein, "AFL-CIO Unit Accused of 'Snooping' Abroad," *Los Angeles Times*, May 22, 1966.

[18] *Christian Science Monitor*, August 24, 1966.

[19] Windmuller, *op. cit.*, 217–18.

U.S. withdrawal from Vietnam, both wanted Hanoi and Peking to learn that they could not attain a military victory, both claimed to favor a solution to be found at the conference table. Reuther, however, claimed to stand between what he called "two extreme positions," those of the "appeasers" on the one hand and the "hawks" who favored unlimited escalation.[20] It did not occur to Reuther that insofar as he accepted the premises of the "hawks," the tactic of negotiation could easily be made to appear untenable. Within the AFL-CIO, Reuther's moderation worked to strengthen the hands of "hawk" Meany.

By the time the Executive Board met eight months later (August 1966), its position had hardened. A statement on Vietnam was adopted unanimously by those board members present. The vote, however, was taken after Reuther had left the meeting to attend another function. The AFL-CIO policy statement supported the growing build-up of U.S. forces, and attacked the Soviet, Chinese, and North Vietnamese governments for blocking a peace settlement. Most important, the board severely condemned American opponents of the war. While claiming to favor the right of dissent, the AFL-CIO executive urged that this right "be neither abrogated nor abused." Any "disruption by even a well meaning minority," it stated, "can only pollute and poison the bloodstream of our democracy. . . . Those who would deny our military forces unstinting support are, in effect, aiding the Communist enemy of our country."[21]

Reuther, who had left before the vote was taken, later attacked the statement as "intemperate, hysterical, jingoistic and unworthy of a policy statement of a free labor movement."[22] Although the gap was growing wider between Meany and Reuther, the UAW chieftain offered little that was constructive to put in place of the pro-war statement. He objected because the statement was clearly an endorsement of the "hawk" position; but Reuther was

[20] *Ibid.*, 219.
[21] *AFL-CIO Free Trade Union News*, September 1966, p. 1.
[22] *New York Times*, August 27, 1966.

not willing to fight for a statement truly in favor of peaceful settlement.

Because of growing dissatisfaction with the Meany-Lovestone analysis, Reuther requested a full-scale AFL-CIO Council meeting to be devoted entirely to a re-evaluation of American foreign policy. The meeting was scheduled for November 14, 1966. Inexplicably, Reuther announced shortly before the session that he would not be able to attend. The necessity of attending a UAW Executive Board meeting in Detroit, concerning urgent contract negotiations, made his attendance in Washington an impossibility. No one believed Reuther's feeble excuse. Perhaps he did not attend because he knew he faced overwhelming defeat, and he did not wish to suffer the personal embarrassment. Yet, as Joseph Curran had wired him, if he did not attend there would be "reason to doubt your sincerity."[23]

The AFL-CIO board met, with Reuther absent, to carry out their review of American foreign policy. As expected, when the board went through nineteen different questions on which the AFL-CIO had taken a position in the previous eleven years, it unanimously reaffirmed all of its existing policy statements, with one minor exception. Had Reuther attended, it is uncertain whether he would have been able to get others to vote with him. It is certain that in his absence, the other members from former CIO unions did not feel strong enough to buck Meany and Lovestone. Reuther, as Windmuller puts it, absented himself "without furnishing a convincing reason." He had abandoned "the field to the majority" and had offended "those who had in the past given him their support."[24]

The unwillingness of Reuther to wage a fight on the foreign policy issue, when the time was most opportune, revealed the fatal flaw in counting on the Reuther wing of

[23] Quoted in Windmuller, *op. cit.*, 221.
[24] *Ibid.*, 221. The sole exception was on AFL-CIO opposition to U.S. recognition of Communist China and her admission to the United Nations. Jacob Potofsky of the Amalgamated Clothing Workers favored support of the so-called "two Chinas" policy.

the labor movement for a change in labor's foreign policy position. Reuther's position corresponds to that advanced by the State Department and sophisticated corporate policy makers. These groups oppose social revolution and revolutionary nationalism in the underdeveloped world, while they seek simultaneously to "build bridges" to the nuclear-armed Soviet bloc nations that are already partially industrialized. Like his counterparts in the European social democratic union movement, Reuther sees a mellowing process at work in Eastern Europe, and he favors increased contacts with unionized workers from these nations. Although he still wages the Cold War, he differs with the "hard line" traditionalists on how to go about it. George Meany sees world communism as a monolithic expansionist force, ruled by men who are totally evil. Reuther views world communism as a system which can only thrive where poverty and degradation are allowed to exist. Once a frontal assault is waged on poverty by the advanced Western capitalist nations, Reuther hopes it will produce a liberalizing trend within the Soviet bloc nations so that mutual relations can be established. Eventually, the mellowing process would lead to an end of Soviet-style Communist governments.

Although Reuther's more flexible analysis bears a close similarity to the views advanced by most postwar administrations, the various Presidents have hesitated to throw their formal support to the liberal-labor wing. The administrations of both John F. Kennedy and Lyndon B. Johnson stood in the same relationship to George Meany as Woodrow Wilson had to Samuel Gompers. The government, as John P. Windmuller points out, desires to achieve orderly relations with organized labor. They need to deal with the men who control AFL-CIO policy. Both Kennedy and Johnson knew that they could pursue their policies toward the Eastern European nations without challenging the more conservative views held by Meany. They could "build bridges" without fearing that Meany, unless he was deliberately provoked, would create difficulties. "Under these circumstances," Windmuller writes, "the very marginal advantage which might have accrued to the administration by openly encouraging a wider hearing in the labor movement for Reuther's more congenial views was hardly worth the certain cost of incurring Meany's profound hostility."[25]

Windmuller, however, exaggerates the extent of the government's differences with the Meany wing. Meany may not have shared administration desires to secure a *modus vivendi* with the Soviet bloc, but in other key areas, the State Department and the executive branch were on the same side as the Meany-Lovestone group. John F. Kennedy wanted to oust Cheddi Jagan from the premiership of British Guiana, and it was the Lovestone-oriented AIFLD which served as the vehicle to carry out AFL-CIO policy. Like Woodrow Wilson, both Kennedy and Johnson did not want to risk support of real social revolution, or even of moderate social democrats like Juan Bosch.

Perhaps it was the crucial lack of firm administration support that led Reuther to stop calling for a reassessment of foreign policy. Today, Reuther and the other unions in the new Alliance for Labor Action follow a moderate anti-Communist policy, one that is adapted to the realities of postwar European stabilization and frankly accepts Soviet strength in Eastern Europe as a given. But Reuther and his associates still believe in the Cold War; many UAW affiliates are in the forefront of support for defense-oriented industries. Reuther's policy is in line with the contemporary needs of a corporate economy which now faces severe competition from Western European nations as well as from many in the Socialist bloc.

Henry W. Berger suggests that Reuther "could possibly provide a different direction for labor's international activities and also restore a portion of a badly damaged democratic labor tradition."[26] But Reuther's time for that has already passed. His criticism has been advanced within

[25] *Ibid.*, 226.
[26] Henry W. Berger, "American Labor Overseas," *The Nation*, January 16, 1967, p. 84.

the framework of existing assumptions, and he has shied
away from any basic challenge to the premises of U.S.
foreign policy.

Moreover, the Nixon Administration's policy is based
upon close liaison with the Meany camp. Washington
journalist Richard Dudman reports that since mid-1968, a
new method of roundabout government financing of AFL-
CIO activity via AIFLD, AALC, and the new Asian-Ameri-
can Free Labor Institute has been developed. Unions are
used as conduits for money funneled by the Agency for
International Development into AFL-CIO international
affiliates which previously received their funds directly
from the CIA. The plan, formulated by Ernest S. Lee, assistant director of the AFL-CIO Department of International Affairs, is based on using AID money as an "instrument to provide financial support to American labor
organizations" for the development of "free" trade unions
abroad.

Lee asked for $1,300,000 in AID funds to allocate to
the three labor institutes. On March 10, 1969, Meany met
with the Labor Advisory Committee on Foreign Assistance.
George P. Delaney, State's internal labor affairs coordina-
tor, told Meany that AID chief John A. Hannah could be
regarded as labor's "friend in court" within the Nixon Administration. Meany acknowledged his friendship with
Hannah, and related as well that President Richard M.
Nixon had recently written J. Peter Grace that he was favorable to AIFLD and looked forward to cooperating on
behalf of common goals. It was also reported that Nelson
Rockefeller had pledged to take Andrew McLellan, AFL-
CIO Inter-American Representative (remembered for his
infamous role in the Dominican Republic) as well as Joseph Beirne, secretary of AIFLD, along on his first Latin
American tour on behalf of the Nixon Administration.[27]

Continuation of dependency on the Meany wing was
combined with a surprising move initiated by Meany in
February 1969—a move that only worked to further isolate

[27] Richard Dudman, "Agent Meany," *The New Republic*, May 3,
1969, pp. 13–16.

Reuther's group. Meany announced that the AFL-CIO was withdrawing from the International Confederation of Free Trade Unions. On the surface, departure from the ICFTU was a reversal of previous policy. Since the end of World War II, the AFL leaders had worked to split the WFTU and to build a new international anti-Communist union federation. The ICFTU was the result, and throughout the 1950's AFL-CIO foreign policy was carried out under its auspices. By the mid 1960's, however, the old shibboleths about a monolithic international Communist conspiracy had worn thin. Western European moderate labor leaders no longer spoke or acted as if they expected a Soviet invasion in the near future. Precisely those anti-Communist unions which Lovestone and Brown had built up between 1945 and 1948 were now taking the Reuther position on a *modus vivendi* with the Eastern European nations. Their leadership had also become increasingly hostile to the interference of men like Brown in their internal affairs. ICFTU affiliates now moved to make contact with Eastern European labor organizations. Meany was unable to stop these overtures. Therefore, he and Lovestone advised the AFL-CIO Executive Council to withdraw from the ICFTU. International anti-Communist activity among trade unionists could now be coordinated entirely through government-supported AFL-CIO institutes like AIFLD, which were securely under the control of the Meany-Lovestone bloc.

Withdrawal from the ICFTU reveals the total bankruptcy of AFL-CIO foreign policy. The very institution meant to carry out AFL foreign policy in Europe had opted for the more moderate and reasonable Reuther position on world communism. But Reuther himself, rather than choosing to take the offensive and use new opportunities to launch American labor on an independent course in foreign affairs, tails behind Meany and throws out only half-hearted criticisms which he fails to follow up.

The total absorption of American labor leaders in the ideology of Cold War liberalism shows little sign of dissipation. Support of American foreign policy has been the chosen path of union leaders desiring to gain acceptance for their unions by corporate capitalists. The leaders' decision to work within the system has deep implications for those who believe that labor has a crucial role to play in movements for fundamental change in America. Particularly, it has implications for those who argue that a new coalition should be forged—a coalition of trade unionists, Negroes, and the poor. This old New Deal labor-liberal coalition, in the words of Tom Kahn (administrative secretary of the League for Industrial Democracy), could transform the Democratic Party "from an amalgam of New Dealers and Slave Dealers into the political instrument of the labor, civil rights and peace movements—and of the poor"; or it might, as Irving Howe has put it, function as a coalition "of Negro, labor, liberal and church groups" that could "stretch the limits of the welfare state."[28]

This position has received its most sophisticated presentation in Michael Harrington's *Toward a Democratic Left*. Harrington believes that a coalition of blacks, liberals, labor and the poor could indeed capture the Democratic Party, remove its reactionary elements, and turn it into an instrument of democratic planning. "The strategy of massive public investments and of governmental persuasion of the private sector," Harrington writes, "can be put into effect at once. They already command the support of a potential new majority in the civil rights, labor, liberal and religious movements."[29]

Harrington's prescription for social change, however, depends upon the illusory hope of uniting disparate groups. The black community has long ago departed from the advocacy of "civil rights" and integration, partially because it has come to realize from bitter experience that the white union worker is not his brother in the true trade union sense of the word.[30] The employed white

[28] Quoted in Hal Draper, "In Defense of the 'New Radicals,'" *New Politics*, IV, no. 3 (Summer 1965), p. 14.

[29] Michael Harrington, *Toward a Democratic Left: A Radical Program for a New Majority* (New York, 1968), p. 141.

[30] Julius Jacobson, "Union Conservatism: A Barrier to Racial Equality"; Marc Karson and Ronald Radosh, "The American Fed-

worker, moreover, still believes that the constantly increasing tax-bite into his hard-earned paycheck is going for governmental hand-outs to the idle poor.

The vaunted coalition has come to mean not a coalition for freedom—but, "coalition now, freedom later." Thus in the pre-1964 presidential election, coalition strategists asked for a moratorium on demonstrations by the civil rights movement, on the ground that the "labor-liberal-Negro coalition" would be harmed, since demonstrations would antagonize whites and send them into Goldwater's camp. Opposition to independent activity by blacks clearly reflected the demand that their action be subordinate to the needs of the coalition. One can only wonder at the value of a coalition whose members hesitate to join when their black "partners" demand their rights!

This could occur because of the total absorption of American unions in the corporate capitalist structure. By suggesting a coalition with these corporate unions, and by failing to urge a vigorous battle to change the unions internally, Harrington sows illusions about a potential for change. To assume that Walter Reuther's UAW is about to join with the peace movement—even the moderate Committee for a Sane Nuclear Policy—in an all-out effort to end the war in Vietnam or to prevent future imperialist conflicts is to disregard the nature of both the UAW and Reuther's consistently moderate course. Even if Reuther and his Alliance for Labor Action did act in a more forthright fashion, any meaningful coalition would have to be based on the majority of the unions still within the AFL-CIO—unions which have not even reached the modest level of "criticism" attained by the UAW.

At the beginning of this work, we addressed ourselves to a question raised by one Arthur Calhoun: how long can American corporate capitalism hand out tangible benefits to labor as a payment for loyalty? When, if at all, will the game be up? Recent developments indicate that the Nixon

---

eration of Labor and the Negro Worker, 1894–1949," in Julius Jacobson, ed., *The Negro and the American Labor Movement* (New York, 1968), pp. 1–26; 155–87.

Administration may move to limit wage increases by exercising new forms of controls over the collective bargaining process. Depending on how severe these controls become, the possibility exists that unions may be pushed into an opposition course. A strong industrial union movement served a purpose during the time of industrial depression. Labor was tamed when the new CIO began functioning as a disciplinary force to integrate blue collar workers into the system. But as wages become an unstable factor in production costs, and as U.S. durable goods industries face increasing foreign competition, corporations may be forced to push up productivity per man-hour in order to meet this new competition.[31] New labor struggles, however, might just as likely take the form of wildcat strikes or organization outside the framework of existing trade unions.

From the days of the First World War to the war in Vietnam, American organized labor has officially supported both the aims and purposes of U.S. foreign policy, in the hope that such support would give the working class a share of the great American pie. Since the end of World War II, this has meant labor support of a permanent war economy, of production for "defense" systems, and participation in Cold War politics throughout the world. Such a stance is determined by the very nature of corporate unionism. Any movement away from a Cold War orientation, therefore, demands creation of a trade union movement whose leadership and membership begin to transcend the existing social system. The end of corporate unionism depends upon a critique of corporation capitalism. Until American labor leaders present a Socialist alternative to American workers, they will not make the long overdue reassessment of American foreign policy that is required in an era of world revolution.

[31] The writer is indebted to the *Guardian* journalist and former labor organizer, Stanley Aronowitz, for this analysis.

INDEX

ABOUT THE AUTHOR

RONALD RADOSH was born in 1937, in New York City, and was educated at the University of Wisconsin, from which he received a B.A. and a Ph.D., and the State University of Iowa, from which he received an M.A. He at present is Assistant Professor of History at Queensborough Community College, City University of New York. He has also taught history at Brooklyn College.

Co-editor (with Louis Menashe) of *Teach-Ins U.S.A., Reports, Opinions, Documents,* Professor Radosh has published widely in *The Nation, Liberation, Monthly Review* as well as in *Studies on the Left,* on which he served as an Associate Editor.

He lives in New York City with his wife and two children.

A free catalogue of VINTAGE BOOKS *will be sent at your request. Write to* Vintage Books, 457 Madison Avenue, New York, New York 10022.